Protected Areas and Tourism in Southern Africa

This volume discusses the complex relationship between Protected Areas and tourism and their impact on community livelihoods in a range of countries in Southern Africa.

Protected areas and tourism have an enduring and symbiotic relationship. While protected areas offer a desirable setting for tourism products, tourism provides revenue that can contribute to conservation efforts. This can bring benefits to local communities, but it can also have a negative impact, with the establishment of protected areas leading to the eviction of local communities from their original places of residence, while also preventing them from accessing the natural resources they once enjoyed. Taking a multi-disciplinary approach, this book addresses the opportunities and challenges faced by communities and other stakeholders as they endeavour to achieve their conservation goals and work towards improving community livelihoods. Case studies from Botswana, Malawi, Namibia, South Africa, Tanzania, Zambia and Zimbabwe address key issues such as human–wildlife conflicts, ecotourism, wildlife-based tourism, landscape governance, wildlife crop-raiding and trophy hunting, including the high-profile case of Cecil the lion. Chapters highlight both the achievements and positive outcomes of protected areas, but also the challenges faced and their impact on how protected areas are viewed and also conservation priorities more generally. The volume gives these issues affecting protected areas, local communities, managers and international conservation efforts centre stage in order inform policy and improve practice going forward.

This book will be of great interest to students and scholars of conservation, natural resource management, tourism, sustainable development and African studies, as well as professionals and policymakers involved in conservation policy.

Lesego Senyana Stone is a Senior Lecturer in Tourism Management in the Department of Tourism and Hospitality Management, University of Botswana.

Moren Tibabo Stone is a Senior Lecturer in the Department of Environmental Science, University of Botswana.

Patricia Kefilwe Mogomotsi is an Associate Professor in Natural Resources Economics in the Department of Economics, University of Botswana.

Goemeone E. J. Mogomotsi is an Associate Professor in International Environmental Policy and Senior Executive Assistant to the Vice Chancellor in the University of Botswana.

Routledge Studies in Conservation and the Environment

This series includes a wide range of inter-disciplinary approaches to conservation and the environment, integrating perspectives from both social and natural sciences. Topics include, but are not limited to, development, environmental policy and politics, ecosystem change, natural resources (including land, water, oceans and forests), security, wildlife, protected areas, tourism, human-wildlife conflict, agriculture, economics, law and climate change.

Humans and Hyenas
Monster or Misunderstood
Keith Somerville

Is CITES Protecting Wildlife?
Assessing Implementation and Compliance
Tanya Wyatt

A Political Ecology of Forest Conservation in India
Communities, Wildlife and the State
Amrita Sen

Ethics in Biodiversity Conservation
Patrik Baard

Protected Areas and Tourism in Southern Africa
Conservation Goals and Community Livelihoods
Edited by Lesego Senyana Stone, Moren Tibabo Stone, Patricia Kefilwe Mogomotsi and Goemeone E.J. Mogomotsi

Women and Wildlife Trafficking
Participants, Perpetrators and Victims
Helen U. Agu and Meredith L. Gore

For more information about this series, please visit: www.routledge.com/Routledge-Studies-in-Conservation-and-the-Environment/book-series/RSICE

Protected Areas and Tourism in Southern Africa

Conservation Goals and Community Livelihoods

Edited by
Lesego Senyana Stone, Moren Tibabo Stone, Patricia Kefilwe Mogomotsi and Goemeone E. J. Mogomotsi

First published 2022
by Routledge
2 Park Square, Milton Park, Abingdon, Oxon OX14 4RN

and by Routledge
605 Third Avenue, New York, NY 10158

Routledge is an imprint of the Taylor & Francis Group, an informa business

© 2022 selection and editorial matter, Lesego Senyana Stone, Moren Tibabo Stone, Patricia Kefilwe Mogomotsi and Goemeone E.J. Mogomotsi; individual chapters, the contributors

The right of Lesego Senyana Stone, Moren Tibabo Stone, Patricia Kefilwe Mogomotsi and Goemeone E.J. Mogomotsi to be identified as the authors of the editorial material, and of the authors for their individual chapters, has been asserted in accordance with sections 77 and 78 of the Copyright, Designs and Patents Act 1988.

All rights reserved. No part of this book may be reprinted or reproduced or utilised in any form or by any electronic, mechanical, or other means, now known or hereafter invented, including photocopying and recording, or in any information storage or retrieval system, without permission in writing from the publishers.

Trademark notice: Product or corporate names may be trademarks or registered trademarks, and are used only for identification and explanation without intent to infringe.

British Library Cataloguing-in-Publication Data
A catalogue record for this book is available from the British Library

Library of Congress Cataloging-in-Publication Data
Names: Stone, Lesego Senyana, editor. | Stone, Moren T., editor. |
Mogomotsi, Patricia Kefilwe, editor. | Mogomotsi, Goemeone E.J., editor.
Title: Protected areas and tourism in southern Africa: conservation goals
and community livelihoods / edited by Lesego Senyana Stone, Moren Tibabo
Stone, Patricia Kefilwe Mogomotsi and Goemeone E.J. Mogomotsi.
Description: Abingdon, Oxon; New York, NY : Routledge, 2022. |
Series: Routledge studies in conservation and the environment |
Includes bibliographical references and index.
Identifiers: LCCN 2021046517 (print) | LCCN 2021046518 (ebook) |
ISBN 9781032044330 (hardback) | ISBN 9781032044347 (paperback) |
ISBN 9781003193166 (ebook)
Subjects: LCSH: Protected areas–Africa, Southern. |
Protected areas–Economic aspects–Africa, Southern. |
Protected areas–Public use–Africa, Southern. |
Sustainable tourism–Africa, Southern. | Wildlife conservation–Africa, Southern.
Classification: LCC S934.S6 P76 2022 (print) |
LCC S934.S6 (ebook) | DDC 333.95/160968–dc23
LC record available at https://lccn.loc.gov/2021046517
LC ebook record available at https://lccn.loc.gov/2021046518

ISBN: 978-1-032-04433-0 (hbk)
ISBN: 978-1-032-04434-7 (pbk)
ISBN: 978-1-003-19316-6 (ebk)

DOI: 10.4324/9781003193166

Typeset in Bembo
by Newgen Publishing UK

Contents

List of figures	viii
List of tables	ix
List of contributors	x
Acknowledgements	xv
List of abbreviations	xvi

1 Protected areas and tourism dynamics in Southern Africa: An overview   1

MOREN TIBABO STONE, LESEGO SENYANA STONE,

GOEMEONE E. J. MOGOMOTSI AND PATRICIA KEFILWE MOGOMOTSI

PART I
Community–PA relations: Impacts on local communities   13

2 Protected areas and tourism development: A historical analysis of the Southern African experience   15

BOGA THURA MANATSHA AND BONGANI GLORIOUS GUMBO

3 Community perceptions of protected areas and tourism amidst poverty: Experiences from Southern Africa   28

HERBERT NTULI AND EDWIN MUCHAPONDWA

4 Ecotourism as a paradigm shift in conservation and community livelihoods in the Southern African region: Opportunities, challenges and lessons learnt   42

SAID JUMA SULUO AND WINEASTER ANDERSON

5 Tolerance for wildlife resources through community wildlife-based tourism: Implications for sustainability   56

CHIEDZA NGONIDZASHE MUTANGA

vi *Contents*

PART II
Protected areas, tourism and human–wildlife conflicts dynamics   71

6 Landscape governance in sub-Saharan Africa   73
   RENE VAN DER DUIM AND ARJAAN PELLIS

7 In the way of wildlife: Contestations between Indigenous
   Peoples' livelihood and conservation   87
   ONTHATILE OLERILE MOETI

8 The socio-economic impacts of wildlife crop-raiding:
   An assessment of the efficacy of conservation and
   agricultural land uses reconciliation   100
   EMMANUEL MWAKIWA

9 Protected areas and community-based tourism:
   The effectiveness of current mitigation techniques in
   human wildlife conflicts   114
   PATRICIA KEFILWE MOGOMOTSI AND GOEMEONE E. J. MOGOMOTSI

PART III
Managing the wildlife economy: Contemporary issues in Southern Africa   129

10 Lifting of the hunting ban and the elephant debate in
    Botswana: Implications for conservation and development
    in Southern Africa   131
    JOSEPH ELIZERI MBAIWA AND EMMANUEL MOGENDE

11 The role of the media and the international community in
    recent conservation issues in Southern Africa: The case of
    Cecil the lion   146
    GARIKAI CHIMUKA

12 Nature-based tourism resources and climate change
    in Southern Africa: Implications for conservation and
    development sustainability   161
    KAITANO DUBE

13 International organisations and the ivory sales ban
    debate: The case of Zimbabwe, Namibia and Botswana   175
    CAROLINE COX

Contents vii

14 The COVID-19 pandemic and nature-based tourism in
Southern Africa 188
SUSAN SNYMAN

PART IV
Protected areas and tourism practices:
Policy and practice 203

15 The adoption of community-based tourism in the
proximity of protected areas: Implications for policy
and practice 205
OLIVER MTAPURI

16 Militarisation of conservation and 'shoot to kill' policies:
An analysis of the rights of African states to protect and
conserve wildlife 218
GOEMEONE E. J. MOGOMOTSI AND PATRICIA KEFILWE MOGOMOTSI

17 Implications of the 'high-value, low-volume' approach in
conservation and tourism resources management 232
LESEGO SENYANA STONE AND MOREN TIBABO STONE

18 Promotion of pro-poor tourism in Southern
Africa: Conservation and development critical issues 245
OWEN GOHORI, PEET VAN DER MERWE, AND ANDREA SAAYMAN

19 Contrasting safari and bushmeat hunting in Southern
Africa: Conservation and development issues 259
JULIA LAURA VAN VELDEN

PART V
Conclusion 271

20 A synthesis of protected areas and tourism contributions to
conservation and community livelihoods goals in Southern
Africa: A conclusion 273
MOREN TIBABO STONE, LESEGO SENYANA STONE,
PATRICIA KEFILWE MOGOMOTSI AND GOEMEONE E. J. MOGOMOTSI

Index 282

Figures

3.1	The link between perceptions, attitudes and behaviour	29
4.1	Concept of ecotourism	43
12.1	Niño 3.4 index for 1990 to 2021, which affected climate in the Southern African region	164
12.2	Annual average maximum temperature trend at Cape Point (Table Mountain National Park) 1978–2018	167
12.3	Monthly average maximum temperature trend at Cape Point (Table Mountain National Park) 1978–2018	167

Tables

3.1	An example of variables affecting how people form perception based on theoretical framework for analysing complex SESs	32
4.1	Study themes and sub-themes	45
5.1	The role of CWBT in enhancing communities' tolerance for wildlife resources and implications for sustainability	60
8.1	List of different conservation and agricultural land conflict drivers	101
11.1	Total lion (Panthera leo) trophy imports (and percentage of imports worldwide) in the top 10 importing countries during 2004–2014	153
14.1	General impacts from COVID-19 related to nature-based tourism	191
14.2	Examples of national level impacts of COVID-19 on tourism in Southern Africa	193

Contributors

Wineaster Anderson (PhD) is Professor of Marketing at the University of Dar es Salaam, Tanzania. She has researched widely in the areas of sustainable tourism, international business and trade, tourism marketing and poverty alleviation; and has published a wide range of articles and books on these subjects. Her current research interests are in the broad field of marketing and sustainable tourism.

Garikai Chimuka is a researcher with interest in sustainable development in the Global South. He holds an MSc in leisure, tourism and environment from Wageningen University, the Netherlands, and the Executive Certificate in Sustainable Development Diplomacy from the Fletcher School of Law, USA. He also holds a Bachelor of Tourism and Hospitality Management from the University of Zimbabwe as well as both the Master of Laws and Bachelor of Laws from the University of London.

Caroline Cox is the lead researcher in the University of Portsmouth's Ivory Project, set up in November 2015 to analyse the sale of illegal ivory through various routes in the UK and overseas. The project works with government, law enforcement, charities and NGOs to advise on the threats of and responses to the illegal wildlife trade.

Kaitano Dube (PhD) is one of the leading tourism geographers from Africa. He has written several journal articles and book chapters on tourism, climate change and sustainability. Given the timely research that he undertakes, his work has received global attention in both academia and mainstream media. Currently, a lecturer at the Vaal University of Technology in South Africa, he holds several qualifications, amongst them a Hons BSC Geography and Environmental Studies from Midlands State University, Zimbabwe, MSc Geography and PhD Environmental Management from the University of South Africa.

Owen Gohori (PhD) is Post-Doctoral Fellow at the North-West University, Potchefstroom campus. He worked in the tourism industry in Zimbabwe for seven years before he became an entrepreneur and ran his travel agency for some years before decided to advance his studies. His research interests

List of contributors xi

include pro-poor tourism, community-based tourism and sustainable tourism. Dr Gohori has extensive knowledge and experience working with inbound tourists and promotes the development of community-based tourism in rural communities as a strategy to benefit disadvantaged local people.

Bongani Glorious Gumbo (PhD) is Senior Lecturer in the Department of History. He obtained his BA, PGDE and MA from the University of Botswana, PhD from the University of Cape Town. His research interests, largely on Economic History, include the livelihoods of riparian communities in Botswana, tourism development, wildlife conservation, Southern African liberation history and Botswana's role therein.

Boga Thura Manatsha (PhD) is Senior Lecturer of History at the University of Botswana (UB). Manatsha obtained his BA in History and English at UB in 2004. He also graduated with a Post-Graduate Diploma in Education in 2005 at the same institution. Manatsha also holds MA and PhD in Cultural and Regional/Asian Studies from Hiroshima University, Japan.

Joseph E. Mbaiwa (PhD) is the Director of the Okavango Research Institute (ORI), University of Botswana. He holds a PhD in Parks, Recreation and Tourism Sciences from Texas A&M University is also a Professor of Tourism Studies. He is widely published in areas of tourism development, community-based natural resource management, rural livelihoods and biodiversity conservation.

Onthatile Olerile Moeti holds a Bachelor of Laws degree from the University of Botswana, an LLM in Human Rights and Democratisation in Africa from the University of Pretoria and a Master of Arts (Politics and International Relations) from the University of Botswana. She is employed as a Lecturer in the Department of Law, Faculty of Social Sciences by the University of Botswana and is currently a full-time student at the University of Glasgow in Scotland pursuing a PhD in Law. Her thesis is on 'The Impact of the Modern Development Agenda on the Indigenous Peoples' Rights in Botswana: The Case of the San'.

Emmanuel Mogende (PhD) is Lecturer in the Department of Environmental Science, Faculty of Science, University of Botswana. He was formerly a Research Scholar in natural resource governance at the Okavango Research Institute, University of Botswana. His research focuses on the political economy of natural resources, in particular wildlife conservation and development in Botswana. His doctoral thesis draws attention to processes that produce the green state in the context of Africa, using the example of the shifting wildlife conservation policy and practices in post-independent Botswana (1966–2018).

Goemeone E. J. Mogomotsi (PhD) is an Associate Professor (International Environmental Policy) at the Okavango Research Institute, University of xii *List of contributors*

Botswana, Botswana. He is also serving on secondment as a Senior Executive Assistant to the Vice Chancellor, University of Botswana, Botswana. He has published in water law, natural resources use and policy, waste management, legal aspects of religious freedom and financial services regulation. Dr Mogomotsi is an admitted attorney, conveyancer and notary public in the Courts of Botswana.

Patricia Kefilwe Mogomotsi (PhD), is Associate Professor (Natural Resources Economics) at the University of Botswana, Department of Economics, Gaborone Botswana. Prof Mogomotsi has published extensively in water institutions and regulation, waste management, tourism economics, climate change adaptation, natural resources management among others.

Oliver Mtapuri (PhD) is Professor in Development Studies at the School of Built Environment and Development in the College of Humanities at the University of KwaZulu-Natal (UKZN) in Durban, South Africa. Mtapuri is also the Interim South African Research Chairs Initiative (SARChI) chair in Applied Poverty Reduction Assessment, funded by the National Research Foundation (grant No. 71220) and the Department of Science and Innovation. He is the Academic Leader, Research in his School. His areas of research interest include tourism, community-based tourism, poverty and inequality, redistribution, climate change and innovation.

Edwin Muchapondwa (PhD) is Professor in the School of Economics at the University of Cape Town, South Africa. He is a guest professor at Luleå University of Technology in Sweden. He participates in the Environment for Development (EfD) Initiative – a global network of environmental economics research centres solving the world's most pressing environmental and development challenges. He serves on the EfD Board. He is a member of the Green Growth Knowledge Platform (GGKP) Expert Working Group on Natural Capital. He is also the country representative for South Africa at the European Association for Environmental and Resource Economists (EAERE).

Chiedza N. Mutanga (PhD) is Senior Lecturer in the School of Hospitality and Tourism at Chinhoyi University of Technology, Zimbabwe. She holds a PhD in tourism and wildlife conservation from Chinhoyi University of Technology, Zimbabwe.

Emmanuel Mwakiwa (PhD) is a researcher specialising in agriculture, environment and resource economics. He has a doctoral degree in environment and natural resource economics, MSc in agricultural economics and BSc in agriculture. His PhD thesis is based on wildlife management by public and private landowners for Kruger National Park and Game Reserves surrounding Kruger National Park in South Africa. He is currently lecturing at the Department of Agricultural Business Development and Economics, Faculty of Agriculture, Environment and Food Systems at the University of Zimbabwe.

List of contributors xiii

Herbert Ntuli (PhD) is Postdoctoral Research Fellow in the School of Economics at the University of Cape Town (UCT) and Wildlife Economics and Policy Analyst at WWF South Africa. He obtained his PhD (Economics) from the University of Cape Town in December 2015. His research interests include Community-Based Natural Resource Management, institutions, evaluation of non-market environmental goods, agriculture and rural development, land tenure issues and Land use economics. Herbert has seven years' research experience in wildlife conservation in the Great Limpopo Transfrontier Conservation Area (GLTFCA) and the Kavango-Zambezi (KAZA) Transfrontier Conservation Area and more than 15 years research experience in agriculture and rural development in the region.

Arjaan Pellis (PhD) is Lecturer at the Cultural Geography Chair Group, Department of Environmental Sciences at Wageningen University & Research. His research focuses on the mapping of conflicts in the nexus of tourism, conservation and development.

Andrea Saayman (PhD) is Professor of Economics at the North-West University (NWU), Potchefstroom Campus, South Africa where she lectures Macroeconomics and Econometrics. She is a visiting professor in Tourism Macroeconomics for the Masters course offered by the University of Bologna, Italy as well as an extraordinary professor at the Kore University of Enna, Italy.

Susan Snyman (PhD) is the Director of Research at the African Leadership University's School of Wildlife Conservation. Previously, Sue worked for Wilderness Safaris, a private sector ecotourism operator, for ten years in various roles, including as Group Sustainability Manager. She is vice-chair of the IUCN WCPA Tourism and Protected Areas Specialist (TAPAS) Group and Coordinator of the Communities & Heritage Working Group in TAPAS. She recently managed the Biodiversity and Protected Areas Management Programme for IUCN in 24 countries in Africa. Her research focus is on sustainable, diversified wildlife economies in Africa.

Lesego Senyana Stone (PhD) is Senior Lecturer at the University of Botswana, Maun, Botswana, Department of Tourism and Hospitality Management, Gaborone, Botswana. Her research interests are in sustainable tourism development with specific reference to nature-based tourism, protected area tourism and community livelihoods, tourism marketing and ecotourism.

Moren Tibabo Stone (PhD) is Senior Lecturer at the University of Botswana, Department of Environmental Science. His interests include community resources and development with a focus on sustainable tourism development and management, ecotourism, community-based tourism, protected areas conservation and community livelihoods improvement through tourism engagements.

xiv *List of contributors*

Said Juma Suluo (PhD) is Lecturer at the University of Dar es Salaam Business School and holds a PhD in Business Administration. His research interest generally lies in the field of corporate sustainability and revolves around topics of sustainable tourism, ecotourism, CSR, financial management and sustainability accounting.

Rene van der Duim (PhD) is Emeritus Professor Tourism and Sustainable Development at the Cultural Geography Chair Group, Department of Environmental Sciences at Wageningen University & Research, the Netherlands. His research focuses on the relation between tourism, conservation and development, and he has executed research projects in countries like Kenya, Uganda, Tanzania Costa Rica, Portugal and the Netherlands. In 2015 he published together with Machiel Lamers and Jakomijn van Wijk the book *Institutional Arrangements for Conservation, Development and Tourism in Eastern and Southern Africa* (Springer)

Peet van der Merwe (PhD) is currently a professor and researcher at the School of Tourism Management, at the Faculty of Economic Management Sciences. He also forms part of the research unit TREES (Tourism Research in Economics, Environs and Society), at the faculty which is the only research unit in South Africa with a focus on tourism-related aspects. His main area of specialisation lies with natural-area tourism, which includes ecotourism, wildlife tourism, adventure tourism, marine ecotourism and sustainable tourism development.

Julia van Velden (PhD) is a South African conservation biologist, with interests in the illegal wildlife trade, community-based conservation and participatory research. She completed her PhD in 2020 at Griffith University, on the topic of bushmeat hunting in Malawi. This work investigates the prevalence and livelihood implications of bushmeat, to further both conservation and development goals. Julia completed her Master's degree in conservation biology at the University of Cape Town in 2016, investigating the conflict between blue cranes and farmers in the Western Cape, South Africa. She has also spent time working in Mauritius to conserve the endangered pink pigeon. Her current work focuses on using participatory processes to explore sustainable futures for the Great Barrier Reef.

Acknowledgements

We would like to thank all the contributors to this volume. We thank them for the time they took to work on their chapters and the efforts they made to contribute to the successful completion of this project. We would like to thank them for their commitment and the patience they demonstrated from the beginning to the end of the project. We also acknowledge our families and thank them for giving us time to complete this task. We also thank the publisher for giving us this opportunity.

Abbreviations

AEMP	Amboseli Ecosystem Management Plan
AET	Amboseli Ecosystem Trust
AP	African Parks
BLF	Big Life Foundation
BNA	Botswana National Archives
BoT	Board of Trustees
BWP	Botswana Pula
CAMPFIRE	Communal Areas Management Programme for Indigenous Resources
CBA	Cost-Benefit Analysis
CBNRM	Community Based Natural Resource Management
CBOs	Community-Based Organisations
CBT	Community-Based Tourism
CECIL	Conserving Ecosystems by Ceasing the Importation of Large Animal Trophies Act
CECT	Chobe Enclave Community Trust
CITES	Convention on International Trade in Endangered Species
CKGR	Central Kalahari Game Reserve
CNP	Chobe National Park
CPR	Common Pool Resources
CWBT	Community Wildlife-Based Tourism
DNPW	Department of National Park and Wildlife
DWNP	Department of Wildlife and National Parks
ES	Ecosystem Services
ETIS	Elephant Trade Information System
EU	European Union
EWB	Elephant Without Borders
GDP	Gross Domestic Product
GEF	Global Environment Facility
GKNP	Greater Kruger National Park
GLTFCA	Great Limpopo Transfrontier Conservation Area
GOB	Government of Botswana
GOK	Government of Kenya

List of abbreviations xvii

G7	Group of Seven
HATAB	Hospitality and Tourism Association of Botswana
HVLV	High-value, Low-volume tourism strategy
HWC	Human Wildlife Conflicts
ICDPs	Integrated Conservation and Development Projects
IKS	Indigenous Knowledge Systems
IUCN	International Union for Conservation of Nature
JVP	Joint Venture Partnerships
KAZA	Kavango-Zambezi
KAZA TFCA	Kavango Zambezi Transfrontier Conservation Area
KNP	Kruger National Park
KRST	Khama Rhino Sanctuary Trust)
KWCA	Kenya Wildlife Conservancies Association
KWS	Kenya Wildlife Service
LWC	Lewa Wildlife Conservancy
LWF	Laikipia Wildlife Forum
MET	Ministry of Environment and Tourism
MEWT	Ministry of Environment, Wildlife and Tourism
MGR	Mbirikani Group Ranch
MIKE	Monitoring the Illegal Killing of Elephants
MPT	Maasailand Preservation Trust
NACSO	Namibian Association of CBNRM Support Organisation
NATO	North Atlantic Treaty Organisation
NEPAD	New Partnership for Africa's Development
NFGA	National Forestry and Grassland Administration
NGO	Non-Governmental Organisation
NRC	Northern Rangeland Company
NRT	Northern Rangelands Trust
PAA	Protected Area Approach
PA	Protected Areas
PCF	Predator Compensation Fund
PPC	Pro-Poor Conservation
PPF	Peace Parks Foundation
PPP	Public-Private Partnership
PPT	Pro-Poor Tourism
REDD+	Direct Payments
SADC	Southern Africa Development Community
SANParks	South Africa National Parks
SDGs	Sustainable Development Goals
SES	Social Ecological Systems
SET	Social Exchange Theory
SGL	Special Game Licenses
SRT	Save the Rhino Trust
SVC	Savé Valley Conservancy
TAC	Technical Advisory Committees

xviii *List of abbreviations*

TFCA	Transfrontier Conservation Area
TIES	International Ecotourism Society
TOSCO	Tourism Supporting Conservation
UN	United Nations
UNDRIP	United Nations Declaration on the Rights of Indigenous Peoples
UNEP	United Nations Environment Programme
UNWTO	United Nations World Tourism Organisation
UNWTO	United Nations World Tourism Organization
USA	United States of America
WMA	Wildlife Management Areas
WTTC	World Travel and Tourism Council
WWF	World Wildlife Fund

1 Protected areas and tourism dynamics in Southern Africa

An overview

Moren Tibabo Stone, Lesego Senyana Stone, Goemeone E. J. Mogomotsi and Patricia Kefilwe Mogomotsi

The conservation and development nexus debate is still ongoing, regardless of research, projects and policy developments that have been undertaken to guide and reconcile the discourse. The ongoing search for solutions that can balance the discourse demonstrates that the conservation and development debate is still open for more research, practical project trials and policy instruments to test those endeavours and bridge the knowledge gap between development plans/strategies and practice. This book came into existence to join debates on the discourse to contribute to this open dialogue. The book is centred on protected areas (PAs) and tourism with a focus on the Southern African region, the emphasis being on conservation goals and community livelihoods. In this book we explore the extent to which conservation and development goals are being met in the Southern African protected region, and outline ways in which performance can be improved.

To provide the conceptual and contextual setting of the book, we give an overview of PAs and tourism dynamic trajectories in Africa, revealing achievements and challenges. While some PAs are excelling, others face significant challenges in their roles as biodiversity hosts and in improving community livelihoods through tourism development. Linkages between PAs and community livelihoods (through tourism development) are inseparable, hence the understanding of their complex relationship has drawn global attention in the twenty-first century (Stone & Nyaupane, 2016). Ever since PAs moved from exclusionary (i.e. fortress conservation) to inclusive approaches (i.e. all-encompassing) that accommodate and involve communities as partners in conservation, conservation–development linkages and dynamics have produced complex relationships (Nyaupane & Poudel, 2011). The complex relationship emanates mainly from the unintended consequences that may not be consistent with conservation and development objectives (Stone et al., 2020a). As demonstrated by different chapters in this volume, while to some extent PAs achieve their conservation and development nexus objectives, loss of biodiversity is still taking place, even though efforts are in place to thwart

DOI: 10.4324/9781003193166-1

this. For instance, a recent report by the United Nations warns about the unprecedented loss of biodiversity, including an 82% decline in the biomass of wild mammals since 1970 (Diaz et al., 2019). Equally, evidence shows that some communities have failed to improve their livelihoods even though they have implemented tourism projects that tap the biodiversity hosted by PAs. Stone et al. (2020b) report that, although the need for community involvement in protected areas-based tourism is extensively supported in the literature, many such projects operate below optimal levels. Some reasons for the failure of PAs in fulfilling their conservation and community development roles point to different trajectories (see Balmford et al., 2015; Stone & Stone, 2020b; Birendra, 2021).

Protected areas, tourism and community livelihoods

From inception, PAs were envisaged to conserve iconic landscapes and wildlife (Watson et al., 2014). However, in the past few decades, PAs have undergone pronounced expansions geographically and conceptually (Diaz et al., 2019). Created not only to conserve iconic landscapes and seascapes and to provide habitats for endangered wildlife, PAs also contribute to the livelihood of local communities, bolster national economies through tourism revenues, replenish fisheries and play a key part in the mitigation of and adaptation to climate change, among many other functions (Dudley & Stolton, 2010). PAs are now expected to promote conservation as well as social and economic objectives. It is not only their functions that have been expanded, but also expectations placed on them by a growing number of diverse stakeholders have dramatically increased (Dudley & Stolton, 2010). These new demands are in addition to, rather than a replacement for earlier motivations (i.e. mainly for conservation); the numerous functions have contributed to a prevalence of trade-offs between competing objectives (White et al., 2012). These expected multi-functional dynamics of PAs contribute to the complex intended and unintended relationship outcomes. Hence, Dudley and Stolton (2010) argue that PAs are constantly changing focus, making them susceptible to failures in their quest to achieve one or more of these objectives.

Although many PAs were set up with the dual mandate of landscape and species protection and public use, it was not until the mid-twentieth century that tourism inside PAs was accelerated (Zeiger et al., 1992) and proved to be economically viable. Therefore, many regions around the world, including Southern Africa, rely on PAs not just to uphold conservation, but also for economic development through tourism. Balmford et al. (2015) estimated that worldwide, 94,238 terrestrial PAs received 8 billion visits annually, generating in-country direct expenditures of approximately US$ 600 billion. This signifies that PAs have the potential to generate revenue that enables development while simultaneously promoting conservation efforts. However, PA conservation and development debates are never-ending. Furthermore, maintaining a balance between conservation and development in PAs is challenging, hence this volume of edited chapters was initiated to contribute to knowledge on this discourse. This idea of promoting biodiversity conservation through PAs and combining that with an economic development model (tourism) has been implemented in many places at varying scales (Birendra, 2021). The increased popularity of PA tourism is well documented in the literature (Das & Chatterjee, 2015; Kim & Park, 2017; Mehmetoglu & Normann, 2013; Stone & Nyaupane, 2016; Stone & Stone, 2020a) but comprehensive statistics on PA tourism are limited, especially economic statistics.

While PA tourism may contribute to both economic development and conservation in Southern Africa, the outcomes from specific PAs are likely to vary based on geographical location, management structures in place and approaches to resource governance (Birendra, 2021). Given this knowledge gap, this volume is geared towards bringing together research work carried out in the Southern Africa region and amalgamating it into one volume with a view to build an understanding and fostering research knowledge and ideas that might provide mechanisms for resolving uncertainties; providing tools for effective decision-making, generating means for getting necessary but fragmented work together to foster joint management activities and for PA stakeholders to deal with challenges of the future.

Sustainability

The debate on PAs and the contribution of tourism to conservation and development is ongoing, facilitated by the lack of solutions in striking a balance between conservation and livelihood development sustenance. Tourism in PAs is advocated for because it has the potential to enhance global biodiversity conservation by providing alternative livelihood strategies for local people, and to alleviate poverty in and around PAs (Liu et al., 2012). Conservation success is often predicated on local support for conservation which is strongly influenced by local communities' perceptions of impacts, management and governance issues (Bennett & Dearden, 2014). PAs serve different stakeholders. As a result, they have been exposed to many transformations, subjected to growing marketisation, experienced multiple competing uses, changing rural economies and technological advances (Nyaupane & Poudel, 2011), threatening their existential sustenance due to overstretching to accommodate a wide range of functions. For communities living within or around PAs, tourism performs multifaceted roles, including financial (Saayman & Saayman, 2006), non-financial, livelihood, empowerment and environmental services (Ashley & Elliot, 2003). Informed by the tenets of social exchange theory, literature commonly supports the view that communities will only support conservation if the benefits of living with natural resources outweigh costs (Mbaiwa & Stronza, 2011). Numerous studies have established that costs associated with conservation such as wildlife depredation of crops and livestock have negative impacts on local community attitudes, whereas benefits may have positive outcomes (Fiallo & Jacabson, 1995; Heinen, 1993; Walpole & Goodwin, 2001).

4 *Moren Tibabo Stone et al.*

As a result, PAs are often considered sustainable if they offer more benefits than costs to their inhabitants and adjacent communities. However, ensuring that more benefits than costs are realised is often a difficult feat to achieve. This can make it difficult to justify the existence of PAs. According to Gossling et al. (2009), moving to more sustainable tourism in PAs is a very difficult task as it requires transformations of well-established and interlocking systems and social practices. Stone and Nyaupane (2016) argue that tourism is often managed with inadequate knowledge, particularly of the approaches in which the entire tourism system functions, and of the science that drives it. Furthermore, PAs, tourism and community livelihoods operate as a complex system, and the relationship contains a myriad of factors and activities that are interdependent (i.e. economic, social, environmental, cultural, political, human and policy factors) (Walker et al., 1998). Therefore, we should conceptualise PAs, tourism and livelihoods as a complex system, consisting of multiple interacting components. We can argue that, at one level, tourism in PAs can be a success given the concept's diffusion among industry, government, academics and policy actors, while on the other, it can be a policy failure given the continued growth of negative environmental and social impacts.

Challenges

Despite making global commitments towards increasing the size and effectiveness of PAs within the Convention on Biological Diversity (CBD) framework (CBD, 2011), there is now significant evidence that some governments are sliding back on their commitments to support PAs. This has been shown through disproportionate funding cuts, reductions in professional staff and by ignoring their own policies (Dudley & Stolton, 2010). While the contribution of PAs to tourism development is in most cases measured by financial indicators, it should be noted that many of the benefits cannot be easily measured in monetary terms. The performance and contributions of PAs to conservation and development objectives should not be subjected to financial indicators alone, but to robust, multi-faceted frameworks and indicators. Furthermore, PAs now face over-tourism, other human-led threats (e.g. illegal hunting, mining, deforestation, fragmentations, alien invasive species, etc.), natural disasters and climate change (Birendra, 2021). These common threats to PAs, however, provide a basis for collaboration, building common ground to promote a shared goal and vision among PAs (Diaz et al., 2015). While human-led threats to PAs should not be overlooked, science has lagged behind in generating data that can inform intervention measures. For example, several tools have been developed based on the IUCN framework to assess the effectiveness of management in individual PAs (Birendra, 2021). However, there are no globally accepted measures with which to assess PAs and their management effectiveness (Chape et al., 2005). This has led to more instinctive management practices that potentially compromise the robustness and achievements of PA's set goals (Birendra, 2021).

Outline of the volume

The diverse themes and viewpoints expressed in the chapters of this volume indicate that, although individual Southern African countries may struggle to have PAs optimally realise their full potential in performance, there is acknowledgement that PAs are central to the future of life on our planet, for both humans and wildlife.

This volume is divided into five parts: Part I provides an overview of the book, conceptualising and contextualising relationships between PAs, tourism, conservation goals and community livelihoods.

Part I, with the theme 'Community-protected areas relations: impacts on local communities' is made up of four chapters. Manatsha and Gumbo provide a historical analysis of PAs and tourism development experiences in Southern Africa. They discuss the Western models of wildlife conservation that influenced the development of PAs, They also discuss the preservation and conservation paradigm shifts and critique Western models of conservation that undermine traditional conservation methods. Ntuli and Muchapondwa discuss community perceptions of PAs and tourism, and how perceptions are increasingly being viewed as being important determinants for the success of conservation in Southern Africa. Their chapter establishes a consolidated theoretical framework for understanding community perceptions of PAs and tourism using Ostrom's social-ecological systems as a conceptual framework to guide their chapter. They argue that it is important to understand how people consider the whole system in forming perceptions, and this in turn influences their attitudes and behaviour in their interactions with natural resources. Suluo and Anderson's chapter examines ecotourism as a tool for improving conservation and communities' livelihoods in the Southern African region. They emphasise that ecotourism in the region is still in its infancy, but demonstrate with evidence that ecotourism is instrumental in the improvement of natural and cultural conservation, while also enhancing the livelihoods of local communities. Nevertheless, they highlight that the sector faces challenges that range from the low capacity of local communities to exploit ecotourism opportunities, poor tourism infrastructure, poor linkages with other economic sectors and inadequate governance mechanisms. The last chapter in Part I is by Mutanga who discusses communities' tolerance for wildlife resources through community wildlife-based tourism (CWBT). The chapter highlights that, while CWBT can generate revenue and provide other opportunities that increase tolerance for wildlife resources, CWBT programmes often face several obstacles that weaken communities' tolerance for wildlife resources. The chapter ends with discussions on how obstacles that weaken communities' tolerance for wildlife resources can be mitigated.

Part II, themed 'protected areas, tourism and human–wildlife conflicts dynamics' has four chapters. Van der Duim and Pellis explore and compare landscape-wide partnerships in Southern Africa by integrating literature on partnerships, governance, power and landscapes into a landscape governance

6   *Moren Tibabo Stone et al.*

perspective. Their analysis demonstrates that partnerships play prominent and complementary landscape governance roles. Furthermore, in practice, power relations play a decisive part in achieving these roles. The chapter further highlights that partnerships represent policy arenas where different interests are negotiated and there are trade-offs between conservation and development; between private, public and community interests; but also, differences between tourism and other sectoral practices are brought to the surface. Lastly, they conclude that partnerships can address direct drivers of biodiversity loss (such as poaching), and to a much lesser extent address indirect drivers such as lasting poverty, land subdivisions or impacts of climate change in targeted landscapes.

The next chapter by Moeti adopts the traditional legal research methodology to discuss the cases of the San in Botswana and the Ogiek in Kenya who frequently have to defend their livelihood against fortress conservation policies. The chapter uses legal perspectives to discuss the treatment of Indigenous Peoples who are perceived as being 'in the way of development' or an inconvenience by the State. Moeti's chapter argues that states use their sovereign right to natural resources to grab Indigenous Peoples' land under dubious policies. Consequently, Indigenous Peoples lose their land and the right to participate in projects and resultant profits. Next, Mwakiwa's chapter discusses the socio-economic impacts of wildlife on crop raiding and the efficacy of conservation and agricultural land. The chapter concludes that, in areas that are adjacent to state PAs, private conservancies and community-based natural resource management (CBNRM) programmes were established as landowners realised managing wildlife is more profitable than managing livestock. Mogomotsi and Mogomotsi's chapter focuses on the effectiveness of current mitigation techniques in human–wildlife conflicts in communities adjacent to PAs. The chapter discusses lethal and non-lethal mitigation strategies. The chapter's main findings reveal that, although there are various approaches to mitigating human–wildlife conflicts, there is no single approach that can adequately deter predators and crop-raiders effectively. Therefore, the chapter concludes that governments and other stakeholders should identify and embrace integrated interventions with an understanding of people's expectations, realities and attitudes to ensure efficacy.

Part III is themed 'managing the wildlife economy: contemporary issues in Southern Africa' and constitutes five chapters. Mbaiwa and Mogende use socio-ecological theory to analyse the lifting of the hunting ban and the elephant debate in Botswana. They further analyse its implications for conservation and development in Southern Africa. In their analysis, they juxtapose the different views held by people in the Global North and South regarding the hunting debate. They provide evidence to indicate that trophy hunting provides incentives for wildlife conservation and rural communities' development in Southern Africa, particularly in Botswana. In concluding, they indicate that any policy shift that affects wildlife conservation and rural livelihoods needs to be informed by socio-ecological approaches. Following that is Chimuka's chapter which addresses the role of the media and the international community in recent conservation issues in Southern Africa. The author argues, that traditionally, the media in Africa have not focused much on environmental issues. In a continent facing major political, economic and social challenges, issues to do with wildlife are mostly covered by special interest groups like non-governmental organisations and academics working on the same. However, the killing of a lion called Cecil in Zimbabwe instantly became a global event. One of the findings of the chapter is that the Western media set the dominant narrative on conservation issues in Southern Africa. Nevertheless, the chapter noted that social media have narrowed the media imbalance between Africa and the West.

Dube's contribution focuses on nature-based tourism resources and climate change in the Southern African region. It highlights that extreme weather events attributable to climate variability and change have increased in occurrence between 2010 and 2020, and equally, the socio-economic cost of such hydro-meteorological incidents have equally risen. The chapter argues that, given its reliance on weather and climate, nature-based tourism is one of the sectors most vulnerable to climate change. The chapter that follows is by Cox. She focuses on international organisations and the ivory sales ban debate, using Zimbabwe, Namibia and Botswana as her case studies. The chapter discusses the issue of lifting the ban on the sale of ivory in order to allow Southern African countries to sell their valuable stockpiles for conservation and development purposes. The chapter highlights a growing demand amongst Southern African states for an end to the international 'one size fits all' legislation which Southern African leaders argue prevents their countries from selling elephant ivory and using the proceeds of such to fund their conservation efforts.

The next chapter by Snyman discusses implications of the COVID-19 pandemic for nature-based tourism in Southern Africa. The chapter posits that nature-based tourism is a key economy activity for most countries in Southern Africa, and provides employment and income to households, communities and governments, and in most cases, supports conservation. The chapter discusses how the COVID-19 pandemic resulted in an abrupt and complete halt to all tourism activities, devastating the Southern African region as many communities and governments rely heavily on tourism and its contributions to local and national economies. The chapter concludes that it is not only livelihoods that have been negatively affected, but there have also been significant impacts on conservation as a large majority of conservation funding in Africa comes from the tourism sector.

Part IV is themed 'protected areas and tourism practices: policy and practice'. The section has five chapters, beginning with Mtapuri's that discusses community-based tourism in proximity to PAs. The chapter highlights the importance of PAs and argues that, to ensure that local communities get maximum benefits, PAs need to be integrated and managed alongside local communities, with them and for them, through assemblages such as community trusts. The chapter cautiously highlights that the interests of communities may collide with the purposes of PAs due to cultural values and traditional practices. The chapter concludes by highlighting how stereotypes of Africans as poachers are created when local communities harvest what their ancestors used to harvest in their normal course of life. Furthermore, the chapter argues that rich people enjoy an exclusive and unfair advantage over natural resources because of their money. Due to their purchasing power, the chapter argues that the rich can hunt animals but are never labelled as poachers. Moreover, they are often supported by laws instituted by national governments to earn money from hunting fees.

Mogomotsi and Mogomotsi's chapter adopts traditional legal research methodologies to analyse environment and conservation policy instruments in Southern Africa, specifically on the militarisation of conservation and 'shoot to kill' policies as viable policy tools for wildlife conservation in Africa. It places the militarisation of wildlife law enforcement and conservation within the legitimate preserve of the sovereignty of states. It further characterises and equates poachers to armed belligerents who can be related to terrorists. Therefore, the chapter argues that international humanitarian law (law of armed conflict) can be lawfully used by nation-states to enforce international wildlife law. The chapter concludes that states have a right to adopt legal frameworks for the execution of militarisation of conservation, and that the shoot-to-kill approach can be an effective part of the wider approach to effectively combat poaching and protect wildlife species for the benefit of future generations. Next, Stone and Stone's chapter focuses on the implications of the 'High-Value, Low-Volume' (HVLV) tourism strategy in conservation and tourism resources management focusing on Botswana. The chapter's discussions reveal that the HVLV tourism strategy has changed Botswana's tourism landscape, resulting in domination by the international tourism market over the domestic market on the consumption of the country's nature-based tourism offerings. The imbalance in Botswana's tourism consumption has led to an unreliable and unsustainable tourism development approach. The main findings of the chapter indicate that although the HVLV tourism strategy has contributed to community livelihoods and the conservation of tourism resources, it has also yielded unintended consequences by stifling and limiting the domestic market from consuming Botswana's most sought-after destinations. It concludes that while the call for the 'Low-Volume' part of the HVLV tourism strategy takes care of resources' conservation, the 'High-Value' part excludes locals, thereby compromising principles of sustainability such as social equity and justice.

The following chapter by Gohori, van der Merwe and Saayman assesses the promotion of pro-poor tourism in Southern Africa. The chapter theorises that Southern African governments came to the realisation that the creation of PAs may be key to poverty alleviation, wildlife conservation and rural development through the involvement of local communities in tourism development. The chapter gives an overview of poverty alleviation, natural resource conservation and community development through community-based natural resource management (CBNRM) initiatives in the Southern African region. The chapter concludes by highlighting the challenges faced by Southern Africa in its endeavour to use tourism as a tool for poverty alleviation, conservation

PAs and tourism dynamics in Southern Africa 9

and development. Possible solutions to the challenges are discussed. Van Velden's chapter follows and centres its arguments on conservation and development issues, with a specific focus on contrasting safari and bushmeat hunting in Southern Africa. The chapter sets the scene by declaring that hunting from PAs, either legal or illegal, can have ramifications on the success of conservation and community development. The chapter provides a conceptual overview of bushmeat and safari hunting via a narrative literature review and uses case studies of Namibia and Malawi to explore their linkages and differences. The chapter concludes that safari hunting and bushmeat hunting are controversial topics in conservation. The chapter's assessment of the two as inter-related issues provides important insights into how to provide win–win situation for both communities and conservation.

Part V is the concluding chapter that synthesises all the chapters in the volume. The chapter weaves in together case studies and conceptual materials presented in the book by accentuating key findings that bring new insights in understanding the relationship between PAs and tourism in Southern Africa and the role they play in contributing to conservation goals and improvements in community livelihoods. The chapter argues that the relationship between PAs and community livelihoods is complex, dynamic and follows evolution pathways due the historical transition of the roles and management regimes of PAs that span from exclusionary (i.e. fortress conservation) to inclusionary (i.e. integrated conservation), preservation to protection, and conservation and development. What the chapter highlights as a take-home lesson is that PAs are not static. They are now expected to achieve conservation, social and economic objectives, extending their functions and meeting expectations placed on them by a growing number of diverse stakeholders. It is a mammoth task for PAs to achieve this new agenda without abandoning their existential role, accentuating conflicts and inconsistencies between conservation and development and leaving a vacuum which science has to fill. Evidently, there are currently no integrated approaches that can harmoniously bring conservation and development in PAs without generating unintended outcomes. Furthermore, as discovered from the contributing chapters in this volume, conceptual frameworks that have explanatory power on how the relationship between PAs, tourism and community livelihoods is structured, nested and/or organised, and how best each constituent can influence each other and ultimately influence desired interactional and resultant outcomes (either intended or unintended, positive or negative) are lacking.

Overall, this chapter summarises findings from this edited volume in an endeavour to contribute to knowledge on integrating PAs, tourism and community livelihoods. The volume brings together different case studies in Southern Africa, focusing on practice, governance and policy instruments. This chapter draws our attention and contributes to knowledge and understanding on why some case studies seem to achieve conservation and development goals while others do not. Different explanations are given, some based on empirical data while others are conceptual.

References

Ashley, C., & Elliott, J. (2003). 'Just wildlife?' or a source of local development? *ODI Natural Resource Perspectives*, 85. Retrieved from www.odi.org/sites/odi.org.uk/files/odi-assets/publications-opinion-files/2790.pdf

Balmford, A., Green, J. M. H., Anderson, M., et al. (2015) Walk on the wild side: Estimating the global magnitude of visits to protected areas. *PLoS Biology*, 13 (2), e1002074.

Bennett, N. J., & Dearden, P. (2014). Why local people do not support conservation: Community perceptions of marine protected area livelihood impacts, governance and management in Thailand. *Marine Policy*, 44, 107–116.

Birendra, K. C. (2021). Complexity in balancing conservation and tourism in protected areas: Contemporary issues and beyond. *Tourism and Hospitality Research*, 14673584211015807.

Chape, S., Harrison, J., Spalding, M., et al. (2005) Measuring the extent and effectiveness of protected areas as an indicator for meeting global biodiversity targets. *Philosophical Transactions of the Royal Society B: Biological Sciences*, 360 (1454), 443–455.

Convention on Biological Diversity (CBD). (2011). *COP 10 Decision X/2: Strategic Plan for Biodiversity 2011–2020*. Accessed 10 June 2021 at www.cbd.int/decision/cop/?id=12268

Das, M., & Chatterjee, B. (2015). Ecotourism: A panacea or a predicament? *Tourism Management Perspectives*, 14, 3–16.

Diaz, J. M., Stallings, K. D., Birendra, K. C. B, & Seekamp, E. (2015) Evaluating multi-institutional partnership sustainability: A case study of collaborative workforce development in renewable energy assessment. *Educational Research and Evaluation*, 21 (5–6), 466–484.

Diaz, S., Settele, J., & Brondizio, E, S. (2019). *Summary for policymakers of the global assessment report on biodiversity and ecosystem services of the intergovernmental Science-Policy Platforms on biodiversity and Ecosystem Services*. Bonn: IPBES.

Dudley, N., & Stolton, S. (Eds.). (2010). *Arguments for protected areas: Multiple benefits for conservation and use*. London: Routledge.

Fiallo, A., & Jacabson, S. (1995). Local communities and protected areas: Attitudes of rural residents towards conservation and Machalilla National Park, Ecuador. *Environmental Conservation*, 22 (3), 241–249.

Gossling, S., Hall, C., & Weaver, D. (Eds.). (2009). *Sustainable tourism futures. Perspectives on systems, restructuring and innovations*. New York: Routledge.

Heinen, J. (1993). Park–people relations in Kosi Tappu Wildlife Reserve, Nepal: A socio-economic analysis. *Environmental Conservation*, 20 (1), 25–34.

Kim, K. H., & Park, D. B. (2017). Relationships among perceived value, satisfaction, and loyalty: Community based ecotourism. *Journal of Travel & Tourism Marketing*, 34 (2), 171–191.

Liu, W., Vogt, C. A., Luo, J., He, G., Frank, K. A., & Liu, J. (2012). Drivers and socio-economic impacts of tourism participation in protected areas. *PloS One*, 7 (4), e35420.

Mbaiwa, J., & Stronza, A. (2011). The effects of tourism development on rural livelihoods in the Okavango Delta, Botswana. *Journal of Sustainable Tourism*, 18 (5), 35–56.

Mehmetoglu, M., & Normann Ø (2013). The link between travel motives and activities in nature-based tourism. *Tourism Review*, 68 (2), 3–13.

Nyaupane, G. P., & Poudel, S. (2011). Linkages among biodiversity, livelihood, and tourism. *Annals of Tourism Research*, 38 (4), 1344–1366.

Saayman, M., & Saayman, A. (2006). Estimating the economic contribution of visitor spending in the Kruger National Park to the regional economy. *Journal of Sustainable Tourism*, 14 (1), 67–81.

Stone, M. T., & Nyaupane, G. P. (2016). Protected areas, tourism and community livelihoods linkages: A comprehensive analysis approach. *Journal of Sustainable Tourism*, 24 (5), 673–693.

Stone, M. T., Nyaupane, G. P., Timothy, D. J., & Stone, L. S. (2020a). Natural resources, sustainable tourism development and community livelihoods relationships: A comparison between Botswana and the USA. In Stone, M. T., Lenao, M., & Moswete, N. (Eds.), *Natural resources, tourism and community livelihoods in southern Africa: Challenges of sustainable development*. New York. Routledge, 221–234.

Stone, M. T., & Stone, L. S. (2020b). Challenges of community-based tourism in Botswana: A review of literature. *Transactions of the Royal Society of South Africa*, 75 (2), 181–193.

Walker, P., Greiner, R., McDonald, D., & Lyne, V. (1998). The tourism futures simulator: A systems thinking approach. *Environmental Modelling & Software*, 14 (1), 59–67.

Walpole, M., & Goodwin, H. (2001). Local attitudes towards conservation and tourism around Komodo National Park, Indonesia. *Environmental Conservation*, 28 (2), 160–166.

Watson, J. E., Dudley, N., Segan, D. B., & Hockings, M. (2014). The performance and potential of protected areas. *Nature*, 515 (7525), 67–73.

White, C., Halpern, B. S., & Kappel, C. V. (2012). Ecosystem service tradeoff analysis reveals the value of marine spatial planning for multiple ocean uses. *Proceedings of the National Academy of Science USA*, 109, 4696–4701.

Zeiger, J. B., Caneday, L. M., & Baker, P. R. (1992). Symbiosis between tourism and our national parks. *Parks Recreation*, 27, 74–79.

Part I

Community–PA relations

Impacts on local communities

2 Protected areas and tourism development

A historical analysis of the Southern African experience

Boga Thura Manatsha and Bongani Glorious Gumbo

Introduction

Tourism is as old as mankind, however the history of nature-based tourism can be traced 'to Aristotle who traveled to the Island of Lesbos in the Aegean Sea to study marine creatures' (Pradhan, 2008, p. 43). In the nineteenth century, many people started taking interest in travelling 'in quest for spectacular and unique scenery' (Pradhan, 2008, p. 43). It was also during this period that national parks and game reserves were introduced worldwide (Bolaane, 2013; Pradhan, 2008). Tourism is a key socio-economic activity, strongly supported by governments and the private sector in many developing countries due to its contribution to economic development, promoting tolerance and appreciation of different cultures (Manatsha, 2014; Telfer & Sharpley, 2008). For this reason, tourism is described as the 'largest peaceful movement of people across cultural boundaries' (Lett cited in Telfer & Sharpley, 2008, p. 1).

The concept of 'protected areas' in sub-Saharan Africa is a colonial creation. However, the concept of conservation is not new to Africa. Western models disparaged and undermined indigenous methods of conservation (Hinz, 2003; Phuthego & Chanda, 2004). During the colonial period, sub-Saharan Africa experienced reckless and wanton hunting of game for hides, meat and trophies by European hunters, explorers, fortune seekers and adventurers (McCormick, 1989, pp. 8–10). The Griquas moved from the Cape Colony, South Africa, into the Bechuanaland Protectorate (Botswana), at the beginning of 1800, and hunted down and slaughtered thousands of elephants using guns imported from Europe (Tlou & Campbell, 1997, pp. 173–176). The Griquas were later joined by the Barolong and Batlhaping (Tswana groups). The inland transportation of elephant tusks, from Botswana to South Africa, fed into the large-scale intercontinental ivory trade. The ivory was destined for the Asian market and Europe (Tlou & Campbell, 1997, pp. 173–176). The illicit trade in ivory dates to this period, though it has only recently attracted international attention (Annecke & Masubelele, 2016; Hess, 2021; Lunstrum, 2015). Hunters from Europe also participated in hunting expeditions for profit-making and leisure (Hess, 2021, p. 3). Upon the near depletion of the elephant population, especially in the

DOI: 10.4324/9781003193166-3

Bechuanaland Protectorate, the same perpetrators turned around and blamed traditional methods of conservation as the root cause (Hinz, 2003). The dismissive attitudes towards traditional methods of conservation were later popularised by Hardin in his article, 'The Tragedy of the Commons' (Hardin, 1968).

Ironically, the near depletion of Africa's game caused uneasiness and alarm on the part of colonial administrators across sub-Saharan Africa. They therefore advocated for the 'protection' and 'preservation' of Africa's flora and fauna through 'Western models' of conservation. Thus, in the twentieth century, national parks and game reserves were created (Bolaane, 2013; Carruthers, 1989). These protected areas invariably conflicted with traditional methods of conservation. In Southern Africa, the concept of national parks and game reserves originated from the United States (USA) Yellowstone model, 'or from British imperial reactions to the predatory hunting of the nineteenth century' (Bolaane, 2013, p. 1; Tlou & Campbell, 1997). These Western models were, and still are, seen as superior. Some scholars, mainly Eurocentric in approach, see 'traditional methods' as romanticised myth (Hinz, 2003), and blame these for ecological disasters and policy failures (Hardin, 1968).

Some, however, argue that traditional methods of conservation are 'ecologically sound' and can lead to the sustainable use of natural resources (Phuthego & Chanda, 2004). Others contend that the much-touted Western models of conservation fail to consider the needs of local communities (Kepe, Wynberg & Ellis, 2005; Robins & van der Waal, 2008; Strickland-Munro, 2010). Thus, conflicts between governments and local communities over access to protected areas always evoke autochthonous emotions. Some have argued that 'many protected-area schemes have overlooked the importance of local specific ways of providing for food, health, shelter, energy and other fundamental needs' (Pimbert & Pretty, 2009, p. 297). Often 'local communities are excluded from managing their local resources leading to serious contestations and conflicts' (Manatsha, 2014, p. 524).

The tourism sector in Southern Africa, as in East Africa, is based on both consumptive wildlife utilisation and non-consumptive utilization. In these regions, therefore, the history of tourism development is inextricably linked to that of wildlife conservation. Historically, wildlife tourism has attracted, and continues to attract, both local and international tourists because of its aesthetic value. Through tourists' visits, these safari connoisseurs have injected the much-needed revenue for economic development in countries that host the wildlife resource and the tourism industry (Rogerson, 2004). To safeguard this natural heritage, governments in these regions set aside large chunks of land dedicated to the protection of wildlife, in the form of protected areas. These protected areas were established in rural or communal areas belonging to peasants, who eked out a living by subsistence agriculture (Kepe, Wynberg & Ellis, 2005). This exacerbated social inequities and compromised community livelihoods.

Feeling alienated and violated, local communities often withhold their support from and/or frustrate the touted Western conservation models (Stone, et al., 2020). Legislations have been employed to reinforce fortress conservation

(Lunstrum, 2015). Throughout Southern Africa, game parks and national parks were created by colonial administrators. Their conservation agenda was shaped by European environmentalism and the emerging threat of extermination of wild animals. Ironically, this has been exacerbated by European trophy hunters engaged in illicit trade in wildlife products (Fisch, 1999; Hess, 2021). However, the concept of wildlife and natural resource conservation was part of the cultural heritage and practice of African communities prior to European colonisation (Gumbo, 2020).

This chapter examines the historical development of fortress conservation in Southern Africa. It looks at its interface with indigenous communities in the colonial and post-colonial periods and encapsulates the region's historical experience. It contends that, from inception, fortress conservation alienated local communities by expropriating their land (Kepe, Wynberg & Ellis, 2005). Protected areas tended to be excessively 'preservationist', and, thus, denied local communities' access to wildlife resources. The exponential increase in the population of wild animals has created enduring human–wildlife conflict. The chapter notes, however, that, over time, post-colonial governments have made modifications that sought to mitigate the excesses of colonial policies, with a view to assuaging the local communities and luring them into partnerships in conservation (Strickland-Munro, 2010). Ironically, even in the post-colonial period, the tourism industry began as an enclave of the resource-rich foreign elites. A few local investors got involved in the ownership and management of tourism enterprises (Gumbo, 2002). In this chapter, two national parks are used as case studies: the Kruger National Park in South Africa and the Chobe National Park in Botswana.

Kruger National Park, South Africa

The creation of the Kruger National Park (KNP) in South Africa in 1926 was done in the context of political and economic nationalism. It was not just a victory of the moral (game protection) against the evil (wanton killing of game animals) (Carruthers, 1989). Politically, it was established to unify the English-speaking white South Africans and Afrikaners. These two groups needed each other's support against the threat from land-starved, politically disfranchised Africans whose land they had violently expropriated since 1652 (Kepe, Wynberg & Ellis, 2005). In the Transvaal, two legal avenues were 'followed by the state for protecting wildlife – "conservation" (hunting restrictions) and "preservation" (game reserves)' (Carruthers, 1994, p. 266). It was due to this legal framework that the KNP was established. Another objective was to protect biodiversity as cultural heritage for posterity (Carruthers, 1994).

The KNP, like many protected areas in Southern Africa, experiences serious contestation from local communities (Anthony, 2007; Kepe, Wynberg & Ellis, 2005; Robins & van der Waal, 2008). Increasing poaching incidents in the KNP may be seen as criminal acts (Annecke & Masubelele, 2016; Lunstrum, 2015), but this could also be due to the discontent of local communities. Annecke and Masubelele argue that, in the KNP, 'rhino poaching exacerbates the thin relations that exist between the Park and the neighbouring communities particularly since the majority of poachers (60%) come from or are sheltered by these communities' (2016, p. 200). Strickland-Munro (2010, p. 193) contends that 'discontented communities can undermine conservation through deliberate contravention of park regulations'. This fits within what has been termed 'everyday forms of resistance' or 'weapons of the weak' by James Scott (1985, p. xvi). Thus, peasants deploy various strategies when responding to what they view as unfair actions by the state (Scott, 1985).

In South Africa, the land issue is so contentious and emotive that protected areas are seen by local communities as depriving them of their land rights and resources (Robins & van der Waal, 2008). Kepe, Wynberg and Ellis (2005, p. 5) assert that: 'The creation of many protected areas around the world has often resulted in the alienation of indigenous populations from their land and resources.' Land is the root cause of local communities' concerns and contestations at KNP. Historically, black communities were evicted from the land. Conflicts between the KNP and local communities worsened during the apartheid era (Carruthers, 1989, 1994). The issue of access by black communities in conservation areas and social inequity dominate such conflicts. From 1926 to 1989, the KNP was only open to white communities. This strengthened the perception held by black communities that their land was unjustly expropriated to satisfy the wants of the minority whites (Kepe, Wynberg & Ellis, 2005).

In post-apartheid South Africa, 'national park managers are increasingly focusing on building positive relationships with local communities' (Strickland-Munro, Moore & Freitag-Ronaldson, 2010, p. 663). For the KNP, some local communities acknowledge economic benefits from park tourism, but it has also been observed that 'the enclave nature of Park tourism keeps local communities separate from the park and makes it hard for them to benefit from it' (Strickland-Munro, Moore & Freitag-Ronaldson, 2010, p. 663). The KNP is inaccessible to local communities because it is fenced; some researchers suggest that its boundaries should be made 'more "permeable" to improve relationships with adjacent communities, while also pragmatically managing community expectations' (Strickland-Munro, Moore & Freitag-Ronaldson, 2010, p. 663). Strickland-Munro (2010, p. 60) asserts that 'apartheid was thus complicit in fostering the physical and psychological separation of black South Africans from the natural environment'.

The conflicts between the KNP and local communities are exacerbated by the low involvement of the latter in the park's activities. There are, however, some miniscule economic projects geared towards empowering them, such as curio sales and car washing. There are also semi-skilled jobs that local communities partake in (Strickland-Munro, Moore & Freitag-Ronaldson, 2010, p. 663). These are, however, seen as less significant economic activities (Strickland-Munro, 2010). Although the KNP provides economic and employment opportunities to local communities, there are concerns about the hiring process. Some residents indicate nepotism is rife, the unfair hiring process excludes deserving people. In addition, some lament that the 'benefits of the Park employment [are] restricted to those employed and [are] not available to other community members' (Strickland-Munro, Moore & Freitag-Ronaldson, 2010, p. 671).

The KNP is bordered by former Bantustans. These areas are largely impoverished, undeveloped and underdeveloped, and social inequalities are high compared to many parts of South Africa. These issues reinforce peoples' perceptions of the park 'as being for tourists, not for them' (Strickland-Munro, Moore & Freitag-Ronaldson, 2010, p. 663). Another issue of concern between local communities and the KNP are human–wildlife conflicts (Anthony, 2007; Strickland-Munro, 2010). A study by Chaminuka, McCrindle and Udo (2012, p. 235) found that 'households in villages close to the park reported higher incidence of livestock depredation (32%) than those further from the park (13%)'. The same study concludes that 'farmers viewed wildlife as an obstacle to cattle farming' (2012, p. 235).

Local communities also complain about high entrance fees. This prevents them from visiting the park. In their view, KNP largely remains a preserve of foreign tourists (Strickland-Munro, 2010). In post-apartheid South Africa, community participation is increasingly considered a critical avenue for improving relations between the park and local communities (Strickland-Munro, 2010). This is also done to 'increase legitimacy' of the KNP, which communities feel sits on their land. South African authorities also realise that 'discontented communities can undermine conservation through deliberate contravention of park regulations, degrading natural environments and through the creation of political instability, which typically disrupts tourism' (Strickland-Munro, 2010, p. 193).

Land conflicts, emanating from the history of the KNP, are incessant. In post-apartheid South Africa, the land restitution programme resulted in the Makuleke community and the Khomani san reclaiming their ancestral land from the KNP (Robins & van der Waal, 2008). The South African government has discontinued the process of returning land to claimants due to the importance of the park in the national and regional economy (Strickland-Munro, 2010). Instead, monetary compensation is preferred. This, however, fuels land conflicts because Africans' attachment to their land for spiritual, psychological, historical, cultural and symbolic reasons is central to the land debate. As elsewhere in the region, land conflicts are also exacerbated by rigid conservation measures instituted by governments (Gumbo, 2002). These measures restrict access to resources found in protected areas. Local communities adjacent to the KNP feel excluded from the park for several reasons, including the 'unresolved' land issue.

Chobe National Park, Botswana

The Chobe National Park (CNP) in Botswana also provides a good case study of how protected areas result in conflicts with local communities. In Botswana, the objectives of establishing protected areas have historically been narrowed to the protection of game animals from reckless trophy hunters and unscrupulous poachers (Bolaane, 2013). With more tourist visits, it was envisaged that more income would be generated to offset recurrent costs incurred by colonial administrators, whose budgetary allocations for the Bechuanaland Protectorate were paltry (Parsons & Crowder, 1988). Revenue would accrue, for instance, from entrance fees, leasing of hunting concession areas to private safari firms and income tax (Botswana National Archives (BNA) S. 568/13/1). The Bechuanaland Protectorate was one of the poorest countries in Africa. It was only after independence, in 1966, with the discovery and exploitation of diamonds that the economic situation got better (Tlou & Campbell, 1997). The income from the nascent tourism industry was still key to the country's economic development.

The CNP became the first game park to be established in Botswana. So crucial was game protection that 17% of the land was designated as national parks and game reserves and 20% as wildlife management areas (Republic of Botswana, 2000). The evolution of the Chobe Game Reserve, as it was called at inception in 1960, dovetails with that of the KNP (Carruthers, 1989, 1994): it was imposed on local communities for economic and political motives and as a source of revenue and prestige for the imperial power. This is evidenced by colonial administrators' disregard for, and replacing of, the existing traditional conservation practices informed by indigenous knowledge systems (see Bolaane, 2013).

The Chobe Game Reserve was a product of the plan of the then British Resident Commissioner, Sir Charles Rey, to protect wild animals in the area (Gumbo, 2010). Charles Rey and other British colonial officials wrongly assumed that African leaders did not appreciate the value of game (Bolaane, 2013). Examples of the nationalists' emphasis on the development of livestock over wildlife in the case of Maasai along the Ngorongoro Crater in Tanzania's Serengeti Park were cited (BNA S. 568/13/5). Thus, Africans were perceived as people who saw game as either food or predators worthy of destruction on sight (BNA S. 568/13/5, 1960). Imbued with such Eurocentric perceptions, colonial administrators used sentiments such as these in considering the establishment of the game reserve in the Chobe area. The scenic beauty of the flora and fauna in this park, like that of the KNP, made it one of Southern Africa's most famous tourist destinations (BNA S. 568/13/1). Its beauty is so renowned that it attracted connoisseurs, such as Elizabeth Taylor, who remarried fellow film actor, Richard Burton, in the CNP in the 1970s (Gumbo, 2002). Former President of the US, Bill Clinton, and his wife, Hillary, also visited the CNP in 1998 (Gumbo, 2002), further catapulting the area to international stardom.

Growing pains for local livelihoods amid plenty

When the Chobe Game Reserve was created, local communities were not consulted, yet they were required to pay tax to colonial administrators. Scott's (1985, 29) analysis of the tendency by the bureaucrats to undermine those

Protected areas and tourism development   21

under their control could not have been more appropriate: 'the peasantry appeared in the historical record not so much as historical actors but more or less anonymous contributors to statistics on … taxes'. In the Chobe, this was the beginning of the marginalisation of local communities' livelihoods. The hunting of any animal or bird within the Game Reserve was prohibited. Even an 'innocent act' of taking away for 'the pot' any wild animal's carcass left by predators became regarded as an unlawful act punishable by law (Gumbo, 2002, p. 50). An animal could only be killed in self-defence. Taylor (2001, pp. 3–4) sums it up: 'considering the means attached to various subsistence options, wildlife assumes a greater importance than simply its nutritional value, an importance of which conservation policies take little cognizance'.

Furthermore, firearms and any type of weapon or trap with the potential to endanger animal life were prohibited in the Chobe Game Reserve. A permit was required to enter the newly established game reserve; permits were not always granted (BNA S. 568/13/2). Local communities were deprived of other resources, such as firewood and access to medicinal plants (Mosetlhi, 2012). Fishing, a major source of livelihood for these riparian communities, was also regulated in parts of the Chobe River, which had become part of the game reserve, especially around Kasane (Gumbo, 2002). The Chobe River is the boundary between Botswana and Namibia. Ironically, Botswana's conservation laws prohibit citizens to fish using nets in the Kasane area, while Namibians, on the other side of the river, are not affected by this law and catch the same fish protected on the Botswana side (BNA S. 568/13/2). In Botswana, the contravention of the above constituted an offence, which was punishable by a fine 'not exceeding one hundred pounds or, in default of payment, to imprisonment for a period not exceeding six months' (BNA S. 568/13/2). Community leaders protested these restrictions to no avail. For communities living adjacent to protected areas, the euphoria that accompanied the attainment of independence from Britain soon wilted as there was not much change insofar as conservation contestations were concerned.

Post-colonial governments not only inherited the status quo, they also found themselves beholden to the whims of the Convention on International Trade in Endangered Species (CITES), which further entrenched the protection of wildlife (Hutton, 1997). Various pieces of legislations on wildlife protection made criminals out of local communities (Othomile, 1997). Taylor (2001, pp. 3–4) avers that communities subsequently acquiesced to state-sanctioned restrictive measures on wildlife conservation but suggests that one can debate the effectiveness of the legislation on stopping 'poaching for subsistence'. The emergence of unscrupulous syndicates of traders in wildlife products and the globalisation of such trade have led to sophisticated poaching networks in Southern Africa (Annecke & Masubelele, 2016; Lunstrum, 2015), often enlisting participants from disgruntled former freedom fighters in neighbouring countries acting in cohort with some members of local communities (Gumbo, 2010).

This negative development has necessitated the strengthening of state institutions responsible for the protection of wildlife. This includes the

22 Boga Thura Manatsha and Bongani Glorious Gumbo

deployment of the Botswana Defence Force, Department of Wildlife and National Parks (DWNP), and other intelligence and security organs (Henk, 2007). Notwithstanding this, local communities have faced enduring challenges because of human–wildlife conflict. The protection of wild animals led to the increase in their population, resulting in the environment's carrying capacity being compromised. Crowded in their space, wild animals have extended their territory to human settlements causing damage to property and life (Ludbrock, 1995). Human–wildlife conflicts persist, and the government is accused of being less than candid in paying compensation for the damage caused. This makes local communities apprehensive of wildlife conservation (Tamuhla, 1997). The process of securing compensation is rigidly bureaucratic as it requires the claimant to ensure that officers from the DWNP satisfy themselves of the merits of the case (Ludbrock, 1995). Examples of human–wildlife conflicts abound: they have mushroomed in all the villages of the Chobe enclave. These include the destruction of property and human life (Gumbo, 2010, 2020).

The lack of support for conservation is exacerbated by the government's annexation of more communal land for the expansion of protected areas, including forest reserves for the protection of flora (Republic of Botswana, 2004). These include the Kasane Forest Reserve, created in 1968, and the following four were declared in 1981: Kasane Extension Forest Reserve, Chobe Forest Reserve, Maikaelelo Forest Reserve, and Sibuyu Forest Reserve. The impact of the Western models of conservation remains a contested arena. Objectives of conservation have been partially met, while livelihoods have been pushed to the fringes due to the losses occasioned by the fortress conservation model (Mosetlhi, 2012). This scenario plays out across Southern Africa (Strickland-Munro, 2010). To lure and secure communities' participation in wildlife conservation and management, the Botswana government introduced Community Based Natural Resource Management (CBNRM) in 1990 (Mbaiwa, 2004; Tamuhla, 1997).

Modelled along Zimbabwe's Communal Areas Management Programme for Indigenous Resources (CAMPFIRE), CBNRM programmes are responsible for the management of wildlife hunting quotas granted by the DWNP in local areas. In return, local communities in the vicinity of wildlife habitats are guaranteed direct economic returns. They benefit in the form of cash acquired through the sale of the wildlife quota to commercial hunting companies, the revenue is shared between the community (35%) and the government (65%) (Keitumetse, 2009). In the Chobe District, the CBNRM project is known as the Chobe Enclave Conservation Trust. It is a new people-centred conservation ethic and communities gradually bought into the project. Other communities living with wildlife have adopted such projects. The wildlife industry also created employment opportunities for people around and beyond parks, contributing to improved livelihoods (Butynski & Von Richter, 1975). Community participation was gradually achieved through increased employment opportunities in the tourism industry, thus providing purchasing power in an otherwise remote district.

Tourism development: an enclave for the elites or livelihood game changer?

As with conservation, tourism development goals and the impact of tourism on livelihoods is another protracted debate. Tourism researchers posit that the industry is an ideal strategy for the 'reorientation of local economies which are marginal in the wider global economy' (Binns & Nel, 2002). Botswana's tourism industry began in the mid-1980s following the end of the liberation wars in Southern Africa (Gumbo, 2010). The government established a Public-Private Partnership (PPP) with Hospitality and Tourism Association of Botswana (HATAB), with the latter representing private sector investors in tourism. The objectives of the industry are articulated in various policy documents, such as the Tourism Policy (1990), Tourism Master Plan (2000), Tourism Act (1992) and Tourism Regulations (1996). These speak to several goals, which address economic diversification because Botswana's economy is heavily dependent on diamond mining, making it vulnerable to global economic shocks.

Historically, the tourism sector has been dominated by elite foreign investors. Local participation is limited to employment opportunities because citizens lack the finances needed for substantial investment in tourism (Gumbo, 2010). The government of Botswana also sets out to achieve economic sustainability with ecological balance to increase the Gross Domestic Product (GDP), without damaging the environment (Republic of Botswana, 2000). In 2020, the tourism industry's direct contribution to the GDP was BWP 9,546.4 million, representing 5.3% of GDP, and 6.6% of total employment (World Travel and Tourism Council, 2020). As with many other tourist destinations globally, the Botswana tourism industry has suffered due to COVID-19, which has restricted international travel. This has caused major disruptions and declines in the industry, job losses and increased poverty (Stone, et al., 2021).

In 2000, it was estimated that approximately 60% of employed people in the Chobe District worked in the tourism sector (Gumbo, 2010). Tourism-related occupations were found largely in hospitality institutions. Other services were introduced, such as banking, health, retail shops, vehicle repair centres and fuel filling stations, all of which boosted local livelihoods through wage labour (Gumbo, 2010). Some citizens have made inroads into the ownership of tourism assets, either individually or through joint venture (Morongwe, 2006). However, the importance of upgrading workers through training has been identified, a critical factor in improving livelihoods of employees in the tourism industry (*Botswana Daily News*, 2013).

The tourism industry has been blamed for many shortcomings. First, the ownership of tourism assets is largely a preserve of foreign investors (Gressier, 2011). This has created enclave tourism. Another group of elite investors are naturalised white citizens, 'conducting high-cost safaris' (Gressier, 2011, p. 355). Most locals only participate in the industry, performing manual work. Senior and management positions are occupied by expatriates (Gumbo, 2010). Secondly, there have been reported to be poor working conditions for most local employees (Mbaiwa, 2003). The employees' situation is exacerbated by the workers not being unionized, since there are no unions for the industry (Gumbo, 2010). Some employees are allegedly dismissed for failing to smile to a customer or asking for clarity if the client spoke a non-English European language (Gumbo, 2010). In some instances, employees are dismissed because of their HIV status (Gumbo, 2010). Nonetheless, tourism has brought profound yet complex impacts to the government and local communities.

Conclusion

This chapter has provided a historical analysis of protected areas and the development of tourism in Southern Africa, using the KNP and the CNP as case studies. It has argued that the Western models of conservation are at variance with local communities' needs and expectations. These opposed stances on conservation lead to lack of support from local communities, as shown with the two case studies. In Botswana's case, to appease local communities and win their participation in the new conservation model, the government introduced CBNRM programmes, which brought in a modicum of shared ownership of wildlife resources. As with the case of the KNP, the issue of land restitution plays a critical role in assuaging local communities, although the issue is complex. The chapter has also shown that, with the KNP and the CNP, the tourism industry has been historically 'exclusive'. However, local communities have somewhat directly and indirectly benefited through employment opportunities and other socio-economic services.

The chapter makes some recommendations for achieving sustainable conservation of wildlife in protected areas. On conservation, both governments should design policies which are sensitive to the needs of conservation and livelihoods. They should not over-stress the protection of wildlife at the expense of livelihoods. There ought to be hunting and culling of some species, such as elephants, which cause irreparable environmental destruction and endanger human life, a concern the residents of the Chobe and Ngamiland often raise with the government (Gumbo, 2010). In the KNP, communities have also raised issues of human–wildlife conflicts (Anthony, 2007). Additionally, to gain the support of local communities in conservation, governments ought to increase the amount of compensation for the property destroyed by wild animals. In Botswana, low compensation contributes to hardening the attitudes of local communities against coexisting with wildlife (Gumbo, 2010). Governments should consult communities as equal partners to achieve sustainable tourism in Southern Africa.

References

Annecke, W. & Masubelele, M. (2016). A review of the impact of militarisation: The case of Rhino poaching in Kruger National Park, South Africa. *Conservation and Society*, 14 (3), 195–204.

Anthony, B. (2007). The dual nature of parks: Attitudes of neighbouring communities towards Kruger National Park, South Africa. *Environmental Conservation*, 34 (3), 236–245.

Binns, T., & Nel, E. (2002). Tourism as a local development strategy in South Africa. *The Geographical Journal*, 168 (3), 235–247.

Bolaane, M. M. M. (2013). *Chiefs, hunters and San in the creation of the Moremi Game Reserve, Okavango Delta: Multiracial interactions and initiatives, 1956–1979.* Osaka: Yubunsha.

Botswana Daily News. (2013). Development of tourism workers critical. 17 November.

Botswana National Archives (BNA) S. 145/3 Game policy.

Botswana National Archives S. 568/13/1: Game reserve-northern, establishment of.

Botswana National Archives S. 568/13/2: Game reserve-northern, establishment. Letter no. 64 from Philip K. Crowe, The Chobe Game Reserve, 10 September 1960.

Butynski, T., & Von Richter, W. (1975). Wildlife management in Botswana. *Wildlife Society Bulletin*, 3, 19–24.

Carruthers, J. (1989). Creating a national park, 1910–1926. *Journal of Southern African Studies*, 15 (2), 188–216.

Carruthers, J. (1994). Dissecting the myth: Paul Kruger and the Kruger National Park. *Journal of Southern African Studies*, 20 (2), 263–283.

Chaminuka, P., McCrindle, C., & Udo, H. (2012). Cattle farming at the wildlife/livestock interface: Assessment of costs and benefits adjacent to Kruger National Park, South Africa. *Society and Natural Resources*, 25 (3), 235–250.

Fisch, M. (1999). *The Caprivi Strip during German colonial period, 1890 to 1914.* Windhoek: Out of Africa.

Gressier, C. (2011). Safaris into subjectivity: White locals, black tourists, and the politics of belonging in the Okavango Delta, Botswana. *Identities: Global Studies in Culture and Power*, 18, 352–376.

Gumbo, B. (2002). The political economy of development in the Chobe: Peasants, fishermen and tourists, 1960–1995. Unpublished MA thesis, Department of History, University of Botswana.

Gumbo, B. (2010). Economic and social change in the communities of the wetlands of Chobe and Ngamiland, with special reference to the period since 1960. Unpublished PhD thesis, University of Cape Town.

Gumbo, G. (2020). Historical evolution of conservation and tourism in Southern Africa. In Stone, M., Lenao, M., & Moswete, N., (Eds.), *Natural resources, tourism and community livelihoods in Southern Africa: Challenges of sustainable development* Abingdon, Oxon: Routledge, 11–25.

Hardin, G. (1968). The tragedy of the commons. *Science*, 162, 1243–1248.

Henk, D. (2007). The Botswana Defence Force and the wars against poaching in southern Africa. *Small Wars and Insurgencies*, 16 (2), 170–191.

Hess, C. S. (2021). Identity, guns, and nineteenth-century globalization: An examination of Botswana. *African Studies Quarterly*, 20 (1), 1–18.

Hinz, M. (2003). *Without chiefs there would be no game: Customary law and nature conservation.* Windhoek: Out of Africa.

Hutton, M. (1997). The impact of international treaties on wildlife management. In F. Monggae (Ed.), *Proceedings of a national conference on conservation and management of wildlife in Botswana: Strategies for the twenty-first century, 13–17 October 1997.* Gaborone: Kalahari Conservation Society. 255–259.

Keitumetse, S. (2009). The eco-tourism cultural heritage management (ECT-CHM): Linking heritage and 'environment' in the Okavango Delta Regions of Botswana. *International Journal of Heritage Studies*, 15 (2), 223–244.

Kepe, T., Wynberg, R. & Ellis, W. (2005). Land reform and biodiversity conservation in South Africa: Complementary or in conflict? *International Journal of Biodiversity Science and Management*, 1 (1), 3–16.

Ludbrock, S. (1995). Problem animal control: A closer look at the issues. Paper presented at a conference on Natural Resources Management Programme, Kasane, Botswana.

Lunstrum, E. (2015). Conservation meets militarisation in Kruger National Park: Historical encounters and complex legacies. *Conservation and Society*, 13 (4), 356–369.

Manatsha, B.T. (2014). The politics of Tachila Nature Reserve in the North East District, Botswana: A historical perspective. *South African Historical Journal*, 66 (3), 521–545. DOI: 10.1080/02582473.2014.954600

Mbaiwa, J. (2003). The socio-economic and environmental impacts of tourism development on the Okavango Delta, north-western Botswana. *Journal of Arid Environments*, 54, 447–467.

Mbaiwa, J. (2004). The success and sustainability of community-based natural resource management in the Okavango delta, Botswana. *South African Geographical Journal*, 100 (1), 41–61.

McCormick, J. (1989). *The global environmental movement: Reclaiming paradise.* London: Belhaven.

Morongwe, M. (2006). Economic impact of tourism in Botswana: Case study of Manu and surrounding villages (Phuduhudu, Toteng and Shorobe), 1960–2000. Unpublished BA dissertation, Department of History, University of Botswana.

Mosetlhi, B. (2012). *The influence of Chobe National Park on people's livelihoods and conservation behaviour.* Unpublished PhD thesis, University of Florida.

Othomile, M. (1997). Illegal offtake and anti-poaching strategies for the 21st century. In F. Monggae (Ed.), *Proceedings of a national conference on conservation and management of wildlife in Botswana: Strategies for the twenty first century, 13–17 October 1997.* Gaborone: Kalahari Conservation Society, 169–175.

Parsons, N., & Crowder, M. (1988). *Monarch of all I survey: Bechuanaland diaries 1929–37 by Sir Charles Rey.* Gaborone: The Botswana Society

Phuthego, T., & Chanda, R. (2004). Traditional ecological knowledge and community-based natural resource management: Lessons from a Botswana wildlife management area. *Applied Geography*, 24, 57–76.

Pimbert, M., & Pretty, J. (2009). Parks, people and professionals: Putting 'participation' into protected area management. In Ghimire, K. B., & Pimbert, M. P. (Eds.), *Social change and conservation.* London: Earthscan, 297.

Pradhan, H. (2008). Ecotourism in Nepal: Status and contributions. In Upadhyay, R. P. (Ed.), *Readings in rural tourism.* Kathmandu: Sunlight, 43–63.

Republic of Botswana. (2000). *Botswana tourism master plan.* Gaborone: Department of Tourism.

Republic of Botswana. (2004). *Forestry statistics.* Gaborone: Central Statistics Office.

Robins, S., & van der Waal, K. (2008). 'Model tribes' and iconic conservationists? The Makuleke restitution case in Kruger National Park. *Development and Change*, 39 (1), 53–72.

Rogerson, C. (2004). Regional tourism in South Africa: A case of 'mass tourism of the South'. *GeoJournal*, 60 (3), 229–237.

Scott, J. (1985). *Weapons of the weak: Everyday forms of peasant resistance*. New Haven, CT: Yale University.

Stone, L., Stone, M., Mogomotsi, P. & Mogomotsi, G. (2021). The impacts of Covid-19 on nature-based tourism in Botswana: Implications for community development. Retrieved from www.scholar.google.com/scholar?hl=en&as-sdt=0%2C5&q=the+impacts+of+covid-19+on+nature+based+tourism+in+botswana%3A+implications+for+community+development&btnG=

Stone, M., Nyaupane, G., Timothy, D., & Stone, L. (2020). Natural resources, sustainable tourism development and community livelihoods relationships: A comparison between Botswana and the USA. In Stone, M. T., Lenao, M., & Moswete, N. (Eds.), *Natural resources, tourism and community livelihoods in Southern Africa: Challenges of sustainable development*. Abingdon, Oxon: Routledge, 221–234.

Strickland-Munro, J. (2010). Understanding the interactions among local communities, protected areas and tourism: Case studies of Kruger National Park and Purnululu National Park. DPhil, School of Environmental Science, Murdoch University.

Strickland-Munro, J. K., Moore, S. A., & Freitag-Ronaldson, S. (2010). The impacts of tourism on two communities adjacent to the Kruger National Park, South Africa. *Development Southern Africa*, 27 (5), 663–678.

Tamuhla, A. (1997). Factors influencing community participation in sustainable wildlife utilisation: A case of the Chobe Conservation Trust, Botswana. Unpublished MSc thesis, Department of Environmental Science, University of Botswana.

Taylor, M., (2001). Government policy and popular values: Basarwa livelihood strategies in Okavango. Unpublished seminar paper, University of Botswana.

Telfer, D., & Sharpley, R. (2008). *Tourism and development in the developing world*. London and New York: Routledge.

Tlou, T., & Campbell, A. (1997). *History of Botswana*. Gaborone: Macmillan.

World Travel and Tourism Council. (2020). Botswana: 2021 annual research: Key highlights. Available at https://wttc.org/Research/Economic-Impact

3 Community perceptions of protected areas and tourism amidst poverty

Experiences from Southern Africa

Herbert Ntuli and Edwin Muchapondwa

Introduction

It is beyond doubt that the perceptions of local communities towards protected areas and tourism developments provide an important means of assessing the perceived value and performance of conservation projects (Abukari & Mwalyosi, 2020). In this chapter, perceptions are defined as the views that people form about something based on their interpretation of what they have experienced or heard from others (Huong & Lee, 2017), while attitudes refer to how they feel given the information at their disposal (Wang & Pfister, 2008). Minton & Khale (2014) define behaviour as an action, mannerisms or the way in which one conducts oneself in relation to others or the environment. Sociologists theorise that such a distinction is valid as perceptions tend to translate into attitudes and then into behaviour (Beedell & Rehman, 2000).

Governed by perceptions, the relationship between people and protected areas is complex and multifaceted (Bragagnolo et al., 2016). First, perceptions are important in understanding the attitudes and behaviours of local people in relation to resource use in protected areas, which in turn has implications for conservation, tourism benefits and the welfare of the people dependent on the resource (Ntuli et al., 2019). If the behaviour of resource users is not consistent with sustainability, then conservation and tourism outcomes will suffer.

Secondly, exploring perceptions of different facets of conservation initiatives, such as governance, management, ecological outcomes and socio-economic impacts can help identify those aspects of the initiatives that are succeeding and those that are failing. Finally, by understanding people's perceptions better, policies may be developed for effective biodiversity management and the well-being of people living near protected areas. This becomes particularly important during a time of intensifying competition for land, where protected areas are coming under increasing pressure to justify their status (Bragagnolo et al., 2016).

DOI: 10.4324/9781003193166-4

Theoretical frameworks linking people's perceptions with protected areas and tourism

Different theoretical frameworks have been proposed in the literature to analyse people's perceptions in relation to protected areas and tourism initiatives (see Ntuli et al., 2019; Snyman, 2014). The frameworks allow researchers to identify and analyse variables that affect this relationship. Bragagnolo et al. (2016) observed a relatively high degree of concordance between studies, with certain variables showing strong associations with attitudes. The authors recommend a more rigorous model-building approach, based on a clear conceptual framework and drawing on the extensive empirical literature, for studying people's perceptions and attitudes towards protected areas. Such an approach would improve the quality of research, increase comparability and provide a stronger basis to support conservation decision-making.

According to Ntuli et al. (2019), it is imperative to begin by acknowledging theories linking people's perceptions, attitudes and behaviour before reviewing the theoretical frameworks that have been developed to examine people's perceptions in relation to protected areas and tourism. Theoretically, the behaviour of local people towards resources inside protected areas is linked to their perceptions of system benefits and costs through the intermediacy of people's attitudes (Snyman, 2012; Ntuli et al., 2020). Theories from psychology and sociology on human behaviour, such as the theory of planned behaviour, rooted in the theory of reasoned action (Fishbein, 1979) and behavioural change (see Munro et al., 2007; Webb et al., 2010), suggest that people develop attitudes based on their perception of the system or environment, which in turn feeds into their behaviour (Figure 3.1).

The building blocks of people's attitudes are the cognitive, affective and behavioural components. Attitude formation is influenced by experience, learning, conditioning, observation and social factors (Webb et al., 2010). People's behaviour is also believed to be linked to intentions, social norms,

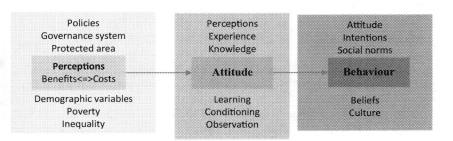

Figure 3.1 The link between perceptions, attitudes and behaviour.
Source: Authors' diagram.

beliefs and culture which also shape people's perceptions (Munro et al., 2007). Understanding people's perceptions about protected areas also helps to shed light on their attitudes and behaviour towards conservation initiatives. The study of perceptions becomes important for the understanding of illegal behaviour, such as poaching, by local communities since it is difficult to collect data on such variables (Ntuli et al., 2020). Viewed as a whole, the literature seems to suggest that we can model perceptions, attitudes and behaviour using the following system of equations:.

$$Perceptions = f\left(system\,benefits\,and\,costs \mid poverty; inequality\right) \tag{1}$$

$$Attitudes = f\left(perception \mid experience; learning; conditioning; observation\right) \tag{2}$$

$$Behaviour = f\left(attitudes \mid social\,norms; beliefs; culture\right) \tag{3}$$

Although understanding the theories of psychology and sociology that link perceptions, attitudes and behaviour is important as a starting point, we need other theories to understand the relationship between people's perceptions and protected areas. Social exchange theory has been used widely to examine individual and community members' perceptions of and attitudes towards protected areas and tourism initiatives (Andereck et al., 2005). This theoretical framework assumes that the perception of potential beneficial outcomes will create positive attitudes towards protected areas or tourism business ventures (Andereck et al., 2005). Like rational choice theory in neoclassical economics, individuals perceiving net benefits from an exchange are likely to view it positively and those perceiving net costs are likely to view it negatively (Snyman, 2012). Evidence shows that residents who depend on tourism for support, or who perceive it as offering net personal benefits, tend to view its impacts more positively than others (Wang & Pfister, 2008).

The needs theory suggests that people with lower household incomes are often less supportive of protected areas and tourism since they depend more on the environment for survival. The creation of protected areas and the establishment of tourism activities might jeopardise their livelihoods if they are not involved in or do not derive benefits from such initiatives (Snyman, 2014). Proponents of this theory argue that an individual's basic needs, such as food and shelter, are attended to first before higher needs, such as supporting community conservation or tourism initiatives, are considered (Emptaz-Collomb, 2009). The implication of this is that people's perceptions are a function of poverty status and as a result poverty enters the framework through equation [1]. The relationship between poverty and perceptions is best understood in the form of a switching function, in which poor people do not support conservation initiatives, while non-poor people do. Therefore, the behaviour of poor households towards the environment is linked to their perception of system benefits and costs.

Recent arguments suggest that inequality in a community, rather than poverty *per se*, could be the driver of people's perceptions, and in turn feed into their behaviour, such as poaching and participation in illegal wildlife trafficking (Duffy et al., 2016). If people think that other people in the community benefit more from the resource than they themselves do, then they are likely to hold negative perceptions about the protected areas or tourism initiatives. For this reason, the literature seems to suggest that a framework might not operate differently in the presence or absence of poverty. This is true when we consider commercial poaching behaviour and illegal wildlife trafficking, which are done by non-poor households, rather than subsistence poaching behaviour, which is thought to be perpetrated by the poor alone (Ntuli et al., 2020).

Another theoretical framework, based on the theory of rationality borrowed from neoclassical economics, that has been used extensively in the literature to understand the behaviour of resource users, such as resource overexploitation and environmental crime, is rational choice theory (Perman et al., 2003), which makes use of the cost-benefit analysis (CBA) framework. The theory assumes that a decision made by an individual is rational since it is based on comparing benefits and costs. Based on people's perceptions of the benefit-cost structure of a system, the necessary incentives are generated for people to behave in a sustainable manner. By extrapolation, we can assume that people form their perceptions by comparing the benefits and costs associated with a system (Ntuli et al., 2019). These variables may be conceptualised as positive or negative impacts of an intervention on various aspects of people's livelihoods, depending on the information at their disposal and their experience with the system. The difference between the perceived benefits and costs can be interpreted as the perceived value of the protected areas.

Ostrom (2007) developed a comprehensive theory for analysing complex social ecological systems (SESs) that allowed researchers to identify and analyse variables that affect people's behaviour. According to Ntuli et al. (2019), the same variables can be used to analyse the drivers of people's perceptions of a system. As shown in Table 3.1, these variables fall into eight core subsystems, namely ecosystem (river, woodlands, wildlife, etc.); resource system (e.g. national park); users; resource units; governance system (institutions, policies, laws, rules and regulations, community-based structure and state-based structures); and environment (political, economic and social variables), which in turn result in an outcome (optimal or suboptimal) via interactions (legal or illegal exploitation). As an example, people are assumed to form their perceptions based on their analysis of these variables as part of a system given the information at their disposal (Ntuli et al., 2019).

Theoretically, the perceptions that people form by analysing all this information is ultimately linked to their perceptions of protected areas and tourism initiatives, which in turn affect community support and the success of protected areas. It is also assumed that, if protected areas and tourism initiatives are successful, then community welfare will increase, while poverty and inequality are diminished. The SES variables also interact with each other in addition to

32 Herbert Ntuli and Edwin Muchapondwa

Table 3.1 An example of variables affecting how people form perception based on theoretical framework for analysing complex SESs

Core subsystems		Variables	Examples
First tier **Environment**	**Political★**	Are basic needs of the community catered for?	Views on resettlement programmes, land expropriation, contested legality
	Economic	Are benefits of living with wildlife greater than costs?	PA benefits and costs
	Social	Who are the winners and losers?	Improvement in rural welfare and community resilience
Second tier **Governance system** **Ecosystem linkages** **Resource system** **Resource units**		Are local communities involved in decision making?	Existence of community structures at grassroots level
		Are benefits distributed from PAs and tourism fairly?	Mechanisms for sharing benefits and resolving conflict
		Are the rules governing the resource system fair?	Origin of rules governing the protected areas
		Are the ecosystem goods and services enhanced?	Flood protection, availability of water
		Do the resource system benefit local communities?	Food security, nutrition
		Who owns the resources?	Rights to resources, attributes of resource units
Third tier **Users** **Interactions** **Outcome**		Who is allowed to benefit and why?	Extent to which communities and tourists benefit from the resource
		User attributes	Number of beneficiaries, age structure, gender etc.
		How do local communities access resources?	Legal, illegal, contested illegality, human–wildlife conflict
		What are the consequences of the current regime?	Sustainability issues, inequitable access, etc.
		Do communities care about the environment?	Competition for land and other resources in PAs Community welfare

Source: Variables in the first column were extracted from the framework for analysing complex ecosystems developed by Ostrom (2007).

Note: ★ Contextual factor.

overlapping between categories. Based on this interpretation, and without loss of generality, we can rewrite equation [1] as follows:

$$Perceptions = f(SES\,variables\mid interactions) \tag{4}$$

While people's perceptions are explained by analysing all variables of the SES which shape their attitudes towards protected areas, their behaviour is captured through interaction with the resource units.

The frameworks discussed earlier are nested under the theoretical framework for analysing complex SESs developed by Ostrom (2007). Social exchange theory is captured in the action domain, where users interact with wildlife to produce an outcome, while the needs theory is addressed by capturing the needs of the community or households in the three different tiers, from basic needs in the first tier to higher needs in the second and third tiers. The CBA is internalised by conceptualising the variables of the SES as benefits if the impact is positive and costs if it is negative. Several other frameworks that have also been applied can be interpreted as either adaptations or variants of the SES framework, e.g. the Ecosystem Management framework (Meffe et al., 2002) and the Ecosystem Services (ES) framework (Bouman et al., 2000).

The SES framework is therefore more robust and comprehensive than earlier frameworks as it allows researchers to identify all the variables in the model as part of a system rather than analyse them as components of different systems. Alternatively, variables could be chosen based on contemporary understandings of the interactions between people and protected areas or of the literature on the social consequences of protected area designation (Agrawal & Redford, 2006).

We have therefore established that the SES is the holistic consolidated framework that could contribute to our understanding of the relationship between people's perceptions of protected areas and tourism by allowing researchers to identify the system variables. In this framework, people consider all the variables of the system in forming their perceptions, and this in turn influences their attitudes and finally their behaviour, which is captured through their interaction with resource units.

Determinants of community perceptions of protected areas and tourism

Previous studies done in the region and elsewhere demonstrate that communities may have positive perceptions of conservation (Sekhar, 2003) and ecotourism development (Lepp, 2007), a neutral or indifferent position (Mutanga et al., 2015), or, in some cases, negative perceptions, especially towards tourism initiatives (Mutanga et al., 2015). Ordinarily, one can comment on attitudes based on data from a perception study since there is a one-to-one correspondence between perceptions and attitudes, i.e. good (bad) attitudes can only come from positive (negative) perceptions. For this reason, the two concepts have been used interchangeably by researchers even though they are different (Ntuli et al., 2019).

A review of the literature of studies conducted in Southern Africa reveal that the important determinants of people's perceptions can be classified into five different categories, namely, (1) socio-economic attributes (such as age, gender, education, household shocks, wealth, poverty and inequality), (2) benefits from conservation, such as wildlife income, employment and environmental resources harvested from protected areas, (3) costs incurred as a result of living with wildlife, such as crop damage, livestock predation and human injuries (Snyman, 2014), (4) institutional variables, such as community-based structures endogenous to the community and state-based exogenous institutions (Ntuli et al., 2019), and (5) ecological characteristics such as wildlife abundance (Ntuli et al., 2019). These drivers perfectly align with the message from our consolidated framework. Perceptions are also influenced by factors invisible to outsiders (Waylen et al., 2009).

The effects of socio-economic variables on perceptions are mixed in the literature. First, there are studies that found either no effects or very little evidence of socio-economic variables influencing the perceptions of local communities towards protected areas and tourism (e.g. Ntuli et al., 2019). Level of education has been observed to have a positive impact on perceptions towards protected areas and tourism, since people with better education are likely to find employment in the area, which also reduces their dependence on the environment (Snyman, 2014). In a study of six countries across Southern Africa, Snyman (2014) found a positive relationship between perceptions of protected areas and variables such as age and income, while Ntuli et al. (2019) found a negative relationship associated with age in the South African and Zimbabwean constituents of the Great Limpopo Transfrontier Conservation Area (GLTFCA). Households with low income are likely to have negative perceptions of protected areas, since poverty increases dependence on the environment (Snyman, 2012). Regarding gender, women were found to have positive perceptions of protected areas and tourism initiatives, while men had negative perceptions. Sundström et al. (2019) found that women's attitudes generally are not divergent from men's, but they found some differences between non-electrified households and those with a dependence on resources.

Other important drivers of people's perceptions and attitudes are the costs and benefits derived from protected areas and tourism initiatives (Ntuli et al., 2019). From both protected areas and ecotourism initiatives, rural households receive direct benefits in the form of wages, employment, wildlife income and the ability to harvest non-timber forest products (Snyman, 2012). They also receive indirect benefits, such as aesthetic, bequest and spiritual benefits (Gren et al., 2018). It is believed that the benefits, if perceived as fair by the communities in question, will generate the incentives necessary for them to care about natural resources, protect wildlife and support conservation initiatives (Gren et al., 2018). Ntuli et al. (2019) found a positive relationship between benefits and perceptions of conservation, while Walpole & Goodwin (2001) failed to establish a correlation between perceptions and economic benefits from tourism. An analysis of the various factors impacting attitudes towards conservation and tourism showed that ecotourism employment positively affects perceptions, though level of education showed the largest impact (Snyman, 2012).

Snyman (2014) identified new skills, broader experiences in managing projects and people, the exchange of ideas, expanded circles of contacts, empowerment and support for community efforts as non-economic benefits that could influence perceptions of and attitudes towards protected areas and tourism. These non-economic benefits are, however, often difficult to measure and assess. Ntuli et al. (2019) established that people perceiving the park as well-managed tend to have more positive perceptions of the benefits from the park, rules governing the park and wildlife conservation in general.

The costs, however, counter or reduce the incentives created by sharing benefits with local people. These costs are usually conceptualised and analysed in the literature in the form of human–wildlife conflict, as people retaliate by killing problem animals that destroy their field crops or prey on livestock (Ntuli et al., 2019). Snyman (2014) observed that human–wildlife conflict negatively impacted perceptions, highlighting important policy focus areas. Human–wildlife conflict also forms part of people's experience with protected areas and tourism initiatives, as well as their historic experience of protected areas and management regimes (Ntuli et al., 2019). Thondhlana & Cundill (2017) studied local people's and conservation officials' perceptions of relationships and conflicts in South African protected areas. They found sharp contrasts in perceptions between reserve managers and local communities. Reserve managers generally perceived that there were no conflicts with local communities and that their relationship with them was positive, while local communities thought otherwise, claiming that conflicts were centred around restricted access to protected areas, inequitable distribution or lack of benefits and communication problems.

According to scholars, benefit distribution is a necessary, but not sufficient, condition for communities to perceive wildlife conservation positively (Snyman, 2012), which implies that other factors come into play. Closely linked to retaliatory behaviour is defiance or resentment displayed by local people because of dissatisfaction with the system, which they perceive as unfair since they suffered through land expropriation during the creation of the protected areas and the establishment of policies and laws that forbid exploitation of environmental resources in the park (Hübschle, 2016. Resentment is usually captured in the literature under 'contextual factors', which are often difficult to measure (Ntuli et al., 2019). Therefore, creating and maintaining positive perceptions towards protected areas is an increasingly important tool in fostering community-based conservation when other mechanisms for changing behaviour, such as regulation, are inappropriate or ineffective (Waylen et al., 2009).

The governance model has a bearing on people's perceptions of and incentives for conservation since it determines whether local communities are included or not in decision-making and benefit sharing (Sas-Rolfes, 2017). The top-down governance model has been criticised because of its exclusionary mechanisms, and bottom-up approaches, which are more inclusive, are now favoured (Muchapondwa & Stage, 2015). Abukari & Mwalyosi (2020) studied four facets of conservation – governance, management, ecological outcomes and social impacts –in protected areas in East Africa (Tanzania) and West Africa (Ghana). Further analysis revealed that governance issues had the most influence on local communities' perceptions of the impact of the two national parks on livelihoods and community development.

Since the establishment of protected areas in Southern Africa, the use of strict regulations has often failed to ensure conservation success, making a more appropriate and effective means of ensuring conservation necessary (Muchapondwa & Stage, 2015). Wildlife policies are known to generate both intended and unintended consequences or externalities for the affected parties. Well-crafted policies generate incentives by creating an enabling environment for people to participate in wildlife conservation (Gren et al., 2018). Endogenous institutions are likely to generate positive incentives and good stewardship through ownership, which, in turn, improves people's perceptions of protected areas and of ecotourism initiatives if they are community-based. State-based exogenous institutions are often viewed as unfair by communities since they are usually not consulted during establishment (Ntuli and Muchapondwa, 2018). Negative perceptions of state-based exogenous institutions affect the relationship between local communities and protected areas (Massé, 2017). Ntuli et al. (2019) found that local communities are likely to have positive perceptions of protected areas if they perceive the management of the park to be good. Furthermore, they found that if people have a negative view of park rules, they are less likely to conserve wildlife.

Ecological factors, such as species diversity and abundance, may also affect people's perceptions of protected areas and tourism initiatives (Ostrom, 2007). Ntuli et al. (2019) observed that local communities are more likely to hold negative perceptions of protected areas if they believe that wildlife is plentiful and that they have been unfairly prevented by the authorities from harvesting the resource. Another study found that people are more likely to have positive perceptions of protected areas if they believe that particular species of wildlife are facing extinction and hence understand the need for those animals to be protected (Bencin et al., 2016). Ntuli et al. (2019) used household expertise in resource extraction as a proxy for local ecological knowledge and found that expertise tends to make people more likely to perceive environmental crime as morally acceptable.

Understanding the drivers of community perceptions of protected areas helps policymakers to devise new policy interventions to insulate protected areas and tourism from existing negative perceptions. The policy regime needs to create an enabling environment for local communities to contribute meaningfully towards conservation through their participation in value-chain opportunities and, most importantly, in monitoring and enforcement. The inclusion of local communities in wildlife management and decision-making directly challenges the current governance models, which are based on a top-down straitjacket approach. In the light of these findings, both the policy regime and governance models could be altered to gain community support and enhance positive perceptions.

Finally, it is also important to highlight that wildlife conservation is happening in the context of poverty in rural and peri-urban communities that are located adjacent to protected areas. Poverty is a cross-cutting issue that has a bearing on how local people form perceptions about protected areas and tourism, especially if the benefits from conservation initiatives are not realised by the communities who incur the costs of living with wildlife (Snyman, 2012). The relationship between poverty and perceptions is not straightforward as poverty affects households through different channels, such as education, health, food security and income (Agrawal & Redford, 2006). These channels create positive and negative feedback loops which also make the analysis complicated (Upton, 2008).

Policy options

Various policy options to improve local communities' perceptions of protected areas and tourism initiatives have been suggested in the literature, ranging from simple tools, such as implementing awareness campaigns and training in the short run, to long-run interventions, such as fashioning park-governance structures that are more inclusive and prioritising the roles and entitlements of local communities (Abukari & Mwalyosi, 2020). The former is meant to enhance the understanding and appreciation of protected areas and tourism initiatives. The latter can help make park-adjacent communities' important stakeholders by instilling in them a sense of ownership, and this may help strengthen their support for conservation. Policy mechanisms to enhance perceptions and incentivise community-based conservation should be embedded in inclusive governance models, e.g. co-management arrangements, beneficiation, market-based schemes to improve financial incentives, conflict mitigation strategies and ownership models.

In a study of perceptions in Zimbabwe, Mutanga et al. (2015) observed that local communities are not fully involved in the management of protected areas and that benefits from natural resources are not fairly shared among stakeholders. They recommended that conservation agencies should: (i) nurture positive perceptions and address the possible determinants of communities' negative perceptions, (ii) enhance community involvement and benefits from tourism, and (iii) consider community heterogeneity in conservation planning.

Ntuli et al. (2019) argue that increased devolution of natural resource management into the hands of local communities can enhance community perceptions of integrated conservation and development projects through increasing their decision-making capabilities and offering a more equitable sharing of benefits. Furthermore, addressing human–wildlife conflict could be a way to manage community relationships and garner long-term support for protected areas and ecotourism (Snyman, 2014).

The need to identify how to enhance community perceptions and incentivise conservation is common across developing countries where conservation must compete with other land uses and livelihood options (Ntuli et al., 2019). Traditionally, initiatives that have been used to incentivise conservation in Africa include governance models, policy mechanisms, beneficiation or market-based schemes, conflict mitigation strategies, financial or tax incentives and ownership models. All these mechanisms treat wildlife income as the main activity. Regional bodies and governments in Southern Africa have experimented with some of these different models to varying degrees and with varying success.

The COVID-19 pandemic has caused the income of communities who normally relied on trophy hunting and wildlife tourism to supplement their livelihood strategies to plummet, creating unprecedented vulnerabilities and threatening local social-ecological resilience and the sustainability of community-based natural resource management in Africa. There is no doubt that local communities' perception of protected areas area has also been affected negatively by the crisis. The COVID-19 pandemic highlights the need for complementary incentives to the income generated by tourism. As a result, there has been an increasing demand for initiatives, beyond tourism, that develop communities without requiring wildlife income to generate incentives for conservation in communities, while at the same time improving their perceptions of protected areas. Such a mechanism could help to deal with shocks, such COVID-19, in the presence of dwindling wildlife income. Alternative nature-based enterprises that might diversify livelihood strategies beyond income from hunting and tourism have been provisionally collated in a Luc Hoffmann Institute study (Roe, 2020).

Conclusion

Understanding the nuances, the history, the interests and values of community members, and the drivers behind poaching (whether intrinsic or driven by transnational organised crime) is imperative if we are to create sustainable and resilient communities on multiple levels that make a substantial positive impact on people's lives, but also conserve wildlife for posterity. The broader objective of the chapter was to shed light on community perceptions of protected areas and tourism initiatives amidst poverty, using Southern Africa as a case study. Our findings show that the most important determinants of community perceptions are the socio-economic attributes of resource users, resource units, governance, policy and institutional variables that can be identified from the SES framework.

The chapter suggested policy options for addressing negative community perceptions of protected areas and tourism, such as awareness campaign programmes, training related to natural resource management, improvement in the benefit-sharing arrangements and governance or co-management models. Previous studies suggest that large-scale collective action can help since perceptions of wildlife benefits, corruption, environmental crime, park management and rules governing the parks all affect local communities' ability and willingness to self-organise. Some of the drivers identified in the literature are interesting because they can be influenced by policy through training and awareness campaigns. These findings have profound implications for rural development and conservation policy, especially considering the importance of getting local people's support in protected area management and tourism initiatives.

References

Abukari, H., & Mwalyosi, R. B. (2020). Local communities' perceptions about the impact of protected areas on livelihoods and community development. *Global Ecology and Conservation*, 22, e00909.

Agrawal, A., & Redford, K. (2006). Poverty, development, and biodiversity conservation: shooting in the dark? New York: Wildlife Conservation Society, Working Paper No. 26.

Andereck, K. L., Valentine, K. M., Knopf, R. C., & Vogt, C. A. (2005). Residents' perceptions of community tourism impacts. *Annals of Tourism Research*, 32 (4), 1056–1076.

Beedell, J., & Rehman, T. (2000). Using social-psychology models to understand farmers' conservation behaviour. *Journal of Rural Studies*, 16, 117–127.

Bencin, H., Kioko, J., & Kiffner, C. (2016). Local people's perceptions of wildlife species in two distinct landscapes of Northern Tanzania, *Journal for Nature Conservation*, 34, 82–92.

Bouman, M., Heijungs, R., van der Voet, E., van den Bergh, J. C. J. M., & Huppes, G. (2000). Material flows and economic models: An analytical comparison of SFA, LCA and partial equilibrium models. *Ecological Economics*, 32, 195–216.

Bragagnolo, C., Malhado, A., Jepson, P., & Ladle, R. (2016). Modelling local attitudes to protected areas in developing countries. *Conservation and Society*, 14 (3), 163–182.

Duffy, R. F., St John, A. V., Buscher, B., & Brockington, D. (2016). Toward a new understanding of the links between poverty and illegal wildlife hunting. *Conservation Biology*, 30 (1), 14–22.

Emptaz-Collomb, J. G. J. (2009). Linking tourism, human wellbeing and conservation in the Caprivi Strip, Namibia. PhD thesis, University of Florida, viewed 15 February 2012, from http://etd.fcla.edu/UF/UFE0041031/emptazcollomb_j.pdf.

Fishbein, M. (1979). A theory of reasoned action: some applications and implications. In Howe, H., & Page, M. (Eds.), *Nebraska symposium on motivation*, Vol 27. Lincoln, NE: University of Nebraska Press, 65–116.

Gren, I. M., Häggmark-Svensson, T., Elofsson, K., & Engelmann, M. (2018). Economics of wildlife management: An overview. *European Journal of Wildlife Research*, 64 (2), 1–16.

Hübschle, A. M. (2016). The social economy of rhino poaching: of economic freedom fighters, professional hunters and marginalized local people. *Current Sociology*, 427–447.

Huong, P. M., & Lee, J. H. (2017). The social economy of rhino poaching: of economic freedom fighters, professional hunters and marginalized local people, *Vietnamese Forum of Science and Technology*, 13 (3), 126–132.

40 *Herbert Ntuli and Edwin Muchapondwa*

Lepp, A. (2007). Residents' attitudes toward tourism in Bigodi village, Uganda. *Tourism Management*, 28, 876–885.

Massé, F. (2017). Securing conservation: The politics of anti-poaching and conservation law enforcement in Mozambique. PhD thesis, York University Toronto.

Meffe, G., Nielsen, L., Knight, R., and Schenborn, D. (2002). *Ecosystem management: Adaptive, community-based conservation.* Washington, DC: Island Press.

Minton, E. A., & Khale, L. R. (2014). *Belief systems, religion, and behavioral economics.* New York: Business Expert Press LLC.

Muchapondwa, E., & Stage, J. (2015). Whereto with institutions and governance challenges in African wildlife conservation? *Environmental Research Letters*, 10 (9), 1–8.

Munro, S., Lewin, S., Swart, T., & Volmink, J. (2007). A review of health behaviour theories: How useful are these for developing interventions to promote long-term medication adherence for TB and HIV/AIDS? *BMC Public Health*, 7 (104), 1–16.

Mutanga, C. N., Vengesayi, S., Gandiwa, E., & Muboko, N. (2015). Community perceptions of wildlife conservation and tourism: A case study of communities adjacent to four protected areas in Zimbabwe. *Tropical Conservation Science*, 8 (2), 564–582.

Ntuli, H., Jagers, S. C., Linell, A. Sjöstedt, M., & Muchapondwa, E. (2019). Factors influencing local communities' perceptions towards conservation of transboundary wildlife resources: The case of the Great Limpopo Transfrontier Conservation Area. *Biodiversity Conservation*, 28, 2977–3003.

Ntuli, H., & Muchapondwa, E. (2018). The role of institutions in community wildlife conservation in   Zimbabwe. *International Journal of the Commons*, 12 (1), 134–169. www.thecommonsjournal.org/article/10.18352/ijc.803/.

Ntuli, H., Sundström, A., Muchapondwa, E., Sjöstedt, M., Linell, A., & Jagers, S. C. (2020). Understanding the drivers of subsistence poaching in the Great Limpopo Transfrontier Conservation Area: What matters for community wildlife conservation? *Ecology and Society*, 26 (1), 18.

Ostrom, E. (2007). A diagnostic approach for going beyond panaceas. *Proceeding of the National Academy of Sciences USA*, 104 (39), 15181–15187.

Perman, R., Ma, Y., McGilvray, J., & Common, M. (2003). *Natural resource and environmental economics*, 3rd ed. Harlow: Pearson Education.

Roe, D., Booker, F., Wilson-Holt, O., & Cooney, R. (2020). *Diversifying local livelihoods while sustaining wildlife: Exploring incentives for community-based conservation.* Gland, Switzerland: Luc Hoffmann Institute.

Sekhar, N. U. (2003). Local people's attitudes towards conservation and wildlife tourism around Sariska Tiger Reserve, India. *Journal of Environmental Management*, 69, 339–347.

Snyman, S. L. (2012). The role of tourism employment in poverty reduction and community perceptions of conservation and tourism in southern Africa, *Journal of Sustainable Tourism*, 20 (3), 395–416.

Snyman, S. (2014). Assessment of the main factors impacting community members' attitudes towards tourism and protected areas in six southern African countries. *Koedoe*, 56 (2), 1–12.

Sundström, A., Linell, A., Ntuli, H., Sjöstedt, M., & Gore, M. (2019). Gender differences in poaching attitudes: Insights from communities in South Africa and Zimbabwe living near the Great Limpopo, *Conservation Letters*, 13 (1), 1–8.

Sas-Rolfes, M. (2017). African wildlife conservation and the evolution of hunting institutions. *Environmental Resource Letters*, 12, 115007.

Thondhlana, G., & Cundill, G. (2017). Local people and conservation officials' perceptions on relationships and conflicts in South African protected areas. *International Journal of Biodiversity Science, Ecosystem Services & Management*, 13 (1), 204–215.

Upton, C., Ladle, R., Hulme, D., Jiang, T., Brockington, D., & Adams, W. M. (2008). Are poverty and protected area establishment linked at a national scale? *Oryx*, 42 (1), 19–25.

Walpole, M. J., & Goodwin, H. J. (2001). Local attitudes towards conservation and tourism around Komodo National Park, Indonesia. *Environmental Conservation*, 28 (2), 160–166.

Wang, Y., & Pfister, R. E. (2008). Resident's attitudes toward tourism and perceived personal benefits in a rural community. *Journal of Travel Research*, 47 (1), 84–93.

Waylen, K. A., McGowan, P. J. K., & Milner-Gulland, E. J. (2009). Ecotourism positively affects awareness and attitudes but not conservation behaviours: A case study at Grand Riviere, Trinidad. *Oryx*, 43 (3), 343–351.

Webb, T. L., Sniehotta, F. F., & Michie, S. (2010). Using theories of behaviour change to inform interventions for addictive behaviours. *Addiction*, 105, 1879–1892.

4 Ecotourism as a paradigm shift in conservation and community livelihoods in the Southern African region

Opportunities, challenges and lessons learnt

Said Juma Suluo and Wineaster Anderson

Introduction

Most Southern African countries have set aside significant land area, protected for conservation and/or tourism activities. Tanzania, for example, has set aside about a third of its land as protected areas, most of these being the country's tourism hotspots (Suluo et al., 2020). However, the local populations, especially poor rural communities, depend on the same protected natural resources for their survival (Torri & Herrmann, 2010). Thus, the conservation efforts result in the shrinkage of traditional economic opportunities for the local population due to restrictions on farming, hunting and firewood collection (Songorwa, 1999; Wells & Bradon, 1992). Unfortunately, the economic benefits of tourism have not been able to compensate for the lost opportunities brought by the protection of such areas – leaving most remote rural communities in extreme poverty (Nelson, 2012). Consequently, conservation efforts are challenged by the intrusion into the protected areas by neighbouring communities in their desperation to sustain their livelihoods.

Ecotourism is considered to have the capacity to address the conflicts between conservation efforts and the livelihood of communities around protected areas (Kavita & Saarinen, 2016). The ecotourism concept, however, has varying definitions (Anderson, 2009). According to Anderson (2009), ecotourism's definitions and synonyms cover green, sustainable, nature-based, alternative and adventure tourism, as well as other elements of environmental education. Anderson (2009) simplifies the complexities of the various definitions and synonyms and considers components of ecotourism to be among six types of holidays (also see Figure 4.1).

The International Ecotourism Society (TIES) (2015) defines ecotourism as a form of responsible travel to natural attractions that ensures environmental conservation and the livelihood of host communities while providing learning experiences to tourists. Therefore, ecotourism does not simply refer to visiting

DOI: 10.4324/9781003193166-5

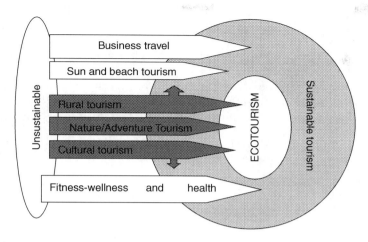

Figure 4.1 Concept of ecotourism.

natural tourist attractions (Medina, 2005), but to ecologically sound tourism (Shores, 1992). Ecotourism focuses on the impact of nature tourism activities on the conservation of the environment, the improvement of the well-being of the host communities and the learning experiences for visitors (Roberts & Thanos, 2003). Ecotourism is viewed as a model that can foster sustainable development, especially in developing countries.

Ecotourism is the fastest-growing component in the tourism industry (Gossling, 2000) and the centre of tourism growth in Africa (Backman & Munanura, 2015). This trend in Africa may be explained by Africa's endowment in wildlife diversity and abundance of charismatic wildlife species (Lindsey et al., 2007). The Southern Africa Development Community (SADC) region, which is famous for housing world-renowned nature-based attractions, attracts almost double the average of African share of tourism expenditure per capita (SADC, 2019), suggesting that the region is the leading beneficiary of ecotourism activities in Africa.

Community-based tourism is the standard approach used to implement ecotourism initiatives in the Southern Africa context (Mnini & Ramoroka, 2020; Stone & Nyaupane, 2018). The community-based tourism model allows village communities to turn some of the village lands over to tourism and conservation and stop utilising it for other economic activities such as farming, hunting and animal grazing which might be detrimental to the sustainability of wildlife species and their habitats (Stone & Nyaupane, 2018). The model also allows communities to share the benefits of tourism activities occurring on their land. The assumption is that, when communities directly enjoy the benefits of tourism from the protected land, they will be willing to conserve the environment and the wildlife (Anderson, 2009; Mnini & Ramoroka, 2020).

Since the early 1990s, countries have instituted community-based eco-tourism enterprises through the Community-Based Natural Resources Management (CBNRM) programme (Mbaiwa, 2015; Stone & Nyaupane, 2018). However, such a move has brought both opportunities and challenges to communities participating in ecotourism initiatives (Stone & Stone, 2020). While studies have explored the challenges or opportunities in specific countries (Stone & Stone, 2020; Mgonja, Sirima & Mkumbo, 2015), none has highlighted the same in the whole of the Southern African region. This chapter therefore aims to review ecotourism opportunities and challenges in the Southern Africa region. The chapter also highlights the lessons learnt and recommends the way forward.

Tourism is a significant economic activity in the SADC region as it contributed about 8% of regional GDP and 2.5 million jobs in 2017 (SADC, 2019). Wildlife tourism is the main form in the region since it houses some of the largest national parks in the world. This suggests that the adoption of ecotourism in the region is crucial to ensure the conservation of these natural resources and to improve the livelihood of people living around them.

Challenges and opportunities of ecotourism in the region

Google Scholar search was used to search recent articles about 'ecotourism' or 'community-based tourism' in the following selected SADC countries of 'Botswana', 'Namibia', 'South Africa', 'Tanzania' and 'Zimbabwe' from the year 2010 to obtain the most recent developments. The Google Scholar platform was preferred since it is very easy to find research publications on any topic through it (Jacsó, 2005), and in terms of recall and precision, it performs better than most of the subscription databases (Walters, 2009). The selected countries, together with Mozambique, receive more than 75% of tourists visiting the SADC region (SADC, 2019). The search was conducted in March and April 2021, and this produced 183 publications which provided data for analysis. Further screening of publications that cover challenges and/or opportunities related to ecotourism in the region produced 41 journal articles.

Thematic analysis (Braun & Clarke, 2006) was employed to analyse the articles. Each paper was first read through to familiarise with its content and an initial list of ideas about what is in each article was generated. Then, articles' contents were coded to identify the meaning that lies beneath the semantic surface of contents. Coding was done by identifying text carrying ideas about the chapter objectives and notes were written beside it for identification. The codes were then reviewed to identify themes. The whole process was repeated to ensure themes are the only existing ones – i.e. recoding and regrouping of codes. This process brought back the same number of themes. The resulting themes formed part of our findings, i.e. opportunities, challenges, and recommendations as indicated in Table 4.1.

Ecotourism as a paradigm shift 45

Table 4.1 Study themes and sub-themes

Themes	Sub-themes	References
Opportunities	Improved livelihood (employment income, conservancies' lease and other income, business opportunities and donations) Improved conservation (Local communities' positive attitude towards conservation, reduced poaching, flourishing wildlife habitats, increased number of wildlife)	Snyman (2012, 2014, 2017); Chirenje (2017); Anderson (2015); Shoo (2020); Mbaiwa (2015); Maude & Readings (2010); Mgonja et al. (2015); Mbaiwa & Stronza (2011)
Challenges	Negative unintended cultural and economic impacts, Inadequate local communities' capacity to exploit ecotourism opportunities, Conflicting demands on protected areas Inefficient governance mechanisms, Low economic linkage between tourism and other economic sectors, Inadequate infrastructure	Mbaiwa (2011); Mgonja et al. (2015); Chirozva (2015); Mbaiwa (2015); Snyman (2012;2014); Pasape et al. (2015a, 2015b); Zanamwe et al. (2018); Saurombe et al. (2018); Stone & Stone (2011; 2020); Lindsey et al. (2007); Lindsey et al. (2013); Mhuriro-Mashapa et al. (2018); Naidoo et al. (2011); Powel et al. (2017); Stone (2015); Shoo (2020); Hoole (2010); Maude & Readings (2010); Mbaiwa & Stronza (2010; 2011); Anderson (2009, 2013, 2015, 2018); Anderson & Juma (2011)
Recommendations	Make tourism sensitive to local cultural norms and beliefs, Allow stakeholders participation in ecotourism policy making, Improve linkage between tourism and other economic sectors, Improve rural literacy, Establish ecotourism financing facilities, Improve quality of local produce, Establishing ecotourism guidelines, standards and certification mechanisms, Establish good governance practices, Improve tourism infrastructure,	Mbaiwa (2011); Mgonja et al. (2015); Stone & Stone (2020); Pasape et al. (2015b) and authors' synthesis

Ecotourism opportunities

Ecotourism presents opportunities for host communities to raise funds to conserve their pristine cultural and natural environments and to improve their livelihoods (Anderson, 2009). The findings indicate that ecotourism programmes in Southern Africa are mostly conducted on lands set aside by village communities for wildlife tourism (Snyman, 2017). Cultural tourism is an add–on instituted later as opportunities emerge (Shoo, 2020). The findings (Table 4.1) indicate that ecotourism improves the livelihood of people by providing them with employment income, leases (and other) income associated with communities' conservancies, business opportunities and donations.

The major contribution of ecotourism to the livelihood of local communities around protected areas is the provision of employment (Snyman, 2017). Ecotourism employment creates income for Zimbabweans, which, according to Chirenje (2017), is higher than income from other formal employment. Snyman (2012) further observes that ecotourism improves the financial security and social welfare of remote rural communities in Southern Africa. It is a reliable source of income that enables communities to meet their domestic, education and health-related needs (Anderson, 2015). Apart from income, Snyman (2014) observes that ecotourism is the first employment for the majority who also benefit from skills training and development opportunities as well as building working experience for other career opportunities.

Additionally, individual members in host communities receive income distributed to communities from leases (and other income) associated with communities' conservancies (Shoo, 2020; Snyman, 2012, 2014). The income generated from conservancies' leases and entrance fees is in turn used to finance communities' infrastructure developments (Shoo, 2020; Mbaiwa, 2015). Moreover, the funds improve the quality of social services such as education and healthcare facilities (Snyman, 2012, 2014; Shoo, 2020; Mbaiwa, 2015). Communities also receive charitable donations for development projects from tourism firms operating in their conservancies (Shoo, 2020; Snyman, 2017).

The findings also indicate that members of host communities enjoy business opportunities associated with ecotourism operations within the conservancies (Snyman, 2017; 2012, 2014; Shoo, 2020). This involves accommodation facilities in the conservancies using local supplies of goods and services, accommodation firms' staff attending schools and clinics in the area, and accommodation firms' staff spending their income at local stores in the villages (Snyman, 2017). Mbaiwa (2015) thus notes that the economic benefits of ecotourism in Botswana's Okavango Delta are high enough to attract communities to participate in tourism at the expense of other traditional economic activities such as farming and hunting. Moreover, the introduction of ecotourism initiatives allows people to earn income that transforms their lifestyles (Mbaiwa, 2015).

Apart from improvements in livelihood directly associated with income derived from tourism, governments have also taken steps to improve the infrastructure and social services of ecotourism areas due to their increased importance (Snyman, 2012, 2017). For example, Anderson (2015) observes that, before the introduction of cultural tourism activities in Kilimanjaro, Tanzania, 'some roads in rural areas were not passable, especially during the rainy season, but after the introduction of cultural tourism, there have been deliberate efforts to improve roads, particularly those leading to various cultural tourism sites' (p. 221). Improvement in infrastructure such as power, roads and telecommunication can highly influence people's mobility and allows them to diversify their livelihoods (Snyman, 2012, 2017).

Ecotourism initiatives have also facilitated improvements in the conservation of the environment and wildlife. Chirenje (2017) observes that the impact of ecotourism in Zimbabwe is positive through the preservation, protection and management of natural resources. In the community-based ecotourism programmes, the conversion of the communities' lands from agricultural purposes to ecotourism has allowed the wildlife and grasslands of these areas to flourish again (Chirenje, 2017). The absence of ecotourism in these areas would most likely result in the primary land use being changed to cattle farming, which would have a detrimental impact on the grassland habitat and the region's biodiversity (Maude & Readings, 2010). According to Maude and Reading (2010), the presence of ecotourism activities in these protected areas acts as a deterrent to poaching (Maude & Readings, 2010).

The conservation strategy involves the change in land use but also employing entrance fees by tourists and/or lease fees by ecotourism operators to promote and protect the wildlife and their habitats (Mgonja et al., 2015; Shoo 2020; Snyman, 2012). The conservation efforts help to increase the wildlife in protected areas and thus bring in more tourists (Maude & Reading, 2010). In addition, the improved livelihood associated with ecotourism in protected areas positively influences the positive attitudes of host communities towards conservation (Mbaiwa, 2015; Snyman 2012, 2014). For example, Mbaiwa and Stronza (2011) observed enhanced positive attitudes towards ecotourism and conservation amongst local communities in Botswana. This was caused by economic benefits residents derived from tourism activities conducted through community-based conservation initiatives. Similarly, ecotourism employment is observed to influence local communities' positive attitudes towards conservation in Namibia (Snyman, 2012).

Ecotourism in the Southern African region has promoted conservation and improved communities' livelihoods. Following the region's endowment with unique and unspoilt cultural and natural resources (Mgonja et al., 2015), there is an opportunity to develop ecotourism activities further to conserve these resources. Communities around these resources live in abject poverty, and perhaps further extension of ecotourism activities in these areas could improve the conservation of local cultures and environment and the livelihood of communities.

Associated challenges

Despite opportunities for conservation and improvements in livelihoods, there are challenges hindering the development of ecotourism and its effective impact. The challenges include socio-cultural impacts to the host communities, inadequate capacity to exploit ecotourism opportunities, conflicting demands on protected areas, inadequate governance mechanisms, low economic linkages, and inadequate tourism infrastructure. These are discussed below.

Socio-cultural impacts on host communities

Ecotourism has socio-cultural impacts on host communities. In Botswana, ecotourism caused the relocation of traditional communities, breaking up the traditional family structure, increase in crime, prostitution, and cultural deterioration (Mbaiwa, 2011). Mbaiwa (2011) further observes that economic gains from ecotourism led local communities to change and forgo traditional economic activities such as subsistence hunting, gathering, crop and livestock farming – which increases livelihood insecurity. The communities also changed their lifestyles – from traditional foods to processed foods and from the use of traditional utensils to modern facilities (Mbaiwa, 2011). While modernisation may be perceived to be a positive step, it destroys the traditional lifestyle and culture which could also be preserved and become a tourism product.

Inadequate capacity to exploit ecotourism opportunities

Local communities in Southern Africa own unique cultural and natural resources that have potential for ecotourism development (Mgonja et al., 2015). Moreover, local communities in the region make efforts to invest in ecotourism business opportunities that arise from their proximities (Chirozva, 2015). However, due to low education levels and poverty, they lack skills and capital to establish competitive and sustainable ecotourism businesses (Mgonja et al., 2015). Mbaiwa (2015) argues that the failure of ecotourism initiatives in Botswana is related to inadequate entrepreneurship, managerial and marketing skills in communities. The low education disadvantage and constrains participation of community members in the formal and highly paying ecotourism job market (Snyman, 2012, 2014). These challenges generally constrain local communities' participation in ecotourism and lead to high leakage of ecotourism benefits.

Moreover, even where local ecotourism businesses are established, most local owners/managers lack skills to incorporate ecotourism in their business operations (Mgonja et al., 2015; Pasape, Anderson & Lindi, 2015a). For example, Zanamwe et al. (2018) argue that, in Zimbabwe, local efforts to establish ecotourism enterprises have been unsuccessful. They argue that local institutions have not been empowered and lack clear policy guidelines on ecotourism. Saurombe, du Plessis and Swanepoel (2018) observe that Zimbabwean tourism firms' managers are aware of ecotourism but do not comply with it. The managers argue that there is a lack of leadership and there is uncertainty in guiding ecotourism principles on all levels of implementation. This challenge seems to be coupled with the non-existence of ecotourism guidelines and certification programmes, at least in the case of Tanzania (Mgonja et al., 2015).

Conflicting demands on protected areas

Land transformation for conservation and ecotourism reduces the communities' access to resources that support their livelihood (Snyman, 2012). Stone and Stone (2011) note that such transformation may disappoint parts of the communities in which ecotourism benefits are minimal and their livelihoods are adversely affected. This leads to heightened human activities in protected areas, resulting in deforestation, poaching and human encroachment. Mgonja et al. (2015) observed the widespread and organised poaching of elephants, which are key species in the Savannah ecosystem, whose extinction could have wider effects in the region. Moreover, communities in many areas suffered the loss of livestock and crops from wild animals, leading to human–wildlife conflicts (Lindsey et al., 2013; Mhuriro-Mashapa, Mwakiwa, & Mashapa, 2018; Naidoo et al., 2011), which jeopardises the conservation and sustainability of ecotourism. For example, Powel et al. (2017) observe that farmers in Namibia have a negative attitude towards predators that kill their livestock and positive attitudes towards meat-producing wildlife species. These attitudes were directly related to communities' decision to support or not support conservation efforts of such species and ecotourism activities in conservancies. However, according to Naidoo et al. (2011), the richness in predators and other destructive species in a conservancy increases ecotourism earnings.

Inadequate governance mechanisms

The most fundamental challenge facing ecotourism activities in the region is related to governance mechanisms (Pasape, Anderson & Lindi, 2015b). The first aspect of governance is related to powers to control resources and decision-making. It is challenging to decide on planning, decision-making, and policymaking about ecotourism development (Pasape et al., 2015b). The community-based tourism model proposes the delegation of powers and control over resources and decision-making to communities (Stone & Stone, 2020). However, multiple stakeholders involved in community-based tourism have varying powers and interests, complicating communities' central role in conservation (Stone, 2015).

In Tanzania, for example, the government holds decision-making powers on resources utilisation and how to share the benefits (Pasape et al., 2015b; Shoo, 2020). This approach turns communities into passive participants (Stone & Stone, 2020) and thus discourages them from participating in conservation. Similarly, Hoole (2010) observes asymmetric power sharing in community–enterprise partnerships in Namibia. Hoole (2010) argues that private enterprises have inherent control over most components of the ecotourism supply chain and make the most revenue generated through partnerships and high-end

50 *Said Juma Suluo and Wineaster Anderson*

employment positions externalised to regional and headquarter operations. This leads to high economic leakage, thus limiting benefits to local communities.

Another aspect of governance relates to accountability and transparency over the affairs of ecotourism enterprises. Studies show that most conservancies withhold key information about their finances from communities and are involved in corruption (Maude & Readings, 2010; Stone & Stone, 2011). Moreover, the ecotourism benefits are distributed across the communities inequitably (Snyman, 2012; Shoo, 2020; Stone & Stone, 2011). For example, Shoo (2020) observes that, in Tanzania, most employment opportunities in lodges are taken by men, non-locals and a few local elites. This situation has marginalised other groups within the communities. The fair distribution of community-based ecotourism benefits is a contentious issue in many conservancy projects (Mbaiwa & Stronza, 2010: Sebele, 2010), although it is critical to the success of community-based ecotourism programmes (Stone & Stone, 2020). Thus, poor governance mechanisms jeopardise the sustainability of ecotourism through unproductive planning, inefficiencies and mismanagement of ecotourism resources (Pasape et al., 2015b).

Low economic linkages

While there have been critical direct economic benefits from ecotourism activities, there are few economic benefits from the linkage of tourism business with other economic sectors (Snyman, 2012). Anderson (2013), for example, observed inadequate local supply sourcing by resorts in Zanzibar. This limits the linkage between local suppliers and tourism businesses in Zanzibar. Anderson and Juma (2011) note low-quality products, high transaction costs and violation of agreements by local suppliers as among the reasons for the challenging linkages between tourism and local suppliers in Zanzibar. Moreover, there are low linkages between tourism and agriculture – the key economic sector in most Southern African countries (Anderson, 2018; Snyman, 2012, 2014). Anderson (2018) argues that this low linkage is due to the product quality mismatch between what is locally produced and what is demanded by tourism firms. This may explain why local communities in Botswana had to forgo traditional economic activities such as subsistence hunting, gathering, crop and livestock farming during the tourism boom (Mbaiwa, 2011).

Inadequate tourism infrastructure

Most ecotourism operations in the Southern African region occur in remote rural localities with inadequate tourism infrastructure (Mgonja et al., 2015). Shoo (2020) indicates that tourists' complaints about poor tourism infrastructure at Lake Natron protected area in Tanzania range from inadequate information centres, sign posting, accommodation, access roads and bird-watching facilities. Inadequate infrastructure makes destinations less attractive and tourists less satisfied. Thus, despite the attractiveness of protected areas, the inadequate

Ecotourism as a paradigm shift 51

infrastructure may result in financially unsustainable ecotourism and thus jeopardise conservation and communities' livelihoods.

Lessons learnt, recommendations and conclusions

This chapter reviews opportunities and challenges of ecotourism in improving conservation and livelihood of local communities in the Southern African region. Evidence suggests that ecotourism is, at least in some parts of the region, instrumental in improving the conservation of natural and cultural resources while also enhancing the livelihoods of local communities. Along with the benefits, ecotourism has also brought unintended detrimental consequences for the culture and traditional economic activities in the region. Moreover, the findings indicate that ecotourism in the Southern African region is in its infancy, with most potential attractions, especially in cultural ecotourism, remaining untapped. In terms of challenges, the sector faces the low capacity of local communities to exploit ecotourism opportunities, inadequate tourism infrastructure, low linkages with other economic sectors and poor governance mechanisms. This chapter notes the potential of ecotourism to enhance the conservation of natural and cultural resources and the livelihoods of local communities. However, this potential can only be achieved if the region addresses the challenges and expands ecotourism to other unexplored areas, particularly cultural attractions.

In response to identified challenges, the following recommendations are made. It was earlier observed that ecotourism is partly responsible for youths adopting a Western lifestyle. Although it is difficult to restrict the adoption of foreign culture, ecotourism needs to be sensitive to local cultural norms and beliefs for it to be accepted by local people and for it to promote sustainable development (Mbaiwa, 2011). This is possible if all the stakeholders (government, operators and local people) collaborate in policy formulation, implementation and monitoring. Moreover, tourism planning should ensure that there are linkages between tourism and other traditional economic activities so that a tourism boom should result in enhanced traditional economic systems and rural livelihood sustainability (Mbaiwa, 2011).

Rural communities are characterised by low education levels which translate to inadequate knowledge and skills to establish and manage ecotourism and conservation initiatives. To enhance the knowledge and skills of local communities, Mgonja et al. (2015) recommend the training of communities on eco tour-guiding as a starting point. The training should provide tour-guides with ecotourism-related techniques that promote local culture and protect natural resources (Mgonja et al., 2015). However, this matter requires long-term solutions where regional governments show commitment to improving rural literacy levels (Stone & Stone, 2020). In addition to literacy problems, local communities also lack the financial muscle to invest in ecotourism enterprises (Mgonja et al., 2015). Governments and financial institutions need to consider establishing ecotourism financing facilities that support communities through micro credits to finance the growth of ecotourism businesses. Tourism actors also need to improve the capacity of local suppliers and the quality of local produce to align with tourism sector demands; this will enhance linkages between tourism and other economic sectors. These steps may also help reduce revenue leakage and improve economic benefits from ecotourism.

Local ecotourism enterprises also lack the necessary skills and guidelines on ecotourism implementation. To address this concern, the first approach should be to create general awareness among existing ecotourism enterprises on how to incorporate ecotourism values and principles in businesses. Tourism actors need to consider the development of ecotourism guidelines and standards during implementation. They also need to develop ecotourism certification mechanisms (Mgonja et al., 2015) that form a basis for awarding ecotourism operators whose initiatives have a significant contribution to the sustainable development goals. This can encourage firms to align their ecotourism practices with sustainable development goals.

The governance mechanisms of ecotourism conservancies need to be addressed. Pasape et al. (2015b) recommended the establishment of good governance practices through transparency, accountability and integration of activities in ecotourism programmes. Central governments and associated institutions need to transfer decision-making powers back to communities. However, they should continue to oversee the undertakings of the ecotourism projects, while building the capacity of local communities to implement these projects. Corruption and other inefficiencies from the managements of the ecotourism projects should be punished accordingly.

Tourism infrastructure requires improvement within and around ecotourism conservancies. Shoo (2020) recommends efforts to improve infrastructure and interpretation facilities should be crucial to ecotourism development. Governments need to include in their policies and plans the improvement of infrastructure within and around protected areas. Moreover, ecotourism firms need financing facilities to enhance their infrastructure – the financial industry should consider ecotourism-related financing schemes. These measures are expected to enhance ecotourism services delivery and tourists' satisfaction.

Governments and other stakeholders must show commitment and be willing to address these challenges, most of which are reversible. Until efforts are made to address the challenges, the contribution of ecotourism to conservation and communities' livelihoods in Southern Africa region will be limited. These findings, however, were based on a literature review of previous studies in some Southern African countries from 2010. Future studies may extend the scope and include a much bigger sample in terms of years and regions.

References

Anderson, W. (2009). Promoting ecotourism through networks: Case studies in the Balearic Islands. *Journal of Ecotourism*, 8 (1), 51–69.

Anderson, W. (2013). Leakages in the tourism systems: Case of Zanzibar. *Tourism Review*, 68 (1), 62–76.

Anderson, W. (2015). Cultural tourism and poverty alleviation in rural Kilimanjaro, Tanzania. *Journal of Tourism and Cultural Change*, 13 (3), 208–224.

Anderson, W. (2018). Linkages between tourism and agriculture for inclusive development in Tanzania: A value chain perspective. *Journal of Hospitality and Tourism Insights*, 1 (2), 168–184.

Anderson, W., & Juma, S. (2011). Linkages at tourism destinations: Challenges in Zanzibar, *ARA Journal of Tourism Research*, 3 (1), 27–41.

Backman, K. F., & Munanura, I. (2015). Introduction to the special issues on ecotourism in Africa over the past 30 years. *Journal of Ecotourism*, 14 (2–3), 95–98.

Braun, V., & Clarke, V. (2006). Using thematic analysis in psychology. *Qualitative Research in Psychology*, 3 (2), 77–101.

Chirenje, L. I. (2017). Contribution of ecotourism to poverty alleviation in Nyanga, Zimbabwe. *Chinese Journal of Population Resources and Environment*, 15 (2), 87–92.

Chirozva, C. (2015). Community agency and entrepreneurship in ecotourism planning and development in the Great Limpopo Transfrontier Conservation Area. *Journal of Ecotourism*, 14 (2–3), 185–203.

Gössling, S. (2000). Sustainable tourism development in developing countries: Some aspects of energy use. *Journal of Sustainable Tourism*, 8 (5), 410–425.

Hoole, A. (2010). Place-power-prognosis: Community-based conservation, partnerships, and ecotourism enterprises in Namibia. *International Journal of the Commons*, 4 (1), 78–99.

Jacsó, P. (2005). Google Scholar: The pros and the cons. *Online Information Review*, 29 (2), 208–214.

Kavita, E., & Saarinen, J. (2016). Tourism and rural community development in Namibia: Policy issues review. *Fennia-International Journal of Geography*, 194 (1), 79–88.

Lindsey, P. A., Alexander, R., Mills, M. G. L., Romañach, S., & Woodroffe, R. (2007). Wildlife viewing preferences of visitors to protected areas in South Africa: Implications for the role of ecotourism in conservation. *Journal of Ecotourism*, 6 (1), 19–33.

Lindsey, P. A., Havemann, C. P., Lines, R. M., Price, A. E., Retief, T. A., Rhebergen, T., van der Waal, C., & Romañach, S. S. (2013). Benefits of wildlife-based land uses on private lands in Namibia and limitations affecting their development. *Oryx*, 47 (1), 41–53.

Maude, G., & Reading, R. P. (2010). The role of ecotourism in biodiversity and grassland conservation in Botswana. *Great Plains Research*, 109–119.

Mbaiwa, J. E. (2011). Changes on traditional livelihood activities and lifestyles caused by tourism development in the Okavango Delta, Botswana. *Tourism Management*, 32 (5), 1050–1060.

Mbaiwa, J. E. (2015). Ecotourism in Botswana: 30 years later. *Journal of Ecotourism*, 14 (2–3), 204–222.

Mbaiwa, J. E., & Stronza, A. L. (2010). The effects of tourism development on rural livelihoods in the Okavango Delta, Botswana. *Journal of Sustainable Tourism*, 18 (5), 635–656.

Mbaiwa, J. E., & Stronza, A. L. (2011). Changes in resident attitudes towards tourism development and conservation in the Okavango Delta, Botswana. *Journal of Environmental Management*, 92 (8), 1950–1959.

Medina, L. K. (2005). Ecotourism and certification: Confronting the principles and pragmatics of socially responsible tourism. *Journal of Sustainable Tourism*, 13 (3), 281–295.

Mgonja, J. T., Sirima, A., & Mkumbo, P. J. (2015). A review of ecotourism in Tanzania: Magnitude, challenges, and prospects for sustainability. *Journal of Ecotourism*, 14 (2–3), 264–277.

Mhuriro-Mashapa, P., Mwakiwa, E., & Mashapa, C. (2018). Socio-economic impact of human-wildlife conflicts on agriculture-based livelihood in the periphery of save valley conservancy, southern Zimbabwe. *Journal of Plant and Animal Sciences*, 28, 12–16.

Mnini, P., & Ramoroka, T. (2020). Challenges of ecotourism and poverty alleviation in South Africa. International *Journal of Economics and Finance Studies*, 12 (2), 184–197.

Naidoo, P., Ramseook-Munhurrun, P., & Seegoolam, P. (2011). An assessment of visitor satisfaction with nature-based tourism attractions. *International Journal of Management and Marketing Research*, 4 (1), 87–98.

Nelson, F. (2012). Natural conservationists? Evaluating the impact of pastoralist land use practices on Tanzania's wildlife economy. *Pastoralism: Research, Policy and Practice*, 2 (1), 15.

Pasape, L., Anderson, W., & Lindi, G. (2015a). Assessment of indicators of sustainable ecotourism in Tanzania. *Anatolia*, 26 (1), 73–84.

Pasape, L., Anderson, W., & Lindi, G. (2015b). Good governance strategies for sustainable ecotourism in Tanzania. *Journal of Ecotourism*, 14 (2–3), 145–165.

Powell, L. A., Kazahe, U., & Kharuxab, R. (2017). Livestock farmers engage in ecotourism as a result of beliefs and attitudes toward wildlife on communal lands in Namibia. *Human Dimensions of Wildlife*, 22 (3), 217–230.

Roberts, T., & Thanos. N. D. (2003). *Trouble in paradise: Globalization and environmental crises in Latin America*. New York: Routledge.

Saurombe, H. A., du Plessis, Y., & Swanepoel, S. (2018). An integrated managerial framework towards implementing an ecotourism culture in Zimbabwe. *Journal of Ecotourism*, 17 (2), 107–122.

Sebele, L. S. (2010). Community-based tourism ventures, benefits and challenges: Khama rhino sanctuary trust, central district, Botswana. *Tourism Management*, 31 (1), 136–146.

Shoo, R. A. (2020) Ecotourism potential and challenges at Lake Natron Ramsar Site, Tanzania. In Durrant, J., et al. (Eds.), *Protected Areas in Northern Tanzania*. Geotechnologies and the Environment, Vol 22. Cham: Springer, 75–90.

Shores, J. N. (1992). *The challenge of ecotourism: A call for higher standards*. Paper presented at the 4th world congress on national parks and protected areas, Caracas, Venezuela.

Snyman, S. (2014). The impact of ecotourism employment on rural household incomes and social welfare in six southern African countries. *Tourism and Hospitality Research*, 14 (1–2), 37–52.

Snyman, S. (2017). The role of private sector ecotourism in local socio-economic development in southern Africa. *Journal of Ecotourism*, 16 (3), 247–268.

Snyman, S. L. (2012). The role of tourism employment in poverty reduction and community perceptions of conservation and tourism in southern Africa. *Journal of Sustainable Tourism*, 20 (3), 395–416.

Songorwa, A. N. (1999). Community-based wildlife management (CWM) in Tanzania: Are the communities interested? *World Development*, 27 (12), 2061–2079.

Southern African Development Community (SADC). (2019). *Tourism Programme 2020 – 2030*. Gaborone, Botswana: SADC.

Stone, L. S., & Stone, T. M. (2011). Community-based tourism enterprises: Challenges and prospects for community participation; Khama Rhino Sanctuary Trust, Botswana. *Journal of Sustainable Tourism*, 19 (1), 97–114.

Stone, M. T. (2015). Community-based ecotourism: A collaborative partnerships perspective. *Journal of Ecotourism*, 14 (2–3), 166–184.

Stone, M. T., & Nyaupane, G. P. (2018). Protected areas, wildlife-based community tourism and community livelihoods dynamics: Spiraling up and down of community capitals. *Journal of Sustainable Tourism*, 26 (2), 307–324.

Stone, M. T., & Stone, L. S. (2020). Challenges of community-based tourism in Botswana: A review of literature. *Transactions of the Royal Society of South Africa*, 75 (2), 181–193.

Suluo, S. J., Mossberg, L., Andersson, T. D., Anderson, W., & Assad, M. J. (2020). Corporate sustainability practices in tourism – evidence from Tanzania. *Tourism Planning & Development*, 1–22.

The International Ecotourism Society [TIES], (2015). Definition and principles of ecotourism. Retrieved from https://ecotourism.org/what-is-ecotourism/ (5 April 2021).

Torri, M. C., & Herrmann, T. M. (2010). Biodiversity conservation versus rural development: What kind of possible harmonization? The case study of Alwar District, Rajasthan, India. *Journal of Human Ecology*, 31 (2), 93–101.

Walters, W. H. (2009). Google Scholar search performance: Comparative recall and precision. *Portal: Libraries and the Academy*, 9 (1), 5–24.

Wells, M., & Bradon, K. (1992). *People and parks: Linking protected area management with local communities*. Washington, DC: World Bank.

Zanamwe, C., Gandiwa, E., Muboko, N., Kupika, O. L., & Mukamuri, B. B. (2018). Ecotourism and wildlife conservation-related enterprise development by local communities within Southern Africa: Perspectives from the greater Limpopo Transfrontier Conservation, South–Eastern Lowveld, Zimbabwe. *Cogent Environmental Science*, 4 (1), 1531463.

5 Tolerance for wildlife resources through community wildlife-based tourism

Implications for sustainability

Chiedza Ngonidzashe Mutanga

Introduction

Southern Africa is home to a diverse and abundant wildlife. Wildlife resources generate revenue and wealth directly and indirectly for many local and national economies (Naidoo et al., 2016). As a result, any detrimental effects on biodiversity may have an impact on a community's ability to thrive. In recent years, several countries in Southern Africa have benefited from strong growth in their tourism sectors (UNWTO, 2015). Wildlife tourism is a form of nature-based tourism that is based on encounters with wild animals and can be both consumptive and non-consumptive in nature (Lovelock, 2008). Community-based tourism (CBT), on the other hand, refers to a form of development that improves the social and cultural benefits of local communities by facilitating social and cultural exchanges with tourists (Zielinski et al., 2020). Community wildlife-based tourism (CWBT) is therefore a form of CBT that enables local communities to generate economic benefits by providing visitors with consumptive or non-consumptive wildlife encounters and at the same time promoting community growth, wildlife conservation and poverty reduction.

The sustainability of several protected areas (PAs) is threatened because many of these PAs forced local people to relocate from their original areas of residence, denying them access to resources such as meat, grazing areas and firewood in the PAs (Fischer et al., 2011). Increased illegal hunting, habitat encroachment and destruction, human–wildlife conflicts (HWC), crime and poverty among indigenous communities have all resulted from such protectionist and oppressive conservation policies, also known as 'fortress conservation' (Romañach et al., 2011). The realisation that, if societies do not embrace PAs, they would resist PA conservation measures led to the creation of integrated conservation and development projects (ICDPs) (Holmes, 2013). Community-based natural resource management (CBNRM) programmes are an example of ICDPs. In Southern African countries such as Botswana, Malawi, Namibia, Mozambique, Zambia and Zimbabwe, there have been several community-based conservation initiatives (Fabricius et al., 2013). CBNRM in Southern Africa started in the 1980s in Zimbabwe with the Communal Areas Management Programme for Indigenous

DOI: 10.4324/9781003193166-6

Resources (CAMPFIRE), with parallel programmes springing up in Namibia, Zambia and Botswana (Dressler et al., 2010). These programmes aimed to support local communities by taking a utilitarian approach to wildlife and to encourage conservation by increasing community tolerance for wildlife resources.

Local support for wildlife management relies heavily on benefit sharing (Tessema et al., 2010). Communities that receive more wildlife-related benefits are more likely to support conservation, while communities that receive less benefits are more likely to show disappointment (Gandiwa et al., 2013). Despite the benefits, Songorwa et al. (2000) argue that the issue of whether community wildlife management effectively provides sufficient incentives to substitute ecologically harmful yet economically rewarding practices such as poaching remains unanswered. This chapter investigates the role of CWBT in increasing community tolerance for wildlife resources based on the study of opportunities and challenges posed by efforts to use CBNRM as a catalyst for conservation and community growth.

Theoretical framework

This chapter is informed by Hardin (1968)'s theory of common pool resources (CPR) and the social exchange theory (SET). The theory of CPR represents a significant and promising approach to natural resource governance that aims to avoid common pool dilemmas (Saunders, 2014). Common pool dilemmas, also known as 'tragedy of the commons', occur when individuals in interdependent circumstances fail to coordinate their behaviour, resulting in outcomes in which everyone loses because CPR are depleted by reasonable, utility-maximising individuals rather than conserved for the good of all (Ostrom, 2008). Individuals who formulate and follow sets of rules that organise their use of the popular pool tools, on the other hand, will achieve better results. As a result, the CPR theory has been instrumental in packaging knowledge to create local natural resource institutions through commons projects (Saunders, 2014). This chapter examines how the conservation and use of wildlife resources for tourism purposes improves communities' appreciation for wildlife resources.

SET on the other hand, is a theoretical structure for explaining host communities' positive and negative attitudes (Rasoolimanesh et al., 2015). The basic premise of the theory is that, in social environments, humans select behaviours that increase their chances of achieving their own self-interests (Emerson, 1976). Among the assumptions that underpin SET are that individuals are generally rational and engage in calculations of costs and benefits in social exchanges, and that those engaged in interactions are rationally seeking to maximise the profits or benefits to be gained from those situations, particularly in terms of meeting basic individual needs (Rasoolimanesh et al., 2015). As a result, SET is critical in determining whether CWBT provides sufficient incentives to motivate tolerance for wildlife resources. The argument is that, if people believe that the benefits of wildlife tourism outweigh the costs of wildlife conservation, they will develop more tolerance for wildlife resources (Mutanga, 2017). The

58   *Chiedza Ngonidzashe Mutanga*

two theories are both important for this study because, to illuminate social ecological systems and design governance institutions that promote sustainable resource use, it is important to understand how and when cooperative human behaviour forms in CPR systems (Klein et al., 2017).

Methodology

Data were gathered using a qualitative method based on a study of applicable literature. A meta-synthesis of current scholarly literature on CBNRM, wildlife conservation and wildlife tourism was performed, based on peer-reviewed journal articles, books, edited book chapters and academic theses. Related literature was found using Google Scholar, Scopus and Web of Science, primarily using the key phrases 'CBNRM', 'community-based tourism', 'wildlife conservation' and 'wildlife tourism'. The descriptive interpretive qualitative approach was used to analyse the collected data on CBNRM and wildlife resources. The role of CWBT in fostering community tolerance for wildlife resources was investigated by evaluating opportunities for wildlife conservation offered by CWBT and the challenges faced by CWBT projects that undermine or have potential to weaken community tolerance for wildlife resources.

Results and discussion

Situating CWBT

Protectionist conservation strategies aided the creation of PAs (Igoe, 2004). The forcible displacement and exclusion of rural communities from wildlife benefits engendered hostility and hostile attitudes toward wildlife resources, leading to increased poaching and habitat encroachment and destruction (Romañach et al., 2011). Due to the rise in illegal resource harvesting, it was realised that the fences and fines strategy was failing to protect wildlife, which led to the introduction of ICDPs (Wilkie et al., 2006). ICDPs became a common method for engaging with communities in and around PAs after they gained local support (Gockel & Gray, 2009). Conservationists believe that wildlife resource conservation will fail unless residents are active in conservation efforts and this has led to the creation of these new community conservation or participatory management strategies (Yeo-Chang, 2009).

The CBNRM model entails a shift from 'top-down' growth approaches to 'bottom-up' approaches involving local communities (Mbaiwa, 2015). Some CBNRM programmes which became popular through local community support in Southern Africa include the Living in a Finite Environment (LIFE) and Wildlife Integration for Livelihood Diversification (WILD) in Namibia, the Administrative Management Design (ADMADE) and Luangwa Integrated Resource Development Project (LIRDP) in Zambia (Fabricius, 2013), Tchuma Tchato in Mozambique and CAMPFIRE in Zimbabwe (Zanamwe et al., 2018). Namibia also has communal conservancies based on trust and co-management while Botswana has community trusts guided by the CBNRM policy promulgated in 2007 by the Botswana parliament (Shereni & Saarinen, 2020). CBNRM programmes are focused on the idea that, if communities benefit financially from wildlife resources, they can value and contribute to their protection (Martin, 1986). CBNRM programmes encourage community growth by promoting independent projects on communal property (Balint & Mashinya, 2006). Their mission is to increase the benefits of alternative livelihood practices to reduce the threat of local people to conservation (Salafsky & Wollenberg, 2000).

CBT can be traced back to the origin of the CBNRM concept, which aims to encourage natural resource protection as well as rural community growth (Stone & Stone, 2020). CBT has been backed to help communities link biodiversity protection and improved livelihoods. Over time, various CBT models, including CWBT, have been developed. CWBT is often developed on a small scale, and includes interactions between tourists and local communities, with the local communities being the primary beneficiaries through the development of their communities, and boosting conservation (Asker et al., 2010).

In Botswana, CWBT is systematised through the formation of a community trust to participate in joint wildlife tourism venture partnerships on behalf of the community, with the aim of generating high-stakes revenue (Cassidy, 2021). Although some reports claim that CWBT has been effective in strengthening local institutions, empowering local communities, improving rural communities' livelihoods and changing community attitudes toward wildlife resource conservation (Stone & Stone, 2020), others claim that CWBT has failed because no real power has been intentionally devolved (Cassidy, 2021; Stone & Stone, 2020). CBWT, according to Cassidy (2021), has been a success in Namibia. The grassroots base of each conservancy is connected through support networks supported by non-governmental organisations (NGOs) to provide an expanded landscape of collective conservation in Namibia's conservancy system. Rather than focusing on generating large amounts at the community level, Namibian conservancies seek to get revenue to participating households, however small it may be (Silva & Mosimane, 2013). In Zimbabwe, poaching was greatly reduced in some areas as communities began to receive economic benefits from CWBT and began to help with wildlife conservation, while in other areas poaching subsided only briefly and then returned after a few years (Fischer et al., 2011). Shereni and Saarinen (2020) stated that the communities surrounding Hwange National Park in Zimbabwe were not receiving any significant benefits from CAMPFIRE, contradicting the entire intent of the CWBT. In Zambia, as in Zimbabwe, community members' attitudes toward CBNRM are generally negative due to crop losses and other wildlife disruption, a lack of compensation mechanisms and the local districts' high percentage of revenue retention (Chisanga, 2016). These examples illustrate that, while CWBT has tremendous potential for inspiring tolerance for wildlife resources, it is often hampered by several challenges that, if tackled, have the potential to improve communities' tolerance for wildlife resources and promote sustainable community livelihoods. Table 5.1 summarises the role of CWBT in promoting tolerance to wildlife resources.

Table 5.1 The role of CWBT in enhancing communities' tolerance for wildlife resources and implications for sustainability

Attribute of CWBT	Opportunities for enhancing community tolerance to wildlife resources	Challenges in enhancing tolerance through CWBT	Implications for sustainability
Offers opportunity for host communities to derive benefits	• Communities are more inclined to support wildlife conservation if they are involved in it • When communities benefit from CWBT: 1. their tolerance for wildlife resources may be increased and they will comply with restrictions on use and extraction 2. they are less likely to engage in activities that are detrimental to wildlife conservation like poaching	• Limited financial investments • Poor market access • Poor governance • Limited capacity to meet tourist requirements • Benefits are site-specific and dependent on unique visitor experiences • Legacy of fortress conservation • Sectoral attributes of tourism • HWC • Unmet expectations and livelihoods • Increasing populations within communities	• Capacity building focused on training in entrepreneurship • Capacity building to enhance skills of local people to effectively manage the CWBT ventures. • Creation of key linkages and partnerships in CWBT projects among all stakeholders • Develop mechanisms for tourists to bring direct benefits to the local area and for money to stay in • Revenues must be distributed in an open, easily understood, and straightforward manner • Allocating lease sites for photographic tourism within PAs for community enterprises
In CWBT, communities are better placed for wildlife resource management than governments	• Stakeholders and intra-group conflicts are limited • With the continuous watchful attention of other community members, individuals' sense of responsibility increases	• Intra-community tensions still exist due to the heterogeneous nature of the communities • Communities may not share the same interests which can lead to some resistance or complications within CWBT projects	• Investment in the establishment of effective mechanisms for the transparent exchange of information and ironing out of grievances between stakeholders • The design and implementation of CWBT should also be based on communities of interest rather than geographical location only.

Local communities have indigenous knowledge required for wildlife resource conservation	• Becomes easier to put into use people's traditional knowledge on conservation • Restores a sense of ownership and responsibility for the wildlife resource among community members	• Lack of important scientific and ecological information to enable communities to make informed decisions	• Enhancing community access to reliable ecological information
CWBT promotes 'bottom-up' development	• Gives communities a voice in issues regarding their welfare which gives them a sense of ownership and responsibility	• In most CWBT in many Southern African countries, the governments still apply a 'top-down' approach where they have most say in natural resources in the countries	• There is need to fully decentralise authority to the local communities as has been the original design of the CBNRM programmes
CWBT projects involve multiple stakeholders	• Reciprocal relationship between stakeholders increases their participation in community development projects • Stakeholders learn to appreciate the legitimacy of each other's views • Multiple stakeholders leads to a greater uptake of conservation measures and fewer conflicts among stakeholders	• Often dilutes the power of the communities to make decisions • Some stakeholders mistrust the communities' ability to manage wildlife resources	• There is need for clarity around the mandates of and relationships to different stakeholders such as traditional leaders, local government and line departments • Ensuring representativeness and accountability of all stakeholders

Sources: Compiled from Barnes (2008); Mogaka et al. | (2001); Songorwa et al. (2000); Bruchac (2014); He et al. (2020); Sterling (2017); Goodwin (2009); Bond & Frost (2005); Tosun (2000); Munalula et al. (2020); Sterling et al. (2017); Mutanga et al. (2017); Stone & Stone (2020).

Opportunities for enhancing community tolerance for wildlife resources through CWBT

Several studies have shown that CBNRM projects support certain communities, such as the Caprivi Strip in Namibia (Barnes, 2008) and Mahenye in Zimbabwe (Mudzengi et al., 2020). As communities begin to reap the benefits of CWBT and become incentivised to restrict poaching and preserve wildlife habitat on their land, tolerance for wildlife resources is anticipated (Balint & Mashinya, 2006). Improvements in local welfare and the provision of measurable local benefits from wildlife resources encourage community tolerance for wildlife resources and minimise unsustainable or illegal wildlife activities (Mogaka et al., 2001). Although the history of being excluded from PAs may have dampened communities' tolerance for wildlife resources, if their expectations are met and they are satisfied, the history may be forgotten. Sustainable wildlife resource management is more likely to occur when local users can maintain and profit from those resources (Kull, 2002).

CWBT communities, rather than governments, are best suited for wildlife resource management because they serve and can act on local concerns directly. This is because, in community-based projects, the number of partners and intra-group disputes are restricted, making inclusion and exclusion rules easier to implement (Songorwa et al., 2000). Furthermore, proponents claim that individuals' sense of duty increases because of the constant watchful interest of other group members, decreasing the issue of shared pool resources.

Local communities in wildlife areas have the traditional or indigenous knowledge needed for wildlife resource protection (Songorwa et al., 2000). Indigenous knowledge is knowledge passed down over generations based on long-term observations of the environments in which the people reside (Bruchac, 2014). Local communities can use indigenous information if resources are placed under their jurisdiction. In other words, when wildlife tourism is community-based, it becomes easier to put into use people's traditional knowledge on conservation. This gives community members a voice in making decisions that concern them, restoring a sense of ownership and responsibility for the wildlife resource.

The promotion of 'bottom-up' development is one of CWBT's tenets. This approach to development empowers communities by giving them a say in matters that affect their well-being, giving them a sense of control and accountability (Cooksey & Kikula, 2005). In CBNRM, communities are involved in designing, planning and taking part in the conservation process from the bottom-up (He et al., 2020). CWBT is therefore a viable method of enhancing wildlife resource tolerance in which community involvement is a means for the community to gain the trust and expertise to fully participate in their wildlife resource management programmes without relying on outside help (He et al., 2020).

A variety of stakeholders are involved in CWBT programmes. Stakeholders' interest in community development programmes is increased when they have a reciprocal partnership. Involving a diverse range of stakeholders in CWBT can result in higher quality decisions that are better suited to local social, cultural and environmental contexts, the creation of common ground, trust and reduced stakeholder conflict, and lower implementation costs (Sterling, 2017). For example, while local and traditional ecological knowledge is important for achieving wildlife conservation goals, knowledge co-production among indigenous groups, scientists and PAs can result in more successful wildlife resource conservation.

Challenges faced in strengthening communities' tolerance for wildlife resources through CWBT

Benefits of CWBT to local communities are affected by (i) lack of financial viability, poor market access, poor governance, lack of human capital, and limited capacity to meet tourists' requirements, (ii) the legacy of fortress conservation which makes it more difficult for communities to participate on an equal basis with their partners, (iii) the sectoral attributes of tourism which pose special challenges to CWBT where communities have to compete for tourists within a large and competitive field with many state-owned PAs and a large private nature tourism industry, and (iv) lack of substantial investment for profitable wildlife tourism – although tourists often pay access fees, the larger share of revenue is garnered through housing, transport and tour management of which communities engaged in CWBT are unlikely to have sufficient funds to set up high-cost tourism ventures on their own (Goodwin, 2009). While CWBT may help rural communities become more tolerant to wildlife resources, this is not a given. The advantages are usually site-specific and based on special visitor experiences (Songorwa et al., 2000). This condition, which stems from lack of benefits from wildlife to communities, may lead to a decrease in community tolerance for wildlife resources, which manifests as revenge destruction of wildlife resources (Ebua et al., 2011). Moreover, HWC compromises communities' tolerance for wildlife resources, even in cases where CWBT is effective. This is because unresolved HWCs ensure the perpetuation of negative perceptions towards wildlife resources, which has negative social effects and threatens the long-term viability of wildlife resources (Holmes, 2013). Although some benefits are received by communities, some community members are dissatisfied, partially due to unmet high standards and livelihoods that are heavily reliant on wildlife resources in an environment marked by an increasing human population chasing declining wildlife resources (Bond & Frost, 2005).

Although some advocates of CWBT claim that communities are best suited for wildlife resource management due to less intra-community disputes, communities are still linked by geography but are heterogeneous, resulting in intra-community tensions (Stone & Stone, 2020). Furthermore, since communities are typically heterogeneous, with various interest groups such as local elites pursuing their own goals, this may lead to conflicting agendas, opposition or problems within CWBT initiatives (Tosun, 2000). On indigenous knowledge needed for wildlife resource protection, communities lack important scientific and ecological information that could help them make informed decisions, especially when it comes to setting hunting quotas, because it is either unavailable or difficult to obtain (Songorwa et al., 2000). This means that, although indigenous knowledge is essential, it may be less so in current circumstances.

Most CWBT in many Southern African countries still use a 'top-down' approach in which governments have a lot of control over the countries' natural resources (Isidiho & Sabran, 2016). This approach includes the state dictating what communities must follow without considering the local contexts in which those resources are found (Munalula et al., 2020). This discourages community engagement in CWBT projects and weakens communities' ability to make decisions on how resources can be handled to maximise community benefits and increase tolerance for wildlife resources (Sabatier, 1986). Furthermore, the presence of numerous stakeholders in CWBT initiatives dilutes communities' decision-making authority. Also, some stakeholders doubt communities' capacity to manage wildlife resources, leaving them voiceless and marginalised (Sterling, 2017).

Implications for sustainability

To provide and market visitor services, communities need investment and capacity building. Capacity building is important, and should focus on providing support to communities, particularly through entrepreneurship training to empower local people to start and manage small CWBT ventures, as well as livelihood activities such as poultry projects to reduce reliance on wildlife resources. Besides helping communities gain benefits, these can also improve community tolerance for wildlife resources. This is because CWBT ventures instil a sense of ownership of the wildlife resources. Following the CPR theory, the establishment of CWBT ventures can lead to better wildlife conservation outcomes since community members are able to devise and adopt sets of rules that coordinate their use of common pool resources and can have clearly defined membership and physical boundaries of the resources.

To improve communities' tolerance for wildlife resources, all stakeholders, including states, local communities, NGOs, government wildlife agencies, universities and private businesses, should form key alliances and linkages in CWBT projects (Sterling et al., 2017). There is, however, a need for clarification about the mandates of various stakeholders. According to SET theory, it is important to consider what each stakeholder is supposed to bring to the relationship, as well as what they hope to gain from it. This ensures representativeness and accountability of all stakeholders.

There must be a mechanism for visitors to bring direct benefits to local destinations, and a mechanism for the money to remain in the community, for CWBT to be worthwhile. Local wildlife tourism revenues must stay in the community, where they can be reinvested in wildlife resource management and community development projects. Revenues must be administered in a transparent and straightforward manner. It is necessary to invest in the development of effective processes for the open exchange of information and the resolution of grievances between stakeholders for this to occur (Mutanga et al., 2017). This condition could be strengthened by allocating lease sites for photographic tourism within PAs to community enterprises under public–private community partnership agreements, resulting in increased community benefits and infrastructure improvements. According to SET principles, with the provision of benefits, individuals may perceive that they are receiving benefits from a relationship approximately equal to what they are putting into the relationship, and this can make individuals comfortable and more tolerant towards wildlife resources. As individuals perceive the presence of reciprocity in their social relationships, they are more likely to feel satisfied with and maintain those relationships.

Access to accurate ecological information is also needed for communities to be inspired and to actively engage in the protection of wildlife resources (Songorwa et al., 2000). To address the issue of intra-community tensions caused by the diverse existence of populations, Stone and Stone (2020) recommend that CWBT be designed and implemented to target groups based on their interests and skills rather than their geographic position alone. Investment is also needed in the creation of effective mechanisms for the open exchange of information and the resolution of grievances among stakeholders.

Governments must decentralise power to local communities, as was the original design of CBNRM programmes. The greater the authority given to communities and the greater the willingness of the state to relinquish control, the more likely the CWBT projects will succeed. It is assumed that if true community control is established, long-term usage and tolerance will follow.

Poaching was greatly decreased in some areas because of CWBT, as communities began to benefit from legal wildlife use and to assist with wildlife conservation (Child, 1995). Poaching, on the other hand, was only briefly reduced in some places before returning after a few years (Fischer et al., 2011). This demonstrates that, while benefit sharing may improve community tolerance for wildlife resources, wildlife benefits alone may not be sufficient to ensure positive outcomes. Other considerations, such as communication and HWC prevention, must also be considered. Open and adequate communication aids in the resolution of conflicts and the management of expectations and perceptions in a way that fosters trust among stakeholders (Mutanga et al., 2017).

Collectively, the challenges discussed in the previous section necessitate the development of successful policies that increase local people's empowerment while also considering the unique characteristics of the areas to be used for wildlife-based tourism. Given the importance of PA-community relationships in the conservation of wildlife resources, it should be acknowledged that SET is important in understanding interactions between PA staff and local communities.

Conclusion

The role of CWBT in fostering community tolerance for wildlife resources is examined in this chapter. Opportunities for enhancing communities' tolerance to wildlife resources through CWBT include providing incentives for host communities to prosper, reducing intra-group conflicts in community-based projects, increasing individuals' sense of responsibility, people's traditional knowledge on conservation, opportunities for communities to be heard, increasing stakeholders' participation, stakeholder appreciation of each other's views and greater uptake of conservation measures due to multiple stakeholders. However, CWBT programmes also face a number of obstacles that weaken communities' tolerance for wildlife resources which include lack of financial investments, poor market access, poor governance, limited capacity to meet tourist requirements, site-specific nature of benefits, legacy of fortress conservation, sectoral attributes of tourism, HWC, the heterogeneous nature of communities, lack of important scientific and ecological information and the 'top-down' approach which is still employed by some governments. To enhance communities' tolerance for wildlife resources, the chapter proposes the need for community capacity building, creation of key linkages and partnerships, mechanisms for tourists to bring direct benefits to local areas, transparent distribution of revenues, designing CWBT ventures based on communities of interest, enhancing community access to reliable ecological information, full decentralisation of authority to local communities and ensuring representativeness and accountability of all stakeholders.

The chapter shows that wildlife tourism activities hold significant potential for local communities to promote long-term conservation of wildlife resources. However, despite opportunities, the question remains whether CWBT effectively provides adequate incentives to promote communities' tolerance for wildlife resources? There is need for more research and more nuanced solutions on how CWBT can enhance community tolerance for wildlife resources.

Acknowledgements

I am grateful to Professor Edson Gandiwa for the initial review of the manuscript and for providing insightful suggestions which were instrumental in the outcome of the chapter.

References

Asker, S. A., Boronyak, L. J., Carrard, N. R., & Paddon, M. (2010). *Effective community based tourism: A best practice manual. Asia Pacific economic cooperation (APEC) tourism working group*. Gold Coast, Australia: Sustainable Tourism Cooperative Research Centre.

Balint, P. J., & Mashinya, J. (2006). The decline of a model community-based conservation project: Governance, capacity, and devolution in Mahenye, Zimbabwe. *Geoforum*, 37 (5), 805–815.

Barnes, J. I. (2008). Community-based tourism and natural resource management in Namibia: local and national economic impacts. In Spenceley, A. (Ed.), *Responsible tourism: critical issues for conservation and development*. London: Routledge, 343–357.

Bond, I., & Frost, P. G. (2005). CAMPFIRE and payments for environmental services. PES-Methods and Design: ZEF/CIFOR 15–18 June workshop, Titisee, Germany.

Bruchac, M. (2014). Indigenous knowledge and traditional knowledge. In Smith, C. (Ed.), *Encyclopedia of global archaeology*. New York: Springer, 3814–3824.

Cassidy, L. (2021). Power dynamics and new directions in the recent evolution of CBNRM in Botswana. *Conservation Science and Practice*, 3 (1), e205.

Chisanga, A. (2016). What explains success and failure in community based natural resource management? A comparison of Botswana and Zambia. Master's thesis, Gothenburg University, Sweden.

Child, G. (1995). Managing wildlife successfully in Zimbabwe. *Oryx*, 29 (3), 54–63.

Cooksey, B., & Kikula, I. (2005). When *bottom-up meets top-down*: The *limits of local participation in local government planning in* Tanzania. Special Paper 17. Research on Poverty Alleviation. Tanzania: Mkuki Na Nyota Publishers.

Dressler, W., Büscher, B., Schoon, M., Brockington, D., Hayes, T., Kull, C. A., Mccarthy, J., & Shrestha, K. (2010). From hope to crisis and back again? A critical history of the global CBNRM narrative. *Environmental Conservation*, 37 (1), 5–15.

Ebua, V., Agwafo, T., & Fonkwo, S. (2011). Attitudes and perceptions as threats to wildlife conservation in the Bakossi area, South West Cameroon. *International Journal of Biodiversity and Conservation*, 3 (12), 631–636.

Emerson, R. (1976). Social exchange theory. *Annual Review of Sociology*, 2 (1), 335–362.

Fabricius, C., Koch, E., Turner, S., & Magome, H. (2013). *Rights resources and rural development: Community-based natural resource management in Southern Africa*. New York: Routledge.

Fischer, C., Muchapondwa, E., & Sterner, T. (2011). Bioeconomic model of community incentives for wildlife management before and after CAMPFIRE. *Environmental and Resource Economics*, 48, 303–319.

Gandiwa, E., Heitkönig, I. M. A., Lokhorst, A. M., Prins, H. H. T., & Leeuwis, C. (2013). CAMPFIRE and human–wildlife conflicts in local communities bordering northern Gonarezhou National Park, Zimbabwe. *Ecology and Society*, 18 (4), 7–23.

Gockel, K., & Gray, L. (2009). Integrating conservation and development in the Peruvian Amazon. *Ecology and Society*, 14 (2), 11–28.

Goodwin, H. (2009). Reflections on 10 years of pro-poor tourism. *Journal of Policy Research on Tourism, Leisure and Events*, 1 (1), 90–94.

Hardin, G. (1968). The Tragedy of the Commons. *Science*, 162: 1243–1248.

He, S., Yang, L., & Min, Q. (2020). Community participation in nature conservation: The Chinese experience and its implication to national park management. *Sustainability*, 12 (11), 4760.

Holmes, G. (2013). Exploring the relationship between local support and the success of Protected Areas. *Conservation and Society*, 11 (1), 72–82.

Igoe, J. (2004). *Conservation and globalization: A study of national parks and Indigenous communities from East Africa to South Dakota*. London and Belmont, CA: Thomson Learning.

Isidiho, A., & Sabran, M. S. B. (2016). Evaluating the top-bottom and bottom-up community development approaches: Mixed method approach as alternative for rural un-educated communities in developing countries. *Mediterranean Journal of Social Sciences*, 7 (4), 266.

Klein, E., Barbier, M., & Watson, J. (2017). The dual impact of ecology and management on social incentives in marine common-pool resource systems. *Royal Society Open Science*, 4 (8), 170740.

Kull, C. (2002). Empowering pyromaniacs in Madagascar: Ideology and legitimacy in community-based natural resource management. *Development and Change*, 33 (1), 57–78.

Lovelock, B. (2008). *Tourism and the consumption of wildlife: Hunting, shooting and sport fishing*. New York: Routledge.

Martin, R. (1986). Communal Areas Management Programme for Indigenous Resources (CAMPFIRE). Revised version. CAMPFIRE Working Document No. 1/86. Harare, Zimbabwe: Branch of Terrestrial Ecology, Department of National Parks and Wild Life Management.

Mbaiwa, J. (2015). Community-based natural resource management in Botswana. In van der Duim, R. et al. (Eds.), *Institutional arrangements for conservation, development and tourism in Eastern and Southern Africa*. Dordrecht: Springer, 59–80.

Mogaka, H., Simons, G., Turpie, J., Emerton, L., & Karanja, F. (2001). *Economic aspects of community involvement in sustainable forest management in Eastern and Southern Africa (No. 8)*. Nairboi: IUCN-The World Conservation Union, Eastern Africa Regional Office.

Mudzengi, B., Gandiwa, E., Muboko, N., & Mutanga, C. N. (2020). Towards sustainable community conservation in tropical savanna ecosystems: A management framework for ecotourism ventures in a changing environment. *Environment, Development and Sustainability*, 23, 3028–3047.

Munalula, M., Siamabele, B., Kalonje, V., & Kaliba, M. (2020). Community based natural resource management: exploring the benefits and challenges. *International Journal of Humanities, Art and Social Studies (IJHAS)*, 5(3), 33–44.

Mutanga, C., Muboko, N., & Gandiwa, E. (2017). Protected area staff and local community viewpoints: A qualitative assessment of conservation relationships in Zimbabwe. *PLoS One*, 12 (5), e0177153.

Naidoo, R., Weaver, L. C., Diggle, R. Matongo, G., Stuart-Hill, G., & Thouless, C. (2016). Complementary benefits of tourism and hunting to communal conservancies in Namibia. *Conservation Biology*, 30 (3), 628–638.

Ostrom, E. (2008). Tragedy of the commons. *The new palgrave dictionary of economics*, 2. Basingstoke: Palgrave.

Rasoolimanesh, S. M., Jaafar, M., Kock, N., & Ramayah, T. (2015). A revised framework of social exchange theory to investigate the factors influencing residents' perceptions. *Tourism Management Perspectives*, 16, 335–345.

Romañach, S., Lindsey, P., & Woodroffe, R. (2011). Attitudes toward predators and options for their conservation in the Ewaso Ecosystem. In Georgadis, N. (Ed.), *Conserving wildlife in African landscapes: Kenya's Ewaso ecosystem*. Washington, DC: Smithsonian Institution Scholarly Press, 85–93.

Sabatier, P. (1986). Top-down and bottom-up approaches to implementation research: A critical analysis and suggested synthesis. *Journal of Public Policy*, 6 (1), 21–48.

Salafsky, N., & Wollenberg, E. (2000). Linking livelihoods and conservation: A conceptual framework and scale for assessing the integration of human needs and biodiversity. *World Development*, 28 (8), 1421–1438.

Saunders, F. (2014). The promise of common pool resource theory and the reality of commons projects. *International Journal of the Commons*, 8 (2), 636–656.

Shereni, N., & Saarinen, J. (2020). Community perceptions on the benefits and challenges of community-based natural resources management in Zimbabwe. *Development Southern Africa*, 38 (6), 879–895.

Silva, J., & Mosimane, A. W. (2013). Conservation-based rural development in Namibia: A mixed-methods assessment of economic benefits. *Journal of Environment & Development*, 22 (1), 25–50.

Songorwa, A. Bührs, T., & Hughey, K. (2000). Community-based wildlife management in Africa: A critical assessment of the literature. *Natural Resources Journal*, 40, 603–643.

Sterling, E., Betley, E., Sigouin, A., Gomez, A., Toomey, A., Cullman, G., … & Porzecanski, A. L. (2017). Assessing the evidence for stakeholder engagement in biodiversity conservation. *Biological Conservation*, 209, 159–171.

Stone, M., & Stone, L. (2020). Challenges of community-based tourism in Botswana: A review of literature. *Transactions of the Royal Society of South Africa*, 75 (2), 181–193.

Tessema, M., Lilieholm, R., Ashenafi, Z., & Leader-Williams, N. (2010). Community attitudes toward wildlife and protected areas in Ethiopia. *Society and Natural Resources*, 23 (6), 489–506.

Tosun, C. (2000). Limits to community participation in the tourism development process in developing countries. *Tourism Management*, 21 (6), 613–633.

UNWTO (2015). *Tourism highlights, 2015 edition.* New York: United Nations World Tourism Organisation.

Wilkie, D, Morelli, G., Demmer, J., Starkey, M., Telfer, P. & Steil, M. (2006). Parks and people: Assessing the human welfare effects of establishing protected areas for biodiversity conservation. *Conservation Biology*, 20 (1), 247–249.

Yeo-Chang, Y. (2009). Use of forest resources, traditional forest related knowledge and livelihood of forest dependent communities: Cases in South Korea. *Forest Ecology and Management*, 257, 2027–2034.

Zanamwe, C., Gandiwa, E., Muboko, N., Kupika, O., & Mukamuri, B. (2018). Ecotourism and wildlife conservation-related enterprise development by local communities within Southern Africa: Perspectives from the greater Limpopo Transfrontier Conservation, South-Eastern Lowveld, Zimbabwe. *Cogent Environmental Science*, 4 (1), 1531463.

Zielinski, S., Jeong, Y., Kim, S. & B Milanés, C. (2020). Why community-based tourism and rural tourism in developing and developed nations are treated differently? A review. *Sustainability*, 12 (15), 5938.

Part II

Protected areas, tourism and human–wildlife conflicts dynamics

6 Landscape governance in sub-Saharan Africa

Rene van der Duim and Arjaan Pellis

Introduction

In response to perceived shortcomings of the dominant Protected Area Approach (PAA) in sub-Saharan Africa, the 1980s and 1990s witnessed an upsurge in people-centred conservation approaches to bridge the conservation–development gap. Many of these approaches were implemented at landscape level to address problems associated with sustainable development. However, despite this growing tendency toward integrated approaches at the landscape level, the inherent complexity of landscapes will always present persistent and significant challenges, such as balancing multiple objectives, equitable inclusion of all relevant stakeholders, dealing with power and gender asymmetries and moving beyond existing administrative, jurisdictional and sectorial silos (Ros-Tonen et al., 2018). Partnerships are seen as key in overcoming such challenges given their potential to bridge different stakeholders' interests and practices.

Therefore, in practice, work on landscape-wide conservation and development approaches in sub-Saharan Africa have largely been organised through different partnership arrangements, varying from conservancies in Namibia and conservation enterprises in Kenya and Uganda (Van der Duim et al., 2015, 2017) to partnerships focusing on entire landscapes such as the Laikipia Wildlife Forum and the Northern Rangelands Trust (see Pellis et al., 2015) and the Amboseli Ecosystem Trust (Mugo et al., 2020). Most of these approaches integrate tourism as an avenue for livelihood improvement (Nthiga et al., 2015).

Although various authors have examined the effectiveness of partnerships, especially at the global level (Visseren-Hamakers, 2013), there is limited understanding of how partnerships contribute to governing integrated landscapes across sub-Saharan Africa. Moreover, in governance and partnership literature, power has often been neglected as a useful concept in analysing and understanding evolving landscape governance processes. In fact, governance and partnerships tend to be presented as depoliticised and consensual policy-making by independent actors in seemingly power-free processes (Kuindersma et al., 2012).

To gain a better understanding of the role of power relations in this context, this chapter explores and compares landscape-wide partnerships in Kenya and

DOI: 10.4324/9781003193166-8

74   *Rene van der Duim and Arjaan Pellis*

Namibia to understand: 1) the role of partnerships in landscape governance in sub-Saharan Africa; and 2) how landscape governance is subject to processes of power and politics. To be able to analyse and compare cases in Kenya and Namibia, this chapter amalgamates literature on partnerships, governance, power and landscapes into a landscape governance perspective.

Landscape governance

Landscapes are socially and culturally constructed entities (Görg, 2007) that provide opportunities for and fulfil multiple needs of diverse actors. A landscape can be defined as a social-biophysical construct that relates to land (or water/air) that invokes a sense of belonging (Arts et al., 2017), and that bridges 'social scales and the biophysical conditions and ecological processes in spaces' (Görg, 2007, p. 955). Given the multifunctional character of landscapes, supporting different actors with multiple and diverse interests, landscape approaches create a need for landscape governance. Following Görg (2007), landscape governance is the way actors, often in the form of partnerships, steer and shape landscapes. To overcome self-interested and self-referential approaches, it can be helpful to explore intersectoral and interdisciplinary approaches to embrace more ambitious, long-term and boundary-crossing partnerships. How to do this through landscape approaches remains unclear given the lack of common systemic practices and understanding of these approaches (Reed et al., 2015).

If we zoom into landscape partnerships, these are defined as collaborative arrangements between multiple actors from public, private and/or civil society sectors, who work towards solving specific societal problems and/or issues of mutual concern (Van Huijstee et al., 2007). As such, partnerships are viewed as specific forms of governance (Visseren-Hamakers et al., 2012), which we define as modes of steering in which multiple societal actors become organised and involved in making and implementing decisions with the aim of addressing societal problems (Kersbergen & Waarden, 2004). These problems can be addressed at different scales, depending on the jurisdiction, the underlying issues at stake, the level of ambition and the capacity (including capital, skills, levels of trust) of landscape partnerships. At the same time, it is key to consider that what is considered as problem-solving by one partnership, and how this may be interpreted differently by a neighbouring partnership. Or what is considered as 'solved' in one location and moment in time may form the stage for yet another problem if we zoom out from one landscape to another (Pellis et al., 2018).

Despite these limitations, landscape partnerships aspire to fulfil several landscape governance roles, such as agenda-setting, policy development, information sharing, capacity building, implementation and meta-governance (Van Huijstee et al., 2007; Mugo et al., 2020; Visseren-Hamakers et al., 2012). Through these diverse landscape governance roles and practices, the capacity of partnerships to address challenges related to sustainable development in complex landscapes grows (Lamers et al., 2014; Mugo et al., 2020). Still, the ability to address such challenges remains reliant on goal and resource dependencies of partners involved. Related landscape monitoring, for instance, is often logically based on organisational-centric procedures that are, foremost, designed to communicate with funding bodies, not with peer organisations or other actors within the same social-biophysical context (Pellis et al., 2015). Besides, partnerships are criticised elsewhere as being elitist (Dubbink, 2013), exclusionary and favouring the interests of specific partners (Rhodes, 1997). This may lead to power imbalances (Visseren-Hamakers, 2009) and the favouring of 'capable' partners, allowing others in governance processes to become excluded (Bitzer & Glasbergen, 2015). Power, without doubt, emerges as an essential aspect deserving further attention in analysing and understanding the role of partnerships in landscape governance (Mugo et al., 2020).

By contributing to more fruitful power analyses in landscape governance, diverse faces of power that may relate to various institutions, socio-economic structures and ideas and perspectives need to be included (Kuindersma et al., 2012). As we will show, power relationships in landscapes are indeed multidimensional and multidirectional. In practice this means that certain landscape ideas, practices and networks gain prominence while others become absent or invisible.

Experiences from Kenya

In Kenya, landscape approaches are gaining momentum, which in part can be explained by national policies (Mugo, 2021). The 2010 Constitution of Kenya has led to a devolved system of governance by landowners for the management of wildlife resources outside formal government-run protected areas (KWCA, 2016). The subsequent Conservation and Wildlife Management Act of 2013 not only enabled the recognition of conservancies as a legal form of land use, but also the foundation of regional conservancy associations and the formation of the Kenya Wildlife Conservancies Association (KWCA) in 2013 (GoK, 2013). KWCA is 'a landowner-led national membership organization that serves the interests and collective voice of community and private conservancies' (KWCA, 2016, p. 10) across Kenya. It focuses on advocacy and policy development, capacity building and mainstreaming women and youth in conservancy operations. To this end KWCA developed a Code of Conduct.

Illustrative examples of landscape governance are – amongst others – to be found in southern and northern regions of Kenya, where various NGOs (nongovernmental organisations) have experimented with different landscape perspectives to better combine wildlife conservation and livelihood enhancements, often in shape of tourism development (see also Pellis et al., 2015).

Landscape partnerships in southern Kenya

At Amboseli, the Amboseli Ecosystem Trust (AET) is a landscape-based partnership that brings together a diverse group of stakeholders, including landowners, NGOs and Kenyan Wildlife Services (KWS), with the aim of simultaneously achieving conservation and development goals through the implementation of the Amboseli Ecosystem Management Plan (AEMP). The AEMP is a policy document developed collaboratively by the AET partners between 2004 and 2008 and launched in 2009, for the purpose of ensuring that wildlife and communities thrive (AET, 2009). A key component of the AEMP is a land-use zoning plan aimed at separating conflicting land uses to address human–wildlife conflicts (HWCs) and wildlife habitat loss. The activities of the AET are undertaken by a Board of Trustees (BoT) consisting of governmental agencies, communities, private investors and civil society representatives.

The Big Life Foundation (BLF) is a partner and member of the AET. BLF is the product of a successive evolution from a three-phased partnership arrangement in the Mbirikani Group Ranch (MGR). The first phase (1986–1992) of the partnership linked the MGR community members and a private investor in tourism. The second phase (1992–2012) concerned the Maasailand Preservation Trust (MPT), a partnership between the MGR community members and Ol Donyo Wuas Trust. The third phase started in 2012, when MPT merged its activities, and the BLF was founded. BLF operations now focus on conservation and development initiatives in the entire Amboseli landscape in collaboration with local communities, NGOs and the Kenyan government. Policy interventions by BLF include a wildlife conservation and security programme, a Predator Compensation Fund (PCF), a wildlife education bursary, healthcare provisions, the Maasai Olympics and empowerment programmes for women (Mugo, 2021).

Landscape partnerships in northern Kenya

The Northern Rangelands Trust (NRT) forms another example of a landscape-wide partnership, in this case exclusively owned and controlled by the communities that it serves (NRT, 2021). NRT started operating in 2004 and later became extended to operations in the North Rift and NRT-Coastal regions of Kenya (Glew, Hudson & Osborne, 2010; Pellis et al., 2015). NRT's aim is to establish conservancies to enable communities to democratically self-organise community-owned land to improve security, livelihoods and conserve biodiversity. Like BLF, NRT has evolved from a partnership between local communities and a private conservancy – in this case the Lewa Wildlife Conservancy (LWC) in the 1980s (Glew et al., 2010) – to a landscape-wide initiative that aims to secure conservation and regional safety for associated communities.

At the time of writing, 39 NRT conservancies have been registered across a territory of over 4 million hectares, uniting approximately 400,000 community members. To support the management of these conservancies, NRT has a subsidiary arm that runs its affairs as an NGO on a wider landscape level: the Northern Rangeland Company (NRC). On a national level the NRT has been one of the founders of the Kenyan Wildlife Conservancies Association (KWCA) of which all NRT conservancies are currently a member. NRT has partially initiated the KWCA to secure legal and national support of conservancies.

So far, the KWCA has helped the voluntary registration of 160 conservancies across Kenya and offers complementary support, either directly to regional organisations like the NRT (and ten other regional conservancy organisations in Kenya) or directly to conservancies.

While community conservancies largely depend on livestock as a livelihood, particularly beadwork and tourism have offered new communal income opportunities that were worth $1.3 million to communities in 2019 (NRT, 2019).

In Laikipia, NRT conservancies have been evolving next to other longstanding landscape partnerships. A well-known example hereof is the Laikipia Wildlife Forum (LWF), a membership-based organisation that since 1992 has aimed to unite the goals and ambitions of smallholders, community groups, conservancies and large landowners focused on integrated natural resources management (LWF, 2021). While NRT conservancies aim at uniting landowners to manage communal landscapes, LWF has focused on the joint promotion of Laikipia as a wildlife destination (Pellis et al., 2014). Furthermore, LWF has been active in supporting private and community members to secure their property rights and tenure, to offer technical support, advocacy and policy advice concerning land and conservation challenges or link (international) funding for member initiatives within the Laikipian landscape.

Experiences from Namibia

In Namibia, a nationwide conservancy movement has formally materialised since Namibia's independence in 1990. However, local nature conservation organisations and traditional leaders in Kunene, a province in North-Western Namibia, already started experimenting with community-managed conservation in the 1980s (Blaikie, 2006; Jones, 2006). Traditional leaders appointed local community game guards to monitor wildlife and participate in anti-poaching patrols (Novelli & Gebhardt, 2007; Pellis, 2011). Today, Namibian conservancies are taken up as an internationally appraised landscape approach that allows rural communities to self-manage and conserve natural resources. Most registered conservancies, like initial experiments from the 1980s, are found in the northern regions. Communities living in these conservancies do not own the land but are offered usufruct rights as granted by the state.

The national conservancy movement is facilitated by the Namibian Association of Community Based Natural Resource Management (CBNRM) Support Organisations (NACSO), which unites the University of Namibia and eight NGOs, but also allies with organisations like the World Wildlife Fund (WWF-Namibia), Tourism Supporting Conservation (TOSCO), and regional community conservancy associations. The idea behind a national unification of diverse practices is:

> that it is unlikely that any single institution houses all of the skills, resources and capacity to provide community organisations with the multi-disciplinary assistance that is required to develop the broad range of CBNRM

initiatives taking place in Namibia. These skills include advice on governance and institutional issues, on natural resources management and assistance with financial and business planning.

(www.nacso.org.na/about-nacso)

Various institutional conditions have allowed Namibian communities to become conservancy beneficiaries. One such condition is the Traditional Authorities Act (1995) by which traditional communities and authorities are legally recognised as far as they do not conflict with the Namibian Constitution or with any other written law applicable in Namibia. Next to such recognition, the state gives communities the right to organise themselves into conservancies. Communal conservancies in Namibia are seen as:

> self-governing, democratic entities, run by their members, with fixed boundaries that are agreed with adjacent conservancies, communities or landowners. ... Communal conservancies are obliged to have game management plans, to conduct annual general meetings, and to prepare financial reports. They are managed under committees elected by their members.
>
> (www.nacso.org.na/conservancies)

The first community conservancy of Nyae Nyae was gazetted by the Ministry of Environment and Tourism (MET) in 1998. By 2021, another 85 conservancies now cover a total of 166,179 km^2 and affect 227,802 residents. Most lucrative commercial partnerships are found in the context of (joint venture) tourism and hunting practices (NACSO, 2019). To form community-private partnerships, private enterprises need to form legally binding agreements with conservancies. This typically entails agreements on the use of land next to benefit-sharing arrangements. Each conservancy is required to operate within the boundaries of state-defined frameworks, including yearly wildlife quota indicating conservancy allowances in terms of hunting, shoot-and-sell permits or own use. To support conservancies in day-to-day conservancy affairs, different NACSO organisations offer technical support, trainings, legal assistance, conservation management and marketing support. Traditional authorities formally do not have a direct say in these affairs, yet often indirectly influence decision-making through their representatives in elected conservancy committees.

Similarities and differences

A comparison between our observations in Kenya and Namibia reveal both striking similarities and differences. To start with the similarities, all the landscape governance initiatives discussed focus on conservation and development outside NPs and include wide-ranging landscape processes (ecological, but also social and economic) where specific boundaries at times fluctuate.

Second, their current existence primarily rests on early experimentation initiated by conservation NGOs. While most arrangements emerged in the

1990s, their origins are to be found much earlier. For instance, between the mid-1980s and 1990, conservationists and community leaders already experimented with community-based approaches with the aim to stop poaching in Namibia. In Kenya, NGOs already experimented with community-based conservation around Amboseli national park in the 1950s. 'Old' institutional arrangements have thus not simply been replaced by 'new' ones; instead, existing arrangements have been transformed, scaled up and altered in novel ways to adapt to a and dynamic context (Van der Duim et al., 2015).

Third, our examples illustrate that governing landscapes through partnerships is in actual sense about 'governance with government', denoting that the government remains a dominant and essential partner in landscape governance. In Amboseli, by using the Protected Area Policy Framework, AET relied on government institutions in the development and gazettement of the plan. BLF needs the support of the government to effectively protect wildlife, since governmental agencies are the ones that prosecute poaching suspects. Similarly, in Namibia, the MET can grant or take away communities' right to institutionalise themselves as a conservancy or limit the amount of wildlife consumption through annual quota. Besides the official government, most regional NGOs have also been seen as governmental agencies given their strong visibility and the long-term relationships they established with communities. NGOs have as such taken on the role of government where the national government is experienced as a 'distant entity' with limited local legitimacy in daily conservancy operations.

Fourth, tourism has been an important source of income to finance landscape aims. For instance, out of 160 Kenyan conservancies, 69 depend on 142 tourism facilities. Results nevertheless remain mixed and uncertain, as for example the current COVID-19 pandemic has shown. This is forcing tourism-dependent partnerships to diversify to sustain livelihoods and conservation activities. As a result, partnerships like AET, BLF, NRT, LWF and NACSO often remain dependent on donors. This could threaten their continuity and they thus require alternative financing mechanisms. NACSO, for instance, has experienced drastic cuts in international funding, after which the initial partnership of 60 organisations became downsized to ten. Available funding has diminished their local presence, forcing NACSO to focus more on regional and national forum associations by which existing conservancy operations ought to become streamlined across larger landscapes (e.g. focusing on important wildlife corridors).

As said, our comparison also revealed interesting differences. First, we found that partnerships operate at different levels of scale. Partnership agreements are signed on the level of individual conservancies, at the level of landscapes (like LWF and AET), at a national level (NACSO) and may even spread to become a transboundary initiative (as shown in the cases of BLF and NRT).

Second, our examples show that partnerships have different configurations, jurisdictions and roles in landscape governance. Especially in Kenya, there is a variety of partnership configurations (e.g. diverse types of private, communal, group or state-owned conservancies); whereas in Namibia, conservancies fit in a national model streamlined by NACSO organisations. In terms of governance roles, in Kenya AET primarily focuses on policy development and LWF on agenda-setting, advocacy and capacity building, while BLF and NRT aim to secure conservation and regional safety for associated communities. Finally, through its advocacy, KWCA promotes favourable national policies for its associated conservancy members by collecting the ideas of conservancies and regional conservancy associations and report those to the Kenyan government to co-shape legislation, such as the review of the 2013 Kenyan Wildlife Act which has led to legal recognition of wildlife conservancies.

Third, although both in Kenya and Namibia partnerships partly rely on tourism-related income, types and volumes of tourism income may differ. For example, whereas sport hunting was banned in Kenya in 1977, trophy hunting has always been central in Namibia's sustenance of CBNRM. Income may also differ depending on the location of the conservancy.

Fourth, partnerships have been subject to unique socio-historical dependencies. Pre-independence socialist discourses in South-West Africa have certainly contributed to community empowerment of a post-apartheid Namibia and contemporary CBNRM in which local people are offered an opportunity to manage the land they live on. At the same time, in Kenya's Laikipia, there has been a long history of Kenya's 'white cowboys' taking charge of large private ranches that have often stimulated partnerships with local communities surrounding them. These examples show how different areas have been subject to different historical developments, and how these enable/constrain how landscape partnerships materialise over time.

Power relations

Although partnerships are often touted as avenues for moderating power inequalities, our examples also reveal instances of the opposite. Here we discuss three examples: domination of and over-reliance on individual partners in landscape governance, the role of local communities, and the growth and overlap of landscape approaches.

Domination of and over-reliance on individual partners

Our examples show how different partners dominate on different issues. For example, in Kenya, AET has mediated between different actors and has been able to control agenda-setting aiming to change institutional settings. This, however, was restrained by the national Kenya Wildlife Service (KWS), who took a leading role in the development of the AEMP as it had expertise in formulating conservation area policies. Additionally, Mugo (2021) indicates an over-reliance on individual AET partners for on-the-ground implementation of the AEMP programmes. This over-reliance poses a risk of powerful partners hijacking AET to further their own interests. This finding echoes the argument

Landscape governance in sub-Saharan Africa   81

by Glasbergen, Biermann & Mol (2007) that partnerships may act as avenues to advance actor-specific goals. Nowadays especially BLF emerges as a powerful actor in the Amboseli landscape, based on its financial resources.

Likewise, in Namibia, there are prominent roles for organisations committed to regional partnerships. In the context of Kunene, for instance, the IRDNC has historically played a key role in capacitating community conservancies next to the Save the Rhino Trust (SRT), an organisation that works with similar communities on conservation objectives. Past personal tensions between founding managers of both NGOs and competition over funding opportunities contributed – according to some community members – to local conflict dynamics as both organisations operate in the same social, financial and biophysical context (Pellis, 2011).

Role of local communities

A recent study by Mugo et al. (2020) showed that AET and BLF have only to a certain degree been able to bridge the conservation and development discourses, and thus have only partly been able to structurally change the positions of local communities involved. For example, migrant communities represent a significant interest at Amboseli – cultivating crops, which exacerbates wildlife habitat loss and human wildlife conflicts – but are excluded from the AET. Local communities have also been underrepresented in BLF's top decision-making level since the Maasailand Preservation Trust merged its activities into BLF, and the organisational set-up evolved from a partnership into an NGO. Accordingly, although local populations in theory have been given a new structural position as landscape stewards, their participation in the governance remained limited even though they own the land.

Likewise, by formalising partnerships within Laikipia, landscape-specific decisions tend to make certain actors and practices present while making others absent. A good example hereof is the exclusion of mobile pastoralists who do not necessarily feel tied to landscape-specific borders and related community arrangements such as new conservancies across the north of Kenya. These 'mobile others' nevertheless make themselves present when they – in terms of contemporary landowners – 'trespass' landscapes and 'illegally' let their cattle graze (Pellis et al., 2018). Such trespassing has become a heated conflict because of recurrent political support of opportunist cattle barons in times of drought and elections, and because of people's memories of similar trespassing and associated violence in Laikipia (Pellis et al., 2018). Consequently, many projects – including heavily funded tourism and wildlife initiatives – have become severely damaged as dependent communities pay a serious price in terms of lost tourism income and encounters with violence.

In the Namibian context, communities have a significant role in natural resource management. In practice there are nevertheless feelings of discontent, not only because local elites often take control of benefits. It is also their discursive and historical affiliation with regional NGOs, next to longstanding clan

82 *Rene van der Duim and Arjaan Pellis*

ties, that make certain members more powerful than others. Another interesting lesson learned from the Namibian context is the way in which communities start to doubt ongoing support from conservation partners. Communities have been resourced by various support organisations in the past 30 years and in the process became more demanding. Some communities even wonder why NGOs continue to benefit from community conservancy operations. NACSO thereby needs to reinvent its role, even though NACSO likes to play a 'mothering' role to their family of conservancy practices across Namibia.

Growth and overlap of landscape governance approaches

Where actor-specific goals may gain prominence in a landscape approach, a landscape partnership may gradually spread and overlap with other landscape partnerships. The prominent success stories of community conservation have become adopted by similar conservancy practices across Namibia and Kenya. The Namibian CBNRM approach has been widely credited as a success story and hence mimicked by similar community-based partnerships elsewhere, as for example in northern Kenya.

However, the spread of the success is also posing new risks, such as the often-missing critical voices that may reflect deeper on challenges and failures (Koot, Hebinck & Sullivan, 2020), or growing demands to diversify centralised landscape objectives. For example, NACSO's initial role to stimulate wildlife conservations through conservancies 30 years ago is increasingly challenged by community voices desiring alternative livelihood developments beyond conservation and tourism. This forms a challenge for affiliated support partnerships who currently see benefit in working with limited partners and a single ministry (the MET). Working on more landscape objectives beyond tourism and conservation, requires partnerships with other ministries and/or organisations given their expertise and capacity to jointly offer alternative landscape wide support.

Conclusion

This chapter demonstrates that partnerships play prominent and complementary roles in landscape governance and that power relations undeniably play a decisive part in achieving these roles. It has also demonstrated that in all these cases partnerships have only been able to effectively fulfil their governance roles with support of the government. These findings therefore reiterate sentiments from authors who argue that, even in instances where the government has shared power with other societal actors, the state always retains authority and control in new governance arrangements (Airey & Chong, 2010).

This chapter also revealed that the partnerships and the landscape in which they operate are dynamic, which introduces new complexities and challenges to landscape governance. Both in Kenya and Namibia, partnerships have been on a dynamic path, whereby some partners have exited as new ones have come on board. The focus of the partnerships has been one of evolution. For example, BLF, which initially sought to address several specific challenges (wildlife security, education, tourism, and livelihood support) in a relatively small landscape – the Mbirikani Group Ranch – is currently covering a larger transboundary landscape encompassing parts of Kenya and Tanzania, presenting an 'all-inclusive' solution (Mugo, 2021). In Namibia, community empowerment facilitated by Kunene-based conservation NGOs has become a nationwide model for having communities govern natural resources. This has inspired and been mimicked in other contexts such as NRT's conservancy practices in northern Kenya or more recent national conservancy advocacy by the KWCA in Kenya. These findings are in line with the hypothesis of Büscher and Dressler (2007, p. 588) that governance 'operates in continuously changing networks and alliances', which calls for continuous meta-governance to ensure durability and effectiveness (Lamers et al., 2014). Accordingly, landscape governance is in actual sense 'an iterative process of trial, adaptation and learning, tailored to the specific socio-spatial conditions of place' (Buizer, Arts & Westerink, 2016, p. 453).

This chapter also raises questions related to the extent of change partnerships can bring. Recently, Dentoni et al. (2018) suggested that partnerships can address complex societal problems, in this case the conservation–development nexus in Kenya and Namibia, by triggering or contributing to systemic change. The persisting challenge that remains, however, is whether partnerships trigger or support *breadth* and *depth* of change to an extent that adequately addresses these complex, fundamental societal problems (Mugo et al., 2020). In relation to Amboseli we argue that AET and BLF have in fact supported systemic change as their work involves multiple spheres and subsectors, since they have targeted conservation, development, tourism, agriculture, health and education. In Namibia, NACSO organisations are under similar pressure from community voices to expand landscape approaches beyond wildlife conservation to explore multiple livelihood alternatives. These examples are typically referred to as *breadth* of change. However, systemic change should also entail a powershift among actors in society and a related redistribution of resources. One could therefore question to what extent these cases in Kenya and Namibia have been able to address the necessary *depth* of change. The persistent poverty, conflicts with community members that halted the AEMP process in the case of Amboseli, the continuous role of the Kenyan government in legitimising wildlife security programmes and the intensification of crop farming raises questions of whether AET and BLF, as forms of collaborative governance, have been fully able to tackle the complex challenges that a region like Amboseli faces (see Mugo, 2021). Similarly, in northern Kenya, existing conservancies are under pressure as other land uses and users recurrently claim centre stage at the expense of longstanding conservation and tourism landscapes (Pellis et al., 2018).

In Namibia, challenges also keep emerging, including intensification of human–wildlife conflicts and limited compensation schemes, ongoing

84 Rene van der Duim and Arjaan Pellis

community rivalry over benefits or longstanding droughts that force communities to relocate to remaining fertile landscapes preserved for wildlife conservation. This debate about breadth and depth of change is fully in line with discussions on the need for transformative change to achieve the Sustainable Development Goals (SDGs) (Díaz et al., 2019; Visseren-Hamakers, 2020). While the partnerships can contribute to addressing direct drivers of biodiversity loss (such as poaching), they contribute to a much lesser extent to addressing indirect drivers, such as poverty, land subdivision or imminent climate change.

More generally speaking, partnerships represent policy arenas where different interests are negotiated and trade-offs between SDGs are brought to the surface. The added value of the partnerships comes from their fulfilment of important meta-governance roles through which partners' views of the landscape – at least to a certain extent – converge and are shaped and reshaped through actors' practices. However, our examples in Namibia and Kenya show that power struggles and power vacuums may seriously affect the capacity of partnerships to strengthen and secure a broad SDG agenda.

References

AET (2009). *Amboseli Ecosystem Management Plan: 2008–2018*. Loitoktok: Amboseli Ecosystem Trust.

Airey, D., & Chong, K. (2010). National policymakers for tourism in China. *Annals of Tourism Research*, 37 (2), 295–314.

Arts, B., Buizer, M., Horlings, L., Ingram, V., Oosten, C. v., & Opdam, P. (2017). Landscape approaches: A state-of-the-art review. *Annual Review of Environment and Resources*, 42 (1), 439–463.

Bitzer, V., & Glasbergen, P. (2015). Business-NGO partnerships in global value chains: Part of the solution or part of the problem of sustainable change? *Current Opinion in Environmental Sustainability*, 12, 35–40.

Blaikie, P. (2006). Is small really beautiful? Community based natural resource management in Malawi and Botswana. *World Development*, 34 (11), 1942–1957.

Buizer, I. M., Arts, B., & Westerink, J. (2016). Landscape governance as policy integration 'from below': A case of displaced and contained political conflict in the Netherlands. *Environment and Planning C. Government and Policy*, 34 (3).

Büscher, B., & Dressler, W. (2007). Linking neoprotectionism and environmental governance: On the rapidly increasing tensions between actors in the environment-development nexus. *Conservation and Society*, 5 (4), 586.

Dentoni, D., Bitzer, V., & Schouten, G. (2018). Harnessing wicked problems in multi-stakeholder partnerships. *Journal of Business Ethics*, 150 (2), 333–356.

Díaz, S., Settele, J., … & Zayas, C. N. (2019). *IPBES, Summary for policymakers of the global assessment report on biodiversity and ecosystem services of the intergovernmental science-policy platform on biodiversity and ecosystem services. Advance unedited version. Plenary of the intergovernmental science-policy platform on biodiversity and ecosystem services*. Paris: IPBES Seventh session, 29.

Dubbink, W. (2013). *Assisting the invisible hand: Contested relations between market, state and civil society*. Dordrecht: Springer Science & Business Media.

Glasbergen, P., Biermann, F., & Mol, A. (2007). *Partnerships, governance and sustainable development: Reflections on theory and practice.* Cheltenham: Edward Elgar Publishing.

Glew, L., Hudson, M. D., & Osborne, P. E. (2010). *Evaluating the effectiveness of community-based conservation in northern Kenya: A report to the Nature Conservancy.* Southampton: Centre for Environmental Sciences, University of Southampton.

GoK (2013). *Conservation and Wildlife Management Act 2013.* Nairobi: Government Printers.

Görg, C. (2007). Landscape governance: The 'politics of scale' and the 'natural' conditions of places. *Geoforum*, 38 (5), 954–966.

Jones, S. (2006) A political ecology of wildlife conservation in Africa. *Review of African Political Economy*, 33 (109), 483–495.

Kersbergen, K. V., & Waarden, F. V. (2004). 'Governance' as a bridge between disciplines: Cross-disciplinary inspiration regarding shifts in governance and problems of governability, accountability and legitimacy. *European Journal of Political Research,* 43 (2), 143–171.

Koot, S., Hebinck, P. & Sullivan, S. (2020). Science for success – a conflict of interest? Researcher position and reflexivity in socio-ecological research for CBNRM in Namibia, *Society & Natural Resources.* doi: 10.1080/08941920.2020.1762953

Kuindersma, W., Arts, B., & van der Zouwen, M. (2012). Power faces in regional governance. *Journal of Political Power*, 5 (3), 411–429.

KWCA (2016). *State of conservancies report 2016.* Nairobi: Kenya Wildlife Conservancy Association.

Lamers, M., Van der Duim, V. R., Van Wijk, J., Nthiga, R., & Visseren-Hamakers, I. (2014). Governing conservation tourism partnerships in Kenya. *Annals of Tourism Research*, 48, 250–265.

Leach, W. D., & Pelkey, N. W. (2001). Making watershed partnerships work: A review of the empirical literature. *Journal of Water Resources Planning and Management*, 127 (6), 378–385.

LWF (2021) History – who we are. Retrieved from https://laikipia.org/history/

Mugo, T., Visseren-Hamakers, I., & van der Duim, V. R. (2020), Landscape governance through partnerships: Lessons from Amboseli, Kenya. *Journal of Sustainable Tourism.* https://doi.org/10.1080/09669582.2020.1834563

Mugo, T. (2021). Governing landscapes through partnerships: lessons from Amboseli, Kenya. PhD thesis, Wageningen University and Research.

NACSO (2019). *The state of community conservation report 2019.* Windhoek: NACSO.

Novelli, M., & Gebhardt, K. (2007) Community based tourism in Namibia: 'Reality show' or 'window dressing'? *Current Issues in Tourism*, 10 (5), 443–479.

NRT (2019) *State of conservancies report.* Retrieved from: https://static1.squarespace.com/static/5af1629f12b13f5ce97ca0b5/t/5e398ee62156d43c562498bf/15808304 99016/LOWRES.FINAL_State+of+Conservancies+Report+2019.pdf

NRT (2021). About NRT. Retrieved from: www.nrt-kenya.org/about-nrt

Nthiga, R. W., Van der Duim, V. R., Visseren-Hamakers, I. J., & Lamers, M. (2015). Tourism-conservation enterprises for community livelihoods and biodiversity conservation in Kenya. *Development Southern Africa*, 32 (3), 407–423.

Pellis, A. (2011). Modern and traditional arrangements in community-based tourism: Exploring an election conflict in the Anabeb Conservancy, Namibia. In Van der Duim, V. R. Meyer, D. Saarinen, J., & Zellmer, K. (Eds.), *New alliances for tourism, conservation and development in Eastern and Southern Africa.* Delft: Eburon.

Pellis, A., Anyango-van Zwieten, N., Waterreus, S., Lamers, M., & Van der Duim, R. (2014). *Tourism captured by the poor: Evaluation of aid investments in the tourism sector of Kenya's ASALs*. Wageningen: Wageningen University.

Pellis, A., Lamers, M., & van der Duim, R. (2015). Conservation tourism and landscape governance in Kenya: The interdependency of three conservation NGOs. *Journal of Ecotourism*, 14 (2–3), 130–144

Pellis, A., Pas, A., & Duineveld, M. (2018). The persistence of tightly coupled conflicts. The case of Loisaba, Kenya. *Conservation & Society*, 16 (4), 387–396.

Reed, J., Deakin, L., & Sunderland, T. (2015). What are 'integrated landscape approaches' and how effectively have they been implemented in the tropics: A systematic map protocol. *Official Journal of Collaborative Environmental Evidence*. Retrieved from: https://link.springer.com/article/10.1186/2047-2382-4-2

Rhodes, R. A. (1997). *Understanding governance: Policy networks, governance, reflexivity and accountability*. London: Open University Press.

Ros-Tonen, M. A., Reed, J., & Sunderland, T. (2018). From synergy to complexity: The trend toward integrated value chain and landscape governance. *Environmental Management*, 62 (1), 1–14.

Van der Duim, R., Lamers, M., & van Wijk, J. (2015). *Institutional arrangements for conservation, development and tourism in Eastern and Southern Africa*. Dordrecht: Springer.

Van der Duim, V.R., van Wijk, J., & Lamers, M. (2017). Governing nature tourism in Eastern and Southern Africa. In Chen, J. S., & Prebensen, N. K. (Eds.), *Nature tourism*. London: Routledge, 146–158.

Van Huijstee, M. M., Francken, M., & Leroy, P. (2007). Partnerships for sustainable development: A review of current literature. *Environmental Sciences*, 4 (2), 75–89.

Visseren-Hamakers, I. J. (2009). Partnerships in biodiversity governance: An assessment of their contributions to halting biodiversity loss. In *Nederlandse Geografische Studies*. Utrecht: Koninklijk Nederlands Aardrijkskundig Genootschap/Copernicus/Institute for Sustainable Development and Innovation, 1–177.

Visseren-Hamakers, I. J. (2013). Partnerships and sustainable development: the lessons learned from international biodiversity governance. *Environmental Policy and Governance*, 23 (3), 145–160.

Visseren-Hamakers, I. J. (2020). The 18th sustainable development goal. *Earth System Governance*. Retrieved from: https://doi.org/10.1016/j.esg.2020.100047

Visseren-Hamakers, I. J., Leroy, P., & Glasbergen, P. (2012). Conservation partnerships and biodiversity governance: Fulfilling governance functions through interaction. *Sustainable Development*, 20 (4), 264–275.

7 In the way of wildlife

Contestations between Indigenous Peoples' livelihood and conservation

Onthatile Olerile Moeti

Introduction

The history of the bloody interaction between Indigenous Peoples and the State is well documented (Barelli, 2018; Ademodi, 2012). Since time immemorial, Indigenous Peoples have been subjugated by forces beyond them, leading to persecution, suppression, exclusion, and conflicts over natural resources with the State and third parties (Jalata, 2012; Clarke, 2001). From the colonial period to the globalisation era, land is at the heart of these disputes.

In the colonial period, settlers arrived with an intent to violently push Indigenous Peoples off their prime land to marginal areas considered economically useless (Everson et al., 2013). Hitchcock, Sapignoli and Babchuk (2015) observe that, with settler colonialism, societies lost their traditional sources of livelihood without being offered alternatives and endured persecution and civilising procedures that devalued the native culture. The systematic violence caused irreversible and irreparable marginalisation of Indigenous Peoples (Hitchcock, Sapignoli & Babchuk, 2015).

In the face of the surging global resource demand, the previously unattractive land has become economically appealing to more players beyond the State. On the other hand, Indigenous Peoples' land is invaluable to them as it is a source of life and represents their wholeness as a people, yet the disregard of this in favour of third parties is recurring. It is right to argue that the dispossession of Indigenous Peoples is a colonial character that remains an indelible feature in the 21st century. In Africa, Indigenous Peoples' dispossession to give way to conservation is common. Aka (2017) rightly observes that tourism forms the mainstay of many African economies which give increased prominence to conservation in their political agendas at the expense of communities. The severity of the contestations between Indigenous Peoples' livelihood and the State in the 21st century has been captured thus:

> Indigenous peoples' territories and cultures remain the final and most sought-after frontier in [globalisation's] latest expansion and their resistance its final obstacle. They stand, both physically and ideologically, at the frontlines of the struggle to transform the globalization model. If

DOI: 10.4324/9781003193166-9

unsuccessful, they stand to be the most profoundly impacted by it. For many, the threats it poses to their cultures and territories puts their very existence as a people at stake. As with previous waves of globalization that occurred during the colonial era, the current model of economic globalization is based on the exploitation of natural resources predominantly located in indigenous territories. What differentiates this latest phase of economic globalization from phases past is the rate at which it is occurring and the geographic and physical extent of its impacts. Unprecedented demands for the world's remaining resources including oil, gas, minerals, forests, freshwaters and arable lands, combined with new technological methods of harvesting what were, in many cases, hitherto inaccessible resources, and speculation on the future value of these resources have created a new development paradigm in which even the remotest and most isolated indigenous community in the world cannot avoid globalization's extended reach.

(Gilbert, 2009, p. 121)

The 21st-century Indigenous Peoples represent a resistance force against resource interested entities, a brutal geographical unlimited system facilitated by technology, a manifestation of globalisation (Gilbert, 2009). Paradoxically, the ability of Indigenous Peoples to organise their resistance against dispossession is a silver lining in the globalising world. Indigenous Peoples continually use resources they have collectively as an advocacy base to resist the 'mighty' State's endeavour to take away what is left of their ancestral land. This has resulted in the perception that Indigenous Peoples are an inconvenience or are in the way of development. To neutralise the resistance from Indigenous Peoples, States invoke sovereign rights to natural resources to facilitate grabbing Indigenous Peoples' land. States equally use conservation policies to justify dispossessing Indigenous Peoples of their ancestral land. The policies used to facilitate the removal of Indigenous Peoples often offend international law (Mogomotsi & Mogomotsi, 2020). Consequently, Indigenous Peoples lose their land, livelihood, the right to participate in the economic activities planned for their ancestral land and resultant profits.

Throughout the world, Indigenous Peoples are on the lowest rung of the socio-economic ladder and exist at the margins of power (Xanthaki, 2003). African Indigenous Peoples face an even bigger challenge as governments refuse to acknowledge their existence (Anaya, 2004). According to Gilbert (2017), Indigenous Peoples in Africa face hardship, discrimination, non-recognition of their rights to land and natural resources, marginalisation and are forced out of their ancestral lands to make room for wildlife reserves, tourism resorts or to allow the extraction of natural resources. Eastern and Southern African countries are indicted for frequently grabbing Indigenous Peoples' land under the guise of conservation (Aka, 2017). When Indigenous Peoples are dispossessed of their ancestral land on account of conservation, they lose more than an economic commodity as classified in the modern economics. Land represents livelihood, identity, religion, source of life, healing and education from their point of view (Xanthaki, 2003). Ancestral land is held by the community in custody for generations yet unborn, so the need to sustainably use the natural resources and preserve the land are inscribed in indigenous genes. The relocations predicated on conservation imperatives cast aspersions on Indigenous Peoples well-known and accepted credentials of being conservationists by nature.

This chapter adopts the traditional legal research methodology to discuss the cases of the San and the Ogiek who frequently defend their livelihood against fortress conservation policies.

Judicialising the contestation between livelihood and conservation

The contestation between Indigenous Peoples' livelihood and conservation is a manifestation of mainstream development and tends to generate conflict between States and ethnic minorities (Clarke, 2001). The implementation of development policies from the colonial period to the post-colonial period is characterised by the need for land. For African countries, land is important for tourism which is the backbone of many economies (Aka, 2017). To facilitate access to land, governments adopt unjust policies that dispossess Indigenous Peoples of their ancestral land. The use of legal apparatus to dispossess Indigenous Peoples is as ancient as the sun (Coates, 2004). Post-colonial governments exacerbated land inequalities occasioned by colonialism, with some territories occasionally fenced under the guise of conservation. In the context of Botswana, contestations over land refuse to rest, with the Government of Botswana (GOB) accused of adopting discriminatory and prejudicial land policies to the detriment of tribes. An example here can be drawn from the recent case *of Malete Land Board v The Registrar of Deeds of Botswana, The Attorney General of Botswana, Kgosi Mosadi Seboko and Gamalete Development Trust (2021)* in which the Balete, a tribe in Botswana successfully challenged a discriminatory post-colonial land legislation. In the *Malete Land Board Case* the court decided that the Balete were unconstitutionally deprived of their property.

Similarly, the Government of Kenya (GOK) grapples with land-related post-colonial conflicts. The policymakers in Kenya acknowledged the historical and ongoing corrosive effects of legislation on access to natural resources and land in the following way:

> Historical injustices are land grievances which stretch back to colonial land policies and laws that resulted in mass disinheritance of communities of their land, and which grievances have not been sufficiently resolved to date. Sources of these grievances include land adjudication and registration laws and processes, treaties and agreements between local communities and the British. The grievances remain unresolved because successive post-independence Governments have failed to address them in a holistic manner. In

90 *Onthatile Olerile Moeti*

the post-independence period, the problem has been exacerbated by the lack of clear, relevant, and comprehensive policies and laws.

(Government of Kenya, 2006, para. 190)

The GOK took legislative steps to address past historical land injustices through the adoption of the 2010 Constitution which recognises public, private and community land ownership. However, the government of Kenya struggles to operationalise Constitutional aspirations to benefit Indigenous Peoples, as illustrated by the Ogiek community cases. In the past, both Botswana and Kenya have experienced internal turmoil because of contestations between the Indigenous Peoples' livelihood and conservation. The GOB and GOK forcefully evicted the San and the Ogiek from their ancestral land to give way to conservation demands. The Indigenous Peoples resisted the evictions through advocacy and dialogue which did not yield positive results. Thereafter, the Indigenous Peoples' resistance took a judicial trajectory consistent with prevailing global trends. Litigation has proven to be indispensable in the promotion and protection of rights and in advancing Indigenous Peoples' agency.

The relocation policies adopted by both the GOB and GOK were said to be intent on ensuring conservation in the CKGR and Mau Forest, respectively. Interestingly, however, neither the GOB nor GOK maintained a consistent position about the basis for the relocation of the Indigenous Peoples. For example, the GOB changed positions from arguing that the relocations were a mining imperative, to that they were a conservation imperative, and later to that it was a developmental imperative. As conservation seemed acceptable and legitimate to international critics, both governments seemed to settle on that as a justification for the relocations.

The following discussion gives an account of the San and the Ogiek's litigation against relocations from their ancestral lands.

The San and the Government of Botswana

In the landmark case of *Roy Sesana, Keiwa Setlhobogwa and Others v Attorney General* (hereinafter referred to as *Sesana case*), the San challenged the decision of the GOB to forcefully remove them from their ancestral land, the Central Kalahari Game Reserve (CKGR) to settlement villages adjacent to the CKGR. Prior to the relocation, the GOB had terminated food, health and water service provision to the San. The GOB also restricted access to the CKGR. As a result, the San could not continue their hunter-gatherer lifestyle within the CKGR or elsewhere, nor could they access their ancestral land at will for any other reason.

The High Court had to determine the following issues; a) whether the termination of the provision of basic and essential services to the residents of the Reserve was unlawful or unconstitutional; b) whether the Government was obliged to restore the provision of such services to the Bushmen; c) whether, subsequent to 31 January 2002, the Bushmen were: i) in possession of the land which they lawfully occupied in their settlements in the Central Kalahari Game Reserve, and (ii) deprived of such possession by the Government forcibly or wrongly and without their consent; and d) whether the Government's refusal to issue special game licences (SGL) to the San (which was necessary to ensure they could pursue their traditional lifestyle) and/or the Government's refusal to allow them to enter the Reserve unless they were issued with such a permit, were unlawful and unconstitutional.

The court constituted by a panel of three judges; Dibotelo J, Dow J and Phumaphi J held that: a) The termination in 2002 by the Government of the provision of basic and essential services to the Applicants in the CKGR was neither unlawful nor unconstitutional. b) The Government is not obliged to restore the provision of such services to the Applicants in the CKGR. c) Prior to 31 January 2002, the Applicants were in possession of the land, which they lawfully occupied in their settlements in the CKGR. d) The Applicants were deprived of such possession by the Government forcibly or wrongly and without their consent. e) The Government refusal to issue special game licences to the Applicants is unlawful. f) The Government refusal to issue special game licences to the Applicants is unconstitutional. g) The Government refusal to allow the Applicants to enter the CKGR unless they are issued with permits is unlawful and unconstitutional. h) Each party shall pay their own costs.

Ogiek community and Government of Kenya

In the celebrated case of *African Commission of Human and Peoples' Rights v Kenya,* the Ogiek sued the GOK in 2009 following a notice to vacate the Mau Forest in 30 days. The Ogiek Peoples' Development Program, Centre for Minority Rights Development and Minority Rights Group International sent a communication to the African Commission on Human and Peoples Rights, arguing that the eviction violated specific rights in the African Charter on Human and Peoples Rights. The Commission issued an interim suspension of the eviction to avoid irreparable harm to the Ogiek community which the GOK ignored. The Commission presented the African Court on Human and Peoples Rights with the Application in 2012.

The legislative framework referenced herein is the African Charter on Human and Peoples Rights. The Ogiek argued that they are Indigenous Peoples in terms of international law and the Charter because of their prolonged stay in Mau Forest, their way of life and how they relate with their land. Denial of this status by the GOK inhibited them from enjoying the right to land communal ownership in breach of Article 14 and international laws. The GOK argued that the Ogiek were not a distinct ethnic group but a mix of different ethnic communities; they opined that the Ogiek are modernised and were like other Kenyans. The Ogiek argued that GOK failed to adopt measures to protect their rights contrary to Article 1, that in dealing with them the GOK adopted unjustified discriminatory and differential treatment in violation of Article 2. The GOK dismissed the allegations as baseless.

The Ogiek argued that denying them access to Mau Forest interferes with their: traditional way of life in violation of Article 4, right to culture under Article 17(2) and their religion under Article 8. The GOK claimed that the Mau Forest Complex was important for all Kenyans. Furthermore, the impact of any economic activity on Indigenous Peoples in Kenya should be consistent with the principle of proportionality. GOK argued that it took reasonable steps to promote the enjoyment of the right to culture by all. Furthermore, the GOK should balance cultural rights and conservation. As a result, it had to limit Ogiek's cultural activities that threaten the environment. Further, the GOK indicated that the Ogiek were modernised and no longer distinct; they have no cultural rights to protect and capacity to protect the environment. The GOK contended that the Ogiek provided no evidence to substantiate this claim. The GOK alleges the Ogiek converted to Christianity, their religious practices are a threat to law and order, necessitating interference. Further, the Ogiek could access the Mau Forest, except at night, and needed a licence to carry out certain activities. The Ogiek argued that their exclusion from using natural resources constitutes a violation of Article 21(1). Regarding their shared life in Mau Forest, they felt their right to development, as protected by Article 22, has been violated. The GOK argued that it reconciled competing interests, exercised its discretion in the interest of all by balancing between conservation, employed a people-centred approach that emphasises access to, rather than ownership over, natural resources, and did not discriminate against the Ogiek in developmental processes.

The Court found that the Ogiek had a communal right to their ancestral land and the forced expulsion from this land, without *prior consultation*, violated their property rights guaranteed by the Charter and the UNDRIP. Further that the failure to recognise the Ogiek as a distinct tribe afforded to similar groups denied them rights availed others and was discriminatory. Moreover, that the Ogiek community could be recognised as an indigenous population that is part of the Kenyan people, with a particular status deserving of protection deriving from their vulnerability. The preservation of the forest could not justify disregarding the Ogiek's indigenous status and rights associated with that status. The court found that the Ogiek could not be held responsible for the depletion of resources in the Mau Forest, nor can the GOK justify their eviction or denial of access to their land to exercise their right to culture. Given the relationship that the Ogiek had with their land, evictions constituted an interference with their right to religion, culture, and to access and occupy the land. Finally, the Court held that the evictions violated the Ogiek's right to development and ordered the government to take all appropriate measures, within a reasonable time, to remedy the violations. The Court was to determine the issue of reparations separately.

Importance of the cases to the discourse

The cases contribute to Indigenous Peoples' rights discourse on indigeneity, rights over ancestral land, mode of engagement between States and Indigenous

Peoples and livelihood and conservation contestations. The cases depict a classic example of people forcefully evicted by use of domestic machineries in contravention of international law and how courts use international law to enforce Indigenous Peoples' rights.

The determination on indigeneity cannot be made outside international law. Indigeneity is a construct of international law that emerged as a response to the perpetual injustice meted out to marginalised and excluded communities. In terms of international law, a determination that a people are indigenous accrues certain rights and privileges in their favour. The ability of the Courts to deduce the violations perpetrated against Indigenous Peoples though camouflaged by States is commendable and is attributable to the appreciation of the power disparity between Indigenous Peoples and the State and further the understanding that dispossession of Indigenous Peoples subtly using the law is one of the problems the UNDRIP seeks to address. The UNDRIP seeks to balance power relations by conferring Indigenous Peoples with certain rights which States ought to fulfil.

The Courts creatively used the right to self-determination and the right to give free, prior and informed consent in the cases and ruled in favour of Indigenous Peoples. The Courts highlighted the different ways in which States and Indigenous Peoples can engage to abet contestations. Effectively, the Courts recognised the importance of candid, honest and respectful engagement between the States and Indigenous Peoples. In so many ways, the Courts acknowledged the Indigenous Peoples' well-documented conservation speciality even where the States sought to discard that in the dustbin of history. The overall outcome of the cases demonstrates that international law can be used to enforce rights and can be an instrument for holding governments accountable for transgressions domestically. Furthermore, international law can augment Indigenous Peoples' rights in any given jurisdiction to improve Indigenous Peoples' lives, improve dialogue between Indigenous Peoples and the State. The cases equally establish international law as a way to balance competing interests between the State and Indigenous Peoples by dictating the bare minimum expected of both parties.

Internationalising the contestations between indigenous livelihood and environmental conservation

The intensification of Indigenous Peoples' participation in the international affairs dates to 1992 when for the first time the United Nations Conference on Environment and Development incorporated Indigenous Peoples in a substantive section of its final document (Burger, 2019). In 1993, the United Nations (UN) instituted the International Year of the World's Indigenous People and in June of that year a series of far-reaching recommendations on Indigenous Peoples were made at the World Conference on Human Rights (Burger, 2019). Thereafter, Indigenous Peoples were engaged in the wider UN processes, standard-setting and policy discussions and more activities relevant to

Indigenous Peoples were introduced (Burger, 2019). Consequently, Indigenous Peoples from all over the world have been participating in the international arena for decades (McMillan, 2014). Increasingly, international instruments address issues affecting Indigenous Peoples and provide specific fora for redressing ongoing injustices. Adherence to these documents can be used as benchmarks to gauge how States protect and promote the rights of Indigenous Peoples (Higgins, 2019).

In addition to international human rights law, the international Indigenous Peoples rights discourse has progressed significantly over the years. Presently, there are arguably coherent Indigenous Peoples' specific legislative framework and institutional mechanisms. These have transformed Indigenous Peoples from an insignificant lot in international law and politics into a group with considerable power, capable of group mobilisation, international standard setting and transnational networks (Kingsbury, 1998). Jurisprudentially, recent developments underscore recognition that Indigenous Peoples experience ongoing marginalisation and dispossession of their land due to historically discriminatory laws. The solution to addressing marginalisation of Indigenous Peoples lies within international human rights and international Indigenous Peoples' rights. To liberate the Indigenous Peoples from the claws of land injustice emanating from dispossession, and to ensure equitable conservation principles and outcome, upholding a rights–based approach is indispensable.

The following discussion seeks to demonstrate the role of UNDRIP in facilitating a mutually beneficial relationship between Indigenous Peoples and the State to ensure trade–offs between livelihoods and conservation. The evolution of international Indigenous Peoples rights is an acknowledgement that the peoples exist as a peculiar entity throughout modern, international legal history, never recognised as legitimate international actors, receiving biased, hegemonic policies which have subjected these peoples to a status quo system masked in the rhetoric of humanitarianism and equal rights (Rajagopal, 2003). UNDRIP seeks to address the difficulty in protecting Indigenous Peoples and their exclusion in policy processes with impunity occasioned by the nature of world politics that clothes States with powers such as sovereignty. Wiessner (2008) notes that sovereignty restricts the ability of international law to affirm Indigenous Peoples' rights and limit the action of States within their asserted spheres of control. The rights espoused in the UNDRIP circumvent the well-known hurdle of State sovereignty because they form part of customary international law. States do not have the prerogative to abstain from compliance with principles that form part of customary international law.

In terms of Article 3 of the UNDRIP, Indigenous peoples have the right to self–determination of their economic, social and cultural development. Self–determination features prominently in contemporary policymaking on Indigenous affairs and has become the dominant motif in the articulation of Indigenous claims and rights (Richardson, 2009). Self–determination is a contested concept, herein it means the right of people to determine their own political status and control their economic, social and cultural development without external compulsion (Richardson, 2009). The self-determination without external compulsion is critical as the power dynamics between Indigenous Peoples and the State is unequal against Indigenous Peoples, renders them susceptible to coercion, compulsion and influence which compromises their role in the decision-making process.

Self-determination plays a pivotal role in balancing contestations between the preservation of livelihoods and the State's interest in conservation. In fact, self-determination is a basis for a candid and fair engagement between Indigenous Peoples and the State. This is because, where Indigenous Peoples enjoy the right to self-determination, they are given platforms to constitute as a community and agree on the trajectory their livelihood should take. In the same breath, they decide as a people how the State can support them and ensure their continued existence. After Indigenous Peoples have taken a position on their interests, they should have a platform to engage with the State with a view to establishing the trade-offs each party should make to attain the desirable end goals. The engagements would dispel the myth that Indigenous Peoples' livelihood and conservation are mutually exclusive. As rightly observed by the Court in the *Joseph Letuya & 21 others v Attorney General & 5 others [2014] eKLR*, there is no better conservationist known to the world, since time immemorial than Indigenous Peoples. Conservation is inherently embodied in the Indigenous Peoples' way of life. In fact, conservation is a prerequisite to Indigenous Peoples' existence on their land, as for them land holds a more complex meaning than a mere economic commodity. With this position well understood by the State, a more meaningful dialogue may begin between the parties.

The State as the policy driver is indicted of many transgressions against Indigenous Peoples. First, there is interference with platforms for Indigenous Peoples to engage as a community. Secondly, no support is provided to Indigenous Peoples to encourage internal engagements to solicit and obtain the community's view. Thirdly, there is hardly a candid platform for the State to engage with Indigenous Peoples' chosen representatives and lastly, the State often adopts paternalistic policies that dictate to Indigenous Peoples the developmental trajectory decided in their absence. These transgressions are the cause of conflict and birth misconceptions that result in unnecessary contestation between livelihood and conservation. The right to self-determination posits Indigenous Peoples as perennial participants in policymaking, implementation and review. This requires States to engage candidly and in good faith with the Indigenous Peoples.

In the context of the San and the Ogiek, the judicial precedents considered above demonstrate how the right to self-determination should serve as a bridging gap between the State and Indigenous Peoples. The preceding position is supported by Mogomotsi and Mogomotsi (2020) who trace the centrality of the right to self-determination and its value to the protection of Indigenous Peoples' ancestral land and natural resources. The gist of the argument is that, if the right to self-determination is respected by the State as envisaged by UNDRIP, there would be no or minimal contestations over livelihood and conservation. If contestations arise anyway, Mogomotsi and Mogomotsi (2020) argue that the right to self-determination forms part of customary international law and thus in resolving the contestations the State is under an obligation to give way to the international customary law dictates and facilitate the full enjoyment of this right.

Closely linked to the right to self-determination, is the Indigenous Peoples' right to give free, prior and informed consent to operations. In terms of Article 32(1) Indigenous Peoples have the right to determine and develop priorities and strategies for the development or use of their lands or territories and other resources. Furthermore Article 32(2) of the UNDRIP provides that States are obliged to consult and cooperate in good faith with Indigenous Peoples, concerned to obtain their free and informed consent prior to the approval of any project in their lands. The wholistic implication of this provision is that consent must be obtained without any coercion of Indigenous Peoples, in advance of the commencement of the project, and allow Indigenous Peoples to consult amongst themselves, seek clarity if need be and they must be furnished with sufficient and accurate information on the intended project to allow them to conclude on its impact on their livelihoods, their lands and their overall being (Lennox & Short, 2016). For Mogomotsi and Mogomotsi (2020) this right entails the recognition of the Indigenous Peoples' inherent rights to their lands and resources as well as third parties' obligation to respect the legitimate authority of Indigenous Peoples when engaging.

Scholars contend that Article 32(2) lacks clarity in that it is not clear as to whether States ought to seek and obtain Indigenous Peoples' consent or States can simply seek consent from Indigenous Peoples (Ward, 2011; Mackay, 2004). Barelli (2018) considers the drafting history of the UNDRIP and concludes that Article 32(2) cannot be interpreted in such a way that States ought to seek and obtain consent from Indigenous Peoples, failing which States cannot proceed with intended projects. The basis for curtailing Indigenous Peoples' powers in Article 32(2) may also be understood from the prevailing world order and the power balance between Indigenous Peoples and the State. The disparity of power between the State and Indigenous Peoples does not allow Indigenous Peoples the leverage to have veto power against States. Despite the foregoing, an argument is made in this chapter that Article 32(2) should be read in the best interest of advancing Indigenous Peoples' rights. Article 32(2) should be read to obligate States to await consent from Indigenous Peoples, especially given the use of the words *shall, in order to, good faith* and *prior*. To seek consent and not obtain it would be an exercise in futility and may serve to negate the mandatory good faith propositioned by the article in question. Furthermore, the use of *in order to obtain* is instructive that the end goal of seeking the consent should be to obtain the consent. Considering the intent of the UNDRIP as an instrument intended to redress Indigenous Peoples' grievances and attempt to balance power scales between Indigenous Peoples and the State, the interpretation that requires the State to seek and obtain consent is persuasive as it serves the aspired end goals.

In the way of wildlife 97

For purposes of the San and the Ogiek, this provision can facilitate consensus between the State and the Indigenous Peoples. This right envisages a situation where the State has interest in relocating Indigenous Peoples from their ancestral land and engages with them through their approved representatives on the relocation, basis for relocation and whether the relocation is an imperative. With the San and Ogiek, an engagement on the conservation necessitated relocation could have potentially resulted in an understanding that Indigenous Peoples are best placed to ensure conservation of their own ancestral land. A trade-off policy would be where the parties involved agree on how modern conservation could be integrated in Indigenous Peoples' conservation for the greater good.

Conclusion

This chapter has noted that Indigenous Peoples around the world share an experience of severe disadvantage, deprivation, discrimination, inequality and violations of unimaginable proportions. The challenges alluded to manifest in various ways, including land dispossession which is a perpetuation of historical wrongs against Indigenous Peoples over centuries. The contestations between Indigenous People and the State have equally dominated the world politics in the 21st century. Governments adopt paternalistic conservation policies and forcefully remove Indigenous Peoples from their ancestral land. Relocation from ancestral land has far-reaching effect on Indigenous Peoples' continued existence. For Indigenous Peoples, their ancestral land is a source of life, health, religion, identity, culture and the backbone of their economy amongst different meanings land hold. Indigenous Peoples are increasingly seeking judicial interventions as exemplified by the San and the Ogiek.

The San and Ogiek's litigation serves to illustrate the utility of international law in promoting and protecting Indigenous Peoples' rights. International Indigenous Peoples law evolved as a direct response to Indigenous Peoples' plight within States. The UNDRIP defines the parameters of engagement between the State and Indigenous Peoples. Thus, the adoption of the UNDRIP was timely and promises more significant changes in favour of Indigenous Peoples if States are to adhere to the bare minimum espoused therein. Guaranteeing the rights discussed herein can ameliorate the contestations between Indigenous Peoples' livelihood and the State's interest in conservation. The UNDRIP acknowledges Indigenous Peoples as critical stakeholders in the decision-making and implementation processes on projects affecting their ancestral land. UNDRIP posits Indigenous Peoples as unparalleled custodians of their ancestral land and by extension put them on the highest pedestal in the conservation frontier rendering the conflict between Indigenous Peoples livelihood and conservation superfluous. Indigenous Peoples' livelihood and environmental conservation are not mutually exclusive. There is a plethora of research that substantiates this argument and even further demonstrates that Indigenous knowledge is the cornerstone of every environmental conservation endeavour. Indigenous Peoples have for centuries adopted the best-known conservation strategies and

98 *Onthatile Olerile Moeti*

thus States must invoke policies with the participation of Indigenous Peoples with a view to come up with mutually beneficial policies. The envisaged policies would allow Indigenous Peoples to possess and inhabit their land whilst they promote conservation. It is in the best interest of both the Indigenous Peoples and the State to ensure natural resources conservation as a source of livelihood and income-generating activity. In a functional democracy, the State ought to engage with the owners of the land and there must be trade-offs in the interest of the greater good of all involved.

References

Ademodi, O. I. (2012). *The Rights and Status of Indigenous Peoples in Nigeria.* Winter Park: Bauu Institute LLC.

Aka, P. C. (2017). Introductory note to African Commission on Human and Peoples Rights v Republic of Kenya (Afr. Ct. H.P.R). *International Legal Materials*, 56 (4), 726–764.

Anaya, S. J. (2004). *Indigenous Peoples in international law,* 2nd ed. Oxford: Oxford University Press.

Barelli, M. (2018). *Seeking justice in international law: The significance and implications of the UN Declaration on the Rights of Indigenous Peoples.* London: Routledge.

Burger, J. (2019). After the declaration: Next steps for the protection of Indigenous People's rights. *International Journal of Human Rights*, 23 (1–2), 22–33.

Clarke, G. (2001). From ethnocide to ethnodevelopment ethics: Minorities and Indigenous Peoples in South East Asia. *Third World Quarterly*, 22 (3), 413–436.

Coates, K. (2004). *A global history of Indigenous Peoples: Struggle and survival.* London: Palgrave Macmillan.

Everson, R., McNeish, J. A., & Cimadamore, A. D. (2013). *Indigenous Peoples and poverty: An international perspective.* London: Zed Books.

Gilbert, J. (2009). Custodians of the land: Indigenous Peoples, human rights and cultural integrity. In Logan, W, Craith, Nic, M., & Langfield, M. (Eds.), *Cultural diversity, heritage and human rights intersections in theory and practice.* London: Routledge, 31–44.

Gilbert, J. (2017). Litigating Indigenous Peoples' rights in Africa: Potentials, challenges and limitations. *International & Comparative Law Quarterly*, 66 (3), 657–686.

Government of Kenya. (2006). *Draft national land policy.* Nairobi: National Land Policy Secretariat.

Higgins, N. (2019). Creating a space for indigenous rights: The universal periodic review as a mechanism for promoting the rights of Indigenous Peoples. *International Journal of Human Rights*, 23 (1–2), 125–148.

Hitchcok, R., Sapignolli, M., & Babchuk, W. (2015). Settler colonialism, conflicts, and genocide: Interactions between hunter-gatherers and settlers in Kenya, Zimbabwe and Northern Botswana. *Settler Colonial Studies*, 5 (1), 40–65.

Jalata, A. (2012). The impacts of English colonial terrorism and genocide on Indigenous/ Black Australians. *Sage Open.* doi:10.1177/2158244013499143

Kingsbury, B. (1998). 'Indigenous Peoples' in international law: A constructivist approach to the Asian controversy. *American Journal of International Law*, 92 (3), 414–457.

Lennox, C., & Short, D. (2016). *Handbook of Indigenous Peoples' rights.* London: Routledge.

MacKay, F. (2004). Indigenous Peoples' right to free, prior and informed consent and the World Bank's extractive industries review. *Sustainable Development Law and Policy*, 4 (2), 43–65.

McMillan, M. (2014). Koowarta and the rural indigenous international: Our place as Indigenous Peoples in the international. *Griffith Law Review*, 23, 110–126.

Mogomotsi, G. E., & Mogomotsi, P. K. (2020). Recognition of the indigeneity of the Basarwa in Botswana: Panacea against their marginalisation and realisation of land rights? *African Journal of International and Comparative Law*, 28 (4), 555–576.

Rajagopal, B. (2003). *International law from below: Development, social movements, and Third World resistance*. Cambridge: Cambridge University Press.

Richardson, B. J., Imai, S., & McNeil, K. (2009). *Indigenous Peoples and the law: Comparative and critical perspectives*. Oxford: Hart Publishing.

Ward, T. (2011). The right to free, prior, and informed consent: Indigenous Peoples' participation rights within international law. *Northwestern Journal of Human Rights*, 10 (2), 54–84.

Wiessner, S. (2008) Indigenous sovereignty: A reassessment in light of the UN declaration on the rights of indigenous peoples. *Vanderbilt Journal of Transnational Law*, 41 (1), 1141–1176.

Xanthaki, A. (2003). The land rights of Indigenous Peoples in South-East Asia. *Melbourne Journal of International Law*, 4 (2), 467–496.

8 The socio-economic impacts of wildlife crop-raiding

An assessment of the efficacy of conservation and agricultural land uses reconciliation

Emmanuel Mwakiwa

Introduction

In Southern Africa, human–wildlife conflicts, which include crop raiding, are rampant and occur where human and wildlife niches overlap (Young et al., 2010). Crop raiding by herbivores and livestock depredation by carnivores reduce communities' tolerance toward wildlife and negatively influences local attitudes towards wildlife (Browne-Nuñez & Jonker 2008). Unaddressed or poorly addressed conflicts are an impediment to effective conservation and management of many wildlife species (Madden & McQuinn, 2014). Some of these conflicts involve situations where various stakeholders clash over land management objectives, especially between conservation and agriculture land uses (Young et al., 2010). The critical drivers of many of these conservation and agricultural land conflicts are given in Table 8.1.

The purpose of this chapter is to discuss various interventions that have been implemented in Southern Africa to mitigate conservation and agricultural land use conflicts. This is done through assessing the efficacy of several case studies of conservation and agriculture land use reconciliation efforts. This will contribute towards informed conservation conflict management.

Method

To perform the assessment of the various interventions, a rigorous literature review of published, unpublished and grey conservation literature related to conservation and agriculture land use interventions in Southern Africa was done. The discussion begins with classifying the conservation and agriculture land use intervention tools. Following that we show how the conservation intervention tools have been applied to mitigate the effects of crop raiding and other human–wildlife conflicts (HWC) through the private sector in private conservancies and the communities in Community-Based Natural Resource Management (CBNRM) programmes. Lastly, we conclude and give recommendations.

DOI: 10.4324/9781003193166-10

Impacts of wildlife crop-raiding 101

Table 8.1 List of different conservation and agricultural land conflict drivers

Conflict drivers	Examples
Wildlife impacts	Human wildlife conflict: human injury/death livestock depredation; crop raiding; retaliatory killing or persecution of wildlife; opposition to conservation efforts
Resource use restrictions	Natural resource related conflict, Illegal wildlife, logging, poaching, unsustainable use, encroachment; fisheries, common-pool resource conflict
Land-use decisions	People-park conflict, environmental justice, indigenous rights, land-use conflict
Conservation governance	Lack of transparency in decision-making process, lack of trust, unequal power dynamics, ineffective governance
Development and economics	Conflicts between poverty and/or economic growth and conservation, commercial or state-sanctioned development in 'green' spaces or protected areas, civic and organisational protest/opposition
Clashing of values	Animal-rights campaigns against lethal control, or trophy hunting; conflicts over different approaches, philosophies or ethics

Source: Adapted from Baynham-Herd et al. (2018).

Conservation intervention tools

The conservation and agriculture land use interventions can be grouped into four categories namely: technical, economic, enforcement and stakeholder conservation interventions (Baynham-Herd et al., 2018; Heberlein, 2012). Each of these interventions are now discussed in turn in this section.

Technical conservation interventions

In cases where conservation conflicts result in human–wildlife impacts, for instance crop or livestock loss, which often lead to retaliatory killing of wildlife, technical conservation interventions are usually recommended (Baynham-Herd et al., 2018). The technical interventions' purpose is to modify human behaviour by changing the external environment (Heberlein, 2012). Proponents of technical interventions are under the assumption that retaliatory killing of wildlife will reduce as the damage exerted by wildlife reduces (Pooley et al., 2016). Some categories of technical conservation interventions include the following: wildlife control, habitat manipulation, livelihoods and people control (Nyhus, 2016). Examples of interventions under wildlife control are use of lethal means (traps, shooting, pesticides, poison), non-lethal means (translocation, deterrents, diversionary feeding and fertility/disease management) (Baynham-Herd et al., 2018). Habitat manipulation interventions include the use of buffer crops, alternative food and barriers (fences, nets, enclosures) (Pooley et al., 2016). Livestock/crop protection, guarding, modifying crops, rotations and immunisation constitute some of the examples of the livelihoods conservation interventions' category; whereas barriers, surveillance systems, modified gear, signposts are examples of people control conservation intervention category (Baynham-Herd et al., 2018).

Barriers are mainly used to reduce wildlife damage, for instance to people and agriculture; barriers can be physically constructed (e.g. fences) or naturally growing (e.g. planted vegetation) (Heberlein, 2012). Fences are used to achieve the following: limiting wildlife from accessing specific areas (e.g. agricultural fields); limiting the movement of undesirable or aggressive species (e.g. predators like lions and hyenas); impeding disease transmission (e.g. foot and mouth); and protecting small, valuable or highly endangered species (e.g. black rhinoceros) (Woodroffe, 2014). In addition to physical barriers, wildlife managers may modify habitats to discourage selected categories of animals through fire management, water or vegetation manipulations (Mwakiwa, 2011). In some cases, alternative food sources could be provided to divert wildlife's attention away from more valuable crops, such as planting secondary crops to divert birds away from primary crops (Conover, 2002). In other cases, other animals can also be used as barriers, e.g. in Kenya, honeybees acting as biological fences have been used to reduce elephant crop raiding, with the added advantage of providing pollination and honey (Shaffer et al., 2019).

Economic conservation interventions

Economic conservation interventions are more common in Africa and other developing countries. The principle behind these interventions is that there are greater odds for success in efforts for wildlife conservation if conservation programmes are associated with economic benefits (Kremen et al., 2000). Economic incentives are used so that communities increase their tolerance for wildlife (Nyhus et al., 2005). Categories of the economic conservation interventions include remuneration, incentives, services and employment. Examples of the remuneration intervention category include compensation and insurance schemes which can come from state, charitable and private players' direct payments (Baynham-Herd et al., 2018). Payments for ecosystem services, tourism income, sustainable use/harvest are examples of the incentive conservation intervention category (Agrawal et al., 2014). On the other hand, the services intervention category has the following examples: education, healthcare and infrastructure (Baynham-Herd et al., 2018). Finally, the employment wildlife intervention category comprises of direct employment and alternative livelihoods (Agrawal et al., 2014).

Compensation involves reimbursing with cash or in-kind to community members who have their crops or livestock damaged by wildlife, or those who have been injured or died from wildlife attack (Baynham-Herd et al., 2018). Compensation can be in terms of market price or proportion of value of lost crop or livestock (Ravenelle & Nyhus, 2017). If they are carried out effectively, compensation programmes can assist in increasing tolerance to wildlife by communities (Nyhus et al., 2005). Some challenges that stem from compensation schemes include moral hazard, risk of fraudulent claims and adverse selection, difficulty in authenticating the cause of damage; sluggish processing, cumbersome and inadequate compensation; and high transaction costs (Nyhus, 2016). Solution to some of the challenges is to let local communities that are represented in the overall management of the challenge participate in determining fair and appropriate compensation.

Enforcement conservation interventions

Enforcement-based conservation interventions are preferred in situations where there is illegal natural resource use, or indirect environmental damage (Baynham-Herd et al. 2018). Enforcement-based interventions are often recommended under the logic that the greater policing of natural resources and stricter regulations will reduce illegal resource use like over-harvesting and illegal behaviour (Baynham-Herd et al., 2018). Categories of enforcement conservation interventions include regulation creating and regulation enforcement. Examples of regulation creating include establishing the following: protective status, land use zoning, land rights, quotas, trade bans, equipment/practice ban (Baynham-Herd et al., 2018; Agrawal et al., 2014).

On the other hand, regulation enforcement includes increased patrols, trials, punishments, reduced corruption and processes; law-making actions, policy reforms or managerial actions can guide enforcement; and policy reforms can create new rights for resources such as the rights to create management plans, or to buy or sell land (Baynham-Herd et al., 2018; Arias, 2015; Agrawal et al., 2014). They can alter land uses directly by changing types of rights, e.g. conservation against agriculture, consumptive against non-consumptive use of resources, or can reallocate rights by excluding groups of users, e.g. removing land use rights from a community to an individual (Agrawal et al., 2014). These shifts in turn affect wildlife use by changing the political-economic relationships among actors, their relative access to assets and their choices over resource use.

Stakeholder conservation interventions

Stakeholder-based wildlife interventions are appropriate where there is undesirable environmental change – such as agriculture land use or recreation expansion – or active opposition to conservation – such as protests, hostility or objections – and in more highly developed countries (Baynham-Herd et al., 2018). It is argued that since social, sometimes non-material factors, sustain the conflict, then stakeholder interventions would be appropriate since they target emotions and aim to increase dialogue and trust, with the idea that shared and agreed-upon problems and solutions can be met (Redpath et al., 2015; Young et al., 2016). Stakeholder-based interventions vary in style and motivation: in some cases, collaborative decision-making or more devolved governance are appropriate, whereas in other cases increasing decision-making transparency or conducting stakeholder consultations would be best (Elston et al., 2014).

104   *Emmanuel Mwakiwa*

Categories of stakeholder conservation interventions include stakeholder engagement, conflict resolution and devolution (Baynham-Herd et al., 2018). Examples of the stakeholder engagement category include participatory planning, knowledge sharing, consultations and deliberations (Baynham-Herd et al., 2018). Trust building, transformation and third-parties conflict resolution are examples of conflict resolution conservation interventions; whilst devolution interventions consist of community-based natural resource management, land rights and power sharing (Young et al., 2016).

Private and community landowners' involvement in conservation and agricultural land uses reconciliation

Community-based natural resource management

An example of community involvement in conservation and agricultural land uses reconciliation is through the CBNRM programmes. CBNRM is important in promoting conservation and agricultural land uses reconciliation, especially in the arid and semi-arid regions in Southern Africa (Gandiwa et al., 2013). CBRNM has been used as a tool to optimise agriculture and conservation land uses, thereby coming up with solutions to minimise crop raiding and other human–wildlife conflicts (Mwakiwa, 2019).

CBNRM models seek to strengthen accountability by local institutions for natural resource use and management, enabling better decisions to be made on the use of land resources (Mwakiwa, 2019). In Southern Africa, CBNRM involves devolution of rights to the community level to make management decisions, and capture benefits, in relation to resources located on communal lands; and it involves some degree of co-management of resources between central authorities, local government and local communities (Mwakiwa, 2019). Apart from Mozambique and South Africa, CBNRM in Southern Africa is based on the common property conceptual framework where there is a strong relationship between local investments in resource management and ownership rights to the concerned resources (Murphree, 1993). Mozambique has substantial resident populations in its protected areas and so has been dealing with natural resource co-management options amongst local communities, private and state (Nhantumbo & Anstey, 2007). For South Africa, CBNRM is commonly associated with local community claims for land compensation – particularly in areas where land was first forcibly taken for national parks creation and expansion (Arntzen et al., 2007). In many cases, where land in protected areas is claimed back, a 'contractual park' is established (Binot et al., 2009).

In Botswana, proponents for CBNRM advocate for legal trust formation by local communities which they use to get quotas from the wildlife department and land leases from District Land Boards, enabling them to enter agreements with the private sector for joint ventures on trophy hunting or photographic tourism (Jones, 2004). At the core of CBNRM initiatives in Southern Africa is that, for wildlife to persist outside protected areas on private and communal

Impacts of wildlife crop-raiding   105

lands, it must be an economically competitive land use option for landowners, when compared to agriculture and livestock (Child, 2004).

Chaminuka (2012) captures some of the criticisms levelled against most of the early CBNRM initiatives: (i) the dependence on donor funding, and limited sustainability of consumptive resource uses; (ii) the commoditisation of natural resources raised concerns about overharvesting, unsustainability and market-related issues such as the proliferation of middlemen who stood to benefit the most in the value chain, disadvantaging rural communities, and the instability of tourism markets; (iii) corruption, nepotism and inequitable distribution of benefits; (iv) being biased towards conservation rather than poverty alleviation and the failure to deliver tangible economic benefits at household level.

Fitzgerald (2015) identified the following factors as requisite for communal conservation programmes to work: (i) community engagement must be voluntary; (ii) communities must be engaged from the beginning of the project and their participation should be institutionalised; (iii) there must be clear conservation targets; (iv) conservation benefits must be tied to conservation responsibility; (v) conservation benefits must be at a scale that deters non-conservation behaviour; (vi) community benefits should be reliable; (vii) communities need to both assume a reasonable level of risk and bring something to the project, such as land, wildlife, money or skills; (viii) project structures must be transparent and set up to ensure equitable distribution of benefits and avoid elite capture; (ix) projects must be economically, ecologically and socially sustainable.

CAMPFIRE programme

The Communal Areas Management Programme for Indigenous Resources (CAMPFIRE) launched in Zimbabwe, on communal areas bordering national parks, is an example of a CBNRM programme (Gandiwa et al., 2013; Taylor, 2009). It is one of the key initiatives adopted to reduce the conflict between agricultural communities and wildlife, while generating benefits, promoting conservation and empowering local communities (Mwakiwa, 2019).

Tchakatumba et al. (2019) analysed the effects of donor withdrawal from CAMPFIRE on wildlife conservation benefits. They found that the aggregate funds allocated to district councils and communities were considerable, compared to what was trickling down directly to households, yet the households are the ones bearing the highest opportunity and transaction costs of wildlife management. They indicated that households were incentivised through direct economic benefits (monetary dividends, employment opportunities and bushmeat provision), and indirect socio-economic benefits (infrastructural facilities like school blocks, clinics, roads) (Tchakatumba et al., 2019; Taylor 2009). Although the direct economic benefits have been limited, the households appreciated the infrastructural facilities from CAMPFIRE. Some households, although limited in number, felt that the programme is still assisting in management of the arresting crop raiding including other types of human–wildlife conflict (Tchakatumba et al. 2019). Both the direct and indirect

106 *Emmanuel Mwakiwa*

socio-economic benefits have been made worse by the donor withdrawal, with a sharp decrease in household dividends, an increased prevalence of human–wildlife conflict and commercial poaching (Tchakatumba et al., 2019). Given that most of the households indicated that they are still benefiting from CAMPFIRE's public infrastructure and community projects, even after the withdrawal of the donor, is a good sign of the project's resilience (Mwakiwa, 2019).

Namibia: a model for CBNRM

Before 1996, rural communities on communal land suffered wide-ranging losses from HWC since they did not have rights over wildlife and in retaliation hunting and poaching were widespread, which resulted in decreasing wildlife populations (Binot et al., 2009). To arrest decline in wildlife populations and HWC, reforms were done which enabled the establishment of communal conservancies in 1996 (Binot et al., 2009). Communities in rural areas were empowered with user rights over the wildlife in their area. Namibia has favourable wildlife bio-physical characteristics which made the communities choose conservation against agricultural land use because of the low population density and high aridity favouring wildlife over crop agriculture (Binot et al., 2009). This saw a sharp increase in the number of conservancies, with about 50 established in 2007, covering 118,704 km^2 of land, about 14.4% of the country, which generated over US$2.5 million of revenue in that year from wildlife-based activities such as tourism and tourist hunting (Binot, 2009). In addition, wildlife populations improved in the conservancies (NACSO, 2006).

According to Binot et al. (2009) the following aspects contributed to the success of the Namibian Conservation model: (i) broad and secure wildlife rights which are not term-limited; (ii) efficient business interaction between community and the private sector; (iii) communities retain 100% of wildlife benefits; and (iv) the programme had experience in development before external players and donors' involvement. The rights over wildlife for the Namibia's version of CBNRM model have not been devolved to local communities anywhere else in Africa, which means Namibia is at a very advanced stage on this aspect in community wildlife management (NACSO, 2006). In addition, the following were key success factors in successfully facilitating the Namibian community wildlife CBNRM reforms: comparatively low levels of institutional corruption and centrally captured revenues from wildlife uses (Binot et al., 2009).

Contractual parks in South Africa

In most of South Africa's national parks, covering over 3 million hectares of land, land was originally taken by force from the native people and they offered very few significant benefits to local communities (Binot et al., 2009). However, there has been a paradigm shift, and it has now been realised that involving local people in wildlife management could be one of the most effective ways of sustainable wildlife conservation while also ensuring that rural livelihoods are enhanced through increased incomes (Prins et al., 2000).

The contractual national park model was developed to meet conservation objectives and expand South Africa's protected area network without heavy investment required by land purchase (Reid, 2001). Joint management agreement formulated by a board comprising representatives of both the landowners and the conservation authority oversees the management of contractual parks (Reid, 2002). The situations for establishment of the contractual parks are varied and include: providing incentives to landowners neighbouring existing PAs who were once involved in other land uses such as agriculture to convert the land use to conservation under PA management without the transfer of title (e.g. Addo Elephant National Park); establishing new PAs on community land also once involved in other land uses (e.g. Richtersveld National Park) and allowing communities formerly evicted from their land for establishment of PAs to claim back their land (e.g. Makuleke land claim) (Reid, 2001; Binot et al., 2009). The Richtersveld National Park is South Africa's only entirely contractual National Park. The community land is contracted by South Africa National Parks (SANParks) which pays rent for using the land for wildlife conservation purposes. However, its remote location and the absence of the big five has constrained generation of income and employment opportunities (Binot et al., 2009).

The Makuleke region was incorporated into Kruger National Park (KNP) in 1969, after eviction of the Makuleke people (Steenkamp, 1999). Following the establishment of the new democratic government, the Makuleke people reached an agreement with the National Parks Board which granted transfer of title for 20,000 hectares of land back to the evicted community in 1996 (Steenkamp, 1999). One of the prominent undertakings that the Makuleke community made was that they would retain the land use of their returned land under conservation and would not convert to any other land use (Steenkamp, 1999). They entered a contractual agreement with Kruger National Park to co-manage their land through the Communal Property Association (CPA) established in 1999 (Binot et al., 2009). All conservation activities are the responsibility of SANParks (Steenkamp, 1999). It has been reported that the Makuleke land claim has operated well (Grossman & Holden, 2009), although in some instances there has been conflict between the traditional chief and the CPA (Binot et al., 2009).

Contractual parks appear to contribute to realising conservation goals; in addition, landowners realise greater benefits that are also available to communities that live adjacent to national parks (Binot et al., 2009). However, operations are not profitable and usually need to be subsidised by central government or other national parks (Binot et al., 2009). Reid (2002) argues that, although there are some failures in contractual parks, these failures are more a problem of implementation than conceptual, and that contractual parks contribute to the realisation of conservation and development objectives, and successful joint management. Thus, the ecological and economic objectives of the conservation

108 *Emmanuel Mwakiwa*

authority and socio-economic objectives of the landowners are met through the contractual parks.

Private conservancies and nature reserves

Private nature reserves are gaining increasing popularity in southern Africa and play a significant role for biodiversity conservation in the region (Fitzgerald, 2015). In contrast to many game ranches and conservancies, private reserves have completely abandoned livestock farming (Fitzgerald, 2015; Krug, 2001). The main intention is to preserve wildlife and natural habitat. While management objectives vary from strict preservation to the wildlife sustainable use, the focus is typically on wildlife-viewing tourism (Krug, 2001). However, some private reserves such as the NamibRand Nature Reserve in Namibia have more ambitious conservation objectives than state-managed national parks, such as strict guidelines on tourism carrying capacity (Odendaal, 2014). In South Africa and Namibia, collaborative nature reserves are common.

Save Valley Conservancy

Save Valley Conservancy (SVC) is in the Lowveld of southwestern Zimbabwe. It is one of the few remaining private conservancies in Zimbabwe. It was formed when landowners converted their properties from agricultural land use (mainly cattle) operations into components of conservation, with internal game fencing having been removed in accordance with a constitution in operation since 1991 (du Toit, 1998). It is situated to the south-eastern lowveld of Zimbabwe, bordering on the Save River on its eastern side, comprising 3,442 km^2 of diverse wildlife habitat (du Toit, 1998). Individual properties operate tourist lodges that offer different types of accommodations in varied ecological settings. The conservancy is a vast and varied natural landscape. Unlike some game reserves where animals are confined to smaller spaces and well habituated to humans, the animals in the conservancy are wild (Lindsey et al., 2008). Visitors to the SVC can view a wide range of Southern African game species, including the Big Five (elephant, lion, leopard, buffalo and rhino) (du Toit, 1998). The SVC is home to one of Africa's largest populations of black and white rhino, and to a healthy population of rare African painted dogs; over 300 species of birds can also be found in the conservancy during the year, including many raptors (Lindsey et al., 2008).

Save Valley Conservancy does not border a national park but rather it is surrounded by communal lands mainly practising agriculture. The SVC has taken several initiatives to incorporate the local community in its decision-making to reduce HWC (Balint & Mashinya, 2008). For example, SVC established a trust in 1999 to foster mutually beneficial and durable economic relations between the conservancy and about 20,000 people in 18 neighbouring communities (Balint & Mashinya, 2008). The purpose of the trust is to attract and administer funds needed to involve the neighbouring communities in the economy created by the conservancy.

However, SVC is at risk because of unplanned settlement and lack of clarity around wildlife user rights and land tenure (Fitzgerald, 2015). The land use transition, of the SVC, from agriculture to conservation has not been an effortless process, due to the changing policy environment during the development of the conservancy. Despite recognition at a technical level of the private conservancy as a model for sustainable land use, the attitudes of government authorities towards commercial wildlife use were not consistent, mainly because of the underlying and intensifying political trends related to land ownership within Zimbabwe (du Toit, 1998). The landowners had justified the development of the conservancy based on three dimensions: ecological, economic and socio-political sustainability when compared to the former agricultural land use. Although the ecological and economic achievements of the conservancy were already clear, its socio-political sustainability was less certain. The policy environment under which the conservancy has evolved, and the policy environment which it must now adapt to, curtailed its effective development (du Toit, 1998).

NamibRand Nature Reserve

The NamibRand Nature Reserve, measuring 172,000 ha, located in southern part of Namibia, is one of the largest private conservation areas in southern Africa. It consists of 16 former livestock farms rehabilitated into a continuous natural conservation area and shares a 100 km border with the Namib–Naukluft National Park (Odendaal & Shaw, 2010). Landowners who form part of the NamibRand Nature Reserve have signed Articles of Association which restrict the land use to conservation and tourism (Odendaal, 2014). It originated when it was realised that farming was unsustainable in the region due to the arid nature of the area. In the 1980s, the Department of Nature Conservation encouraged the formation of the NamibRand Nature Reserve as an additional conservation area between the park and livestock farming areas so that it would act as a buffer between the two land uses. The project is financially self-sustaining mainly through high-quality, low-impact tourism (Odendaal, 2014). There are partnerships with local and regional neighbours, and government and other organisations. When purchased, the former livestock farms had an average of three employees but the nature reserve has over 150 employees (Odendaal, 2014). The reserve maintains a conservation policy of minimal interference with constant monitoring, implemented through an environmental management plan. Wildlife populations have stabilised and have recovered significantly from numbers recorded when intensive conservation efforts began (Odendaal, 2014). The reserve also reintroduced species that had historically occurred in the area but were hunted to the point of local extinction when the land was used as a freehold farmland (Odendaal & Shaw, 2010).

The NamibRand Nature Reserve Association is a successful example of the application of good governance, innovative management systems and the pooling of resources to reach common biodiversity conservation objectives

110 *Emmanuel Mwakiwa*

(Odendaal, 2014). NamibRand Nature Reserve shows that it is possible to run a large, well-managed and well-functioning private nature reserve which is funded privately without donor and government aid.

Criticism of the conservancy approach

Conservancies are in arid and semi-arid regions which are generally unsuitable for agriculture due to low rainfall and/or poor soils and livestock-ranching enterprises have tended to be unprofitable (Lindsey et al., 2008). Wildlife-based land-use generates income through safari hunting and tourism that have higher revenues than agricultural land use and contribute to national food security. This income is complemented by the live game sale that is a huge industry in South Africa and Namibia. Wildlife conservation does not heavily reliant on rainfall as agriculture and is less vulnerable to drought. The sale of affordable meat to local communities from trophy-hunted animals and through the annual harvest of overabundant species also contributes to local protein requirements; and both the quantity and quality of employment opportunities is greater for wildlife production systems than for livestock (Lindsey et al., 2008). A criticism levelled against the private conservancies is that the electric fencing erected around some of the conservancies is a symbol of exclusion of the poverty-stricken communities (Lindsey et al., 2008). However, the practical significance of fencing must also be considered in preventing crop raiding and other human–wildlife conflict and preventing poaching of wildlife. Furthermore, the fencing around such conservancies as the Save Valley Conservancy are legally required to prevent disease transmission to livestock occurring in neighbouring areas. If surrounding communities especially those involved in less productive agriculture misunderstand the intentions of the private conservancies' objectives, they will raise the criticisms above and as such there will tend to be a proliferation of HWC.

Conclusions and recommendations

Technical, economic, enforcement and stakeholder conservation interventions are the various tools aimed at mitigating conservation and agricultural land conflicts. In the arid and semi-arid areas especially those which are adjacent to state protected areas, private conservancies and CBNRM projects were established as landowners realised managing wildlife in arid zones was more profitable than managing livestock, so they shifted their land use from agriculture to conservation. Conservancies assist in increasing land under conservation and directly benefit communities and landowners, when properly managed. According to Schwartzman et al. (2000), conservancies in Africa share the following benefits: (i) they supplement state government-owned protected areas by providing additional wildlife habitat; (ii) they broaden the tourism products through offering a different type of tourism packages, such as walking safaris and cultural interaction; (iii) they diversify land management, expanding a wide habitat range which supports different wildlife and ecosystems; and (iv) there is direct involvement and empowering of communities and private land-owners which ensures they benefit from conservation, thereby incentivising them to be involved in wildlife and habitat conservation and decreasing HWC including crop raiding.

The private conservancies and CBNRM programmes need to maximise the livelihood benefits whilst at the same time minimising crop raiding and other forms of HWC. This could be achieved through having well-defined property, land and wildlife user rights. They should also ensure active partici-pation of all parties through equitable contribution of requisite resources such as money, land and risk sharing. Governments and other stakeholders should ensure that there is strong legislative structure which would support good gov-ernance, transparency, adherence to conservation parameters, code of conduct, undertaking of membership obligations and equitable revenue sharing. In add-ition, good management plans based on science, and which are frequently updated should be adopted and used. Furthermore, the private conservancies should ensure that they have amicable relationships with the neighbouring communities, and they should actively involve them in their ecological and economic activities.

References

Agrawal, A., Wollenberg, E., & Persha, L. (2014). Governing agriculture-forest landscapes to achieve climate change mitigation. *Global Environmental Change*, 29, 270–280.

Arias, A. 2015. Understanding and managing compliance in the nature conservation context. *Journal of Environmental Management*, 153, 134–143.

Arntzen, J., Setlhogile, T., & Barnes J. (2007). *Rural livelihoods, poverty reduction and food security in Southern Africa: Is CBNRM the answer?* Washington, DC: USAID.

Balint, P. J., & Mashinya, J. (2008). CAMPFIRE during Zimbabwe's national crisis: Local impacts and broader implications for community-based wildlife management. *Society & Natural Resources*, 21, 1–14.

Baynham-Herd, Z., Redpath, S., Bunnefeld, N., Molony, T., & Keane, A. (2018). Conservation conflicts: Behavioural threats, frames, and intervention recommendations. *Biological Conservation*, 222, 180–188.

Binot, A., Blomley, T., Coad, L., Nelson, F., Roe, D., & Sandbrook, C. (2009). Community involvement in natural resources management in Africa – regional overviews. In Roe, D., Nelson, F., & Sandbrook, C. (Eds.), *Community management of natural resources in Africa: Impacts, experiences and future directions*. Natural Resource Issues, 18. London: International Institute for Environment and Development, 13–54.

Browne-Nuñez, C., & Jonker, S. A. (2008). Attitudes toward wildlife and conservation across Africa: A review of survey research. *Human Dimensions of Wildlife*, 13, 47–70.

Chaminuka, P. (2012). Evaluating land use options at the wildlife/livestock interface: An integrated spatial land use analysis. PhD thesis, Wageningen University.

Child, B. (2004). The Luangwa integrated rural development project, Zambia. In Fabricius, C., Kock, E., Magome, H., & Turner S. (Eds.), Rights, resources and rural development. Community-based natural resource management in Southern Africa. London: Earthscan, 235–247.

112 Emmanuel Mwakiwa

Conover, M. R. (2002). *Resolving human–wildlife conflicts: The science of wildlife damage management*. Boca Raton, FL: CRC Press.

du Toit, R. (1998). Case study of policies that support sustainable development in Africa: Save Valley Conservancy, Zimbabwe. Paper presented at Scandinavian Seminar College Workshop African Experiences with Policies and Practices Supporting Sustainable Development, 28–30 September, Harare.

Elston, D. A., Spezia, L., Baines, D., & Redpath, S. M. (2014). Working with stakeholders to reduce conflict: Modelling the impact of varying hen harrier Circus cyaneus densities on red grouse Lagopus lagopus populations. *Journal of Applied Ecology*, 51, 1236–1245.

Fitzgerald, K. H. (2015). The silent killer: Habitat loss and the role of African Protected Areas to conserve biodiversity. In Wuethner, G., Crist, E., & Butler, T. (Eds.), *Protecting the wild: Parks and wilderness, the foundation for conservation*. Washington, DC: Island Press, 170–188.

Gandiwa, E., Heitkönig, I. M. A., Lokhorst, A. M., Prins, H. H. T., & Leeuwis, C. (2013). CAMPFIRE and human–wildlife conflicts in local communities bordering northern Gonarezhou National Park, Zimbabwe. *Ecology and Society*, 18 (4), 7.

Grossman, D., & Holden, P. (2009). Towards transformation: Contractual parks in South Africa: Evolution and innovation. In Suich, H., Child, B., & Spenceley, A. (Eds.), *Wildlife conservation: Parks and game ranches to transfrontier conservation areas*. London: Earthscan, 357–372.

Heberlein, T. A. (2012). *Navigating environmental attitudes*. Oxford: Oxford University Press.

Jones, B. (2004). *CBNRM, poverty reduction and sustainable livelihoods: Developing criteria for evaluating the contribution of CBNRM to poverty reduction and alleviation in southern Africa*. Harare and Cape Town: CASS/PLAAS.

Kremen, C., Niles, J. O., Dalton, M. G., Daily, G. C., Ehrlich, P. R., Fay, J. P., Grewal, D., & Guillery, R. P. (2000). Economic incentives for rain forest conservation across scales. *Science*, 288, 1828–1832.

Krug, W. (2001). *Private supply of protected land in Southern Africa: a review of markets, approaches, barriers and issues*. Report to Environment Directorate. Paris: Organisation for Economic Co-operation and Development (OECD).

Lindsey, P., du Toit, R., Pole, A., & Romanach, S. (2008). Savé Valley Conservancy: A large-scale African experiment in cooperative wildlife management. In Child, B., Suich, H., & Spenceley, A. (Eds.), *Evolution and innovation in wildlife conservation in southern Africa*. London: Earthscan, 164–184.

Madden, F., & McQuinn, B. (2014). Conservation's blind spot: The case for conflict transformation in wildlife conservation. *Biological Conservation*, 178, 97–106.

Mwakiwa, E. (2011). Cooperation or competition: Dilemma for resource managers in sustainable wildlife utilisation. PhD thesis, Wageningen University.

Mwakiwa, E. (2019). Optimisation of benefits from agriculture and wildlife land uses by wards in CAMPFIRE areas in Zimbabwe. *African Journal of Agricultural and Resource Economics*, 14 (2), 120–136.

Murphree, M. W. (1993). *Communities as resource management institutions*. Gatekeeper series, 36. London: IIED.

NACSO. (2006). *Namibia's communal conservancies: A review of progress and challenges in 2005*. Windhoek: Namibian Association of CBNRM Support Organisations.

Nhantumbo, I., & Anstey, S. (2007). Community based natural resource management in Mozambique: Progressive policy framework but challenging implementation. Unpublished report.

Nyhus, P. J. (2016). Human–wildlife conflict and coexistence. *Annual Review of Environment and Resources*, 41, 143–171.

Nyhus, P. J., Osofsky, S. A., Ferraro, P., Fischer H., & Madden, F. (2005). Bearing the costs of human–wildlife conflict: The challenges of compensation schemes. In Woodroffe, R., Thirgood, S., & Rabinowitz, A. (Eds.), *People and wildlife, conflict or co-existence?* Cambridge: Cambridge University Press, 107–121.

Odendaal, N. (2014). Governance of the NamibRand nature reserve: A model for private conservation. In IUCN (Ed.), *Twenty-two stories of conservation in Africa: Key elements for effective and well and governed protected areas in* sub-Saharan Africa. Gland, Switzerland: IUCN, 25–28.

Odendaal, N., & Shaw, D. (2010). Conservation and economic lessons learned from managing the NamibRand nature reserve. *Great Plains Research*, 20 (1), 29–36.

Pooley, S., et al. (2016). An interdisciplinary review of current and future approaches to improving human–predator relations. *Conservervation Biology*, 31 (3), 513–523.

Prins, H. H.T., Grootenhuis, J. G., & Dolan, T.T. (2000). *Wildlife conservation by sustainable use*. Boston, MA: Kluver Academic Publishers.

Ravenelle, J., & Nyhus, P. J. (2017). Global patterns and trends in human–wildlife conflict compensation. *Conservation Biology*, 31, 1247–1256.

Redpath, S. M., Gutiérrez, R. J., Wood, K. A., & Young, J. C. (Eds.) (2015). *Conflicts in conservation: Navigating towards solutions*. Cambridge: Cambridge University Press.

Reid, H. (2001). Contractual national parks and the Makuleke Community. *Human Ecology*, 29 (2), 135–155.

Reid, H. (2002). Contractual national parks: Meeting conservation and development objectives in South Africa and Australia. PhD thesis, Durrell Institute of Conservation and Ecology, University of Kent at Canterbury.

Schwartzman, S., Moreira, A., & Nepstad, D. 2000. Rethinking tropical forest conservation: Perils in parks. *Conservation Biology*, 15, 1351–1357.

Shaffer, L. J., Khadka, K. K., van Den Hoek, J., & Naithani K. J. (2019). Human–elephant conflict: A review of current management strategies and future directions. *Frontiers in Ecology and Evolution*, 6, article 235.

Steenkamp, C. (1999). *The Makuleke land claim: Power relations and CBNRM, evaluating Eden*. London: IIED.

Taylor, R.D. 2009. Community based natural resource management in Zimbabwe: The experience of CAMPFIRE. *Biodiversity Conservation*, 18 (10), 2563–2583.

Tchakatumba, P. K., Gandiwa, E., Mwakiwa, E., Clegg, B., & Nyasha, S. (2019). Does the CAMPFIRE programme ensure economic benefits from wildlife to households in Zimbabwe? *Ecosystems and People*, 15 (1), 119–135.

Woodroffe, R., Hedges, S., & Durant, S. M. (2014). To fence or not to fence. *Science*, 344, 46–48.

Young, J. C., Marzano, M., White, R. M., McCracken, D. I., Redpath, S. M., Carss, D. N., Quine, C. P., & Watt, A. D. (2010). The emergence of biodiversity conflicts from biodiversity impacts: characteristics and management strategies. *Biodiversity Conservation*, 19, 3973–3990.

Young, J. C., Searle, K., Butler, A., Simmons, P., Watt, A. D., & Jordan, A. (2016). The role of trust in the resolution of conservation conflicts. *Biological Conservation*, 195, 196–202.

9 Protected areas and community-based tourism

The effectiveness of current mitigation techniques in human wildlife conflicts

Patricia Kefilwe Mogomotsi and Goemeone E. J. Mogomotsi

Introduction

Over the years, various scholars have proposed the development of several systematic approaches to conservation to guide the efficient allocation of scarce resources available for protecting biodiversity and combating conflicts over natural resources (McIntosh et al., 2017; Young et al., 2016). Protected areas are often viewed as one of the most effective measures for conserving the integrity of the natural environment, ecosystems and natural resources. Globally, 16.64% of the land area has been designated as conserved and protected areas (United Nations Environment Programme (UNEP), 2021). These areas are crucial in conserving natural resources and promoting ecosystem diversity. They are used as important tourist attractions. The World Tourism Organisation (WTO, 2004) defines sustainable tourism in protected areas as tourism 'leading to management of all resources in such a way that economic, social and aesthetic needs can be fulfilled while maintaining cultural integrity, essential ecological processes, biological diversity and life support systems'.

Tourism in protected areas has both positive and negative consequences for natural resources and socio-economic livelihoods of communities living adjacent to protected areas. On the one hand, successful instances of tourism in protected areas have been applauded for the creation of jobs for local communities, generation of revenues for the maintenance of protected areas (Thompson et al., 2014), conservation of local biodiversity as well as natural and cultural heritage and offsetting the cost of conservation (Eagles et al., 2002). It also leads to the promotion of social welfare through strengthening the local economy (Brown, 2001). On the other hand, some negative impacts of tourism in protected areas include the imposition of financial and economic loss to poor people living adjacent to protected areas (Brown, 2001), unfair distribution of profits accrued from tourism in favour of the private sector (Bosselman et al., 1999) and adverse impacts on the environment which can pose challenges in managing the ecology, environment and economy (Leung et al., 2018).

DOI: 10.4324/9781003193166-11

Mitigation techniques: human wildlife conflicts 115

Studies have argued that the proximity of some communities to protected areas and the uneven scale of distribution of benefits from tourism in protected areas have consequently led to, and fueled, human–wildlife conflicts in some areas in Africa and globally (Mogomotsi et al., 2020a, 2020b; Treves et al., 2006). Human–wildlife conflicts are loosely defined as tensions between people and wildlife caused by increasing overlaps between resource demands of humans and wild animals, prompting competition for food, land and water (Woodroffe et al., 2005). These conflicts do not only undermine the mutual well-being of humans and wildlife, but they also threaten the sustainability of some wildlife resources. Human–wildlife conflicts are viewed as a major challenge for conservation (Treves et al., 2006; Woodroffe et al., 2005) as they lead to negative attitudes toward wildlife conservation and general aversion toward wildlife resources (Mogomotsi et al., 2020b).

As argued by Snijders et al. (2019, p. 2), for time immemorial, human–wildlife conflicts had been contentious issues, as exemplified by a quote by Titus Plautus (254–184 BC): 'Where there are sheep, the wolves are never very far away.' Equally, human–wildlife conflict resolution approaches, practices and mechanisms have evolved throughout the years. The interventions range from lethal to non-lethal. The efficacy of these interventions in Southern Africa remains under-researched.

In rural Southern Africa, communities living adjacent to protected areas are often exposed to various costs. These include loss of livestock due to predation, crop destruction, loss of human lives due to human–wildlife conflicts and livestock diseases due to livestock–wildlife interactions (Matseketsa et al., 2019). The costs are even more pronounced for communities residing close to protected areas housing large to very large-bodied herbivores, such as the African buffalo (*Syncerus caffer*), common hippopotamus (*Hippopotamus amphibius*) and African elephant (*Loxodonta africana*), and large carnivores, for example lion (*Panthera leo*), spotted hyena (*Crocuta crocuta*) and leopard (*Panthera pardus*) (Matseketsa et al., 2019). The permeable boundaries of protected areas exacerbate human–wildlife conflicts in Southern Africa, leading to negative impacts on livelihoods.

This chapter underscores the need for more studies to understand the effectiveness of various approaches to mitigating human–wildlife conflicts in Southern Africa. Specifically, this chapter seeks to (i) determine factors influencing the choice of human–wildlife conflict mitigation strategies in Southern Africa, (ii) discuss lethal approaches to mitigating human–wildlife conflicts and (iii) discuss non-lethal approaches to mitigating human–wildlife conflicts. The discussions of the lethal and non-lethal interventions are biased towards analysing reviews on their effectiveness. Understanding the effectiveness, or lack thereof, of these conflict mitigation approaches is paramount in determining the appropriate approaches for communities to promote human–wildlife coexistence.

Methods

This chapter used a systematic literature review to identify, select and critically appraise literature sources to answer clearly formulated research questions. It follows a predefined search protocol for identifying studies and to synthesise literature. The systematic literature review focused on mitigation approaches to human–wildlife conflicts. The focus was narrowed down to human–wildlife conflicts in protected areas and against community-based tourism in southern Africa for a period of 20 years between 2000 and 2020. The systematic review process was performed over a period of four weeks in May 2021. The available literature sources were systematically identified in electronic databases such as Google Scholar, ProQuest, EBSCO Discovery Service and African Journal Index. The search used keywords such as human–wildlife conflicts, human–wildlife interactions, effectiveness of countermeasures of human–wildlife conflicts, conflicts in protected areas, hunting in conservation areas, ecotourism, community-based tourism and sustainable rural tourism, among others. The chapter adopted a systematic review process designed by Best et al. (2014). Through the process, the available literature directly related to the research objectives of this chapter was collated and catalogued. The cataloguing exercise is crucial for addressing policy-based questions. The selected papers were then screened, and relevant papers were selected using the systematic search strategy.

Factors influencing the choice of human–wildlife conflict mitigation strategies

In Southern Africa, there are no studies that analyse factors influencing the choice of human–wildlife conflict mitigation strategies by communities living adjacent to protected areas. Some factors influencing the choice of conflict mitigation strategies are, however, implied in some studies. The factors often vary according to the species of wildlife in conflict, level and frequency of crop raiding or livestock depredation, the actual and perceived costs of conflict, and social acceptability (Dickman, 2010; Mogomotsi, 2019).

Dickman (2010) conceptualises the process of identifying appropriate human–wildlife conflict as a three-assumptions process. These assumptions are that: '(A) the level of wildlife damage is directly related to the level of conflict engendered; (B) the level of conflict elicits a proportionate response; (C) altering the response to conflict will have proportionate conservation effects' (Dickman, 2010, p. 459). The process has an impact on the overall conservation efforts and success.

Lethal approaches to mitigating human–wildlife conflicts

Over the years, lethal approaches have been commonly used in managing and mitigating human–wildlife conflicts in Africa. Lethal means are often used in controlling abundant and problem wildlife species. Researchers also argue that lethal approaches are justifiable in selectively removing aggressive animals that pose as direct threats to human life (McManus et al., 2015; Matseketsa et al., 2019) or to the livelihoods of people living adjacent to protected areas. Often, the main justification for lethal conflict mitigation intervention is conflict prevention (McManus et al., 2015). This reasoning follows the underlying assumption that conflicts decline when wild animals are permanently removed. However, eradication is not a straightforward exercise as it may lead to unpredictable and unintended consequences (Treves & Naughton-Treves, 2005). There are various forms of lethal means to mitigating human–wildlife conflicts. These include physical techniques, chemical and biological methods, as well as governance approaches using regulated and unregulated hunting (Rochlitz et al., 2010; McManus et al., 2015).

Physical techniques used in some African countries include firearms and traps such as neck snares and rotating-jaw snares (Treves & Naughton-Treves, 2005; Matseketsa et al., 2019). In a study by McManus et al. (2015), it was established that farmers in South Africa eradicate carnivores and other problem animals using such physical methods as gin-traps and gun traps. However, in most cases, the physical measures have proven to be largely ineffective as depredation persists in pastoral communities, with indications that financial losses and losses to livelihoods are escalating (Avenant & du Plessis, 2008, McManus et al., 2015). In Kenya, ranchers conceal themselves in blinds at the site of fresh livestock kills to shoot and kill suspected culprit lions as a way of mitigating depredation (Treves & Naughton-Treves, 2005). A study by Matseketsa et al. (2019) revealed that in some communities in Zimbabwe, farmers set snares on the outskirts of fields, mainly to stop small to medium body-sized crop raiding wild ungulates. Although snares have been effective in capturing some problem animals in Zimbabwe and other African countries, some researchers caution that captures in snares pose a danger to people and other animal species, leading to proneness to extinction and injury of untargeted species (Distefano, 2005). This is because snares are not discriminatory in injuring, endangering and killing humans, livestock and untargeted wildlife species. The largely indiscriminate killing of non-target species, humans and livestock reflects the ineffectiveness of snares in mitigating conflicts.

Chemical and biological methods such as pesticides and other chemicals can be used as fear-provoking stimuli to repel, startle or divert problem animals as a way of mitigating human–wildlife conflicts in some communities in Africa. When the chemicals lead to killings of targeted and non-targeted wildlife species, they are viewed as lethal. However, when the chemicals merely deter, repel and are aversive, they are classified as non-lethal (Mason, Shivik & Fall, 2001). In South Africa, the use of poisons and other chemicals in killing problem animals has posed threats of extinction to species such as Cape vultures (*Gyps coprotheres*), leading to costs in conserving such species for future generations (Bamford et al., 2007). The indiscriminate nature of the approach has often led to unintended outcomes of perturbation effects (Tuyttens & Macdonald, 2000; McManus et al., 2015), due to an increased risk of 'an influx of replacement individuals, potentially increasing the local predator population and the risk of depredation' (McManus et al., 2015, p. 688). It has been argued that there has been an increase in the demand for chemicals as a human–wildlife conflict management approach (Mason et al., 2001). However, the evidence of effectiveness of such an approach remains virtually non-existent (Mason et al., 2001) largely due to the indiscriminate nature of the approach, posing danger to livestock, humans and non-target species.

In most countries in Southern Africa, institutions are used to govern the acts of regulated hunting and to guard against poaching and other unregulated hunting activities. The use of institutions and governance tools combines monitoring and lethal approach to mitigating human–wildlife conflicts and achieve conservation objectives (Nyhus, 2016). In some countries in Southern Africa, sanctioned lethal control, such as safari and sport hunting, is often both a preventative and remedial measure to shift the attitudes of people living adjacent to protected areas positively. In Africa, the roots of safari hunting can be traced back to the colonial era (Wilkie & Carpenter, 1999). During this period, many protected areas in Africa were established as sanctuaries for the remaining populations of trophy animals that had escaped the white hunters, and proceeds from safari hunting were used to finance colonisation (Wilkie & Carpenter, 1999).

In recent years, safari hunting activities and rights have taken various forms in Southern Africa. For example, in Zimbabwe, through the Communal Areas Management Programme for Indigenous Resources (CAMPFIRE), rural district councils, on behalf of communities on communal land, are given the authority to act as intermediaries providing market access for wildlife to safari operators (Frost & Bond, 2008). The programme allows for the sale of hunting rights predominantly to foreign sport hunters and eco-tourists (Frost & Bond, 2008). Although the rural district councils are mandated by the government to receive and manage the revenues collected from safari hunting activities, 'the principal service sellers in CAMPFIRE are the farming communities, whose land- and resource-use decisions ultimately determine the fate of wildlife' (Frost & Bond, 2008, p. 778). However, Dube (2019) argues that the contribution of CAMPFIRE to local economic development has proven to be less effective due to market challenges and the exclusion of the local communities who are the producer constituency. Moreover, the killing of Cecil the Lion in Zimbabwe by an American hunter in 2015 sparked multi-pronged and polarised debates on the effectiveness of safari hunting. On the one hand, hunters and pragmatic conservationists support safari hunting as its benefits trickle down to communities, which is imperative for wildlife conservation (Mbaiwa, 2017). On the other hand, animal rights groups and protectionists fear that safari hunting, no matter its intended impacts, threatens the sustainability of wildlife resources and may lead to the extinction of some wildlife species (Mbaiwa, 2017). A model like Zimbabwe's CAMPFIRE in Botswana is the Community-based Natural Resource Management (CBNRM) programme.

The CBRNM programme recognises the rights of local communities in managing and deriving benefits from natural resources and wildlife conservation. The CBNRM policy reflects the Botswana government's recognition that 'sustainable and viable tourism and conservation efforts will only succeed if local communities have a stake in the preservation of wildlife and supporting ecosystems' (Chevallier & Harvey, 2016, p. 2). Communities involved in CBNRM programmes get organised through manageable and registered groups known as community-based organisations (CBOs) which are commonly called community trusts. To generate income, these CBOs usually enter joint venture partnerships (JVPs) with private tourism operators (Stone et al., 2021). Most CBOs sublease the tourism rights to a JVP tour operator and derive revenue in the form of rental fees (Cassidy, 2020; Stone et al., 2021). They also generate income by selling their hunting rights for consumptive tourism through the hunting quota system controlled by the government. It has been observed that revenues derived from safari hunting account for two-thirds of the revenue for the majority of CBOs in Botswana while photographic tourism generates only a third of community revenue (Mbaiwa, 2017). Sanctioned hunting through the hunting quota system used in Botswana is effective in not only supporting livelihoods in respective communities (Mbaiwa, 2017), but also in empowering communities, solidifying local institutions in wildlife management areas and providing employment opportunities (Stone & Stone, 2020; Stone et al., 2021). However, the effectiveness of the programme in reducing the incidence of human–wildlife conflicts is not well researched.

Through such as programmes CAMPFIRE and CBNRM, it can be argued that some governments in Southern Africa acknowledge that farmers experiencing human–wildlife conflict tend to have negative attitudes against wildlife if the conflict is not managed effectively (Mogomotsi et al., 2020b). Human–wildlife conflicts do not only continuously disempower communities living adjacent to protected areas, but they also normalise perpetual disutility (Mogomotsi & Madigele, 2017; Dube, 2019; Mogomotsi et al., 2020b), leading to negative attitudes towards wildlife, wildlife conservation and tourism development dependent on wildlife and wilderness. The disutility and negative attitudes towards wildlife consequently lead to the active participation of community members in the destruction of wildlife to compensate for reduced livelihoods (Mogomotsi et al., 2020b). Therefore, they often resort to retaliatory killings of predators and other problem animals to prevent depredation (Mogomotsi, Saayman & Saymaan, 2019). This chapter argues that the retaliatory killings of wildlife due to negative attitudes by those affected by human–wildlife conflicts are arguably one of the lethal approaches to mitigating the conflicts. The effectiveness of retaliatory killings of wildlife is far less clear because these killings have rarely been properly evaluated. However, what is clear is that the killings threaten the sustainability of wildlife resources and devalue the nature-based tourism product offered. It is, therefore, necessary for governments to invest in positively shifting the attitudes of communities in favour of wildlife conservation.

In addition to retaliatory killings of wildlife, another form of unsanctioned lethal approach to mitigating human–wildlife conflicts in some countries in Southern Africa is poaching. In this chapter, poaching is loosely defined as the killing of wild animals for subsistence, commercial or both purposes without a permit (Mogomotsi, 2019; Mogomotsi, Saayman & Saymaan, 2019). The disutility and loss of livelihoods due to human–wildlife conflicts in some communities in Southern Africa have led to the active participation of some community members in poaching activities to generate income and mitigate livelihood losses. For instance, in a study in the Okavango Delta region, Botswana, Mogomotsi et al. (2020a), argued that some communities resort to either poaching or enabling poachers to access wildlife for a fee as way of channelling their frustrations against human–wildlife conflicts as well as retaliating against the impositions of contemporary institutions that restrict hunting which were designed and implemented without prior consultation with hunting communities.

Prior to the introduction of the CBNRM programme and other contemporary conservation institutions in Botswana, some tribal groups were traditionally involved in hunting, gathering, fishing, and farming, among other activities in their customary land (Mogomotsi, 2019). Some of the traditional livelihood activities such as hunting were, however, abandoned in favour of hunting quotas and commercial hunting under CBNRM. The involvement in poaching activities as lethal approach to mitigating human–wildlife conflicts and in retaliation to contemporary institutions was also noted in communities adjacent to the Kruger National Park, South Africa (Hübschle-Finch, 2016). According to Hübschle-Finch (2016, p. 1), through killing certain wildlife species without a permit, 'The poacher is claiming back his right to hunt by poaching in modern-day conservation areas, which were the traditional hunting grounds of his forefathers'. The effectiveness of poaching by affected community members in mitigating human–wildlife conflicts in Southern Africa remains under-researched. This chapter, however, argues that poaching leads to arrests or killings of perpetrators, including affected community members. Moreover, poaching poses a serious conservation concern for many species.

Non-lethal approaches to mitigating human–wildlife conflicts

To address and counter the effects of lethal approaches to addressing human–wildlife conflict, there are several non-lethal alternatives available. These include, although they are not limited to, the translocation of problem animals, proactive guarding and herding, public education, the use of chillies, immunocontraception and other methods to control reproduction in wildlife, as well as the use of barriers and exclusionary devices. Public education is usually used to increase knowledge about human–wildlife conflicts and preventative measures for farmers and other community members (Mogomotsi, 2019).

In some countries in Southern Africa, trained dogs are used as guard animals to safeguard livestock from attacks by carnivores. In a study assessing the perceived effectiveness of guard dogs placed on Namibian farms, it was discovered that 73% of the farmers reported a significant decline in losses after the acquisition of guard dogs (Marker, Dickman & Macdonald, 2005). Similarly, 73% of the farmers reported an increase in livelihoods and an improvement in economic benefits after acquiring a guard dog (Marker et al., 2005). In a study on the perceived efficacy of livestock guarding dogs in South Africa, it was argued that livestock depredation ceased in 91% of guarding dog placements (Rust, Whitehouse-Tedd & MacMillan, 2013). One of the limiting factors to the effectiveness of guard dogs as non-lethal mitigation tools is the cost of food and general care provided by the farmer, such as the cost of preventing premature death (Nyhus, 2016). The other problems with guard dogs include the need for extensive training and control of behavioural problems (Rust et al., 2013).

Kraals serve as inexpensive non-lethal controls. They are passive barriers that require little or no technology (Sitati & Walpole, 2006). Farmers in Botswana and other Southern Africa often enclose their livestock in kraals during the night (Hoare, 2001). Strong kraals are usually 'game proof' as they prevent lions from predating on livestock (Mogomotsi, 2019). However, the long-term maintenance costs of kraals should not be ignored. Another form of barriers used in Southern Africa is the cultivation of chilli trees around fields (Hoare, 2001) and the use of traditional fencing around ploughing fields to avoid crop raiding (Nyhus, 2016). However, fences have proven to be less effective in situations where large animals such as elephants damage fences to circumvent barriers and access farms (Nyhus, 2016). The farmers are consequently faced with the costs of reconstructing and maintaining fences, which has direct implications on their livelihoods.

Some farmers use repellents such as chillies (*Capsicum* spp.) as non-lethal methods to mitigating human–wildlife conflict. For example, in Mozambique, some farmers mix ground chillies with elephant dung and then burn the dried mixture along the boundaries of fields to create an essence that deters elephants from raiding fields (Osborn and Anstey, 2002). In the Okavango Delta region in Botswana, farmers burn the chilli pepper to create an essence that serves as an active deterrent, especially for elephants (Mogomotsi, 2019). Similarly, in Kenya, the use of chillies has been found to be effective in deterring African elephants (*Loxodanta africana*) from raiding crops (Sitati & Walpole, 2006).

Governments may also resort to using translocations as non-lethal tools. This entails selectively moving wildlife away from locations where human–wildlife conflict is occurring or likely to occur (Nyhus, 2016). Due to their non-lethal nature, translocations are generally viewed as more humane, leading to general acceptance and advocacy in their favour. However, the effectiveness of translocations is often questioned due to the low rates of survival of relocated wildlife species (Massei et al., 2010). The costs related to acclimatisation and reduction of mortality post-relocation contribute to the ineffectiveness of translocations. Furthermore, translocations are often associated with the

Way forward and implications for conservation

Although there are various approaches to mitigate human–wildlife conflicts ranging from lethal to non-lethal, there is no single deterrent that can adequately deter predators and crop raiders effectively. No intervention has proven to be without negative consequences either to the livelihoods of communities living adjacent to protected areas, untargeted wildlife species or livestock. In some cases, mitigation interventions, such as the use of chemicals, pose threats to communities, livestock and wildlife.

Generally, there have been controversies surrounding the use of lethal approaches in managing wildlife damage to farms. These methods usually cause social perturbation, attracting outcries against the killing and movement of some wildlife species from their territories, exposing them to increased chances of mortality at host locations. There is dearth of research on the long-term effectiveness of lethal approaches in mitigating human–wildlife conflicts in Southern Africa. Nyhus (2016) argues that selective lethal control may increase the likelihood of human–wildlife conflict. Similarly, lethal approaches to mitigating human–wildlife conflict may exacerbate conflicts, especially among African elephants, as crop raiders are often replaced by new recruits (Chiyo et al., 2011). The indiscriminate killing with some chemicals and biological methods not only threatens biodiversity but also exposes communities to danger.

Where the government uses governance and institutional mechanisms to mitigate conflicts, the interests of communities form the central tenet, and the aim is generally to shift the attitudes of communities living near protected areas in favour of conservation. In Botswana, the promotion of consumptive tourism through the CBNRM programmes has led to income generation for communities, communities' empowerment, strengthening of local institutions in wildlife management areas and the provision of employment opportunities. However, the question of whether sanctioned hunting and consumptive tourism have succeeded in serving as deterrents and mitigation approaches to conflicts remains due to a dearth of research analysing the effectiveness of these approaches in Botswana. Some studies on the effectiveness of CAMPFIRE programme in mitigating conflicts in Zimbabwe have, however, cautioned that, although the programme is effective in promoting positive attitudes of communities towards conservation (Dube, 2019), the efficacy of the programme in mitigating conflicts in the long run is questioned (Treves and Naughton-Treves, 2005). For example, heavily hunted populations stimulate more conflict as their age structure shifts towards younger, inexperienced predators, which may turn to predictable but risky foods like livestock (Treves & Naughton-Treves, 2005). Moreover, when trophy hunting is carried out by less trained hunters, it may result in higher frequencies of injured animals. The injured animals especially carnivores, in turn, cause more conflicts (Treves & Naughton-Treves, 2005).

The ineffectiveness and lack of social acceptability of some lethal control methods have focused attention on possible non-lethal interventions. One of the main advantages of non-lethal interventions is that although they alter the behaviour of wildlife, they have reduced chances of mortality. Furthermore, non-lethal approaches are generally feasible and less costly when employed in small-scale farms and ranches (Gehring et al., 2010). As argued by Stone et al. (2017, p. 34), 'the question then becomes not just whether nonlethal deterrents can work but whether they are feasible in large landscapes'. Some scholars have dismissed non-lethal methods as impractical and limited in their effectiveness due to the habituation of targeted wildlife species to deterrent stimuli over time (Smallidge et al., 2008: Stone et al., 2017).

The lack of efficacy for all the discussed mitigation strategies reflects the absence of a perfect approach. This chapter, therefore, argues that governments and other stakeholders should embrace integrated interventions with an understanding of the people's expectations, realities and attitudes to ensure efficacy. Effective human–wildlife conflict resolution processes necessitate a balance of practical solutions, outreach and a better understanding of both the ecology of the species concerned and the social psychology of the people affected. Ineffective conflict mitigation strategies often lead to retaliatory killings of problem animals. These killings are detrimental to the sustainability of wildlife and biodiversity conservation. For example, in a study of leopards (*Panthera pardus*) in South Africa, it was discovered that retaliatory killings of problem animals led to high levels of leopard mortality compared to recreational sport hunting (Swanepoel, Somers & Dalerum, 2015). This posed increased risks to leopard population viability. In addition, the lack of efficacy of conflict mitigation approaches often leads to increased expectations on the government to compensate affected farmers (Campbell, 2000; Hill, 2004), which puts added pressure on the government's resources. 'If such expectations are not met, any alternative mitigation strategies may be ignored or discounted by farmers' (Hill, 2004, p. 283), leading to a vicious cycle of unsatisfied farmers who may resort to retaliatory killings of problem animals.

Conclusion

In Southern Africa, some communities living adjacent to protected areas are faced with costs to livelihoods due to high incidences of human–wildlife conflicts. Consequently, these communities often develop negative attitudes towards wildlife and nature-based tourism, especially if they do not receive any benefits from the resources and their respective activities. These negative attitudes undermine conservation efforts as they may lead to such acts as retaliatory killings of problem animals and/or the enabling or direct involvement of poaching within communities. To break this vicious cycle, there is a pressing need to counter-balance losses instigated by human–wildlife conflicts with benefits, protect the livelihoods of communities living adjacent to protected areas and to promote positive attitudes towards wildlife conservation. These

124 *Patricia Kefilwe Mogomotsi and Goemeone E. J. Mogomotsi*

require attaining an intricate balance between promoting biodiversity sustainability and protecting communities' livelihoods through employing conflict management interventions that work well for both communities and wildlife. This prompts a need for both correlation-based and quantitative studies assessing the efficacy of conflict mitigation approaches, paying due regard to community attitudes and degree of acceptance. Effective human–wildlife strategies are crucial in contributing to sustainable tourism, community development, improved livelihoods and protection of biodiversity. This chapter has not, however, exhausted all the conflict mitigation strategies used in southern African farms. Research is needed to assess the effectiveness of all the lethal, non-lethal and integrated approaches to mitigating conflicts in Southern Africa. Additional research is needed to evaluate factors that influence the choice of mitigation strategies address the research gap identified by this chapter.

References

Avenant, N. L., & Du Plessis, J. J. (2008). Sustainable small stock farming and ecosystem conservation in Southern Africa: A role for small mammals? *Mammalia*, 72, 258–263.

Bamford, A. J., Diekmann, M., Monadjem, A., & Mendelsohn, J. (2007). Ranging behaviour of Cape Vultures Gyps coprotheres from an endangered population in Namibia. *Bird Conservation International*, 17, 331–339.

Best, P., Manktelow, R., & Taylor, B. (2014). Online communication, social media and adolescent wellbeing: A systematic narrative review. *Children and Youth Services Review*, 41, 27–36.

Bosselman, R., Chon, K., Teare, R., & Costa, J. (1996). Review of graduate education and research in hospitality and tourism management. *International Journal of Contemporary Hospitality Management*, 8 (4): 37–40.

Brown, C. R. (2001). *Visitor use fees in protected areas: Synthesis of the North American, Costa Rican and Belizean Experience*. Arlington, VA: The Nature Conservancy. Retrieved from nature.org/aboutus/travel/ecotourism/resources/

Campbell, B. (2000). Animals behaving badly: Indigenous perceptions of wildlife protection in Nepal. In Knight, J. (Ed.), *Natural enemies: People–wildlife conflicts in anthropological perspective*. London: Routledge, 124–144.

Cassidy, L. (2020). Power dynamics and new directions in the recent evolution of CBNRM in Botswana. *Conservation Science and Practice*, 3 (1), e205.

Chevallier, R., & Harvey, R. (2016). *Is community based natural resource management in Botswana viable?* Johannesburg: South African Institute of International Affairs (SAIIA).

Chiyo, P., Moss, C., Archie, E., Hollister-Smith, J., & Alberts, C. (2011). Using molecular and observational techniques to estimate the number and raiding patterns of crop-raiding elephants. *Journal of Applied Ecology*, 48 (3): 788–796.

Dickman, A. J. (2010). Complexities of conflict: The importance of considering social factors for effectively resolving human–wildlife conflict. *Animal Conservation*, 3, 458–466.

Distefano, E. (2005). *Human–wildlife conflict worldwide: Collection of case studies, analysis of management strategies and good practices*. Rome: Food and Agricultural Organization of the United Nations (FAO), Sustainable Agriculture and Rural Development (SARD).

Dube, N. (2019). Voices from the village on trophy hunting in Hwange District, Zimbabwe. *Ecological Economics*, 159, 335–343.

Eagles, P. F., McCool, S. F., & Haynes, C. (2002). *Sustainable Tourism in Protected Areas: Guidelines for Planning and Management.* Best Practice Protected Area Guidelines Series No. 8. Gland, Switzerland: IUCN.

Frost, P. G., & Bond, I. (2008). The CAMPFIRE programme in Zimbabwe: Payments for wildlife services. *Ecological Economics*, 65 (4): 776–787.

Gehring, T. M., Vercauteren, K. C., Provost, M. L., & Cellar, A. C. (2010). Utility of livestock-protection dogs for deterring wildlife from cattle farms. *Wildlife Research*, 37, 715–721.

Hill, C. M. (2004). Farmers' perspectives of conflict at the wildlife–agriculture boundary: Some lessons learned from African subsistence farmers. *Human Dimensions of Wildlife*, 9 (4), 279–286.

Hoare, R. E. (2001). *A decision support system for managing human–elephant conflict situations in Africa.* Nairobi: IUCN African Elephant Specialist Group.

Hübschle-Finch, A. (2016). Wildlife crime: Why do local communities poach? Retrieved from http://pubman.mpdl.mpg.de/pubman/faces/viewItemOverview Page.jsp?itemId=escidoc:23

Leung, Y., Spenceley, A., Hvenegaard, G., & Buckley, R. (2018). *Tourism and visitor management in protected areas: Guidelines for sustainability.* Gland, Switzerland: IUCN.

Marker, L. L., Dickman, A. J., & Macdonald, D. W. (2005). Perceived effectiveness of livestock-guarding dogs placed on Namibian farms. *Rangeland Ecology and Management*, 58, 329–336.

Mason, J. R., Shivik, J. A., & Fall, M. W. (2001). Chemical repellents and other aversive strategies in predation management. *Endangered Species Update*, 18, 175–181.

Massei, G., Quy, R. J., Gurney, J., & Cowan, D. P. (2010). Can translocations be used to mitigate human–wildlife conflicts? *Wildlife Research*, 37 (5), 428–439.

Matseketsa, G., Muboko, N., Gandiwa, E., Kombora, D. M., & Chibememe, G. (2019). An assessment of human–wildlife conflicts in local communities bordering the western part of Save Valley Conservancy, Zimbabwe. *Global Ecology and Conservation*, 20, e00737.

Mbaiwa, J. E. (2017). Poverty or riches: Who benefits from the booming tourism industry in Botswana? *Journal of Contemporary African Studies*, 35 (1), 93-112.

McIntosh, E. J., Pressey, R. L., Lloyd, S., Smith, R. J., & Grenyer, R. (2017). The impact of systematic conservation planning. *Annual Review of Environment and Resources*, 42, 677–697.

McManus, J. S., Dickman, A. J., Gaynor, D., Smuts, B. H., & Macdonald, D. W. (2015). Dead or alive? Comparing costs and benefits of lethal and non-lethal human–wildlife conflict mitigation on livestock farms. *Oryx*, 49 (4), 687–695.

Mogomotsi, G. E. J., & Madigele, P. K. (2017). Live by the gun, die by the gun: Botswana's 'shoot-to-kill' policy as an anti-poaching strategy. *South African Crime Quarterly*, 60, 51–59.

Mogomotsi, P. K. (2019). An institutional framework for the sustainable co-existence of tourism and agriculture in Botswana. PhD thesis, North-West University, Potchefstroom.

Mogomotsi, P. K., Mogomotsi, G. E. J, Dipogiso, K., Phonchi-Tshekiso, N. D., Stone, L. S., & Badimo, D. (2020a). An analysis of communities' attitudes toward wildlife and implications for wildlife sustainability. *Tropical Conservation Science*, 13. https://doi.org/10.1177/1940082920915603.

Mogomotsi, P. K., Saayman, M., & Saayman, A. (2019). The analysis of conflict and coexistence of traditional and contemporary land uses. In Stone, M. T., Lenao, M., & Moswete, N. (Eds.), *Natural resources, tourism and community livelihoods in Southern Africa: Challenges of sustainable development*. London: Routledge, 93–107.

Mogomotsi, P. K., Stone, L. S., Mogomotsi, G. E. J., & Dube, N. (2020b). Factors influencing community participation in wildlife conservation. *Human Dimensions of Wildlife*, 25 (4), 372–386.

Nyhus, P. J. (2016). Human–wildlife conflict and coexistence. *Annual Review of Environment and Resources*, 41, 143–171.

Osborn, F. V., & Anstey, S. (2002). *Elephant/human conflict and community development around the Niassa Reserve, Mozambique*. Harare, Zimbabwe: Mid Zambezi Elephant Project.

Rochlitz, I., Pearce, G. P., & Broom, D. M. (2010). *The impact of snares on animal welfare*. Cambridge: Cambridge University Press.

Rust, N. A., Whitehouse-Tedd, K. M., & MacMillan, D. C. (2013). Perceived efficacy of livestock-guarding dogs in South Africa: Implications for cheetah conservation. *Wildlife Society Bulletin*, 37 (4): 690–697.

Sitati, N. W., & Walpole, M. J. (2006). Assessing farm-based measures for mitigating human–elephant conflict in Transmara District, Kenya. *Oryx*, 40 (3), 279–286.

Smallidge, S. T., Halbritter, H., Ashcroft, N. K., & Boren, J. C. (2008). *Review of livestock management practices to minimize livestock depredation by wolves: Applicability to the Southwest*. Las Cruces, NM: New Mexico State University.

Snijders, L., Greggor, A. L., Hilderink, F., & Doran, C. (2019). Effectiveness of animal conditioning interventions in reducing human–wildlife conflict: A systematic map protocol. *Environmental Evidence*, 8 (suppl 1), 10.

Stone, M. T., & Stone, L. S. (2020). Challenges of community-based tourism in Botswana: A review of literature. *Transactions of the Royal Society of South Africa*, 75 (2), 181–193.

Stone, L. S., Stone, M. T., Mogomotsi, G. E. J, & Mogomotsi, P. K. (2021). The impacts of Covid-19 on nature-based tourism in Botswana: Implications for community development. *Tourism Review International*, 25 (2–3), 263–278.

Stone, S. A., Breck, S. W., Timberlake, J., Haswell, P. M., Najera, F., Bean, B. S., & Thornhill, D. J. (2017). Adaptive use of nonlethal strategies for minimizing wolf–sheep conflict in Idaho. *Journal of Mammalogy*, 98 (1), 33–44.

Swanepoel, L. H., Somers, M. J., & Dalerum, F. (2015). Functional responses of retaliatory killing versus recreational sport hunting of leopards in South Africa. *PLoS One*, 10, e0125539.

Thompson, A., Massyn, P. J., Pendry, J., & Pastoreli, J. (2014). *Tourism concessions in protected natural areas: Guidelines for managers*. New York: UN Development Programme.

Treves, A., Andiamampianina, L., Didier, K., Gibson, J., Plumptre, A., Wilkie, D., & Zahler, P. (2006). A simple, cost-effective method for involving stakeholders in spatial assessments of threats to biodiversity. *Human Dimensions of Wildlife*, 11 (1), 43–54.

Treves, A., & Naughton-Treves, L. (2005). Evaluating lethal control in the management of human–wildlife conflict. In Woodroffe, R., Thirgood, S., & Rabinowitz, A., *People and wildlife, conflict or coexistence?* Cambridge: Cambridge University Press, 86–106.

Tuyttens, F. A., & Macdonald, D. W. (2000). Consequences of social perturbation for wildlife management and conservation. In Gosling, L. M., & Sutherland, W. J. (Eds.), *Behaviour and conservation*. Cambridge: Cambridge University Press, 315–329.

United Nations Environment Programme, World Conservation Monitoring Centre & International Union for Conservation of Nature. (2020). *Protected planet report 2020*. Cambridge: Protected Planet Report 2021.

Wilkie, D. S., & Carpenter, J. F. (1999). The potential role of safari hunting as a source of revenue for protected areas in the Congo Basin. *Oryx*, 33 (4): 339–345.

Woodroffe, R., Thirgood, S., & Rabinowitz, A. (2005). *People and wildlife, conflict or coexistence?* Cambridge: Cambridge University Press.

WTO. (2004). *Concepts and definitions: Sustainable development of tourism conceptual definition*. Washington, DC: World Tourism Organisation (WTO).

Young, J. C., Thompson, D. B., Moore, P., MacGugan, A., Watt, A., & Redpath, S. M. (2016). A conflict management tool for conservation agencies. *Journal of Applied Ecology*, 53, 705–711.

Part III

Managing the wildlife economy

Contemporary issues in Southern Africa

10 Lifting of the hunting ban and the elephant debate in Botswana

Implications for conservation and development in Southern Africa

Joseph Elizeri Mbaiwa and Emmanuel Mogende

Introduction

For several years, Botswana has been widely acclaimed as a success story in conservation circles due to its commitment to biodiversity conservation and sustainable utilisation of natural resources. This commitment is reflected in setting aside 17% of the country's land as national parks and game reserves, with an additional 22% of land dedicated to wildlife management areas (WMAs), making Botswana one of the most well conserved countries in the world (Death, 2016; Lindsey et al., 2007). These protected areas have an abundance of wildlife, for instance, the country has the largest elephant population which feature prominently in the country's tourism and conservation profile, attracting thousands of tourists from afar (Chase, 2011). Wildlife conservation has significantly contributed to the country's economy, with wildlife-based tourism coming second after diamond mining (Mbaiwa, 2018). It is also considered key towards driving the country's green economy (Mogende & Ramutsindela, 2020). Wildlife-based tourism activities in Botswana include consumptive (trophy hunting) and non–consumptive activities (photographic/game viewing) (Mbaiwa, 2018).

Despite Botswana's commitment towards wildlife conservation, the consumptive use of wildlife, mainly through trophy hunting remains a contested and controversial issue. In 2014 the government of Botswana led by the former president Lieutenant General Ian Khama, well known for his commitment and passion for wildlife conservation worldwide, imposed a nation–wide moratorium on trophy hunting, which was reversed in 2019 by his successor President Mokgweetsi Masisi. The decision to recommence hunting by President Masisi reignited intense debates around trophy hunting among conservationists and caused an international uproar on social media from animal welfare rights activists in the Global North, with some calling for a tourism boycott of Botswana (Mkono, 2018; Bornfree, 2019). Elephants, often considered as gentle and charismatic species by the Western audiences (Garland, 2008), are at the centre in the debate over the reintroduction of hunting. Voices often neglected in the debates, however, are those from the local communities who bear the

DOI: 10.4324/9781003193166-13

cost of living with these charismatic species (Mkono, 2019). Indications are that the views on trophy hunting are polarised among scholars and conservationists. On one side are the hunting lobby groups whose arguments highlight the socio-economic benefits of hunting for wildlife conservation and local communities (Lindsey et al., 2007; Rust & Verissimo, 2015; Di Minin et al., 2016). On the other side are anti-hunting groups who view trophy hunting as unpalatable or unethical and argue that the socio-economic benefits are insignificant (Batavia et al., 2018; Campbell, 2013; Flynn, 2019). We contribute to these debates by arguing that trophy hunting is relevant for wildlife conservation and the improvement of livelihoods of communities adjacent to conservation areas who bear the cost of living with elephants. In addition, trophy hunting can help reverse the negative attitudes adjacent communities have developed towards wildlife that threaten conservation efforts. Although there is a global campaign against trophy hunting, we are of the view that the call for the ban on this industry should not be applied indiscriminately without consideration for the variations of species management that exist in different parts of the world, as is the case with the high elephant population in Botswana.

The chapter draws on qualitative fieldwork by both authors, before and after the hunting ban. This includes a series of key informant interviews with government officials at the Ministry of Environment, Natural Resources Conservation & Tourism, local chiefs and farmers in wildlife areas, review of materials by government and community-based organisations, sustained engagement with domestic and international media reports and social media content (Facebook and Twitter). Most of the social media posts were made by citizens from Western countries voicing out their opposition to trophy hunting.

The chapter is structured as follows. The section that follows discusses the social-ecological systems that underpin the theoretical framework for the chapter. Next, we provide arguments for and against trophy hunting as debated in the conservation literature. From there we analyse the conservation and development implications of the hunting ban introduced in 2014. Next, the chapter analyses the lifting of the hunting ban with a focus on the controversial elephant debate that clouded the anti-hunting lobby group.

The social-ecological systems (SESs) theoretical framework

The social-ecological systems (SES) framework evolved from the recognition of the needed close interactions between society, in terms of social-economic systems and natural systems (Petrosillo et al., 2015). Ostrom (2014) notes that SESs recognise that local communities should be able to derive sufficient benefits from a resource that outweigh the costs of damage caused by the resource (e.g. wildlife damage to people, crops, livestock and property), as well as the costs of managing and monitoring the resource. The SES is the cornerstone of a community conservation framework for policymakers and conservationists (Fynn et al., 2019). If resources are not highly valuable to local communities, they will not have an incentive to conserve them (Fynn et al., 2019). Wildlife ecosystems are not merely ecological systems, driven only by ecological factors but are also social-ecological systems where social and political forces play a major role in determining the character and sustainability of wildlife populations and their associated habitats (Fynn et al., 2019).

If the conservation of wildlife in Botswana is to be sustainable and successful, it must be managed under the SES framework. The SES argues that ecosystems are components of social-ecological systems where biodiversity is affected not only by ecological factors but also social and political factors (Anderies et al., 2004; Agrawal, 2001; Meinzen-Dick et al., 2002; Ostrom, 1990; Poteete et al., 2010; Wollenberg et al., 2007). If social and political factors are ignored, then conservation actions may be ineffective or fail. For example, large wildlife declines have been observed across Africa because local communities resist conservation objectives (Fynn et al., 2019). Policies governing wildlife resources are not explicitly aligned with the principles of the SESs framework (Fynn et al., 2019). Under these circumstances, poaching becomes extremely difficult to contain as local communities become involved in it and resist against top-down control of wildlife resources by government agencies (Fynn et al., 2019). The SES is therefore applied in this chapter to inform the interpretation human wildlife interactions, trophy hunting and wildlife conservation in Botswana. It will also be used to analyse the Global North and South debate on the ban of trophy hunting in the Global South.

Arguments for and against trophy hunting

Trophy hunting is a type of selective recreational hunting of animals done to obtain their body parts as a representation of success or memorial (Pospisil, 2017). Trophy hunting in Africa can be traced back to the arrival of European explorers, traders and hunters around the 1800s, a period in which the continent was under colonialism (Mbaiwa 2002; Ochieng et al., 2020). It is mainly practised in 23 countries in Africa, with the largest industries occurring in Southern Africa (Lindsey et al., 2007). Trophy hunting is a controversial and contested issue. The killing of Cecil the Lion in 2015 by an American hunter in Zimbabwe and the lifting of the hunting ban in Botswana in 2019 reignited the intense debates among conservationists worldwide.

For those who support trophy hunting, their arguments highlight the economic significance to conservation and local development (Dickman et al., 2019; Di Minin et al., 2016; Gunn, 2001; Lindsey et al., 2007; MacDonald et al., 2016; Rust & Verissimo, 2015). Trophy hunting is considered a source of financial support for meaningful conservation success (Di Minin et al., 2016; Naidoo et al., 2015). Di Minin et al. (2016) argue that developing countries do not often have enough funds to support conservation hence proceeds generated from trophy hunting can be channelled towards conservation efforts. For instance, countries can employ more wildlife rangers to combat the surge of commercial poaching. Capecchi and Rogers (2015) argue that, if trophy hunting is done responsibly, 'the selling of expensive licenses to big game hunters can help pay for efforts to protect endangered species' (www.nytimes.com/2015/07/30/us/cecil-the-lion-walter-palmer.html). With regards to local development, it is argued that it boosts local economies and further encourages local communities to participate in conservation (Rust & Verissimo, 2015; Dickman et al., 2019). It should be considered that hunting takes place in marginal areas where photographic tourism is not viable. Studies have shown that communities tend to support conservation when they reap financial rewards (Lindsey et al., 2007; Naidoo et al., 2015; Mbaiwa, 2018). Booth (2010) observes that, in Namibia, there has been an increase in wildlife populations in areas where trophy hunting is taking place. As a result, trophy hunting is presented as a means of achieving biodiversity conservation and rural development simultaneously.

Despite the arguments advanced above, trophy hunting has come under strong criticism from animal rights groups. Critics point out that trophy hunting is immoral and abhorrent because animals have intelligence, emotions and social knowledge critical for their survival (Batavia et al., 2018; Ghasemi, 2020; Nelson et al., 2016). Trophy hunting will result in the extinction of animal species. For instance, in Tanzania, Packer et al. (2011) observe that lion and leopard populations have higher rates of decline in areas where trophy hunting is being practised. Batavia et al. (2018, p. 3) assert that animals are commodified and 'relegated to the sphere of mere things when they are turned into souvenirs, oddities and collectibles'. Against this backdrop, there is a growing movement calling for the industry to be banned (McNamara et al., 2015). Opponents of trophy hunting have also questioned the associated socio-economic benefits (Campbell, 2013). They argue that the evidence provided is not sufficient to conclude that trophy hunting contributes to economies of the countries. For instance, Lindsey et al. (2007) argues that hunting generates 15% of tourism revenues from only 1% of tourist arrivals, making it one of the lowest forms of tourism in Botswana. Additionally, safari hunting contributed 0.13% to Botswana's GDP (Lindsey et al., 2007). In terms of job creation, hunting employs less people in comparison to photographic safaris (Lindsey et al., 2007).

Hunting ban and its implications in Botswana

Before we dwell on the hunting ban and its implications for local development and conservation, we briefly recount the history of hunting in Botswana. Hunting in Botswana dates to the pre-colonial and colonial era and has always been inscribed in national policies. Hunting is integral to the cultural fabric of indigenous Batswana. During the pre-colonial period, hunting was considered a customary right for Batswana (Spinage, 1991). With the advent of colonialism, the hunting rights were curtailed by the British administrators and traditional leaders. Certain animals such as elephants, giraffes and eland were viewed as royal game so people were not allowed to hunt them (Spinage, 1991; Hitchcock, 2001). In post-colonial Botswana, the government introduced Special Game Licences (SGL) under the 1979 Unified Hunting Regulations (Hitchcock,

2001). The licences were issued to persons whose traditional livelihoods depended on hunting and gathering of veld products, particularly those living in remote areas such as the Basarwa (Hitchcock, 2001).

The government held the view that the sustainable utilisation of wildlife would improve the welfare of rural households as a source of animal protein and income, through the sales of trophies and curios (BNARS, 1988). However, the SGL programme faced several challenges. According to Hitchcock (2001) some politicians argued that SGLs granted special rights to a specific class/ group of elites at the expense of all citizens. Others invoked moral and animal rights-based arguments suggesting that the hunting authorised by the SGL was inhumane (Hitchcock, 2001). Against this backdrop, SGL became null and void in 1996. For indigenous populations to benefit from hunting, they were encouraged by the government to participate in community-based natural resource management (CBNRM), where a quota system for hunting was introduced. Through CBNRM, individual hunting rights were exchanged for communal access to wildlife resources through community-based organisations (Taylor, 2002). Commercialisation of safari hunting took precedence and became a cornerstone of CBNRM. Community-based organisations sub-leased their hunting rights – the communal quota – to a private hunting operator at a fee. Literature on hunting in Botswana concurs that safari hunting played a crucial role in local economies (Mbaiwa, 2018; van der Merwe & Mokgalo, 2020). Van Der Merwe and Mokgalo (2020) reported that the industry employed approximately 1,000 people, received 350 hunters annually and sold more than 5,500 hunting days per year. They further highlight that, in 2011, safari hunting generated US$20 million in revenue from 2,500 animals sold to trophy hunters (van der Merwe & Mokgalo, 2020).

Although the industry profoundly contributed to the local economy through CBNRM, things began to change in 2014, the year in which we witnessed a transition from sustainable utilisation to a preservationist approach in wildlife conservation practice in Botswana. During his state of the nation address in November 2013, President Ian Khama announced an indefinite suspension on hunting in all controlled hunting areas save for private land with effect from 1 January 2014, citing declining wildlife numbers (Khama, 2013). A study conducted by Elephant Without Borders (EWB) reported declines in ostriches, wildebeest, tsessebe, warthogs, kudus and giraffes (Chase, 2011). Against this background, the Ministry of Environment issued a press release arguing that the decision came into effect due to the 'realization that the shooting of wild game purely for sport and trophies is no longer seen to be compatible with either our national commitment to conserve and preserve local fauna or long-term growth of the local tourism industry' (MEWT, 2013). In keeping with international trends, the government argued that the ban will facilitate the sustainable growth of the tourism sector, as hunting zones are converted into photographic areas (MEWT, 2013). With the resultant move to photographic tourism, Botswana was to attract ethical tourists to complement the high-cost, low-volume tourism model. The shift in conservation policy towards preservation was well received by the international community and animal rights groups. Through this, Botswana was viewed by many conservation organisations and animal rights groups as a 'safe haven', a 'world saver' and 'darling' of conservation (LaRocco and Mogende, forthcoming). LaRocco and Mogende (forthcoming) argue that Botswana 'painstakingly cultivated reputation into a position where Botswana was seen as one of the most valued African interlocutors in global conservation and environmental governance'.

The decision to ban hunting was viewed as serving the interests of the governing elites. For instance, having announced the hunting ban, it was speculated that former president Ian Khama was promoting his personal interests in the photographic industry where he had financial stakes (LaRocco, 2016; Mogende & Ramutsindela, 2020). Ian Khama was well known for his strong aversion to hunting. Furthermore, he appointed his young brother, to oversee the Ministry of Environment hence Mogende and Ramutsindela (2020) argue that they micro-managed the tourism industry in Botswana. Such deployments often extend patronage networks that serve certain sectional interests, in this case those who are in the photographic industry. Botswana's luxurious eco-tourism is controlled by a small white and foreign elite, but alliances are growing between this group and the traditional Tswana elite (i.e. the bureaucratic, military, business and political elite) (Swatuk, 2005; Mogende and Ramutsindela, 2020). Commentators (e.g. LaRocco, 2016; Mbaiwa & Hambira, 2020) also believed that the former president was influenced by international conservation organisations which he is affiliated to. For example, at the time Ian Khama was a board member of Conservation International. For a long time, such organisations have shaped and influenced nature conservation in Africa.

Although the ban was highly celebrated by the international community, the move was not universally popular among local conservation adjacent communities (LaRocco, 2016). For many years, safari hunting was integral to community-based organisations (CBOs) participating in the CBNRM programme (LaRocco, 2016; Mbaiwa, 2018). According to Mbaiwa (2018), the CBRNM approach was adopted by the government of Botswana in the 1980s to promote conservation and sustainable utilization of natural resources while at the same time promoting rural development and improvements in livelihoods. It is anticipated that communities living with wildlife should receive higher benefits than those who do not because they bear the cost of conservation. Although hunting does not make a significant contribution to the national economy, it directly benefited local communities (Lindsey et al., 2007). CBOs owe most of their financial income to safari hunting. Therefore, the hunting ban disrupted the pro-community CBNRM programme. Many CBOs faced financial hardship leading to pay cuts and the retrenchment of workers while some collapsed. For instance, Mbaiwa (2018) notes that in the first 12 months after the hunting ban, CBOs in Ngamiland District lost approximately BWP7 million and 200 jobs. Furthermore, the Centre for Applied Research (2016) notes that CBOs directly involved in hunting experienced revenue reductions from BWP11.3 million in 2012 to BWP5.6 million in 2015. As a result of the sharp decline in revenue, CBOs were unable to continue social and development projects. The profits accumulated from trophy hunting were mostly used to fund projects such as housing for the most vulnerable groups, water reticulation, income to households, purchasing for vehicles, campsite maintenance and construction of lodges (Mbaiwa, 2018). In addition, the hunting ban deprived local communities of meat which is a source of protein (LaRocco, 2020). It is worth mentioning that hunting is integral to the cultural fabric of many local communities and particularly so for the Basarwa community (LaRocco, 2020).

Due to reduced socio-economic benefits, Mbaiwa (2018) argues that local communities developed a negative attitude towards conservation, paving the way for illegal hunting and indiscriminate wildlife killings, e.g. through wildlife poisoning (Fynn & Kolawole, 2020). Rogan et al. (2017) reported a rise in illegal poaching, in what they refer to as bush meat hunting in the Okavango Delta, Botswana. The authors suggest that bush meat hunting threatens wildlife populations and may ultimately undermine local tourism. Not only did conservation adjacent communities' attitude towards wildlife decrease, they also developed negative attitude towards the state, resulting in tension between local communities, the private photographic tourism companies and the state (Mbaiwa, 2018).

Hunting and the elephant debate

Prior to the highly contested 2019 elections, the incumbent, President Mokgweetsi Masisi reversed the five-year moratorium on hunting. Following a motion in parliament calling for a review of the hunting ban, Masisi constituted a sub-committee of Cabinet to undertake the task. After wide consultations with various stakeholders, the government decided to reinstate hunting, giving primacy to human–wildlife conflict. This decision sparked international outrage, mainly via social media platforms (Twitter and Facebook) by citizens of the Global North as well as animal rights groups (France24, 2019; Somerville, 2019). While some considered it unethical and scandalous, some viewed it as 'Blood law', arguing that wildlife was no longer safe in Botswana (Joubert, 2019). For others, they chalked it up to a populist ploy for Masisi to win the 2019 national elections. Some social media users viewed the decision as 'senseless', 'upsetting', 'reckless', 'evil' and 'disgusting'. In short, President Masisi was portrayed as a villain to the international conservation movement (LaRocco & Mogende, forthcoming). In the aftermath, thousands of tweets originating from Western audiences began pushing for a tourism boycott of Botswana (Bornfree, 2019; Joubert, 2019).

The campaigns were led by celebrities mainly from the USA and animal rights groups such as the Humane Society of the US, Bornfree and the UK campaign to Ban Trophy Hunting. In advancing their campaigns and propaganda, Somerville (2019) asserts that such organisations often use two kinds of propaganda techniques: 1) 'card stacking' – selection and use of facts or falsehoods, illustrations or distraction to give the best or worst possible case for an idea; 2) 'cherry picking' – use of only facts and details that support their arguments and conclusions. These campaigns illustrate a dominant repetitive pattern in thinking about biodiversity conservation where the Global North proposes, and the South reacts and adapts (Kotsakis, 2016). In this way, citizens in the Global North consider their countries and global conservation non-governmental organisations such as World Wide Fund for Nature (WWF), International Union for Conservation of Nature (IUCN) and Conservation International to have superpowers, meaning that they are able to dictate how conservation should be carried out in countries in the Global South such as Botswana. Social media users from the Global North called for the intervention of these organisations to stop the reintroduction of hunting in Botswana.

More often, policies in the Global South are initiated from the global level through the formalisation of international agreements and treaties. Although countries in the Global South participate in these agreements, the discussions are usually dominated by and serve the interests of social actors from the Global North (Compagnon, 2010; Duffy, 2010; Ramutsindela & Mickler, 2020). Thus, countries from the Global South do not enter into these agreements on equal grounds with those from the Global North (Duffy, 2010). This deepens the already existing inequalities between the Global North and Global South. For instance, the contest over whether to allow ivory trade through the Convention on International Trade in Endangered Species (CITES) reveals the power imbalance between the Global North and Global South. Duffy (2010) laments the role of Northern environmental NGOs within CITES' negotiation processes, reminiscent of a colonial present shrouded beneath a veil of interstate cooperation. To illustrate this point, in 2019, CITES rejected the proposal to relax trade restrictions of ivory by Southern African countries. The proposal was rejected by 101 votes, a decision that resulted in Southern African countries threatening to withdraw their membership from CITES (News24, 2019; Down to Earth, 2019). CITES adopts a one-size-fits-all approach for all countries, without taking into consideration the variations of elephant population and management between member states and how this affects marginalised groups who live with these charismatic species. The increase in elephant population has been associated with increased human–elephant conflict in developing countries (Hoare, 2000; Mosojane, 2004).

Citizens of the Global North and anti-hunting groups overlook dissenting voices of the Global South who live in poverty and bear the associated negative costs of living with wildlife such as wildlife crop damage, property damage, livestock predation and loss of human life (Fynn et al., 2019; Mbaiwa, 2018). Ramutsindela (2016, p. 27) asserts that 'nature conservation privileges one form of knowledge system about nature above the other; this often leads to the condemnation of the ways in which marginalised groups relate to, and interact with, their physical environment'. In response to the criticism from citizens and animal rights groups of the Global North, President Masisi (2019) argued that:

> it bamboozles me when people sit in the comfort of where they come from and lecture us about the management of species they don't have. They

want to admire from a distance and in their admiration of those species, they forget that we too, the people of Botswana, are a species, they talk as if we are trees and the grass that elephants eat.

The president was applauded and defended by his citizens on social media platforms, they appreciated his stance to rebuke what they perceived as a neo-colonialist attempt by citizens of the Global North to impose their values on Botswana's system of natural resource management.

Botswana currently holds approximately 130,000 elephants, in an area that ecologically, should support fewer than 25,000 to 50,000 elephants (Government of Botswana, 2018). Chase et al. (2016, p. 18) note that Botswana is among countries in Southern Africa that 'have relatively large elephant populations and show either increasing trends or mild and non-significant declines recently'. These gentle giants are now found in areas which previously did not support elephants. For instance, elephants are now found roaming in areas not common to them such as the Central Kalahari Game Reserve and in districts such as Ghanzi, Kgalagadi, Kweneng, Kgatleng and Southern and many other villages in Botswana including Nkange, Maitengwe, Mmadinare (Mbaiwa & Hambira, 2021).

Due to an increase in the elephant population, conservation adjacent communities have experienced conflict with these gentle giants as they share space and nature resources. The increasing elephant population has resulted in extreme crop losses, property damage and injury or fatality to humans. The destruction caused by elephants was noted by communities during public consultation by the Cabinet sub-committee. For example, at Gumare Village, (Government of Botswana, 2018, p. 15), a community member remarked: 'the number of elephants has increased alarmingly since the hunting ban and has since encroached into human settlements, posing a serious threat to lives and livelihoods ... the number of human fatalities have increased'. In Maun, (Government of Botswana, 2018, p. 14), a community member remarked: 'wildlife is seemingly encroaching into human settlements'. At Plateau Kgotla, the report (Government of Botswana, 2018, p. 22) noted: 'the numbers of elephants have swelled to such large proportions that they frequently destroy property, threaten human lives as well as causing great destruction of trees and other vegetation, thus destroying food sources for other animals'. Elephants are reported to have killed 45 people in Botswana between 2009 and 2018, with 14 deaths and many serious injuries recorded since February 2018 (Dr Cyril Taolo, Acting Director of the Department of Wildlife & National Parks).

Against this backdrop, local communities developed negative attitudes towards elephants, with some local people resorting to indiscriminate wildlife killings, i.e. through wildlife poisoning thus undermining conservation efforts (Fynn and Kolawole, 2020). Roe (2020), the chair of Species Survival Commission of the International Union for Conservation of Nature (IUCN) argues that 'from the perspective of the poor rural farmer, wildlife is more a liability than an asset. To live alongside it, and tolerate it, to put up with it killing livestock and destroying crops, there need to be sound financial incentives'. Roe (2020) further argues that

140 *Joseph Elizeri Mbaiwa and Emmanuel Mogende*

'if you ban hunting but don't address human wildlife conflict in another way, the killing translates into other means – the indiscriminate killing' (see https://justc onservation.org/dossier-hunting-and-human-wildlife-conflict). That is, if crop farmers fail to see the value of wildlife resources that destroy their crops and their livelihoods, this will result in farmers failing to promote wildlife conservation. Therefore, to compensate for crop damage, farmers should be made to benefit from wildlife especially in mixed land use areas where wildlife and agricultural production are carried out in Botswana. Rather than spend funds on conservation efforts, more money has since been spent on compensating local communities for damages caused by elephants. The Acting Director of Department of Wildlife and National Parks noted that the department compensation bill has increased from BWP5 million in 2015 to BWP24 million in 2019 (Dr Cyril Taolo, personal communication, 2021). In view of the escalating compensation bill, it is not surprising that human–elephant conflict was the motivating factor to the recommencement of hunting in Botswana.

Trophy hunting as a land use tool

Most of the critics of trophy hunting do not consider trophy hunting as a land use option that can be used to promote wildlife conservation, especially in marginal areas where photographic tourism is not viable (Batavia et al., 2018). For example, the failure to utilise marginal areas for hunting in Botswana has resulted in these areas being encroached by other land uses which in turn displace wildlife resources (Verlinden et al., 1998). For example, there has been an expansion of the cattle industry into the Schwele region located in the Kalahari system. This cattle encroachment has resulted in the blockage of wildlife corridor between the northern and southern parts of the country (Verlinden et al., 1998). The former wildlife corridor has now become a cattle industry zone. The history of wildlife die-offs and their disappearance in the Schwele region in the Kalahari ecosystem and the expansion of the cattle industry is well documented (e.g. Owens & Owens, 1984; Verlinden et al., 1998; Williamson & Williamson, 1984). The expansion of the cattle industry into the Schwele region resulted in the drilling of boreholes for watering cattle, erection of veterinary fences to control livestock diseases and the establishment of ranches. This caused the blocking of wildlife migratory routes by veterinary cordon fences and subsequent wildlife deaths (Owens & Owens, 1984; Verlinden et al., 1998; Williamson & Williamson, 1984). Owens and Owens (1984) estimate the number to be 800,000 wild animals, whereas Williamson and Williamson (1981), Williamson and Mbano (1988), and Mordi (1989) put the figure at 50,000 animals. Williamson and Williamson (1984) and Murray (1988) argue that the wildebeest die-offs constitute a massive reduction in large herbivore biomass in the Kalahari system. This demonstrates that ignoring trophy hunting as a critical land use option results in marginal lands being turned into agricultural and settlement areas. As a land use option, sustainable hunting has the potential to

Lifting of hunting ban in Botswana 141

promote wildlife conservation in marginal wildlife areas. The failure to legitimize trophy hunting in the Schwele region resulted in the area becoming a cattle zone to the detriment of wildlife resource conservation. The lesson to be learned is that marginal wildlife areas are good for sustainable hunting if these wild lands are to be preserved for wildlife for future generations.

As is the case with the Schwele region in the Kalahari system, if rural communities are not deriving benefits from the wildlife in their community areas, they will encroach into these areas and turn them into agricultural land for crop and livestock production. The result will be a lost wildlife habitat which might never be recovered. Trophy hunting should be carried out as a land use option in marginal areas which cannot support photographic tourism. It is from this background that the ban on hunting or ban on trophies from wildlife imports from Africa and Botswana will not serve as a conservation means but a devastating blow to wildlife conservation in the country. The IUCN (2016) argues that 'habitat loss and degradation is a primary driver of declines in populations of terrestrial species'. The IUCN argues that 'if we ban hunting and stop managing land for the survival of wildlife, that land would inevitably be converted for other uses – in most cases to agriculture or urban settlements'.

Conclusion

In this chapter, we examined the debates over the reintroduction of hunting tourism in Botswana and what it means for wildlife conservation and local development. Elephants are a significant touchstone in the debates over hunting in Botswana and intersect with the Global North–South dynamics. Although there is a global campaign against trophy hunting, the ban on this industry should not be applied indiscriminately without consideration of cases in different parts of the world. For example, in Botswana, trophy hunting is selective and regulated. It is also carried out in a particular time of the year, termed hunting seasons. It is also carried out in marginal areas which do not support photographic tourism. As shown in this chapter, Botswana currently has the largest population of elephants: these charismatic species have put enormous pressure on conservation adjacent communities. Any ban on hunting as proposed by the Global North reverses the sustainable use and conservation of wildlife. Therefore, any policy shift that affects wildlife conservation and rural livelihoods needs to be informed by socio-economic and ecological research. This participatory and scientific approach to decision-making has the potential to contribute to the sustainability of livelihoods and wildlife conservation in Botswana and southern Africa.

References

Agrawal, A. (2001). Common property institutions and sustainable governance of resources. *World Development*, 29, 1649–1672.

142 *Joseph Elizeri Mbaiwa and Emmanuel Mogende*

Anderies, J. M., Janssen, M. A., & Ostrom, E. (2004). A framework to analyze the robustness of social-ecological systems from an institutional perspective. *Ecology and Society*, 9 (1), 18.

Batavia, C., Nelson, M., Daromont, C., Paquet, P., Ripple, W., & Wallach, A.. (2018). The elephant (head) in the room: A critical look at trophy hunting. *Conservation Letters,* 12 (1), 12565.

Booth, V. R. (2010). *The Contribution of Hunting Tourism: How Significant is this to National Economies.* CIC Technical Series Publication. Rome: FAO.

Bornfree (2019). Statement on trophy hunting. www.bornfree.org.uk/trophy-hunting

Botswana National Archives and Record Services (BNARS). (1988). Address by His Excellency Dr Q K J Masire, President of the Republic of Botswana on the official opening of the Gaborone Game Reserve, 1st March. WNP 14/24.

Campbell, R. (2013). *The $200 million question: How much does trophy hunting really contribute to African communities? A report for the African Lion Coalition.* Melbourne: Economists at Large.

Centre for Applied Research (2016). Review of community based natural resource management in Botswana. Report prepared for Southern African Environmental Programme (SAREP).

Chase, M., Schlossberg, S., Griffin, C., Bouche, P., Djene, S., Elkan, P., Ferreira, S., Grossman, F., Kohi, Z., Landen, K., Omondi, P., Peltier, A., Selier, S., & Sutcliffe, R. (2016). Continent-wide survey reveals massive decline in African savannah elephants. *PeerJ*, 4, e2354.

Chase, M. J. (2011) *Dry season fixed-wing aerial survey of elephants and wildlife in northern Botswana.* Kasane, Botswana: Elephants Without Borders.

Capecchi, C., & Rogers, K. (2015). Killer of Cecil the lion finds out that he is a target now, of internet vigilantism. *New York Times*, 29 July. www.nytimes.com/2015/07/30/us/cecil-the-lion-walter-palmer.html

Compagnon, D. (2010). Global governance and the South: Blind spot or terra incognita? *International Studies Review*, 12, 710–715.

Death, C. (2016). *The green state in Africa.* New Haven, CT: Yale University Press.

Dickman, A., Cooney, R., Johnson, P. J., Louis, M. P., & Roe, D. (2019). Trophy hunting bans imperil biodiversity. *Science*, 365, 874.

Di Minin, E., Leader-Williams, N., & Bradshaw, C. J. A. (2016). Banning trophy hunting will exacerbate biodiversity loss. *Trends in Ecology & Evolution*, 31, 99–102.

Down to Earth. (2019). CITES CoP 2019: Proposals to resume sales of ivory stockpiles rejected. *Wildlife and Biodiversity.* www.downtoearth.org.in/news/wildlife-biodiversity/cites-cop-2019-proposals-to-resume-sales-of-ivory-stockpiles-rejected-66313

Duffy, R. (2010). Global environmental governance and North-South dynamics: The case of CITES. *Environment and Planning C: Government and Policy*, 31, 222–239.

Flynn, M. (2019). Trophy hunting: Can it really be justified by conservation benefits? 29 October. https://theconversation.com/trophy-hunting-can-it-really-be-justified-by-conservation-benefits-121921.

France24 (2019). Fierce divide as Botswana lifts hunting ban. 23 May. www.france24.com/en/20190523-fierce-divide-botswana-lifts-hunting-ban

Fynn, R., & Kolawole, O. D. (2020). Poaching and the problem with conservation in Africa. Commentary. *MONGABAY: New & Inspiration from Nature's Frontline*, 3 March. https://news.mongabay.com/2020/03/poaching-and-the-problem-with-conservation-in-africa-commentary/

Fynn, R., Thakadu, O. T., & Mbaiwa, J. E. (2019). Conservation of African wildlife: Implementing scientific best practice for a sustainable future. Unpublished paper, Okavango Research Institute, University of Botswana.

Garland, E. (2008). The elephant in the room: Confronting the colonial character of wildlife conservation in Africa. *African Studies Review*, 51 (3), 51–74.

Ghasemi, B. (2020). Trophy hunting and conservation: Do the major ethical theories converge in opposition to trophy hunting? *People and Nature*, 3, 77–87.

Government of Botswana. Sub-Committee of Cabinet on Hunting Ban (2018). *Report of the Cabinet Sub Committee on Hunting Ban Social Dialogue*. Gaborone, Botswana: Ministry of Local Government and Rural Development, Unpublished Report, Government of Botswana.

Gunn, A. (2001). Environmental ethics and trophy hunting. *Ethics and Environment*, 6 (1), 68–95.

Hitchcock, R. K. (2001). Hunting is our heritage: The struggle for hunting and gathering rights among the San of Southern Africa. In Anderson, D. G., & Ikeya, K. (Eds.), *Parks, property, and power: Managing hunting practice and identify within state policy regimes*. Osaka: National Museum of Ethnology, 139–156.

Hoare, R. (2000). African elephants and humans in conflict: The outlook for co-existence. *Oryx*, 34 (1), 34–38.

IUCN. (2016). Informing decisions on trophy hunting. Briefing paper. www.iucn.org/sites/dev/files/iucn_sept_briefing_paper__informingdecisionstrophyhunting.pdf

Joubert, D. (2019). Great Plains stance to Botswanas proposed blood law. 22 February. https://mailchi.mp/greatplainsconservation/bloodlaw?fbclid=IwAR2A2Li Glh0iMAAu_wn17yHbcMd3Pf29G0LeD9eeh9E0qJISty-C5laVRUk

Khama, I. (2013). *State of the nation address by His Excellecy Lt. Gen Seretse Khama Ian Khama, to the fifth session of the tenth parliament, 4th November 2013*. Gaborone: Government Printers.

Kotsakis, A. (2016) The historical roots of the North–South dynamic in biodiversity conservation and its imprint on the Convention on biological diversity. In Razzaque, J., & Mrgera, E. (Eds.), *Biodiversity and nature protection law*. Cheltenham: Edward Elgar Publishing, 44–57.

LaRocco, A. (2016). The comprehensive hunting ban: Strengthening the state through participatory conservation in contemporary Botswana. In Ramutsindela, M., Miescher, G., and Boehi, M. (Eds.), *The politics of nature and science in Southern Africa*. Basel: Basler Afrika Bibliographien, 179–207.

LaRocco, A. (2020). Botswana's hunting ban and the transformation of game-meat cultures, economies and ecologies. *Journal of Southern African Studies*, 46 (4), 723–741.

LaRocco, A., & Mogende, E. (forthcoming). Fall from grace or back down to Earth? Conservation and political conflict in Africa's 'miracle' state. *Environment and Planning: Nature and Space*.

Lindsey P. A., Roulet, P. A., & Romanach, S. S. (2007). Economic and conservation significance of the trophy hunting industry in sub-Saharan Africa. *Biological Conservation*, 134, 455–469.

Macdonald, D. W., Johnson, P. J., Loveridge, A. J., Burnham, D., & Dickman, A. J. (2016). Conservation or the moral high ground: Siding with Bentham or Kant. *Conservation Letters*, 9, 307–308.

Masisi, K. (2019). President considers culling options. www.news24.com/citypress/news/botswana-president-considers-culling-as-villagers-battle-the-wild-to-survive-on-their-land-20190403

Mbaiwa, J. E. (2002). Past and present perspectives on the sustainable use of wildlife resources among basarwa communities in Ngamiland district: The case of Khwai and Mababe. *Botswana Journal of African Studies*, 16 (2), 110–122.

Mbaiwa, J. E. (2018). Effects of the safari hunting tourism ban on rural livelihoods and wildlife conservation in Northern Botswana, *South African Geographical Journal*, 100 (1), 41–61.

Mbaiwa, J. E. & Hambira, W. L. (2020) Enclaves and shadow state tourism in the Okavango Delta, Botswana. *South African Geographical Journal*, 102 (1), 1–21, DOI: 10.1080/03736245.2019.1601592.

Mbaiwa, J. E., & Hambira, W. L. (2021). Can the subaltern speak? Contradictions in trophy hunting and wildlife conservation trajectory in Botswana. *Journal of Sustainable Tourism* (forthcoming).

McNamara, T., Claasen, C., & Descubes, I. (2015). Trophy hunting in Namibia: Controversial but sustainable? A Case Study of Hunters Namibia Safaris. Working Paper, 16 November. Rennes: ESC Rennes School of Business.

Meinzen-Dick, R. S., Raju, K. V., & Gulati, A. (2002). What affects organization and collective action for managing resources? Evidence from canal irrigation systems in India. *World Development*, 30 (4), 649–666.

MEWT (Ministry of Environment, Wildlife and Tourism). (2013). Press statement from Ministry of Environment, Wildlife and Tourism on Suspension of hunting. 29 November. EWT 6/33/6 X (22). Gaborone: MEWT.

Mkono, M. (2018). The age of digital activism in tourism: Evaluating the legacy and \ limitations of the Cecil anti-trophy hunting movement. *Journal of Sustainable Tourism*, 26 (9), 1608–1624.

Mkono, M. (2019). Neo-colonialism and greed: Africans' views on trophy hunting in social media. *Journal of Sustainable Tourism*, 27 (5), 689–704.

Mogende, E., & Ramutsindela, M. (2020). Political leadership and non-state actors in the greening of Botswana. *Review of African Political Economy*, 47 (165), 399–415.

Mordi, R. A. (1989) The future of animal wildlife and its habitat in Botswana. *Environmental Conservation*, 16, 147–156.

Mosojane, S. (2004). Human elephant conflict along the Okavango Panhandle. Unpublished master's thesis, Department of Zoology and Entomology, Faculty of Agriculture and Natural Sciences, University of Pretoria.

Murray, M. (1988). *Management plan for Central Kalahari and Kutse Game Reserves*. Gaborone, Botswana: Kalahari Conservation Society.

Naidoo, R., Weaver, C. L., Diggle, R. W., Matongo, G., Stuart-Hill, G., & Thouless, C. (2015). Complementary benefits of tourism and hunting to communal conservancies in Namibia. *Conservation Biology*, 30 (3), 628–638.

Nelson, M. P., Bruskotter, J. T., Vucetich, J. A., & Chapron, G. (2016). Emotions and the ethics of consequence in conservation decisions: Lessons from Cecil the Lion. *Conservation Letters*, 9, 302–306.

News24 (2019). Southern African nations threaten to quit wildlife trade monitor. 1 September. www.news24.com/news24/africa/news/southern-african-nations-threaten-to-quit-wildlife-trade-monitor-20190901

Ochieng, A., Visseren-Hamakers, I. J. & Van Der Duim, R. (2020). Sport hunting to save nature? The case of Uganda. *Conservation and Society*, 18 (4), 340–354.

Ostrom, E. (1990). *Governing the commons*. Cambridge: Cambridge University Press.

Ostrom, E. (2014). Do institutions for collective action evolve? *Journal of Bioeconomics*, 16 (1), 3–30.

Owens, M., & Owens, D. (1984). *Cry of the Kalahari*. Boston, MA: Houghton-Mifflin.

Packer, C., Brink, H., Kissui, B. M., Maliti, H., Kushnir, H., & Caro, T. (2011). Effects of trophy hunting on lion and leopard populations in Tanzania. *Conservation Biology: The Journal of the Society for Conservation Biology*, 25 (1), 142–153.

Petrosillo, I., Aretano, R., & Zurlini, G. (2015). Socioecological systems. Reference Module in Earth Systems and Environmental Sciences, Elsevier, 22 July.

Pospisil, H. (2017). Trophy hunting. In J. Urbanik & C. L. Johnston (Eds.), *Humans and animals: A geography of coexistence*. Santa Barbara, CA:, 330–332.

Poteete, A.R., Janssen, M. & Ostrom, E. (2010) *Working together: Collective action, the commons, and multiple methods in practice*. Princeton, NJ: Princeton University Press

Ramutsindela, M. (2016). Political dynamics of human-environment relations. In Ramutsindela, M., Miescher, G., & Boehi, M. (Eds.), *The politics of nature and science in Southern Africa*. Basel: Basler Afrika Bibliographien, 20–38.

Roe, D. (2020). Dossier: Hunting and human-wildlife conflict. 5 June. https://justconservation.org/dossier-hunting-and-human-wildlife-conflict.

Rogan, M., Miller, J., Lindsey, P., & Weldon McNutt, J. (2017). Socioeconomic drivers of illegal bushmeat hunting in a southern African savanna. *Biological Conservation*, 226, 24–31.

Rust, N., & Verissimo, D. (2015). Why killing lions like Cecil may actually be good for conservation, The Conversation, 29 July. www.theconversation.com/why-killing-lions-like-cecil-may-actually-be-good-for-conservation-45400.

Somerville, K. (2019). Propaganda and the trophy hunting debate: The case of 'Conservation before trophy hunting'. 17 May. https://africasustainableconservation.com/2019/05/17/propaganda-and-the-trophy-hunting-debate-the-case-of-conservation-before-trophy-hunting/

Spinage, C. A. (1991). *History and evolution of the Fauna conservation laws of Botswana*. Gaborone: Botswana Society.

Swatuk, L. A. (2005). From project to context: community base natural resource management in Botswana. *Global Environmental Politics*, 5 (3), 95–124.

Taylor, M. J. (2002). The shaping of San livelihood strategies: Government policy and popular values. *Development and Change*, 33 (3), 467–488.

Van Der Merwe, P., & Mokgalo, L.L. (2020). Banning trophy hunting can put wildlife at risk: a case study from Botswana. 25 August. https://theconversation.com/banning-trophy-hunting-can-put-wildlife-at-risk-a-case-study-from-botswana-144156

Verlinden, A., Perkins, J. S., Murray, M., & Masunga, G. (1998) How are people affecting the distribution of less migratory wildlife in the southern Kalahari of Botswana? A spatial analysis. *Journal of Arid Environments*, 38, 129–141.

Williamson, D. T., & Mbano, B. (1988). Notes and records: Wildebeest mortality during 1983 at Lake Xau, Botswana. *African Journal of Ecology*, 26, 341–344.

Williamson, D., & Williamson, J. (1981). An assessment of fences on the large herbivore biomass in the Kalahari. *Botswana Notes and Recors*, 31, 91–94.

Williamson, D. & Williamson, J. (1984). Botswana's fences and the depletion of Kalahari wildlife. *Oryx*, 18 (4), 218–222.

Wollenberg, E., Merino, L., Agrawal, A., & Ostrom, E. (2007). Fourteen years of monitoring community-managed forests: learning from IFRI's experience. *International Forestry Review*, 9 (2), 670–684.

11 The role of the media and the international community in recent conservation issues in Southern Africa

The case of Cecil the lion

Garikai Chimuka

Introduction

The media is just as critical a stakeholder in wildlife conservation as any other agency working in the field. With many African species facing extinction, and the negative impact of poaching on nature, the media must play its role in sensitizing the public.
(Chinje, 2015)

Southern Africa is a region with one of the greatest wildlife endowments in the world. Her treasures have been a source of interest since the advent of European explorers in the 19th century (Western, 2003). Initial efforts to conserve wildlife during the colonial era focused on creating wildlife reserves or national parks where the local indigenous people were excluded from benefiting from their heritage (McIvor, 1994). Therefore, the relationship between wildlife and local people was that of competing interests (Mwakiwa, 2011). Locals were driven out from their land to make way for wildlife reserves but still suffered attacks on their livestock, crops and persons when the wildlife escaped from the parks, resulting in a relationship of conflict (McIvor, 1994).

Strides have been made with new initiatives such as community-based natural resources management (CBNRM) programmes like the Communal Areas Management Programme for Indigenous Resources (CAMPFIRE) in Zimbabwe. However, the vestiges of the colonial architectural ownership and control of wildlife resources are still present (McIvor, 1994).

Sustainability is now topical globally. Wildlife resources especially those endangered like the 'Big 5' which are abundant in Southern Africa are viewed as a global public good. This invites global and Western interest in how this wildlife resource is utilised in the same way, for example, as the Amazon rainforest in Brazil is called the 'lungs of the earth' (Phillips, 2019).

To this end, the media and international community play an important role in shaping the conservation discourse in the region. The media, at least in liberal democracies, is central in educating society, narrative setting, holding public

DOI: 10.4324/9781003193166-14

officials and citizens accountable, galvanising public opinion and applying public pressure (Halloran, 1970; Lang & Lang, 1968). In the context of conservation, this can presumably incentivise improved conservation behaviour and rally the international community to act as if indispensable in the policy outcomes.

However, the African media have not always given high priority to reporting wildlife-related issues. Mutere (1991) in Boafo (1991) notes that;

> Environmental issues constitute a relatively marginal concern in most African newspapers, radio and television news, and current affairs programs. Much more attention is given to national politics, labour disputes, the arts and business.

This preceded the killing of a lion called Cecil in Zimbabwe in 2015 which became one of the greatest media events in the world. This chapter will use Cecil as a lens in analysing the role of the media and international community in conservation issues in Southern Africa. Cecil has been described as a turning point in the role of the media in highlighting wildlife issues at a global scale, resulting in some scholars terming it a 'movement' (MacDonald et al., 2016).

Why Cecil?

The killing of Cecil led to intense media coverage, demonstrations by outraged citizens and several policy initiatives in the West including in the US Congress and the European Union (EU) (Chimuka, 2019).

Cecil galvanised the media in Africa and the West to improve their coverage of wildlife and conservation issues. Post-Cecil, on issues like poaching (Newburger, 2020); differences over the sale of ivory stockpiles at the 18th meeting of the Convention on International Trade in Endangered Species (CITES) in 2019, with Zimbabwe, Botswana, Zambia and Namibia in support and Kenya against (Busani, 2019); export of baby elephants from Zimbabwe to China (Cockburn, 2019; Mutsaka, 2019); the mysterious deaths of elephants in Zimbabwe and Botswana (Somerville, 2020); South Africa's proposal to ban caged lion hunting (Gerber, 2021) among others, the media have shone a light on wildlife management practices in Southern Africa at a global scale.

As Chimuka (2019) noted, what was striking about Cecil was the opposite reactions by ordinary Southern Africans who were surprised by the Western media coverage and therefore lost the window of opportunity to create new policy for wildlife conservation. This dichotomy between massive action by the media and policymakers in the West and the lack of the same in Southern Africa which is the home of not only Cecil but others like the Big 5 deserves critical analysis to come up with informed policy options.

This chapter will start by defining what the media are. Understanding what constitutes the media is important since it informs us what motivates issues they cover. As Chagutah (2010) argues, what determines what makes it into the media is a complex interplay of various factors. These include the influence of

148 *Garikai Chimuka*

issue proponents, proprietary power, the editorial policy with its influence on the value judgments of gatekeepers, exposure of the issue in other media, spectacular news events and extreme events that may result in disaster.

It will also define the term 'international community' to establish a proper basis for the analysis of the issues that emerge. Whilst the media can play its role, it is the policymakers who act. Given that wildlife in Southern Africa is on the world radar, the international community has a role to formulate and execute policy.

Post-Cecil, policy initiatives only occurred in the West and not in Southern Africa (Macdonald et al., 2016). What does this say about the role of the media and international community and Southern Africa itself, where not much was done in policy terms? The discussion will be grounded within the theoretical concept of a focusing event which is a sudden, attention-grabbing event which alongside other factors can create a policy window, during which the conditions for policy reform are particularly favourable (Baumgartner and Jones, 1993).

Background

Cecil was a 13-year-old lion and one of the top tourist attractions in Zimbabwe's Hwange National Park. Walter Palmer, an American, killed Cecil for a trophy (Winter, 2020). A search for Cecil the lion on the internet during the period 10 to 15 December 2018 yielded on average 18,800,000 results (Chimuka, 2019). Macdonald et al. (2016) determined that during 1 July–30 September 2015, Cecil generated a total of 94,631 distinct editorial news items and 695,983 distinct social media posts across 125 languages.

In response to Cecil's death, the US Fish and Wildlife Service listed lions as threatened, under the Endangered Species Act. This action requires that permits be granted before the import of trophies and only upon showing that the import will enhance the survival of the species (Carpenter & Konisky, 2019). In the US Congress, three bills were proposed with each mentioning Cecil's name in their titles. These are Conserving Ecosystems by Ceasing the Importation of Large (CECIL) Animal Trophies Act (S.1918) 2015,[1] Cecil the Lion Endangered and Threatened Species Act of 2015 (H.R.3448) 2015[2] and CECIL Act (H.R.3526).[3] The first two bills would have banned all trophy imports and the third bill would have extended existing import protections under the Endangered Species Act, but all the bills were not adopted into law.

The EU enacted a new policy to require the issuance of import permits for lion trophies (along with five other species) only after a demonstration that the activity meets a set of sustainability criteria. France went further and banned the import of lion trophies (Carpenter & Konisky, 2019). More than 40 airlines, including the three biggest American airlines (Delta, United and American), adopted or reaffirmed bans on the shipment of animal trophies (Carpenter & Konisky, 2019).

The media

You are innovative, technologically gifted and fearless more than the generations that liberated us from colonialism. Can you imagine, the level of impact Nelson Mandela, Kwame Nkrumah, Julius Nyerere, Patrice Lumumba and other renowned young Pan African leaders would have generated, if they had WhatsApp, Facebook, Twitter or Instagram?

(Sebunya, 2020)

The media are among the most powerful influencers of society today. As noted earlier, the media did not always cover environmental issues with the same prominence as politics, arts, sports among others pre-Cecil, especially in Africa. Much coverage of environmental issues relied on practitioners, academics and educators. As outlined by Holl et al. (1995, p. 1553), 'it would be grossly inadequate to rely on academics, practitioners and educators alone to help augment awareness'. Hence, increasing public awareness is among the three priorities for environmental education outlined by the UN Conference on Environment and Development (Kassas, 2002). This puts the media at the centre of the conservation discourse: it is vital in this task.

One can divide the media into the Western and African media. Whilst there is a thin line distinguishing the two, since most Western media have global tentacles and reach and are consumed in Africa, a salient distinction can be made to aid analysis. For example, international media like the *BBC, CNN,* the *Independent,* the *Guardian,* etc. have local chapters in Southern Africa. They share the same umbilical cord to the Western parent and so might be influenced by the global editorial policy. Hence globally there were a total of 94,631 distinct editorial news items in the aftermath of the killing of Cecil (Carpenter & Konisky, 2019). In the West, the story was on television, talk shows, newspapers and social media, thus creating a critical mass that made Cecil a global story.

In the African media, radio, television, and newspapers are the major outlets of information. Radio, for instance, with its ability to reach almost any rural area, is vital in developing countries. Through radio, rural communities learn of events in their region and issues on government policies and plans are brought to their notice (Bennet, 2002). However, with high mobile penetration in Africa, social media is increasingly important especially for the younger generations. In Cecil, social media dominated conservations in Africa. Initially, the old African media covered the Cecil story in a similar way to the Western media. (Chimuka, 2019). After trending on social media, the old African media started to ask critical questions based on the viral issues on social media (Chimuka, 2019).

International community

Some people say the international community is only a fiction. Others say it is too elastic a concept to have any real meaning. Still others say it is a mere vehicle of

150   *Garikai Chimuka*

> *convenience, to be trotted out only in emergencies or when a scapegoat for inaction is needed.*
>
> (Annan, 1999)

The term 'international community' is widely used in government and inter-governmental organisations like the United Nations (UN), North Atlantic Treaty Organisation (NATO), Group of Seven (G7) among others. However, its definition is highly contested.

In Cecil, one can categorise the international community into the originalist and realist definitions. The originalist definition is the one articulated in the Cambridge Dictionary which defines the international community as 'a phrase used especially by politicians and in newspapers to describe all or several of the countries in the world, or their governments, considered as a group'.[4]

Former UN Secretary General, Koffi Annan (1999) favoured such a definition when he argued that:

> Op-ed pages refer routinely to the 'so-called' international community. And news reports often put the term in quotation marks, as if it does not yet have the solidity of actual fact. What binds us into an international community? In the broadest sense there is a shared vision of a better world for all people, as set out, for example in the United Nations Charter.

Noam Chomsky articulates a realist view. He alleges that the term is used to refer to the United States and its allies and client states, as well as allies of those states in the media (Chomsky, 2002). Jacques (2006) adds that:

> We all know what is meant by the term 'international community', don't we? It's the West, of course, nothing more, nothing less. Using the term 'international community' is a way of dignifying the West, of globalizing it, of making it sound more respectable, more neutral and high-faluting.

Focusing event

> *Most focusing events change the dominant issues on the agenda in a policy domain, they can lead to interest group mobilization, and groups often actively seek to expand or contain issues after a focusing event.*
>
> (Birkland, 1998)

Carpenter and Konisky (2017) argue that Cecil is a focusing event. A focusing event is a sudden, attention-grabbing event which alongside other factors can create a policy window, during which the conditions for policy reform are particularly favourable (Baumgartner & Jones, 1993). Birkland (1998) adds that it is

> sudden; relatively uncommon; can be reasonably defined as harmful or revealing the possibility of potentially greater future harms; has harms that

Role of the media   151

are concentrated in a particular geographical area or community of interest; and that is known to policymakers and the public simultaneously.

This chapter will not delve into the details and various theories of a focusing event for it is not assessing whether Cecil is a focusing event. It starts from the premise shared by Carpenter and Konisky (2019) who researched Cecil and determined that it is a focusing event. What it does is to use Cecil as a framework for analysing various post-Cecil actions in the West and in Southern Africa to come up with a discussion on why actors in the two different regions acted in different ways.

Methods

This chapter used secondary or desktop research, especially journal articles, policy documents and newspaper articles on Cecil. Research about Cecil has been published by scholars such as Chimuka (2019), Carpenter & Konisky (2017) and MacDonald et al. (2016) among others. There are also blog posts, newspaper articles and editorial pages. Primary methods were not used because most of the referred articles like Chimuka (2019) used primary methods. For a critical analysis of the role of the media and international community in conservation issues in Southern Africa, a synthesis and critical examination of secondary data is enough to interrogate the subject.

Discussion

We must recognise that conservation is about people as much as it is about species or ecosystems.

(Mascia, 2003)

Cecil's death was a focusing event that triggered a potential policy window in both the West and Southern Africa. The role of the media and the international community was critical in making it a focusing event. However, this research sought to understand the salient and underlying dynamics that led to varying policy outcomes in Southern Africa and the West. Policy literature often mentions the agenda-setting influence of focusing events, but few policy studies systematically examine the dynamics of these events (Birkland, 1998). Thus, this research found interesting discussion points in the foregoing.

The Western media still set the dominant narrative on wildlife and conservation issues

Policy action as a direct response to the killing of Cecil occurred in the US and Europe. In the US, at federal level, three pieces of legislation were formulated. The proposed legislation imposed a ban of wildlife trophy imports which was popular in editorial pages in the US and Europe. Therefore, the media was successful in agenda-setting and putting public pressure on authorities. However, banning wildlife trophy imports though the dominant narrative in the media was contested in the West. There was also a counter narrative by some organisations which argued that trophy hunting is important in generating revenues in poor regions like Southern Africa which can be ploughed back into conservation (MacDonald et al., 2017).

The fact that the federal initiatives failed to be promulgated into law also shows that, while the media can set a narrative and agenda to spur policymakers into action, its power has limits. In the West, there are also other stakeholders that are important like lobbyists who represents special interests and can affect the passage of a new law. This is one of the reasons why the proposed legislations at federal level failed to pass into law.

On the other hand, the Southern African media did not set any agenda both in the region and in the West. For in the Southern African media, there was an outcry that the coverage of Cecil and the legislative and policy initiatives in the West showed more concern about animals ahead of people (Chimuka, 2019). One can thus argue that, since there was no policy and legislative actions in Southern Africa, the governments were not moved to implement bans to trophy hunting which was not a popular theme in the Southern African media.

However, this might not be the only factor for policy inertia since we did not see any post-Cecil initiatives that spoke to the inclusion of locals in the management of wildlife (Chimuka, 2019). This was a popular theme in the Southern African media. One can argue that it was either the usual governmental indifference in Southern Africa or at worst the Southern African elites realised that trophy hunting bans which were being initiated in the West would create opportunity for them to engage in the wildlife grey and black markets where there is corruption, self-enrichment and lack of transparency and accountability.

Social media have narrowed the media asymmetry between Africans and the world

The African media industry has been weak historically. Ordinary African voices have for too long been excluded in narrative shaping on issues that affect them. This power disequilibrium means that the African voice is usually missing in topical global issues and policies formulated at global level for Africa in most cases fail because there is no ownership, since they are not based on the practical lived reality on the continent. However, social media are giving Africans a voice. As noted by Chimuka (2019), African voices in Cecil were amplified by social media. In groups on WhatsApp, Facebook, popular blogs and Twitter among other platforms, Africans expressed shock on the coverage of Cecil since many Zimbabweans did not know about the existence of the lion (Chimuka, 2019).

Most traditional print and electronic media in Southern Africa usually parrot the stories published in mainstream Western media without contextualising them within the reality of the African experience. However, social media platforms now give power to Africans to set the agenda outside the editorial rooms of major newspapers. Therefore, when an issue is 'trending' on social media, it is now difficult for editors of traditional media to ignore it and remain relevant. This explains why some private media in Southern Africa started to come up with headlines about Cecil that were different from those in Western media that they used to copy before the age of social media. Hence, some private traditional print media in South Africa, for example, came up with headlines like 'What Lion?' (news24.com, 2015). What is now missing is for the major traditional Western multinational media to take advantage of this social media feedback loop and use it to give balance to stories about Africa. Only then will the media and international community have power to create a focusing event that can result in successful policy formulation in Southern Africa.

The West is no longer the only 'international community' in conservation issues in Southern Africa

As noted earlier, policy initiatives were carried out in the West. This fits with Chomsky's definition of the international community as the West. Whilst one can argue that such was to be expected, given for example, that the US is the biggest importer of wildlife trophies from Southern Africa, one cannot ignore other emerging giants on the wildlife trophy scene outside of the West. One important nation is China.

The CITES official figures of imports in the year 2016 show the top trophy importing nations (Table 11.1).

While China ranks ninth on official CITES figures, there is also a general acknowledgement that there is a multi-billion illegal wildlife trade flourishing in Southern Africa that has left some African species on the brink of extinction

Table 11.1 Total lion (Panthera leo) trophy imports (and percentage of imports worldwide) in the top 10 importing countries during 2004–2014

Country	Total lion trophy imports (2004–2014)	% worldwide trophy imports (2004–2014)
USA	7,586	58.4
Spain	1,002	7.7
France	444	3.4
Russia	376	2.9
Canada	310	2.4
South Africa	272	2.1
Germany	237	1.8
Mexico	211	1.6
China	**186**	**1.4**
Czech Republic	183	1.4
Rest of world	2,189	16.8
TOTAL	**12,996**	**100**

Source: CITES (2016) trade database.

(Institute for Global Dialogue, 2018). China is the largest market for illegal wildlife products and the market continues to grow (Kirschke-Schwartz, 2016).

This is reinforced by press reports of non-CITES-approved sales of various wildlife to China from Zimbabwe (Cockburn, 2019; Mavhunga, 2019; Wilson-Spath, 2020). In Namibia, the Namibian Chamber of Environment (2017) wrote a letter to the Chinese Ambassador, Xin Shunkang in which it alleged that

> As Chinese nationals moved into all regions of Namibia, setting up businesses, networks, acquiring mineral prospecting licenses and offering payment for wildlife products, the incidence of poaching, illegal wildlife capture, collection, killing and export has increased exponentially.

Gabriel (2020) further notes that:

> While international commercial trade in rhino horn is prohibited by the Convention on International Trade in Endangered Species of Wild Fauna and Flora (CITES), South Africa allows foreigners to hunt rhinos and ship the horns overseas as trophies. Taking advantage of this legal loophole, criminal gangs employ Thai and Vietnamese prostitutes to pose as big game hunters to obtain fake trophy hunting permits to smuggle horns from poached rhinos.

There are various such reports from all countries in Southern Africa. This means that when referring to the role of the international community, we must begin to view it as based on its originalist definition as articulated by Koffi Annan, including all nations of the world working together in concert for a common good.

Such initiatives seem to be under way with regards to China. For example, China's National Forestry and Grassland Administration (NFGA) and World Wide Fund for Nature (WWF), supported by the Chinese Embassies in Nairobi and Gaborone, concluded two advocacy workshops raising awareness on wildlife trafficking amongst Chinese nationals living and working in Kenya and Botswana (Chinadaily, 2016). Similar initiatives have also been undertaken with a Memorandum of Understanding (MoU) between the Chinese government and South Africa (Institute for Global Dialogue, 2018).

Southern African countries as the source and exporting market need to play a focal role in these initiatives. They must view the region as the fulcrum of the international community in terms of wildlife conservation. It does not matter that the region is poor. Being a global wildlife powerhouse must translate into greater interest and activism in matters to do with this heritage. This must start with an honest internal understanding that wildlife is not only for one generation, but future generations also. Therefore, it is in the region's interests to promote the rule of law, economic opportunity and good governance to minimise corruption that promotes illegal wildlife trade and for once turn the

Role of the media   155

wildlife resources into an asset and not a resource curse. As Western (2003, p. 17) observed:

> The will to tackle the formidable obstacles facing African conservation must arise from within the continent; without that will, no amount of international aid will solve the problems.

Without this conviction from the region, opportunities for policy presented by rare focusing events such as Cecil will be lost due to policy inertia.

Policy decoupling between poor wildlife exporting and rich wildlife trophy importing countries destroys conservation efforts

The media sets a narrative that is influenced by societal debates that are topical to its target market (Chagutah, 2010). There is a highly polarised debate about the killing of wildlife for trophies in the West. It seems the movement that argues that it is morally repugnant to kill wildlife for trophies was dominant at least during demonstrations and in the media narrative. Hence the legislative efforts that were initiated in the US and Europe centred on outright banning of trophy hunting.

In the proposed bans on wildlife trophy imports, there was no mention of alternative arrangements to help Southern African nations to finance conservation. This shows that Western policymakers care only about their constituencies even in areas where proposed policy has ramifications outside the West. Trophy hunting involves two parties which are the exporting and the importing nations. Any sound policy must pass the litmus test on both sides, if it is to be effective. There was no attempt by the Western media to understand Cecil from the viewpoint of Southern Africa. Hence most editorials in the West described Cecil as having been popular because of its 'English name', while in Zimbabwe the name was viewed as offensive given that it was the name of the coloniser, Cecil John Rhodes (Chimuka, 2019). The media echo chamber then feeds to the policymakers who naturally respond to any focusing event.

As noted by MacDonald et al. (2017, p. 251):

> Who has the right to make decisions about trophy hunting? How should the weight of opinions held on lion hunting in countries without lions, such as the US (which has a thriving domestic hunting market), be ranked against the opinions held in African countries where lions occur (and where the financial consequences of a cessation of trophy hunting might bite the hardest)?

Therefore, when there is policy asymmetry between the rich importing countries of the West and the poor exporting countries of Southern Africa, conservation efforts suffer. A colonial discourse where former colonial powers

156 Garikai Chimuka

act in isolation without consulting and cooperating with Southern African countries is self-defeating. For if the Western media had incorporated views of Southern Africans, they would have realised that inclusion in wildlife resource management of historically excluded groups was more important than banning trophy hunting (Chimuka, 2019).

Woke corporations are now a huge factor in conservation issues

When talking about major interest groups in conservation a few years ago, one would have expected to hear about UN agencies focusing on the environment, wildlife and sustainability; international non-governmental conservation and environmental organisations; community-based conservation and environmental movements; indigenous groups and First Nations and academics among others. One would not have expected private companies to be a factor. Traditionally, private companies focus on maximising shareholder value through maximising profits.

With the UN coming up with the UN Guiding Principles on Business and Human Rights (2011), corporates started to worry about the impact of their activities not only on shareholders but on stakeholders who include the environment (Muswaka, 2014). Recently, we are increasingly seeing the rise of the 'woke' corporates. These are corporates that are actively involving themselves in societal issues of the day. This means that corporations must no longer be ignored in messaging through the media. The example already noted of 40 airlines that have banned wildlife trophies is instructive. Whilst millionaire hunters use private jets for their Southern Africa hunting jaunts, the upper middle-class trophy hunters use these airlines. Bans such as those implemented by the airlines have a massive impact on wildlife conservation. The only problem with woke corporates is that at times they are not experts in subject matters they engage in but are driven usually by media headlines.

Conclusion

> *Our destiny will not be written for us but by us and all those who are not content to settle for the world as it is but have the courage to remake the world as it should be.*
> (Obama, 2008)

This chapter has argued that sustainable wildlife conservation in Southern Africa and other places in the Global South can better succeed if the media and international community include the views of local people and institutions who were historically and to a greater extent are still excluded from benefiting from and managing wildlife. The media and the international community in its originalist meaning have a great role to play. First, the media can zero in on issues such as poaching and its destructive effects on wildlife in a way that mobilises the world to work together to root out such practices. The media

Role of the media 157

have power to take what might ordinarily be a normal event and through relentless coverage make it a focusing event, thus creating a window for policy change or the formulation of new policy.

The Southern African people must not be bystanders in setting the media narrative. They can effectively harness the power of social media so that their voices are heard and taken into consideration in policy formulation. For it is not only important for a focusing event such as Cecil to lead to policy change, but the policy crafted must be beneficial to the interests of the region.

If Southern African governments, academics and civil society remain spectators of content generation through the media, other nations will impose policies that worsen the situation. Therefore, Southern Africa must utilise the media in an effective way to put across its views in the international arena. Gone are the days when Southern Africa did not view itself as part of the international community. As a wildlife superpower, Southern Africa must assert its voice in as far as the conservation of its wildlife is concerned.

Notes

1 S. 1918 (114th): Conserving Ecosystems by Ceasing the Importation of Large (CECIL) Animal Trophies Act. Available at: www.govtrack.us/congress/bills/114/s1918. Accessed on 5 March 2021.
2 H.R.3448: Cecil the Lion Endangered and Threatened Species Act of 2015. Available at: www.congress.gov/bill/114th-congress/house-bill/3448/cosponsors. Accessed on 10 March 2021.
3 H.R.3526: CECIL Act 114th Congress (2015–2016). Available at: www.congress.gov/bill/114th-congress/house-bill/3526/text. Accessed on 10 March 2021.
4 Cambridge Dictionary (2021). Available at: https://dictionary.cambridge.org/dictionary/english/international-community. Accessed on 4 May 2021.

References

Annan, K. (1999). Secretary-general examines 'meaning of international community' in address to dpi/ngo conference. Available at: www.un.org/press/en/1999/19990915.sgsm7133.doc.html. Accessed 4 May 2021.
Baumgartner, F., & Jones, B. (1993) Agendas and instability in American politics. In M. Lodge, M., Page, E. C., & Balla, S. J. (Eds.), *The Oxford handbook of classics in public policy and administration.* Oxford: Oxford University Press.
Bennet, N. (2002) Connecting farmers worldwide through radio. *Magazine on Low External Input and Sustainable Agriculture (LEISA),* 18 (2), 20–21.
Birkland, T. (1998) Focusing events, mobilization, and agenda setting. *Journal of Public Policy,* 18 (1), 53–74.
Busani, B. (2019) 'Let us trade': Debate over ivory sales rages ahead of CITES summit. *Mongobay.* Available at: https://news.mongabay.com/2019/07/let-us-trade-debate-over-ivory-sales-rages-ahead-of-cites-summit/. Accessed on 3 May 2021.
Carpenter, S. & Konisky, D. (2019) The killing of Cecil the Lion as an impetus for policy change. *Oryx,* 53 (4), 698–706.

158   *Garikai Chimuka*

Chagutah, T. (2010) Communicating sustainability: The apparent and latent features of environmental reporting in the Zimbabwean press, *Journal of Sustainable Development in Africa*, 12 (2), 352–367.

Chimuka, G. (2019) Western hysteria over killing of Cecil the lion! Othering from the Zimbabwean gaze. *Tourist Studies*, 19 (2), 336–356.

Chinadaily (2016) China calls on citizens in Africa: Stop wildlife trafficking. Available at: www.chinadaily.com.cn/a/201903/26/WS5c99e6e6a3104842260b2ac1.html. Accessed on 2 May 2021.

Chinje, E. (2015) African Media Initiative launches project with African Wildlife Foundation to strengthen media's role in supporting wildlife conservation. Available at: www.awf.org/news/partnership-strengthen-media-coverage-conservation-issues. Accessed on 1 May 2021

Chomsky, N. (2002) The crimes of 'Intcom'. *Foreign Policy*. Available at: https://chom sky.info/200209__/ Accessed on 23 March 2021.

Cockburn, H. (2019) Outrage as 30 wild baby elephants 'flown from Zimbabwe to China for lifetime in captivity'. *Independent*. Available at: www.independent.co.uk/news/world/africa/baby-elephants-zimbabwe-sold-china-captivity-zoo-wildlife-drought-a9170886.html. Accessed on 6 May 2021.

Gabriel, G. (2020) Will China say no to wildlife trade? *UN Chronicle*. Available at: www.un.org/en/chronicle/article/will-china-say-no-wildlife-trade. Accessed 24 March 2021.

Gerber, J. (2021) Is govt about to ban canned lion hunting? *News24.com*. Available at: www.news24.com/news24/SouthAfrica/News/end-in-sight-for-canned-lion-hunting-20210502. Accessed on 6 March 2021.

Halloran, J., Elliott, P., & Murdock, G. (1970) *Demonstrations and communication: A case study*. Harmondsworth: Penguin Books Ltd.

Holl, K., Daily, G., & Ehrlich, P. (1995) Knowledge and perceptions in Costa Rica Regarding environment, population and biodiversity issues. *Conservation Biology*, 9, 1548–1558.

Institute for Global Dialogue (2018) China's role in wildlife conservation in Africa. Available at: www.igd.org.za/infocus/11641-china-s-role-in-wildlife-conservation-in-africa. Accessed on 16 March 2021.

Jacques, M. (2006) What the hell is the international community? *Guardian*. Available at: www.theguardian.com/commentisfree/2006/aug/24/whatthehellistheinternati. https://www.theguardian.com/commentisfree/2006/aug/24/whatthehellisthein ternati Accessed on 5 March 2021.

Kassas, M. (2002) Environmental education: Biodiversity. *The Environmentalist*, 22, 345–351.

Kirschke-Schwartz, E. (2016) Wild laws: China and its role in illicit wildlife trade. *Wilson Center*. Available at: www.wilsoncenter.org/event/wild-laws-china-and-its-role-illicit-wildlife-trade. Accessed on 7 March 2021.

Lang, K., & Lang, G. (1968) *Politics and television*. Chicago, IL: Quadrangle Books.

MacDonald, D., et al. (2016) Cecil: A moment or a movement? Analysis of media coverage of the death of a lion, Panthera leo. *Animals*, 6, 26.

MacDonald, D., et al. (2017) Lions, trophy hunting and beyond: Knowledge gaps and why they matter. *Mammal Review*, 47 (4), 247–253.

Mascia, M. (2003) Conservation and the social sciences. *Conservation Biology,* 17 (3), 649–650.

Mavhunga, C. (2019) Zimbabwe sells elephants to China and Dubai for $2.7 million. CNN. Available at: https://edition.cnn.com/2019/05/14/africa/zimbabwe-sells-elephants-intl/index.html. Accessed on 25 January 2021.

McIvor, C. (1994) Management of wildlife, tourism and local communities in Zimbabwe. United Nations Research Institute for Social Development, Discussion Paper No. 53.

Muswaka, L. (2014) The corporate responsibility for human rights: A conceptual framework. *Mediterranean Journal of Social Sciences,* 5 (3), 219–225.

Mutere, A. (1991) Health and environmental concerns in Africa. In Boafo, K. S. T (Ed.), *Module on specialised reporting.* Nairobi: African Council for Communication Education, 39–46.

Mutsaka, F. (2019) Zimbabwe sent 30 baby elephants to China, says rights group. ABCNews. Available at: https://abcnews.go.com/International/wireStory/zimbabwe-30-baby-elephants-china-rights-group-66526788. Accessed on 6 March 2021.

Mwakiwa, E. (2011) *Cooperation or competition: Dilemma for resource managers in sustainable wildlife conservation.* PhD thesis, Wageningen University.

Namibian Chamber of Environment (2017) China must take responsibility for its citizens' wildlife crimes in Africa. Ecologist. Available at: https://theecologist.org/2017/jan/06/china-must-take-responsibility-its-citizens-wildlife-crimes-africa. Accessed on 7 March 2021.

Newburger, E. (2020) 'Filthy bloody business': Poachers kill more animals as coronavirus crushes tourism to Africa. CNBC. Available at: www.cnbc.com/2020/04/24/coronavirus-poachers-kill-more-animals-as-tourism-to-africa-plummets.html. Accessed on 6 March 2021.

News24.com (2015) 'What lion? Zimbabweans ask amid global Cecil outrage'. Available at: www.news24.com/Green/News/What-lion-Zimbabweans-ask-amid-global-Cecil-outrage-20150730. Accessed on 1 March 2021.

Obama, B. (2008) Speaking after his Iowa Caucus Victory. Available at: www.youtube.com/watch?v=Pvo2twG6_EY. Accessed on 1 May 2021.

Phillips, T. (2019) Merkel backs Macron's call for G7 talks on Amazon fires. *Guardian.* Available at: www.theguardian.com/world/2019/aug/23/amazon-rainforest-fires-macron-calls-for-international-crisis-to-lead-g7-discussions. Accessed on 5 January 2021.

Sebunya, K. (2020) Conservation story is yet to be well told by African media. *The East African.* Available at: www.theeastafrican.co.ke/tea/oped/comment/conservation-story-is-yet-to-be-well-told-by-african-media--3207220. Accessed on 2 May 2021.

Somerville, K. (2020) Why are elephants dying in Zimbabwe and Botswana? *Talkinghumanities.* Available at: https://talkinghumanities.blogs.sas.ac.uk/2020/09/10/why-are-elephants-dying-in-zimbabwe-and-botswana/. Accessed on 3 March 2021.

United Nations (2011) *Guiding principles on business and human rights.* Available at: www.ohchr.org/documents/publications/guidingprinciplesbusinesshr_en.pdf. Accessed on 20 March 2021.

Western, D. (2003) Conservation science in Africa and the role of international collaboration. *Conservation Biology,* 17, 11–19.

Wilson-Spath, A. (2020) CITES silent as Zimbabwe dooms elephants to living hell in China. *Daily Maverick*. Available at: www.dailymaverick.co.za/article/2020-08-12-cites-silent-as-zimbabwe-dooms-elephants-to-living-hell-in-china/ Accessed on 6 February 2021.

Winter, A. (2020) Dentist who killed Cecil the lion slammed for slaughtering rare sheep in Mongolia. *The Sun*. Available at: www.thesun.co.uk/news/12092692/dentist-killed-cecil-lion-slaughtering-rare-sheep-mongolia/. Accessed on 20 February 2021.

12 Nature-based tourism resources and climate change in Southern Africa

Implications for conservation and development sustainability

Kaitano Dube

Background and introduction

The past decade has witnessed a steady rise in levels of environmental degradation across the world (World Meteorological Organization, 2021). Various reasons have been put forward as critical drivers of the environmental upheaval being experienced worldwide. Among them are global environmental change, increased human consumption, population growth, increased pollution, rapid urbanisation and climate change. Franklin et al. (2016) indicate that global change has had a devastating impact on global terrestrial vegetation crucial to the biogeochemical cycle process. Consequent to global climate change, vegetation, invasive species and land use have been altered in many regions across the world (Armarego-Marriott, 2020). Terrestrial vegetation acts as a crucial biodiversity reserve crucial for animal habitat and livelihood security in many respects.

Nowhere has the impact of such environmental degradation been felt more than in sub-Saharan Africa. This is because the livelihoods of many people in the region depend on nature (Wisely et al., 2018). Therefore the environmental degradation warrants severe and immediate attention.

Southern Africa is richly endowed with natural resources. These range from rivers, mountains, forests, wetlands, deltas, pristine coastal beaches, majestic mountains, world-renowned waterfalls and national parks (Dube & Nhamo, 2020a). All form part of a rich heritage on which a robust nature-based tourism industry could be based. However, despite an immense potential for tourism that could be the panacea to the region's developmental needs and assist in meeting Sustainable Development Goals (Siakwah et al., 2020), imminent threats to nature tourism might scupper this developmental promise. A spate of climate change-induced extreme weather occurrences has been identified as a threat to nature-based tourism in the Southern Africa region and beyond.

Other than the COVID-19 pandemic, no other natural occurrence has challenged the efficacy and sustainability of the tourism sector more than recent droughts in the region. Nature-based tourism destinations such as national parks and water-based tourism resorts like the Kruger National Park, Okavango Delta

DOI: 10.4324/9781003193166-15

162 *Kaitano Dube*

and Victoria Falls are vulnerable to direct and indirect impact climate change-induced droughts. (Dube & Nhamo, 2018; Hambira et al., 2020). Evidence shows that droughts have adversely affected tourism and recreational activities in lakes, such as Lake Kariba, located in north-western Zimbabwe (Dube & Nhamo, 2020b). Droughts attributed to climate variability have also negatively impacted iconic tourist destinations such as Cape Town. The Day Zero drought (2017–2019) resulted in a significant decline in tourist arrivals to the country's most populous Cape Town resorts and other tourist destinations (Dube et al., 2020b). A decrease in tourist arrivals was witnessed in Table Mountain's National Parks Cape Point, Chapman's Peak Drive and other nature tourism destinations such as Kirstenbosch Botanical Gardens and Grootbos Nature Reserve (Dube et al., 2020a).

Besides droughts, nature-based tourism resorts have also suffered immensely from the impacts of intense rainfall activities (Smith & Fitchett, 2020) that often result in flooding. Such floods have caused extensive damage to tourism infrastructure, consequently undermining tourism development and activities across the region (Dube & Nhamo, 2020a). With the anticipation that climate change will further worsen these events going forward, critical questions are being asked about the sustainability of the tourism industry and the implications for conservation practice in nature-based tourism establishments such as national parks. These questions are particularly pertinent in Southern Africa, where tourism and climate change knowledge gaps are still vast (Mushawemhuka et al., 2018). Against this backdrop, this study explores nature-based tourism's vulnerability to climate change and considers the implications of climate change on conservation practice and the sector's sustainability. The study endeavours to answer the following key questions (1) What are the key drivers of vulnerability to nature-based tourism in protected areas such as national parks? (2) How does climate change shape conservation practice in protected areas to ensure sustainability?

Research approach

The study used secondary archival data and previous work by the author on nature-based tourism and climate change. The constructivism theory largely informed the study. Published, secondary data was sourced and accessed from the Google Scholar search engine. Google Scholar has a rich catalogue with more than 389 million articles in its catalogue (Gusenbauer, 2019). The other advantage of using Google Scholar is to catalogue invaluable grey literature (Maviza & Ahmed, 2021). The search was limited to articles that were published between 2010 and April 2021. The key search terms used for the initial search were climate change and tourism in Africa. This search criterion yielded 472,000 articles without a time limitation. When a custom time filter was placed in the search, a total of 122,000 outcomes emerged. Since the data set was still too big to handle, further refinements were made to source only articles focusing on countries in Southern Africa. A country approach was used as a search term to identify studies that used the key search: 'country name_climate change impact

Nature-based tourism and climate change   163

national parks'. In some instances, prominent national park names were also used to ensure that no study was missed.

In addition to secondary data, archival data such as meteorological data were also utilised from various authoritative and reliable sources like Meteo France and South African Weather Services. Meteorological organisations are tasked with collecting and archiving daily weather data in their various regions; they are considered authoritative climate data sources.

For weather and climate data from South African Weather Services, XLSTAT 2021 software was used to conduct time series analysis using the Mann Kendal trend analysis. For the latter, significance was set at 5%, and the confidence interval at 95%. Content and thematic analysis were used as the main form of data analysis. The themes were developed using the key questions as a guiding principle to both theme and analysis development. Dictates advised by Roberts et al. (2019) were followed in the analysis process.

Results and discussion

Climatic patterns in Southern Africa between 2010 and 2021

A study by the World Meteorological Organization found that the Southern African region experienced several severe weather events in the period 2010 and 2021 (World Meteorological Organization, 2021). Such weather events were of such a magnitude that they curtailed tourism operations and activities in the region. An analysis of severe weather events experienced, which focused on intensity, duration, extent of flooding and temperatures, revealed that the region experienced some of the most intense tropical cyclones ever witnessed during the past few years. The most severe tropical cyclones were Kenneth and Idai, which occurred in 2019 (Nhamo & Dube, 2021).

The compounded effect of climate change and climate variability events have worsened the impact and cost of climate variability and change in the Southern African region in the past decade. Due to climate variability and change, the region also witnessed the most intense El Niño events between 2015 and 2016 (see Figure 12.1). During the same time, the region witnessed a rise in the number of heatwaves and extremely hot days, with far-reaching consequences for nature-based tourism. As Figure 12.1 attests, the frequency and occurrence of El Niño events seem to have increased over the past ten years. This is a factor that most likely attributable to climate change. El Niño events often bring about droughts and other adverse weather events in the region. The so-called El Niño years are generally warmer than other years. There is evidence that global warming tends to increase fire frequency and occurrence in the region (Phillips & Nogrady, 2020). Like in any other part of the world, Southern Africa has witnessed record high temperatures over the past decade (World Meteorological Organization, 2021). This increase in temperature has coincided with some catastrophic fires during the same period, resulting in the destruction of flora and fauna in some protected areas such as

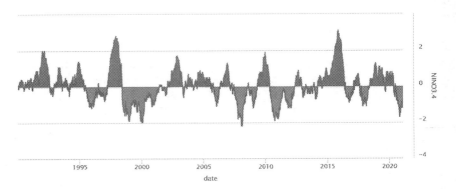

Figure 12.1 Niño 3.4 index for 1990 to 2021, which affected climate in the Southern African region.
Source: SADC (2021).

Table Mountain National Park and Garden Route National Park. This led to disruptions to tourism activities and the destruction of infrastructure.

Figure 12.1 shows the frequency and magnitude of El Niño, which is linked to climate variability. The El Niño has been worsened by climate change, with devastating impacts on various types of nature-based tourism in the Southern African region. In the following sections, the impacts of extreme weather events on nature tourism are examined. Following that there is a discussion on possible conservation measures in the context of climate change and Sustainable Development Goals (SDGs).

Impacts of climate change on nature-based tourism in national parks and other protected areas in Southern Africa

Southern Africa has several national parks, which are significant nature-based tourism destinations for regional and international tourists. One of the countries with the highest number of national parks is South Africa. Van Wilgen et al. (2016) found that national parks in the country are experiencing rapid temperature increases, with arid and semi-arid parks experiencing the worst temperature increase. Current evidence analysed during the study also revealed that several of South Africa's national parks face numerous climatic challenges. The increase in temperature in national parks continues to be of concern and has been observed as a challenge to national parks such as Kruger National Park. Malherbe et al. (2020) observed that recent droughts in the Kruger National park were characterised by higher than usual temperatures. Temperature increases are particularly worrying as they adversely affect some species and contribute to species die-offs in some national parks. The subsequent decline of flora and fauna would ultimately affect tourist appeal and appetite for such destinations. A study by Dube and Nhamo (2020a) found that temperature was a major concern for tourists and tourism staff alike as it affected tourism activities and tourists' comfort.

As previously highlighted, one of the climatic challenges faced by national parks and other nature tourism facilities has been the impact of recurring droughts. Recent droughts have particularly been blamed for the loss of animal populations in South African national parks (Malherbe et al., 2020). MacFadyen et al. (2018) report that climate change has also led to increased aridity and a shift in seasonal rainfall patterns. Such changes have implications for the river regime system in the park and can affect the distribution pattern of aquatic and game species. This would have dire consequences on the tourism season, game viewing experience and, eventually, tourist arrivals at parks such as the Kruger National Park (Dube & Nhamo, 2020a).

At Botswana's Kgalagadi Transfrontier National Park, tour operators have also voiced serious concerns about the impacts of prolonged droughts and increased temperatures over the years. Saarinen et al. (2012) document that some establishments in the area reported low arrivals due to increased temperatures in the transfrontier park. On the other hand, Hoogendoorn and Fitchett (2018) noted a possible disturbance to animal migration patterns within the Kgalagadi Transfrontier National Park. This has the potential to alter animals' spread within the park, and it may also affect fortunes made by various tourism stakeholders in both South Africa and Botswana.

Archibald et al. (2010) observe that the fire regime in protected areas such as Kruger National Park, Etosha (Namibia), Pillanesburg (South Africa) and Hwange National Park (Zimbabwe) seems to follow the rainfall regime and aridity of the area. Prolonged dry spells were also found to be problematic and contribute to the fire frequency in the parks. Pricope and Binford (2012) found that continued rises in global temperature and reduced rainfall activities are responsible for increased fire frequency in one of the richest and largest nature tourism hubs that comprises several national parks and other protected areas in the Kavango Zambezi Transfrontier Conservation Area (KAZA TFCA). The KAZA region has 848 tourism establishments and 619 cultural sites. It incorporates different protected areas from five different countries – Zimbabwe, Zambia, Angola, Botswana and Namibia – and spans over 300,000 km^2 (KAVANGOZAMBEZI, 2021). Fires are disastrous by nature, and their impacts cannot be limited to biodiversity alone. They are likely to have far-reaching negative impacts on destination perception and image. Fires also have a negative and costly impact on tourism infrastructure. They can have deadly consequences to fire rescue teams and tourism personnel.

Besides the impact on the tourist experience, fires have detrimental ecological impacts on protected areas. They have been responsible for vegetation die-offs in some protected areas and hurt vegetation succession. Fires have often been blamed for contributing to bush encroachment (Dube & Nhamo, 2020a). They can drastically reduce the animal population capacity of various protected areas. O'Connor et al. (2014) argue that the challenge of bush encroachment is

166   Kaitano Dube

particularly problematic in small establishments such as small game farms and game reserves.

Furthermore, they report that this problem of encroachment in Southern Africa is also compounded by climate change. Given the cost of correcting such an unwanted development, bush encroachment is likely to drive costs of managing protected areas in the region through increased maintenance costs. Such a development could result in a rise in conservation fees for tourists.

Field observations, experience and archival data have shown that fires have been problematic at mountain destination resorts such as Cape Town's Table Mountain National Park. Wildfires directly and indirectly attributed to climate change have often caused disruptions to Table Mountain National Park's tourism activities. Massive fires often result in the cancellation of hiking activities and disruption in rides on the famous Cableway, one of the most visited spots in Cape Town. Other activities that have been affected by fires on Table Mountain include cable car operations, hiking operations and helicopter views around the mountain. The fires in April 2021 caused extensive damage to several tourist attractions in and around Table Mountain National Park and led to closures of certain parts of the park.

Although the fires have been attributed to human error, weather conditions are also believed to have played a critical role in driving the fire's magnitude and intensity. A statement from the South African National Parks, the management agency in charge of Table Mountain National Park, indicated that the extreme fire danger index of red, characterised by high temperatures of 36°C and very low humidity of less than 10%, was responsible for the rapid spread of the fire (South African National Parks, 2021). Such low humidity is puzzling for such a coastal town. The vulnerability of nature-based tourism destinations to extreme weather events is evident in this particular incident. A temperature of 36°C is too high for the month of April; normally, the temperature would be in the early to mid-20s. The temperature recorded was also a significant deviation from the annual average expected maximum temperature (see Figure 12.2 and 12.3). The fires followed weeks of extremely high temperatures along the coastal areas of South Africa that attracted international media and meteorologists' attention. Extremely high temperatures for April were recorded in Vioolsdrif (Duncan, 2021) and Buffalo City. The latter recorded a temperature of 43.9°C, breaking a 1955 record of 42.6°C (Buffalo City, 2021). Temperature extremes have been a natural phenomenon in the past couple of years, with record high temperatures being reported in 2016, 2019 and 2020 (World Meteorological Organization, 2021). Despite the year 2020 being a La Niña when temperatures were expected to be subdued due to the cooling effect of the phenomenon, in April 2021, this was not so.

On the other hand, in Zimbabwe's Hwange National Park, Mpakairi et al. (2020) voice concerns that the increased reoccurrence of drought in the area has the potential to reduce the habitat's threshold for elephants. Water stress and temperature increases have been cited as one of the biggest threats to elephants in one of biggest elephant sanctuaries in the world and, indeed,

Nature-based tourism and climate change 167

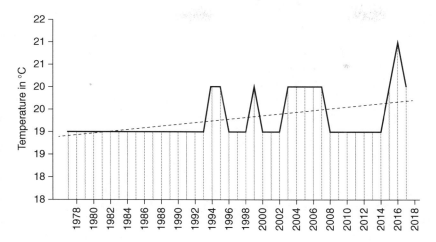

Figure 12.2 Annual average maximum temperature trend at Cape Point (Table Mountain National Park) 1978–2018.
Source: Author Data from South African Weather Services (SAWS).

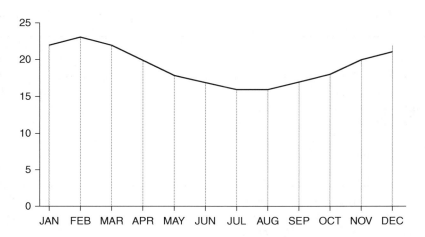

Figure 12.3 Monthly average maximum temperature trend at Cape Point (Table Mountain National Park) 1978–2018.
Source: Author Data from South African Weather Services (SAWS).

Africa. Mushawemhuka et al. (2018) bemoan the impact of extreme rainfall events in the park. They report that the gravel roads in the park often become impassable after heavy rainfall. Intense rainfall often causes localised flooding that disrupts movement by both tourists and tour operators in the park, hence cutting supplies by road. In another of Zimbabwe's national parks, Gonarezhou, droughts and abnormal increases in temperature have also raised concern due to their inadvertent impact on waterholes and vegetation. According to Musakwa et al. (2020), cyclones and erratic rainfall in the park have led to changes in vegetation patterns, loss of biodiversity and soil quality in the park.

Extreme weather events such as tropical cyclones and intense rainfall have been blamed for infrastructural damage caused by flooding in the Kruger National Park and Great Limpopo Transfrontier Park (Dube & Nhamo, 2020a). Flooding causes disturbance in parks. Occasionally, when flooding events occur, certain sections of parks in Southern Africa become inaccessible, affecting tourism operations and tourists' movements alike. Given the paths followed by cyclones in the 2020/2021 rainfall season, the Greater Limpopo Transfrontier Park includes the Kruger, Gonarezhou and Limpopo national parks; these wild-life reserves are particularly vulnerable to the impact of tropical cyclones. After tropical cyclone Idai buffeted and battered the national parks of Gorongosa (Mozambique) and Nyanga (Zimbabwe) in 2021, extensive flooding was reported (Nhamo & Dube, 2021). The 2021 cyclone season was yet another reminder of the vulnerability of national parks to the impact of tropical cyclones in the region.

At least two tropical cyclones affected national parks in the Southern Africa region in the 2020/2021 rainfall season alone. At least five national parks were exposed to at least two of the numerous cyclones that hit Southern Africa. Tropical cyclone Eloise, which started on the 12 January and dissipated on 25 January 2021, severely affected the Kruger, Limpopo, Gonarezhou and Mapungubwe national parks. Consequently, several parts of the Kruger National Park were closed off to visitors. Other tropical cyclones that affected national parks in 2021 include Cyclone Guambe that caused significant rain-fall in St Lucia Wetlands Park in South Africa, and Limpopo National Park in Mozambique. Since it is anticipated that tropical cyclones will become more intense due to climate change (Gupta, Jain, Johari, & Lal, 2019), the cost of cyclone-induced damage to national parks is expected to increase.

In Tanzania, the Serengeti National Park is also reported to be under pressure from the impact of climate change. Kilungu et al. (2017) note that climate change has led to disruptions in the migration of some animal species and the loss of the park's aesthetic values. This could affect seasonal visitor patterns to the park. Changes in migratory patterns caused by irregular rainfall patterns can result in migratory animals spending more time in some sections of the park than others (Fyumagwa et al., 2013). This could trigger some ecosystem challenges and precipitate environmental degradation in certain parts of the park due to grazing and browsing pressure.

A study conducted by Coldrey and Turpie (2020) on South Africa's 19 national parks revealed that some of the major parks could see a decline of 4% in tourist arrivals by 2050. Such a development would negatively impact nature-based tourism in the region. Despite this possible development that could affect host tourism-dependent communities, little is known about how nature-based tourism will be affected by climate change in most national parks across the Southern African region. However, preliminary evidence suggests that climate change will most likely result in decreased tourist arrivals, as highlighted by evidence from Cape Town's Day Zero period (Dube et al., 2020b). Already declines in tourist arrivals caused by COVID-19 have negatively impacted conservation efforts. Other adverse impacts of climate change have been witnessed in Gonarezhou, where increased incidents of drought have led to increases in small-scale poaching activities (Musakwa et al., 2020) in the park. This development is extremely worrying from a conservation perspective.

Conservation and sustainability thinking in nature-based tourism destinations

One of the biggest threats faced by parks in the region is recurring drought, disturbing biodiversity in several protected areas. The vegetation destruction of both grass and tree and/or bush stratum is a significant threat to the habitat of some key species. Other consequences of droughts are increased erosion and desertification in parks, particularly in arid and semi-arid areas. Droughts also pose a significant threat to the riverine environment and aquatic life already battling pollution and over-harvesting in some areas. To ensure sustainability, there is a need to ensure that ecological capacity is respected regarding the number of grazers and herbivores. This is important if grazing and browsing pressure is to be reduced. More so, as many areas gear towards a new adjusted ecological capacity. Such ecological capacity is in most cases lower than envisaged capacities before the advent of anthropogenic climate change. Therefore, in that respect, a timeous census of wildlife at game reserves and national parks must respect new environmental thresholds and ensure sustainability.

There are also fears that prolonged drought poses a significant threat to aquatic life since these creatures suffer the most from the impact of droughts. Droughts are becoming more impactful and are compounded by increased damming (Di Baldassarre et al., 2018) and abstraction in most catchments. Conversely, humanity battles to respond to increased water demand from growing urbanisation and agricultural demands (Sinclair-Smith & Winter, 2019). Consequently, water shortages attributed directly and indirectly to climate change pose a severe threat to water allocated for the environment, threatening aquatic life and other animals dependent on natural water for survival. Given this, an integrated water resources management approach that ensures an adequate water supply is imperative to ensure that environmental water needs are met even amidst growing demands from human beings inside and outside the park. Therefore, there is a need to rethink some of the water infrastructures and evaluate their impact on biodiversity and downstream ecology in the context of climate change. Evidence shows that some water streams can be cut off from the water supply at the end of the hydrological system because of upstream damming in instances where artificial water sources have been used. The spread of water bodies might need to be rationalised to ensure that watering points do

170   *Kaitano Dube*

not worsen the erosion challenge in some national parks and other protected areas, as that would further worsen already heavy siltation levels.

One of the challenges caused by an extended drought in savanna biomes is bush encroachment caused by both injudicious uses of fire and droughts. Bush encroachment can reduce the grazing population and spread of animals, which might affect animals such as cats that are popular with tourists. In the same breath, bush encroachment in some areas could result in increased grazing pressure in areas where bush encroachment is not a problem and create a vicious cycle of encroachment in the park (O'Connor et al., 2014). Bushes are also not ideal for good game viewing, particularly in the summer months when these can blur sightings. Strategic effort must therefore ensure more resources are allocated towards addressing bush encroachment through appropriate actions and interventions. Given the cost of clearing a unit of land, there is a need to set aside more resources towards the maintenance of biodiversity and continued production per unit area in protected areas.

Other smaller protected areas, such as game reserves, also face unique challenges due to climate change. Given the earlier observation on bush encroachment that some enterprises' holding capacity might be rendered too small due to changes brought by climate change, there is a need to ensure that small game establishments adopt adaptation measures to cope with the new challenges. Initiatives for such interventions include joining small establishments and cutting down fences. This will facilitate sustainable wildlife migration corridors that have been disturbed over the years. These could be opened to allow animals to move across searching of places with adequate water and food in times of droughts. Such a move would assist in maintaining and boosting gene pools, accordingly, mitigating against inbreeding depression which has been one of the problems found in small reserves (de Jager et al., 2020). The dual benefit of ensuring that weak gene pools are not reproduced and that strong genes capable of withstanding climate pressures are produced would thus be attained.

Small establishments closer to big national parks can also remove fencing in favour of an open system. However, such an approach must create a win-win situation where small private enterprises reap the benefits of having concessions with large enterprises. The implementation of such measures must be based on empirically sound research (Gandiwa & Zisadza, 2010) and innovation aimed at improving the sustainable management of enterprises. Due to the obvious and possible legal challenges associated with the joining of protected areas, some legislative frameworks might need to be revised to ensure there are no losses to owners of the game when such initiatives are instituted (Blackmore, 2020).

Zimbabwe's Communal Areas Management Programme for Indigenous Resources (CAMPFIRE) model could be used to address community needs and achieve sustainable environmental conservation. However, there is a need to address challenges of CAMPFIRE that have been noted, including community ownership and poor community inclusion in decision-making, which have previously brought the model into disrepute among community members (Shereni & Saarinen, 2020). To address the challenges mentioned above, lessons could be derived from Agenda 2030's SDG target 16.6 that calls for the development of effective, accountable and transparent institutions at all levels, while Target 16.7 calls for responsive, inclusive, participatory and representative decision-making at all levels. Such approaches are crucial in improving operational efficiency and community buy-in.

Conclusion

This study examined the vulnerability of nature-based tourism in protected areas in Southern Africa and discussed possible conservation ramifications and solutions. The study found that, despite there being wide knowledge gaps concerning the state and impact of climate variability and change in nature-based tourism in protected areas in Southern Africa, current evidence points to the huge vulnerability of the sector to climate change. The major threats to nature-based tourism include increased frequency and prolonged droughts, global warming, intense rainfall activity, fires, desertification, and increased frequency of wildfires.

Some of the major nature-based tourism destinations, such as the Kruger National Park, have also suffered flooding threats. Climate change has led to the loss of animals and vegetation in some nature-based tourism destinations. Flooding in protected areas continues to pose a threat to heritage sites. The threat of climate change calls for new conservation approaches in protected areas that are modelled to ensure nature-based tourism destinations embrace green tourism ethos and adopt conservation measures that address climate change mitigation and adaptation to ensure nature-based tourism resilience. Addressing climate change in nature-based tourism destinations is imperative and should address SDG13 on climate change action and the Paris Agreement. There is a strong need to ensure continuous monitoring and research in current and future conservation practices if they are to be responsive to climate change. In some instances, policy and conservation practices need to be revised to reduce mismatches brought about by climate change and proposed solutions.

References

Archibald, S., Nickless, A., Govender, N., Scholes, R. J., & Lehsten, V. (2010). Climate and the inter-annual variability of fire in southern Africa: A meta-analysis using long-term field data and satellite-derived burnt area data. *Global Ecology and Biogeography*, 19 (6), 794–809.

Armarego-Marriott, T. (2020). Climate or biodiversity? *Nature Climate Change*, 10 (5), 385–385.

Blackmore, A. (2020). Climate change and the ownership of game: A concern for fenced wildlife areas. *Koedoe*, 62 (1), 1–5.

Buffalo City. (2021). Record Heat. Retrieved 25 April 2021, from www.facebook.com/buffalocitytourism/photos/a.704209272955941/3866566240053546/

172   *Kaitano Dube*

Coldrey, K. M., & Turpie, J. K. (2020). Potential impacts of changing climate on nature-based tourism: A case study of South Africa's national parks. *Koedoe*, 62 (1), 1–12.

de Jager, D., Harper, C. K., & Bloomer, P. (2020). Genetic diversity, relatedness and inbreeding of ranched and fragmented Cape buffalo populations in southern Africa. *PLoS One*, 15 (8), e0236717.

Di Baldassarre, G., Wanders, N., AghaKouchak, A., Kuil, L., Rangecroft, S., Veldkamp, T. I., & Van Loon, A. F. (2018). Water shortages worsened by reservoir effects. *Nature Sustainability,* 1 (11), 617–622.

Dube, K., & Nhamo, G. (2018). Climate variability, change and potential impacts on tourism: Evidence from the Zambian side of the Victoria Falls. *Environmental Science & Policy*, 84, 113–123.

Dube, K., & Nhamo, G. (2020a). Evidence and impact of climate change on South African national parks. Potential implications for tourism in the Kruger National Park. *Environmental Development,* 33, 100485.

Dube, K., & Nhamo, G. (2020b). Vulnerability of nature-based tourism to climate variability and change: Case of Kariba resort town, Zimbabwe. *Journal of Outdoor Recreation and Tourism*, 29, 100281.

Dube, K., Nhamo, G., & Chikodzi, D. (2020a). Climate change-induced droughts and tourism: Impacts and responses of Western Cape province, South Africa. *Journal of Outdoor Recreation and Tourism*, 100319. doi:10.1016/j.jort.2020.100319

Dube, K., Nhamo, G., & Mearns, K. (2020b). &Beyond's response to the twin challenges of pollution and climate change in the context of SDGs. In Nhamo, G., Oularo, G., & Mjimba, V. (Eds.), *Scaling up SDGs Implementation*. Sustainable Development Goals Series. Cham: Springer, 87–98.

Duncan, S. (2021). Historic moment. Retrieved 25 April 2021, from www.facebook.com/photo?fbid=393511668697835&set=pcb.393511715364497

Franklin, J., Serra-Diaz, J. M., Syphard, A. D., & Regan, H. M. (2016). Global change and terrestrial plant community dynamics. *Proceedings of the National Academy of Sciences,* 113 (14), 3725–3734.

Fyumagwa, R., Gereta, E., Hassan, S., Kideghesho, J. R., Kohi, E. M., Keyyu, J., & Røskaft, E. (2013). Roads as a threat to the Serengeti ecosystem. *Conservation Biology,* 27 (5), 1122–1125.

Gandiwa, E., & Zisadza, P. (2010). Wildlife management in Gonarezhou National Park, Southeast Zimbabwe: Climate change and implications for management. *Nature and Faune,* 25 (1), 95–104.

Gupta, S., Jain, I., Johari, P., & Lal, M. (2019). Impact of climate change on tropical cyclones frequency and intensity on Indian coasts. *Proceedings of international conference on remote sensing for disaster management*. Cham: Springer, 359–365.

Gusenbauer, M. (2019). Google Scholar to overshadow them all? Comparing the sizes of 12 academic search engines and bibliographic databases. *Scientometrics*, 118 (1), 177–214.

Hambira, W. L., Saarinen, J., Atlhopheng, J., & Manwa, H. (2020). Climate change, tourism and community development: Perceptions of Maun residents, Botswana. *Tourism Review* International, 25 (2–3), 105–117. doi:10.3727/154427220X16059054538773

Hoogendoorn, G., & Fitchett, J. M. (2018). Tourism and climate change: A review of threats and adaptation strategies for Africa. *Current Issues in Tourism*, 21 (7), 742–759.

KAVANGOZAMBEZI. (2021). *KAVANGO Zambezi*. Retrieved 21 April 2021, from https://kavangozambezi.org/en/maps

Nature-based tourism and climate change   173

Kilungu, H., Leemans, R., Munishi, P. K., & Amelung, B. (2017). Climate change threatens major tourist attractions and tourism in Serengeti National Park, Tanzania. In Leal Filho, W. (Ed.), *Climate change adaptation in Africa*. Cham: Springer, 375–392.

MacFadyen, S., Zambatis, N., Van Teeffelen, A. J., & Hui, C. (2018). Long-term rainfall regression surfaces for the Kruger National Park, South Africa: A spatio-temporal review of patterns from 1981 to 2015. *International Journal of Climatology*, 38 (5), 25.

Malherbe, J., Smit, I. P., Wessels, K. J., & Beukes, P. J. (2020). Recent droughts in the Kruger National Park as reflected in the extreme climate index. *African Journal of Range & Forage Science*, 37 (1), 1–17.

Maviza, A., & Ahmed, F. (2021). Climate change/variability and hydrological modelling studies in Zimbabwe: A review of progress and knowledge gaps. *SN Applied Sciences*, 3 (5), 1–28.

Mpakairi, K. S., Ndaimani, H., Tagwireyi, P., Zvidzai, M., & Madiri, T. H. (2020). Futuristic climate change scenario predicts a shrinking habitat for the African elephant (Loxodonta africana): Evidence from Hwange National Park, Zimbabwe. *European Journal of Wildlife Research*, 66 (1), 1–10.

Musakwa, W., Mpofu, E., & Nyathi, N. A. (2020). Local community perceptions on landscape change, ecosystem services, climate change, and livelihoods in Gonarezhou National Park, Zimbabwe. *Sustainability*, 12 (11), 4610.

Mushawemhuka, W., Rogerson, J. M., & Saarinen, J. (2018). Nature-based tourism operators' perceptions and adaptation to climate change in Hwange National Park, Zimbabwe. *Bulletin of Geography. Socio-economic Series*, 42 (42), 115–127.

Nhamo, G., & Dube, K. (2021). *Cyclones in Southern Africa*. Foundational and Fundamental Topics, vol. 2. Cham: Springer. doi:10.1007/978-3-030-74262-1

O'Connor, T. G., Puttick, J. R., & Hoffman, M. T. (2014). Bush encroachment in southern Africa: Changes and causes. *African Journal of Range & Forage Science*, 31 (2), 67–88.

Phillips, N., & Nogrady, B. (2020). The race to decipher how climate change influenced Australia's record fires. *Nature*, 577 (7791), 610–613.

Pricope, N., & Binford, M. (2012). A spatio-temporal analysis of fire recurrence and extent for semi-arid savanna ecosystems in southern Africa using moderate-resolution satellite imagery. *Journal of Environmental Management*, 100, 72–85.

Roberts, K., Dowell, A., & Nie, J. B. (2019). Attempting rigour and replicability in thematic analysis of qualitative research data; A case study of codebook development. *BMC Medical Research Methodology*, 1 (19), 66.

Saarinen, J., Hambira, W. L., Atlhopheng, J., & Manwa, H. (2012). Tourism industry reaction to climate change in Kgalagadi South District, Botswana. *Development Southern Africa*, 29 (2), 273–285.

Shereni, N. C., & Saarinen, J. (2020). Community perceptions on the benefits and challenges of community-based natural resources management in Zimbabwe. *Development Southern Africa*, 1–17. doi:10.1080/0376835X.2020.1796599

Siakwah, P., Musavengane, R., & Leonard, L. (2020). Tourism governance and attainment of the Sustainable Development Goals in Africa. *Tourism Planning & Development*, 17 (4), 355–383.

Sinclair-Smith, K., & Winter, K. (2019). Water demand management in Cape Town: Managing water security in a changing climate. In Scott, D., Davies, H., & New, M. (Eds.), *Mainstreaming climate change in urban development: Lessons from Cape Town*. Cape Town: UCT Press, 100–131.

Smith, T., & Fitchett, J. M. (2020). Drought challenges for nature tourism in the Sabi Sands Game Reserve in the eastern region of South Africa. *African Journal of Range & Forage Science,* 37 (1), 107–117.

South African National Parks. (2021). Media release: Rhodes Memorial fire update. Retrieved 23 April 2021, from www.sanparks.org/about/news/?id=58213

van Wilgen, N. J., Goodall, V., Holness, S., Chown, S. L., & McGeoch, M. A. (2016). Rising temperatures and changing rainfall patterns in South Africa's national parks. *International Journal of Climatology,* 36 (2), 706–721.

Wisely, S. M., Alexander, K., & Cassidy, L. (2018). Linking ecosystem services to livelihoods in southern Africa. *Ecosystem Services,* 30, 339–341.

World Meteoorological Organization. (2021). State of the global climate 2020. Retrieved 23 April 2021, from https://library.wmo.int/index.php?lvl=notice_display&id=21880#.YH18CO8zZBw

13 International organisations and the ivory sales ban debate

The case of Zimbabwe, Namibia and Botswana

Caroline Cox

Introduction

6 September 2005, Kruger National Park, South Africa: It is our third drive out into the Bushveld with our ranger, Patrick. We move slowly along a dusty, potholed track as the sun slowly begins to get lower in the wide African sky. The rich smell of the African bush surrounds us. The vegetation is rich but there are wide areas of open ground. We are hunters of a sort, but our weapon of choice is a camera, not a gun. We have already seen giraffe, rhino and hyena. Patrick points out a lioness to our right. She is suckling two cubs and my husband snaps a photo for the holiday album. Patrick stops the land rover. She looks nervous, he says, as the lioness' head comes up and she sniffs the air. She stands, gathers her cubs to her and slowly makes for cover. Patrick holds up his hand. Quiet. We wait. Almost unperceivably at first, I feel the ground begin to shake. Next comes an undeniable rumble, like a deep belly laugh, which increases steadily in volume and intensity. I feel it reverberate through my bones. Patrick smiles. You are very lucky, he says, as a herd of 20 or so elephants steam over the hill in front of us.

This was the first time I saw elephants in the wild and when I think about that late afternoon, it still evokes profound emotions. Memories of an adventure in Africa that will never leave me. Later that same drive, we came across an elephant's corpse. The animal had been dead only a few days but was already decaying rapidly in the heat. Patrick was uneasy about showing it to us. The smell was atrocious, and the vultures had taken up their positions on the body. Its tusks were clearly visible at the sides of its huge sunken head and Patrick used his two-way radio to call it into his office. Rangers, he said, would come and remove the tusks so as not to encourage poachers while the corpse would remain in Bushveld to continue the circle of life. This is the reality of Southern Africa. On that first visit to the Kruger, we were privileged to stay at an historic, private concession in the southern part of the National Park. The Lodge is unique, not just in the astounding fauna and flora that visitors come to see but also in its approach to the conservation, protection of its wild neighbours and its commitment to the employment of local people. Patrick himself had had a

DOI: 10.4324/9781003193166-16

176 *Caroline Cox*

very different life prior to joining the Lodge team. This quiet, knowledgeable man had been a poacher. His tracking skills were excellent – when the Lodge was looking to recruit rangers, he was an obvious choice.

As well as providing on the ground ranger support to the SANParks team, the Lodge contributes to several conservation projects (including the Black Rhinoceros Guardianship Program and the Savannah Vulture Project) in line with its mission to preserve and protect wildlife and wilderness areas (Caleo Foundation, 2021). It represents the best of Southern Africa's 'tourism for conservation' ethos – to protect, restore and sustain its wildlife and flora. Unlike its neighbours, South Africa has not raised the issue of a lifting of the ban on the international commercial sale of ivory. In this chapter, we will seek, through a review of the available literature and reports, to understand and analyse the arguments put forward by Zimbabwe, Botswana and Namibia in favour of such a move.

The first section of this chapter will give a brief history of CITES and the reasons behind the global ban on the sale of ivory. The second section will consider the workings of CITES, the poaching crisis and elephant surveys across Africa. The third section will ask whether elephants can (or should) be conserved through the sale of ivory and the fourth section considers the reasons behind CITES' continuing opposition to this idea. The final section of the chapter brings together some discussion points and concludes that the frustrated southern African states are likely to continue to press for a lifting of the ivory sales ban.

A brief history of CITES: the 'magna carta for wildlife' and the reasons behind the global ban on the sale of ivory

The Convention on International Trade in Endangered Species of Wild Fauna and Flora (CITES) is often cited as one of the world's most successful multilateral environmental agreements (Wijnstekers, 2011). Drafted following a resolution adopted in 1963 at an International Union for Conservation of Nature (IUCN), the text of the convention was agreed in 1973, and the Convention came in to force on 1 July 1975 (Corn, 2016).

Hailed by some commentators as 'a magna carta for wildlife' (Layne, 1973, p. 99), CITES is an international trade agreement which protects the world's fauna and flora by listing endangered species under either Appendix I, II or III – with Appendix I affording the most protection to those species considered to be at risk of extinction (CITES, 2021a, b). CITES' objectives may appear straightforward, but they exist in a world of complicated human nature and powerful economics that makes its implementation and enforcement considerably more arduous. Few would argue against CITES' intentions but counter to those are the formidable forces of human greed and the desire to own or exploit rare and exotic species.

Zimbabwe, Botswana and Namibia, together with 180 other states, are bound by the provisions of the CITES which prohibits the trade in more than 38,700 species of endangered flora and fauna, including some of Southern Africa's most iconic animals. Zimbabwe's President Mnangagwa has been vocal in his belief that CITES should be commending his country for the steps taken to grow its elephant populations by allowing a trade in ivory that would work alongside conservation incentives. However, the Africa's elephant population is declining, and this is due in the most part to illegal poaching (Hauenstein et al., 2019).

The destruction of the African elephant population is a tale that runs parallel to the history of European exploration of the African continent. While in the 1500s, there were estimated to be 26 million elephants roaming the African savannah, by the beginning of the 20th century this had dropped to 10 million (Muskopf, 2021). By the 1950s, the killing of elephants had drastically increased, with estimates that 250 elephants were killed every day (Allen, 2016). Global fears of losing not only Africa's most iconic species but many others besides led to the CITES being signed on 3 March 1973.

In 1977, the African elephant was listed on the CITES Appendices; however, international trade for commercial purposes continued under CITES regulation (CITES, 2021a, b). As the numbers of elephants in the wild continued to fall, in 1979, Dr Iain Douglas-Hamilton led the first Pan-African elephant survey and reported that the elephant population had fallen to 1.3 million (Great Elephant Census, 2021). By the mid-1980s, it was clear that after ten years of regulated trade in ivory, that CITES regulation was not working effectively. The African elephant population had decreased by more than half in only ten years, from 1.3 million in 1978, to only 600,000 in 1988 (Humane Society International, 2013). By 1988, more than 90% of the ivory in the international trade was estimated to have come from poached elephants (Humane Society International, 2013).

In 1989, CITES responded by listing the African elephant on Appendix I, thereby banning the international commercial trade in African elephant ivory as of 20 January 1990 (Humane Society International, 2013). In 1997, with their in-country populations stable and growing, CITES transferred the African elephant populations of Botswana, Namibia and Zimbabwe to CITES Appendix II, with an 'annotation' to the transfer that the international ivory trade for commercial purposes would not be permitted (Humane Society International, 2013). However, CITES agreed to a 'one-time, experimental' export of 49 metric tons of government-stockpiled ivory from Botswana, Namibia and Zimbabwe to Japan in 1997, which took place in 1999 (Lemieux & Clarke, 2009). The following year the South African elephants were also transferred to Appendix II, with a similar 'annotation' (Humane Society International, 2013).

The 1997 'one off, experimental' export of ivory was followed in 2000 with an approved second export of 60 metric tons of government-stockpiled African elephant ivory from South Africa, Botswana and Namibia to unnamed 'trading partners' approved by CITES (Humane Society International, 2013). The export took place until 2008 and in the same year CITES increased the amount of government-stockpiled ivory that could be exported to 108 metric tons and included Zimbabwe among the African countries that could take part in the

178 *Caroline Cox*

export (Humane Society International, 2013). Additionally, CITES approved Japan and China to receive ivory but agreed not to approve any additional international commercial ivory trade for nine years (CITES Secretariat, 2016). This decision saw South Africa, Botswana, Namibia and Zimbabwe export 102 metric tons of ivory to Japan and China in November 2008 (Humane Society International, 2013). This decision was credited (or blamed) for reinvigorating the Chinese government's approved ivory-carving industry, which had been waning since the 1989 CITES ivory trade ban was established. The Far East remains the main destination for poached African ivory, proving that the 'experimental' exports of the 1990s have not been effective in stopping the illegal trade. Poaching is, once again, threatening the survival of the species, with an estimated 415,000 African elephants now left in the wild (Tusk.org, 2021).

CITES, poaching and elephant surveys

While CITES has reported that 'overall' elephant poaching in Africa has been in a gradual decline for the past five years, in some parts of the continent it is increasing – specifically, Central Africa, where dramatic losses of elephant populations have been reported over the last ten years, and levels of illegal killing remain very high (Yuan, 2017). However, in May 2019, Botswana, Namibia and Zimbabwe, taking advantage of the more positive news coming from CITES on the Southern African region, appealed to the Convention to lift the restrictive measures on the trade in raw ivory and allow them to resume their commercial international trade (Chingono, 2019a, b).

In 2019, Botswana, Zimbabwe and Namibia submitted a proposal to the CITES CoP18 Conference of the Parties to amend Annotation 2 to the Appendix II listing of African elephants, seeking to reopen international commercial trade in ivory and other elephant specimens sourced from their own elephant populations (CITES, 2019).[1] At the same meeting of the parties, another proposal was submitted on behalf of the African Elephant Coalition in direct opposition to that of the Southern African states. It sought to strengthen the protection of African elephants by placing all African elephant populations in Appendix I (CITES, 2019).

Arguments against Botswana, Zimbabwe and Namibia's proposal included that it failed to recognise the devastating consequences that a legal ivory market can have on elephant populations (Environmental Investigation Agency, 2019). Indeed, it was these consequences which resulted in the CITES Conference of the Parties making a call to all members to close their own domestic ivory markets (CITES, 2017). Additionally, conservation groups and policy advisers argued that there was growing evidence showing that the previous CITES 'one-off' ivory sales had had a significant impact on stimulating the demand for ivory in China and Asian markets, leading to an increase in poaching and trafficking (Gabriel, 2021). Further, it was argued that the poaching crisis was continuing to threaten elephant populations across the African range states (Monitoring the Illegal Killing of Elephants (MIKE), 2019).

Of course, the elephant populations of Botswana, Namibia and Zimbabwe (as well as South Africa) may be Appendix II animals, but those countries share borders with states whose elephants are listed under Appendix I, including Angola, Mozambique and Zambia (Lindsay et al., 2017). The MIKE (2019) Report submitted to CoP18 found that there had been an increase in the proportion of illegally killed elephants (PIKE) for Southern Africa states since 2016. This included elephants in the Chobe National Park in Botswana and Kruger National Park in South Africa. In addition, the 2016 IUCN African Elephant Status Report noted that, 'While overall, poaching has not had the same impact in Southern Africa as in other regions it has severely affected populations in Zimbabwe, Angola, Mozambique and to a lesser extent, Zambia' (Thouless et al., 2016, p. 6). The Report referred to the 'poaching of elephants by armed gangs' as an increasing threat in northern Botswana and found a 'notable increase' of carcass ratio since 2012 in Botswana and to the increase in poaching in the Zambezi Region of Namibia since 2006 (Thouless et al., 2016). Finally, the Elephant Trade Information System (ETIS), the CITES-mandated tool that tracks the illegal trade in elephant ivory and other elephant products, reported in May 2016 that they had identified Namibia as a country of origin for export for illegally worked ivory, and Botswana and Zimbabwe as sources of ivory to the illegal trade in raw ivory (Milliken et al., 2004). Botswana, with over 130,000 elephants living within its boundaries, is home to the world's largest elephant population, but despite the country's incredible conservation cache, reports suggest that, regrettably, Botswana's airports and border crossings are a major hub for traffickers to export their spoils of the illegal wildlife trade (UNODC, 2020).

While the 'open/don't open the ivory market' debate continues across Africa and beyond, what is clear from the proposals put to the CoP18 Meeting of the Parties is that Botswana, Namibia and Zimbabwe are in the minority in wanting the ban on international commercial trade in ivory lifted (Dalton, 2019). The proposal submitted to the CoP18 by the African Elephant Coalition, testify to the fact that most of the African elephant range states are in favour of closing all domestic ivory markets and that there is very little international appetite for resuming an international commercial trade in ivory at a time when countries outside Africa are taking active steps to close their domestic ivory markets (Department for the Environment, Food and Rural Affairs, 2018). Against this continuing divergence, the next Conference of the Parties is expected to take place in June 2022, and it is likely that Botswana, Namibia, and Zimbabwe will make a fresh application there.

Conservation through ivory sales?

The Southern African range states together are home to 70% of the population of African Savannah elephants (Thouless et al., 2016) and the inability to sell their stockpiles of ivory is causing growing irritation (Chingono, 2019a, b). Ndabaningi Nick Mangwana, Zimbabwe's Permanent Secretary in the Ministry of Information, Publicity and Broadcasting Services said in 2019 that: 'Our ivory stockpile is worth over $300m [£235m], which we can't sell because countries without elephants are telling those with them what to do with their animals' (Chingono, 2019b). While his statement to the press was not entirely true and that in fact most of the African range states oppose a lifting of the ivory sale ban, Mangwana's unhappiness at the current position is echoed by many of his countrymen. Zimbabweans (together with Botswana and Namibians) believe that, if the international commercial ban on the sale of ivory was removed, it could, as their governments promise, provide much needed funding for conservation and community projects. The Zimbabwean president, Emmerson Mnangagwa, told delegates at the Africa Wildlife Economy Summit in 2019, that while Zimbabwe 'remain[ed] committed to the adherence of [CITES'] protocols and rules ... We are gravely concerned ... by the one-size-fits-all approach' and called on CITES 'to resist the temptation to be a policing institution but instead to be a developmental organisation to promote conservation communities and sustainable utilisation of all wildlife resources' (Chingono, 2019a).

However, it is not just the opportunity to use ivory money for conservation prompting the demand that CITES reconsider the current position. Zimbabwe and Namibia are also reporting increasing conflict between the human population and wildlife (Gandiwa, 2021). Zimbabwe has a large elephant population, approximately 83,000 animals, but its human population is also growing. As a result, elephants are being restricted to ever smaller protected areas, which are not large enough to accommodate them. As the elephant population expands, they instinctively move out of their designated habitat in search of food and water (Conservation Action Trust, 2015). Consequently, the species come into contact (and conflict) with their human neighbours. Farmers report elephants raiding crops and threatening lives and the Zimbabwe Parks and Wildlife Management Authority report that the country has an elephant population that cannot be effectively homed within its national park protected areas (Conservation Action Trust, 2015).

There is no doubt that the work Zimbabwe has done to increase its elephant population from a low of 4,000 animals in 1900 to its current figure of 83,000 is remarkable but, it is argued by many Zimbabweans, it has come at a cost to its delicate ecosystem (Zimbabwe Parks and Wildlife Management Authority, 2020). Indeed, another frequently heard rationale put forward for limiting elephant numbers is to reduce the impact they have on biodiversity and woodland habitats (Coneybeare, 2004; Cumming, 1982). The reality is that Zimbabwe's elephant population is considerably higher than was envisaged in the 1980s when the target was to maintain a population of about 35,000 elephants (Cumming, 1983). Zimbabwe's experience is shared by that of Namibia and Botswana.

Namibia's desert elephants migrate from one waterhole to another, following traditional routes across the Namib desert in search of food and water and their decline is largely due to human–elephant conflict incidents (Platt, 2014 & Griffin, 2009). In the mid-1990s, people moved into the area following

Namibia's independence and many of the new residents had no experience of living with wild elephants (Chase & Griffin, 2009). Reports of elephant/human conflict increased as the competition for land and water resulted in conflict situations between the desert elephants and the people living along-side them (Elephant Wildlife Volunteer Project, 2021). The reality for desert-based farmers is that a herd of ten elephants can empty a water reservoir that is meant for livestock, crops, and family needs (Elephant-Human Relations Aid, 2021). The Namibian situation has declined to such an extent that, in March 2021, Namibian Minister Shifeta, told the country's lawmakers that they were facing unprecedented human–wildlife conflict exacerbated by drought (Nyaungwa, 2021).

Botswana, home to the spectacular Okavango Delta, is also Africa's elephant stronghold (Rice, 2020). The country has the world's largest population of elephants, estimated at 130,000 thousand (Sutcliffe, 2019). However, while Botswana is lauded as a haven and a shining example of conservation, it is not without its problems with its giant inhabitants. Botswana's farmers and residents in the north of the country are struggling to coexist with elephants who, similarly to in Namibia and Zimbabwe, destroy crops and threaten livelihoods (DeMotts, 2010).

In Botswana, more than 70% of elephants roam outside the country's protected areas (Thouless et al., 2016). This being the case, it is perhaps of little surprise that the main reasons given by the Botswana government for, first, lifting its hunting ban and secondly, supporting Zimbabwe and Namibia in their application to CITES to lift the ban on international commercial trade in ivory, were the growing human–elephant conflict and habitat destruction (BBC News, 2019). President Khama introduced the ban on hunting elephant in 2014 (Mbaiwa, 2017). However, in February 2019, President Mokgweetsi Masisi's committee, set up to review the ban, recommended that Botswana allow hunting again on the basis that 'there is a negative impact of the hunting suspension on livelihoods, particularly for community-based organizations' (Bale, 2019). There was criticism following the decision, not least from ex-President Khama, who described it as a political move and an attempt by them to shore up the rural vote. Conversely, proponents of safari hunting argue that, if controlled, it holds financial benefits for the country and is an important form of selective culling of over populated herds – and as such is an important and useful conservation tool (Baker, 1997; Baldus, 2004).

In the months leading up to the 2019 CITES Conference of the Parties, elephants did not stray far from the headlines as Zimbabwe lobbied for support in their efforts to sell their stockpiled ivory (Chingono, 2019a). This, together with Botswana's change of policy on international ivory sales saw it, alongside Zimbabwe and Namibia, seeking to resume ivory trading (Sheldrick Wildlife Trust, 2019). With the political manoeuvrings that had gone on in the lead-up to CoP18, it came as little surprise when the three countries submitted proposals to decrease elephant protection and restart the international ivory trade (CITES Management Authority of Zimbabwe, 2019; EIA, 2019).

182   *Caroline Cox*

CITES says 'no'

The first proposal, submitted by Botswana, requested the CITES parties to allow a sale of stockpiled ivory. Although supported by Southern African nations, it exposed divides on elephant conservation on the continent. Citing the reason for the proposal as a need to raise funds for conservation and community development, it was defeated with 101 votes against 23 in support and 18 abstentions (Agade, 2019). The CITES parties explained their decision on the grounds that any legal international trade in ivory would have an impact on elephant populations by acting to conceal the illegal ivory trade and defeat the years of work carried out by campaigns in consumer countries in the Far East and that any release of stockpiled ivory would risk accelerating illegal sales in places like Vietnam where illegal markets are thriving and in Japan, where there remains a legal trade for ivory (Nuwer, 2018; CITES, 2019).

Discussion and conclusion

Given mankind's rampant consumption of natural resources, there is a natural tension between conservationist groups opposed to any trade in ivory and countries wishing to use the natural resources at their disposal for profit or, as in the case of Zimbabwe, Namibia and Botswana, their conservation efforts. No one can doubt the incredible privilege of being home to world's most iconic species but when that species is a 6,000 kg giant that can eat 400 kg of food a day, we need to consider the negative effects on its close, human neighbours (International Elephant Foundation, 2021). The witness accounts of rural communities tell of the destruction caused by elephants to crops and the wider ecosystem. Additionally, and very sadly, people have lost their lives to marauding elephants (Madzwamuse, 2020). This has regrettably led to increased human–elephant conflict across Southern Africa that has seen clashes between farmers and the pachyderms occur anywhere that elephants and people live in proximity (Warner, 2008). Forget the idealised 'Out of Africa' landscape of an unpopulated wilderness. The reality for African conservation is much more complicated. It takes place in human-dominated landscapes which brings with it questions of citizens' rights, ownership of land and political power which are increasingly overlooked in international public conservation discussions and policy processes. Human–elephant conflict is a growing concern of both governments and conservationists across Africa.

Zimbabwe, Namibia and Botswana have benefitted economically from their ecotourism industries (Polakow, 2001). Safaris to their achingly beautiful national parks costs thousands of pounds and visitors want to see Africa's most famous inhabitants. However, what visitors do not see, and perhaps do not realise, is that population growth in the Southern African states has led to the elephants' traditional range areas shrinking to accommodate human activity (Madzwamuse, 2020). As a result, two competing ideological approaches have emerged in African wildlife conservation. On the one hand is the exclusionary approach that is aligned with the, mostly Western, animal protection and conservation movement (Schramlc, 2018). On the other, there is the approach being taken by our three Southern African states, which can be described as a human rights-based approach (Greiber et al., 2009). This sees governments reflecting the opinions and advocating for the rights of their citizens (Madzwamuse, 2020).

We can see these same two ideologies going head-to-head in the ivory sales debate. On the one hand, the (mostly Western) parties to CITES preventing Southern African states from using their stockpiled natural resources in a bid to prevent a new poaching crisis and on the other, Southern African countries, with stockpiles of ivory worth millions of dollars desperate for access to this great, untapped resource to fund community and conservation projects.

Decisions that affect our fragile planet and its wildlife have become a hot political issue. We have witnessed wins and losses for elephants at the various CITES conferences over the years. The calls made by the Southern African states to lift the ban on international commercial sales of ivory will, likely continue and the gulf between them and the outside world on this issue will widen. Zimbabwe will continue to feel their hands are tied by outsiders who do not understand the real situation and that they are wrongly being prevented from using the $600 million worth of ivory in their stockpile. While their government tells them that they have enough ivory to fund community and conservation projects for the next 20 years, it is not surprising that Zimbabwean farmers believe 'animals have more rights' than the human population (Chingono, 2019b).

As the argument continues, this writer's mind cannot help but return to an evening in early September 2005 on a game drive in the Kruger. After an emotional first encounter with the great African Savannah elephants the wise words of Patrick, ranger and ex-poacher are recalled; these animals are the past, present and future of Southern Africa – their survival is our survival.

Note

1 They also included South Africa in this application.

References

Agade, H. (2019). Africa Live. 23 August. Retrieved from CGTN: https://africa.cgtn.com/2019/08/23/cites-reject-proposal-to-allow-legal-ivory-sales/

Allen, P. G. (2016). *Great elephant census*. Seattle, WA: Vulcan.

Baker, J. E. (1997). Development of a model system for touristic hunting revenue collection and allocation. *Tourism Management*, 18 (5), 273–286.

Baldus, R. (2004). Tourist hunting and its role in development of wildlife. Proceedings of the 6th International Game Ranching Symposium, Paris.

Bale, R. (2019). Botswana lifts ban on elephant hunting. 22 May. Retrieved from National Geographic. www.nationalgeographic.com/animals/article/botswana-lifts-ban-on-elephant-hunting

184 *Caroline Cox*

BBC News. (2019). Botswana lifts ban on elephant hunting. 22 May. Retrieved from BBC News: www.bbc.co.uk/news/world-africa-48374880

Caleo Foundation. (2021). Black rhinoceros guardian programme. 3 March. Retrieved from Caleo Foundation: www.caleo-foundation.org/projects/jock-safari-lodge/conservation-projects/

Chase, M., & Griffin, C. (2009). Elephants caught in the middle: Impacts of war, fences and people on elephant distribution and abundance in the Caprivi Strip, Namibia. *African Journal of Ecology*, 47 (2), 223–233.

Chingono, N. (2019a). Lift 'unfair' ban on ivory trade, southern African leaders urge summit. Retrieved from Guardian, 26 June. www.theguardian.com/global-development/2019/jun/26/lift-ban-ivory-trade-southern-african-leaders-summit#:~:text=Southern%20African%20leaders%20have%20renewed,the%20%E2%80%9Cunfair%E2%80%9D%20embargo%20escalates.&text=Cites'%20rules%2C%20which%20co

Chingono,N.(2019b).Rawivorysales:Zimbabwe,BotswanaandNamibiacallforendtoban. RetrievedfromGuardian,21May.www.theguardian.com/global-development/2019/may/21/raw-ivory-sales-zimbabwe-botswana-and-namibia-call-for-end-to-ban

CITES. (2017). Implementing aspects of resolution conf. 10.10 (rev. COP17). 1 December. Retrieved from CITES: https://cites.org/sites/default/files/eng/com/sc/69/E-SC69-51-02.pdf

CITES. (2019). CITES – Decisions of the Conference of the Parties to CITES in effect after the 18th meeting. Retrieved from CITES: https://cites.org/sites/default/files/eng/dec/valid18/E18-Dec.pdf

CITES. (2019). CoP18 Prop. 11. 8 March. Retrieved from Convention on International Trade in Endangered Species: https://cites.org/sites/default/files/eng/cop/18/prop/19032019/E-CoP18-Prop-11.pdf

CITES. (2019). CoP18 Prop. 12. 8 March. Retrieved from Convention on International Trade in Endangered Species: https://cites.org/sites/default/files/eng/cop/18/prop/060319/E-CoP18-Prop-12.pdf

CITES. (2021a). African elephant. 14 March. Retrieved from CITES: https://cites.org/eng/gallery/species/mammal/african_elephant.html

CITES. (2021b). The CITES appendices. 11 February. Retrieved from CITES: https://cites.org/eng/app/index.php

CITES Management Authority of Zimbabwe. (2019, May 23). Consideration of proposals for amendment of appendices I and II. Retrieved from Convention on International Trade in Endangered Species: https://cites.org/sites/default/files/eng/cop/18/prop/19032019/E-CoP18-Prop-11.pdf

CITES Secretariat. (2016). Current rules on commercial international trade in elephant ivory under CITES and Proposals to CITES CoP17. 21 July. Retrieved from CITES: https://cites.org/eng/news/Current_rules_commercial_international_trade_elephant_ivory_under_CITES_Proposals_CITES_CoP17_200716

Coneybeare, A. (2004). Elephant impacts on vegetation and other biodiversity in the Four Corners Area. *Biodiversity of the Four Corners Area: Technical*, 477–508.

Conservation Action Trust. (2015). *Zimbabwe national elephant management plan (2015–2020)*. Harare: Zimbabwe Parks and Wildlife Management Authority.

Convention on International Trade in Endangered Species of Wild Fauna and Flora. (1973). 993 U.N.T.S. 243, Art. 3. Convention on International Trade in Endangered Species of Wild Fauna and Flora.

Corn, P. A. (2016). *The convention on international trade in endangered species of wild fauna and flora*. Washington, DC: Congressional Research Service.

Cumming, D. (1982). The influence of large herbivores on savanna structure in Africa. In Huntley, B. A. (Ed.), *Ecology of tropical savannas*. Berlin: Springer Verlag, 217–245.

Cumming, D. (1983). The decision-making framework with regard to the culling of large mammals in Zimbabwe. In Owen-Smith, N., *The management of large mammals in African conservation areas*. Pretoria: Haum, 173–186.

Dalton, J. (2019). Global wildlife regulator to consider relaxing ivory trade bans, prompting fears of huge rise in elephant poaching. Retrieved from *Independent*, 9 January. www.independent.co.uk/climate-change/news/elephant-ivory-sales-ban-poaching-africa-botswana-namibia-zimbabwe-stockpiles-decline-extinction-wildaid-ifaw-cites-a8717456.html

DeMotts, R. (2010). Whose elephants? Conserving, compensating, and competing in Northern Botswana. *Society and Nature Resources*, 25 (9), 837–851.

Department for the Environment, Food and Rural Affairs. (2018). World-leading UK Ivory Bill becomes law. 20 Decembber. Retrieved from Department for the Environment, Food and Rural Affairs: www.gov.uk/government/news/world-leading-uk-ivory-bill-becomes-law--2

Edson Gandiwa, P. G. (2021). Living with wildlife and associated conflicts in a contested area within the Northern Gonarezhou National Park, Zimbabwe. *Journal of Sustainable Development in Africa,* 14 (6), 252–260.

EIA. (2019). Eyes wide shut. Retrieved from Environmental Investigation Agency: https://eia-international.org/news/eyes-wide-shut-southern-africas-elephants-now-in-the-firing-line/

Elephant Wildlife Volunteer Project. (2021). Volunteer with EHRA and help desert elephants. 14 April. Retrieved from Elephant-Human Relations Aid. www.ehranamibia.org/volunteer-with-elephants-namibia

Environmental Investigation Agency. (2019). *EIA briefing document to CoP18*. August. Retrieved from Environmental Investigation Agency. https://eia-international.org/wp-content/uploads/EIA-Briefing-Document-CITES-CoP18.pdf

Gabriel, G. G. (2021). Will China say no to wildlife trade? *United Nations Chronicle,* 15 April.

Great Elephant Census. (2021). Conservation. 2 June. Retrieved from Great Elephant Census. www.greatelephantcensus.com/background-on-conservation

Greiber, T., Janki, M., Orellana, M., Savaresi, A., & Shelton, D. (2009). *Conservation with justice: A rights based approach*. Geneva: IUCN Publications.

Griffin, M. C. (2009). Elephants caught in the middle: Impacts of war, fences and people on elephant distribution and abundance in the Caprivi Strip, Namibia. *African Journal of Ecology*, 47 (2), 223–233.

Hauenstein, S., Kshatriya, M., Blanc, J., Dormann, C. F., & Beale, C. M. (2019). African elephant poaching rates correlate with local poverty, national corruption and global ivory price. *Nature Communications,* 10, article 2242.

Humane Society International. (2013). Elephant ivory trade-related timeline. Retrieved from Humane Society International. www.hsi.org/wp-content/uploads/assets/pdfs/Elephant_Related_Trade_Timeline.pdf

International Elephant Foundation. (2021). Elephant facts. 8 July. Retrieved from International Elephant Foundation. https://elephantconservation.org/elephants/just-for-kids/

186   *Caroline Cox*

Layne, E. N. (1973). Eighty nations write magna carta for wildlife. *Audubon Magazine,* 99, 73.

Lemieux, A. M., & Clarke, R. V. (2009). The international ban on ivory sales and its effects on elephant poaching in Africa. *British Journal of Criminology,* 49 (2), 451–471.

Lindsay, K., Chase, M., Landen, K., & Nowak, K. (2017). The shared nature of Africa's elephants. *Biological Conservation,* 215, 260–267.

Madzwamuse, M. (2020). Contested conservation: Implications for rights, democratization,. *Journal of the Society for International Development,* 63, 67–73.

Mbaiwa, J. E. (2017). Effects of the safari hunting tourism ban on rural. *South African Geographical Journal,* 100 (1), 41–61.

Milliken, T., Burn, R. W., Underwood, F. M. & Sangalakula, L. (2004). *The Elephant Trade Information System (ETIS) and the illicit trade in ivory: A report to the 13th meeting of the Conference of the Parties to CITES.* CITES, 20 August. Retrieved from CITES.

Monitoring the Illegal Killing of Elephants (MIKE). (2019, June 3). Report on Monitoring the Illegal Killing of Elephants (MIKE) – CoP18 Doc. 69.2. Retrieved from CITES: https://cites.org/sites/default/files/eng/cop/18/doc/E-CoP18-069-02.pdf

Muskopf, S. (2021). African elephant – change over time. 31 May. Retrieved from Libre Texts. https://bio.libretexts.org/@go/page/19911

Nuwer, R. (2018). How Japan undermines efforts to stop the illegal ivory trade. *National Geographic,* 24 September.

Nyaungwa, N. (2021). Human-wildlife conflicts surge in Namibia – environment minister. 11 March. Retrieved from Reuters: www.reuters.com/article/uk-namibia-wildlife-idUSKBN2B3197

Platt, J. (2014). Why is Namibia killing its rare desert elephants? Retrieved from *Scientific American,* 9 July. https://blogs.scientificamerican.com/extinction-countdown/why-is-namibia-killing-its-rare-desert-elephants/

Polakow, D. (2001). Ecotourism ventures: Rags or riches? *Annals of Tourism Research,* 28 (4), 892–907.

Rice, M. (2020). Botswana's elephant crisis – no time for pride and arrogance. 6 July. Retrieved from Environmental Investigation Agency: https://eia-international.org/blog/botswanas-elephant-crisis-no-time-for-pride-and-arrogance-with-such-a-pressing-need-for-action/

Schramlc, O. S. (2018). Making sense of protected area conflicts and management approaches: A review of causes, contexts and conflict management strategies. *Biological Conservation,* 222, 136–145.

Sheldrick Wildlife Trust. (2019). Botswana lifts hunting ban. 24 May. Retrieved from Sheldrick Wildlife Trust. www.sheldrickwildlifetrust.org/news/updates/botswana-lifts-hunting-ban?gclid=Cj0KCQjwpdqDBhCSARIsAEUJ0hPAcx_EaMWsSAXpWy8uBHj-oYN7LArs_0V9ZmezUHfWUtBbJj76VlwaAhZcEALw_wcB

Sutcliffe, M. J. (2019). Evidence of a growing elephant poaching problem in Botswana. *Current Biology,* 29, 2222–2228.

Thouless, C. R., Dublin, H. T., Blanc, D. P., Skinner, T. E., Daniel, R. D., Taylor, F., Maisels, H., Frederick, L., & Bouche, P. (2016). *African elephant status report. An update from the African elephant database.* Retrieved from International Union for Conservation of Nature. https://portals.iucn.org/library/sites/library/files/documents/SSC-OP-060_A.pdf

Tusk.org. (2021). African Savanah Elephant. Retrieved from Tusk: www.tusk.org/species/african-elephant/?gclid=Cj0KCQjw38-DBhDpARIsADJ3kjmz384PMefaGOxUjjUrmrecMdbPcERpE2uOi9F24NNrA7IRbU4tzSMaAgBcEALw_wcB

UNODC. (2020). *World wildlife crime report: Trafficking in protected species.* Vienna: United Nations Office on Drugs and Crime.

Warner, M. Z. (2008). Examining human–elephant conflict in Southern Africa: Causes and options for coexistence. *Master of Environmental Studies Capstone Projects.* Vol 22. University of Pennsylvania. https://repository.upenn.edu/mes_capstones/22

Wijnstekers, W. (2011). *The evolution of CITES – 9th edition.* Budapest, Hungary: International Council for Game and Wildlife Conservation.

Yuan, L. (2017). CITES: African elephant poaching down, ivory seizures up and hit record high. 24 October. Retrieved from CITES. https://cites.org/eng/news/pr/African_elephant_poaching_down_ivory_seizures_up_and_hit_record_high_24102017

Zimbabwe Parks and Wildlife Management Authority. (2020). *Zimbabwe national elephant management plan (2015–2020).* Harare: The Zambezi Society.

14 The COVID-19 pandemic and nature-based tourism in Southern Africa

Susan Snyman

Introduction

Tourism has over the years shown a general resilience to economic, health and natural shocks, with recovery periods varying from weeks to a few months. The COVID-19 pandemic, however, is the largest shock to date, with a complete halt to all tourism. The uncertainty around the pandemic's course, differing vaccine plans and rates of vaccination, as well as the new strains of the virus being detected, have resulted in difficulties in terms of planning for tourism operators as well as for tourists. The uncertainty as to how long the pandemic and its after-effects will last is causing insecurity, intense pressure on funding available to sustain tourism operations and the knock-on effects of this on tourism employees and suppliers of goods and services to the tourism industry.

Tourism scholars (Rylance, 2017; Snyman, 2019, Spenceley & Meyer, 2016) have written a large amount on the positive impacts of the tourism value chain and the large multiplier effects of tourism, which in times of tourism growth are extensive and have large positive economic and social impacts. These same multiplier impacts are now having a large negative impact on economies as the sources of stimulus to them, tourists, are absent: highlighting the vulnerability of these value chains and multipliers (UNCTAD, 2020). A positive aspect of this is the realisation of how far tourism reaches within local and national economies and a broader understanding of these impacts on livelihoods, welfare and socio-economic development. If there was any doubt before as to the contributions of tourism to local and national economies and to funding conservation and development in many rural areas of Africa, the large gaps in funding because of the pandemic have put these to rest. Traditionally, tourism is seen as one of the key components, if not the only activity, and a major export sector of the wild-life economy of many countries, but the COVID-19 pandemic has highlighted the risks associated with this approach and the important need to diversify and make wildlife economies as a whole, and tourism itself, more resilient (Snyman et al., 2021).

Nature-based tourism relies on nature (fauna and flora, marine and ter-restrial) and the conservation of this 'asset' to ensure sustainability. Investment in nature is, therefore, critical. The *Dasgupta Review* (HM Treasury, 2020)

DOI: 10.4324/9781003193166-17

COVID-19 and nature-based tourism 189

highlights the importance of the economics of biodiversity and the negative impacts of declining natural capital, as does the latest Global Risks Report (WEF, 2021) which includes biodiversity loss as one of the top five global risks. A large amount of nature-based tourism revenue is reinvested in nature, directly through conservation levies, park fees, etc., but also through investment by tourism companies in conservation activities in their areas of operation (Spenceley & Snyman, 2017), as well as philanthropic conservation activities (Snyman & Spenceley, 2019). COVID-19 has bought most of this to a halt as well as large amounts of conservation funding being diverted to health initiatives, further highlighting the vulnerability of conservation financing. Protected and conserved areas were, pre-COVID, already under-funded (IUCN ESARO, 2020; Lindsey et al., 2018), now with more serious funding issues due to this lack of tourism-related funding (Lindsey et al., 2020).

The impacts of COVID-19 have been devastating for Africa. In the first half of 2020, international tourist arrivals in Africa declined 57%, with an estimated 99% drop in the second quarter (World Tourism Organisation, 2020). In many countries in Southern Africa tourism comprises a combination of both consumptive (hunting), as well as non-consumptive (photographic) tourism. Both have been equally heavily hit by the pandemic.

According to the WTO (2021) tourism arrivals to sub-Saharan Africa in 2020 were down 87% and WTO's extended scenarios for 2021–2024 pointed to a rebound in international tourism by the second half of 2021, but given current vaccination rates and further lockdowns, this is looking unlikely. A return to 2019 levels in terms of international arrivals could take two and a half to four years (WTO, 2020). One of the main barriers weighing on the recovery of international tourism, according to the UNWTO Panel of Experts is travel restrictions, together with slow virus containment and low consumer confidence (WTO, 2020).

Building forward better will require innovation, collaboration, an ability to be flexible and to adapt on an ongoing basis, resilience and the promotion of sustainable practices. Through an extensive literature review and using the sustainable development framework, this chapter looks at the social, economic and environmental impacts of COVID-19 in Southern Africa as a result of the impacts on nature-based tourism and discusses ways to build forward better, ensuring greater resilience for communities, governments and for conservation.[1]

Tourism in Africa

To understand the impacts of the COVID-19 pandemic on tourism, it is important to understand tourism pre-COVID. In 2018, Africa was the second-fastest growing tourism region, with 5.6% growth in tourism and travel against a global average growth rate of 3.9% (WTTC, 2020).

In Africa in 2018, over a third of all direct tourism contributions to GDP and 3.6 million jobs were attributed to wildlife tourism (Oxford Economics in WTTC, 2019). Before the COVID-19 pandemic, nature-based tourism used to generate more than 10% of GDP for countries such as Tanzania, South Africa and Namibia, and more than 20% for several small island countries (IPBES, 2020, in Lehmann et al., 2021). Pre-COVID, Africa only received a small amount (5%) of global tourism arrivals, indicating that there is a significant amount of room for growth in the tourism economy (WTTC, 2020) at the level of international tourism, but also domestically and regionally. Economic data on nature-based tourism is scarce, and largely inconsistent, so assessing the impacts of COVID has, to date, largely been based on broader tourism figures.

However, wildlife resources are often what initially attracts international tourists to Africa – for example, gorillas in Rwanda, or the Big Five experience in Kruger National Park, South Africa – and the opportunity then exists to provide additional tourism opportunities, such as cultural, historical or other wildlife-related elements, which in turn encourages tourists to stay longer and spend more money in the country or region (Snyman et al., 2021). The World Bank (2020) also highlights that wildlife is an essential drawcard for tourists who visit protected and conserved areas; this therefore needs investment in the region's/country's wildlife to improve the attraction (asset).

Impacts of COVID-19 on tourism

The impacts of the COVID-19 have been devastating for Africa, not only in terms of the impacts on nature-based tourism businesses, but on conservation and lives and livelihoods in general (cf. Spenceley, 2020, for numerous resources specifically related to tourism, as well as the UNWTO tourism dashboard). Table 14.1 provides some examples of the impacts of COVID on nature-based tourism in Southern Africa, as well as more broadly.

Table 14.2 illustrates examples of some national-level impacts of COVID-19 in Southern Africa.

Spenceley (2021a) conducted extensive surveys of tourism businesses in Africa to understand the impact of COVID-19 on wildlife tourism in protected areas. According to her research, environmental crime is one of the immediate concerns of most operators (80%) and a majority predict that levels will increase due to the pandemic (87%). She also found that the likely reduction of operator expenditure on local environmental services by US$ 25.5 million, due to lower tourism turnover, would compound this situation. The research also found that, if the crisis continues, over 17,000 local employees working for tourism operators surveyed will be adversely and directly affected, as well as their dependents, and procurement of local produce, hospitality services and payments to community initiatives by respondents was predicted to be US$ 80.9 million lower than in the previous financial year. These losses will have far-reaching impacts on households and lives.

Some countries which allowed tourism in national parks during different stages of lockdown saw massive increases in visitation, highlighting the importance of nature and tourism to local well-being. Issues with managing these large tourist numbers have also arisen and highlighted even further the need to

COVID-19 and nature-based tourism 191

Table 14.1 General impacts from COVID-19 related to nature-based tourism

General impacts from COVID-19 related nature-based tourism	Positive impacts	Negative impacts
Economic impacts	Awareness has been raised related to the breadth and depth of the tourism value chain, and the huge impact of direct, indirect, and induced impacts (Lindsey et al., 2020)	**Revenues**: Border closures and stopping of flights resulted in no tourism arrivals: resulting in little to no revenue from tourism – this has impacted tourism businesses, governments, community associations, individuals working directly in tourism, as well as those in the value chain, and all dependents (Spenceley, 2021a) **Loss of FOREX/GDP contributions:** general loss of income to governments, which comes from taxes, visa fees, and various other revenue streams related to tourism **Employment**: there have been extensive lay-offs and reductions in salaries (Saunders, 2020; Spenceley, 2021a), resulting in general increased levels of unemployment and poverty According to the International Air Transport Association (IATA), Africa's air transport industry contributes up to US$ 55.8 billion (2.6%) to Africa's GDP and supports 6.2 million jobs. By 11 March 2020, African airlines had lost US$ 4.4 billion in revenue due to fallout from the pandemic (African Union, 2020). Under the average scenario developed by the African Union (2020), the tourism and travel sector in Africa could lose at least US$ 50 billion due to the COVID-19 pandemic and at least 2 million direct and indirect jobs.
Environmental impacts	Reduced carbon emissions from travel (Lehmann et al., 2021; Newsome, 2020; Spenceley, 2021b)	Decreased funding for conservation, from tourism revenues, donors, philanthropy. This funding contributed to direct conservation efforts, but also anti-poaching and other protection efforts (Waithaka, 2020).

(continued)

192 *Susan Snyman*

Table 14.1 Cont.

General impacts from COVID-19 related nature-based tourism	Positive impacts	Negative impacts
	Increased awareness in terms of carbon emissions related to travel (because of the lack of travel during the pandemic) Recovery of conservation areas which had previously been negatively impacted by over-tourism, or unsustainable tourism operations (Spenceley, 2021b)	Increased cases of poaching in some areas (with reductions in others, largely due to border closures) and increased deforestation (Hockings et al., 2021; IPBES, 2020; Lindsey et al., 2020; Marshall, 2020; Spenceley, 2021b) Increased subsistence hunting for survival
Social impacts	Lockdowns have given more time for families to spend together, especially as many people working in nature-based tourism are often away from home for long periods of time	Due to job losses, increasing COVID-19 cases and other related economic hardships, people moving from urban areas back to their rural homes to survive (Waithaka, 2020), as subsistence becomes a livelihood strategy again. This has, in some cases, increased pressure on natural resources, but has also reunited families. Given high dependency ratios in most African countries (Snyman, 2014), large numbers of people have been negatively affected by the increase in unemployment The uncertainty of when nature-based tourism will return results in long-term stress as companies are unable to inform staff as to when they will either return to their employment or their salaries will return to their full amount (many employees have been on reduced salaries for more than a year) (Spenceley, 2021b)

Source: Author's compilation.

Table 14.2 Examples of national level impacts of COVID-19 on tourism in Southern Africa

In **Botswana**, trophy hunting was set to resume in 2020 but was delayed due to the pandemic, resulting in huge financial losses, for example, US\$ 2.2. million raised by the government through the auction of hunting quotas is no longer guaranteed (Lindsey et al., 2020).

In **Kenya**, 70% of the Kenya Wildlife Service's budget is sourced from tourism and in Zimbabwe, Zimparks relies fully on tourism revenues for its operational budget (UN, 2020). Similarly, in South Africa, 80% of SANParks' revenue comes from tourism (SANParks, 2019). The COVID-19 pandemic impacts have thus put the operations of many national protected area authorities in jeopardy due to a lack of funding from tourism (Snyman et al., 2021).

Madagascar: Madagascar National Parks, because of a 100% decline in tourism due to park closures, anticipated a financial loss of US\$ 2.5 million in 2020 (Vyawahare, 2020).

In **Malawi**, Baulch et al. (2020) found that the declining tourist spending accounts for a fifth of short-term losses in GDP.

Namibia: Initial estimates suggested Namibia's communal conservancies could lose US\$ 10 million in direct tourism revenues, threatening funding for 700 game guards and 300 conservancy management employees, and the viability of 61 joint venture tourism lodges employing 1,400 community members (WWF-Namibia, 2020).

South Africa: Some 50,000 businesses have closed temporarily, with many in danger of closing permanently, putting nearly 600,000 jobs at risk. 58% of surveyed firms reported being unable to service their debt and 54% were struggling to cover fixed costs at the end of March 2020 (Republic of South Africa, 2020)

In May 2020, the average future bookings for lodges and protected areas were 70% lower than in 2019; 61% of lodges were fully closed (Saunders, 2020). A third of game lodges surveyed by Saunders (2020) furloughed more than 50% of their staff and the closure of lodges was estimated to result in a loss of over 33,600 jobs and US\$ 214 million in local salaries, procurement, conservation and community project contributions.

Kitshoff-Botha (2020) estimates a loss of ZAR 3.8 billion/US\$ 245 million to wildlife ranchers because of cancellations in 2020 and a further loss of ZAR 3.1 billion/US\$ 200 million in terms of a decline in new bookings from April to December 2020.

Zambia: Despite not closing its borders, Zambia, in the first three months of 2020, saw a drop of over 14,000 international visitors (Tabetando, 2020). A snap poll of members of the Eco-Tourism Association of Zambia (ETAZ) suggests that Zambia's safari tourism and allied sectors such as airlines and charters would suffer a loss in income of US\$ 100 million in 2020. Out of 257 lodges and camps, 165 have closed down already. Over 7,000 jobs are likely to be lost. 165 tourism businesses in Livingstone and Zambia's protected areas face bankruptcy (Tabetando, 2020)

Zimbabwe: The Zimbabwe Parks and Wildlife Management Authority projected that due to reduced tourism-related spending there would be a US\$ 3.8 million (approx. 50%) shortfall in the second quarter of 2020 (Lindsey et al., 2020).

Source: Author's compilation.

194 *Susan Snyman*

have policies, practices and protocols in place to manage over-tourism and the potential related negative impacts on conservation as well as the overall tourism product through more effective planning, monitoring, evaluation and management (Spenceley, 2021b).

Lindsey et al. (2020) highlight that the net conservation impacts of COVID-19 will be strongly negative and that it is critically important to conserve habitat and regulate unsafe wildlife trade practices to reduce the risk of future pandemics. Their paper also emphasises that supporting conservation efforts will assist national and local African economies to recover from the COVID-19 pandemic by diversifying economies, creating employment in rural areas and protecting ecosystem services (Lindsey et al., 2020). This will also support the reopening of nature-based tourism, which depends on the effective conservation of natural resources.

Building forward better

Despite the current collapse of tourism, the tourism sector cannot, and should not, be written off, as its resilience and ability to rebound presents an opportunity for the future (Snyman et al., 2021). There needs to be innovative rethinking and reimagining about tourism models; these need to be redesigned to maximise benefits for conservation, people and local, national and regional economies. These innovations can include strengthening links between pastoralist livestock production, rangeland management, wildlife ranching and overall wildlife conservation – and amplifying the value of healthy rangeland to livestock in these savannah landscapes – which will make community conservation areas more resilient (Kaelo et al., 2020). This is key, given the huge negative impacts that have resulted from an over-reliance of nature-based tourism to support community conservancies.

Although there has been a move over the years to ensure that tourism is more sustainable, now there is no choice. There is also the potential now to build a tourism sector that is more diversified, innovative and sustainable and, therefore, that will be more resilient.

In terms of tourism recovery post-COVID-19, the World Bank (2020), WTO (2020, 2021), WTTC (2020), ATTA (2020) and the UN (2020), amongst others, all provide various strategies and plans for tourism recovery in Africa and globally to rebuild sustainable tourism, as well as build greater resilience going forward. Many countries have also developed national tourism recovery strategies – for example, Kenya, South Africa, Rwanda and Botswana – and have injected funding to support the sector (Snyman et al., 2021). Supportive policy, legislation and an enabling environment are key for the successful building forward better as well as the long-term development and growth of the tourism sector. 'Resilience' in terms of tourism means safeguarding the health of visitors, local people and staff; creating more diverse income streams for the local economy; greater attention to equity and inclusiveness; and better understanding of the large-scale context for tourism, globally, such as changes affecting the airline industry (Nunes, in Spenceley et al., 2021, p. 112).

Waithaka's (2020) report on the impacts of COVID on protected areas in Africa emphasised that a post-COVID-19 strategy will need to invest in capacity development, increased awareness, better land-use planning, appropriate infrastructure and technology to empower communities and to maximise opportunities for diversification of revenues and improve returns from their investments. Waithaka (2020) said further that, as part of diversifying income sources, more attention should be given to sustainable use of biodiversity resources to benefit local people and conservation. This is cognisant of the fact that, although tourism will remain an important source of revenue for protected areas and local people, overreliance on traditional tourism must be diminished in the new post-COVID-19 era (Waithaka, 2020). Key is rethinking traditional tourism and developing new, innovative models which are more resilient, for example, the engagement of local tourists in conservation and development projects, resulting in extended stays and a connection to a place or community.

Despite all the evidence and numerous reports highlighting the linkages between human and environmental health, there still seems to be some resistance to large-scale investment in nature and natural resources. The Healthy Parks Healthy People Initiative (Townsend et al., in Waithaka, 2020) has formally demonstrated the crucial link between healthy ecosystems and human health and well-being – and more specifically the role that parks and protected areas can play in improving human health and well-being (Waithaka, 2020). This connection has never been clearer than it is right now amid the COVID-19 pandemic. The Healthy Parks Healthy People Initiative is one that is well understood in Africa, as it is the continent that has more people interacting directly with nature and relying on nature for livelihoods than any other (Waithaka, 2020). Nature-based tourism directly focuses on this key connection between people and nature.

According to Spenceley et al. (2021) the way forward for tourism could entail five dimensions: (1) fostering openness to change, with a willingness to embrace new ways of thinking and acting; (2) developing a vision for the tourism offer of the future; (3) protecting biodiversity for its importance to the ecology of the area and peoples' dependency on tourism; (4) recovering and rebuilding local livelihoods and the health of residents and visitors; and (5) reframing tourism, including the resources it uses, to achieve productive and healthy livelihoods without degrading the biodiversity upon which it depends.

All tourism businesses, now and in the future, must ensure that they have greater resilience, by creating more diverse livelihood options for staff and local communities, and diversification in their businesses (Snyman et al., 2021). For example, operating a carbon project or beekeeping business on the same property as the tourism business allows for alternative revenues for staff, related communities and the tourism industry itself. Protected and conserved areas

196 *Susan Snyman*

also need to diversify their income sources to avoid reliance on tourism and to build greater resilience (Snyman et al., 2021). Governments also need to diversify their conservation and development finance options to build resilience and reduce the current heavy dependence on tourism (Snyman et al., 2021).

Recovery and building forward better need a focus on both the demand and supply sides of tourism to ensure sustainability and to build resilience. The demand–side focus needs to include raising awareness amongst tourists in terms of the conservation impacts of tourism, both positive and negative, and ways to boost the positive impacts and mitigate the negative impacts (Spenceley & Rylance, 2016). The supply side also needs to include raising awareness, improving systems and processes to ensure greater long-term sustainability and effective monitoring and evaluation to mitigate negative development and impacts.

Based on her surveys of tourism businesses, Spenceley (2021a) highlighted five key areas to encourage sustainable tourism recovery through:

i **Stimulus**: Establishing a stimulus package for protected areas to protect the livelihoods of tourism and conservation staff and communities in the tourism and conservation value chain.
ii **Finance:** Creating a combination of grant and low-interest loan finance, which is decentralised to support operations including the informal sector and micro enterprises.
iii **Support criteria**: Designing sound criteria for those supported, including investment in sustainable tourism practices, the protection of wildlife and biodiversity, support for conservation-based organisations, vulnerability, community beneficiaries, gender and youth, and climate-friendly technologies.
iv **Sustainability of interventions:** Planning interventions to minimise unintended negative impacts (e.g. organisations furloughing more staff to obtain financial support).
v **Coherence amongst recovery measures:** Ensuring coherence with national measures.

Bhammer et al. (2021) suggest three key focus areas for assisting the nature-based tourism sector to recover sustainably. These include: i) protecting the natural asset on which tourism is built; ii) growing and diversifying tourism businesses to generate positive economic impact; and iii) sharing the benefits with local communities living in and around protected areas. They also emphasise that collaboration between governments, the private sector and communities is critical for putting this approach into action and achieving the triple bottom line: economic growth, poverty reduction and biodiversity conservation.

In summary, some of the key measures to be considered as Southern Africa builds forward better include the following.

Economic

- **Business of conservation** – less reliance on tourism for conservation funding and greater diversification of financing and funding options to build resilience. As nature forms the asset base on which nature-based tourism depends, it is essential that there are more diversified, resilient funding sources found for conservation.
- **Diversification of the wildlife economy** – not only does tourism itself need to diversify to build resilience, but there also needs to be a general diversification of wildlife economy activities, to ensure that there is a suite of options available, which will build greater long-term resilience. Diversification can include combining nature-based tourism with wildlife ranching, carbon projects, non-timber forest products, real estate, film and photography and other innovative activities.
- **Promotion of domestic and regional tourism** – the importance of this has been highlighted through the pandemic as domestic and regional travel has been more feasible due to international travel bans, but it also results in less long-haul travel and, therefore, reduced carbon emissions and overall negative impacts on the planet. The marketing and promotion of tourism at local, national and regional levels will require a common vision and working together. There should be a catalysing of domestic demand through informative and inspiring marketing (Republic of South Africa, 2020), as well as differential pricing for domestic travel to increase numbers. Regional tourism can be promoted through prioritising cooperation with neighbouring destinations towards a regional value proposition, joint marketing and offering a seamless visitor experience (Republic of South Africa, 2020).
- **Diversification of the tourism product** – to increase the length of stay of tourists as people start travelling again and if they prefer to travel only to one destination rather than a few on one trip. This should include cultural, historical, urban and other tourism offerings as part of a nature-based tourism package to increase length of stay and spend.
- **Financial support** – create an investment and market-entry facilitation programme to stimulate capital investment, sector transformation and product diversification (Republic of South Africa, 2020). Coordination between governments, banks and other donors to provide further financial support in the form of cheap and accessible credit for tourism businesses to restart and rebuild (Bohlmann, 2020; Spenceley, 2021a).
- **Tourism insurance** – improvements to current systems, which have largely left tourism businesses with little to no protection. The removal of restrictive clauses which prevent payouts to tourism businesses should be investigated.
- **Fiscal incentives** – tax breaks or other forms of tax incentives for tourism businesses which invest in, or contribute to, conservation and development.

198   *Susan Snyman*

- **Resilience funds** – trust funds, blue and green bonds and other financial instruments to provide reserve funding for tourism and conservation in the event of future shocks.
- **Benefit-sharing** – the sharing of benefits from tourism are important in terms of the long-term sustainability of natural resources. The importance of local ownership and rights are more important now than ever and highlight the importance of legal and policy reform to ensure local ownership over wildlife and other natural resources (Kaelo et al., 2020) and an ability to benefit from the associated nature-based tourism.

Environmental

- **Carbon calculators and offsetting of emissions** – legislation and mandatory inclusion of this in future long-haul travel could assist with giving back to the planet and result in 'doing no harm'.
- **Promotion of healthy parks, healthy people** – the inter-connectedness between people, the environment and health must not be forgotten as the world recovers but should be a key focus of all national strategies to build forward better.
- **Importance of conservation and investment in it** – to prevent future pandemics (WEF Global Risks Report, 2021). The foundation of all nature-based tourism is nature. The importance of investing in this key strategic asset should, therefore, be at the forefront of all recovery plans and strategies.
- **Better planning and management plans** – with appropriate research, planning and the development, and implementation, of sustainable management plans, tourism managers can redistribute visitors to avoid overtourism in the future (Spenceley, 2021b), reduce pollution and develop and maintain high standards of environmental integrity to promote long-term sustainability.

Social

- **Safety** – health and safety protocols as well as health insurance adaptations for tourism staff and travellers. See Spenceley (2020) for guidance on operating tourism during COVID-19 times. Countries should look at introducing national norms and standards for safe tourism operations. These should be inspired by globally recognised biosecurity protocols and standards across the value chain to enable safe travel and rebuild traveller confidence (Republic of South Africa, 2020; Spenceley, 2021b).
- **Innovation** – recovery options could include innovation in more efficient plane engines and flight routes (Lehmann et al., 2021), product design and development and experiences offered to tourists (see the next point).
- **Virtual tourism experiences** – ensure a continued connection with places previously visited, but also to entice new travellers in the future.

These may work for specific experiences such as gorilla group viewing, but it will be difficult to charge a fee for general game viewing experiences in the long run, unless the activity includes something unique, a learning experience or inclusion of a conservation activity such as collaring an animal for research purposes.

- **Collaborations and partnerships** – partnerships and collaborations are going to be even more important going forward. Partnerships between conservation, development and health organisations/ministries is key to improving livelihoods, health and conservation outcomes going forward. Should health ministries be investing in/contributing to conservation to promote human health?

Conclusion

Nature-based tourism depends on conservation and an important part of long-term conservation is the related benefit-sharing with communities living in and around protected areas. To-date most of the benefits shared with communities have come from tourism, through revenue shares, lease fees, employment and supply chain benefits. In order to ensure greater long-term sustainability and the related support of local communities for conservation, more resilient benefit-sharing models should include a diversified benefit-sharing portfolio, including benefits from carbon projects, sustainable resource use, non-timber forest products (e.g. mopane worms in Kruger National Park) and payments for other ecosystem services, such as water. See Snyman et al. (2021) for more information on these and other wildlife economy activities such as wildlife estates and wildlife ranching.

Newsome (2020) emphasised that nature-based tourism has in the past and can still lead to a constructive valuation of wildlife, a deeper understanding of our place in the natural world, encourage positive conservation efforts and provide employment and revenues for many people (especially in areas where there are few alternatives). It is, therefore, without doubt, important that sustainable nature-based tourism is included in the suite of recovery options as the world starts to build forward better.

Note

1 The next two sections are adapted from Snyman et al., 2021.

References

Adventure Travel Trade Association (ATTA) (2020). Adventure travel COVID-19 health and safety guidelines. Retrieved from www.adventuretravel.biz/ covid19guidelines.

African Union (2020). *Impact of the coronavirus (COVID 19) on the African economy.* Retrieved from https://au.int/sites/default/files/documents/38326-doc-covid-19_impact_on_african_economy.pdf.

200 Susan Snyman

Baulch, B., Botha, R., & Pauw, K. (2020). Short-term economic impacts of COVID-19 on the Malawian economy, 2020–21: A SAM multiplier modeling analysis. Retrieved from https://massp.ifpri.info/2020/10/20/event-recap-the-economic-impacts-of-covid-19-on-the-malawian-economy-2020-2021-a-sam-multiplier-model/.

Bhammer, H., Li, W., Molina, C. M. M., Hickey, V., Pendry, J., & Narain, U. (2021). Framework for sustainable recovery of tourism in protected areas. *Sustainability,* 13, 2798. https://doi.org/10.3390/su13052798

Bohlmann, H. (2020). *Macroeconomic assessment of the impacts of COVID-19 on tourism in Namibia and strategic recommendations for the recovery and revival of the sector.* 20 April. Retrieved from http://the-eis.com/elibrary/sites/default/files/downloads/literature/Namibia%20Tourism%20Final%20Report%2020201217.pdf

HM Treasury. (2020). *The Dasgupta review: Independent review on the economics of biodiversity: Interim report.* 26 April. Retrieved from https://assets.publishing.service.gov.uk/government/uploads/system/uploads/attachment_data/file/882222/The_Economics_of_Biodiversity_The_Dasgupta_Review_Interim_Report.pdf

Hockings, M., et al. (2021). Editorial essay: COVID-19 and protected and conserved areas. *Parks,* 26 (1). Retrieved from https://parksjournal.com/wp-content/uploads/2020/06/Hockings-et-al-10.2305-IUCN.CH_.2020.PARKS-26-1MH.en_-1.pdf.

IPBES (2020). IPBES workshop on biodiversity and pandemics. Retrieved from https://ipbes.net/sites/default/files/2020-12/IPBES%20Workshop%20on%20Biodiversity%20and%20Pandemics%20Report_0.pdf [Accessed 9 April 2021].

IUCN ESARO (2020). *Closing the gap. The financing and resourcing of protected and conserved areas in Eastern and Southern Africa.* Nairobi: IUCN ESARO; BIOPAMA.

Kaelo, D., Sopia, D., Bell, D., Diggle, R., & Nelson, F. (2020). From crisis to solutions for communities and African conservation (commentary). Retrieved from https://news.mongabay.com/2020/05/from-crisis-to-solutions-for-communities-and-african-conservation-commentary/

Kitshoff-Botha, A. (2020). Impact assessment of COVID-19 on the South African wildlife ranching industry. Retrieved from www.wrsa.co.za

Lehmann, I., Rodriguez, J. C., & Spenceley, A. (2021). *COVID-19 and conservation: Crisis response strategies that benefit people and nature.* Bonn: German Development Institute.

Lindsey, P. A., et al. (2018). More than $1 billion needed annually to secure Africa's protected areas with lions, *Proceedings of the National Academy of Sciences*, 115 (45), E10788–E10796.

Lindsey, P. A., et al. (2020). Conserving Africa's wildlife and wildlands through the COVID-19 crisis and beyond. *Nature Ecology and Evolution,* 4, 1300–1310. Retrieved from www.nature.com/articles/s41559-020-1275-6#citeas

Marshall, C. (2020). How the Covid-19 pandemic is threatening Africa's wildlife. *BBC News*, 7 May. Retrieved from www.bbc.com/news/av/world-africa-52564615/how-the-covid-19-pandemic-isthreatening-africa-s-wildlife

Newsome, D. (2020). The collapse of tourism and its impact on wildlife tourism destinations. *Journal of Tourism Futures,* 7 (3), 295–302. DOI: 10.1108/JTF-04-2020-0053.

Republic of South Africa. (2020). Tourism sector recovery plan: COVID-19 response. August. Retrieved from www.gov.za/sites/default/files/gcis_document/202008/tourismrecoveryplan.pdf [Accessed 5 April 2021].

Rylance, A. (2017). Reducing economic leakages from tourism: A value chain assessment of the tourism industry in Kasane, Botswana. BEST EN Think Tank XVII. Retrieved

COVID-19 and nature-based tourism 201

from https://researchonline.jcu.edu.au/50855/1/TTXVII%20Proceedings%202 017%20FINAL.pdf#page=48 [Accessed 24 April 2021].

SANParks. (2019). *Annual report 2018/19.* Retrieved from www.sanparks.org/assets/ docs/general/annual-report-2019.pdf

Saunders, G. (2020). The impact of COVID-19 on the game lodge sector in South Africa. Inbound tourism recovery team for South Africa. In Spenceley, A. (Ed.), *The future of nature-based tourism: Impacts of COVID-19 and paths to sustainability.* Gland, Switzerland: Luc Hoffman Institute, 2021.

Snyman, S. (2014). The impact of ecotourism employment on rural household incomes and social welfare in six southern African countries. *Tourism and Hospitality Research,* 14 (1–2), 37–52. DOI: 10.1177/1467358414529435

Snyman, S. (2019). African tourism industry employees: Expenditure patterns and comparisons with other community members. *Journal of Sustainable Tourism,* 27 (6), 788–804. DOI: 10.1080/09669582.2017.1408634

Snyman, S., & Spenceley, A. (2019). *Private sector tourism in conservation areas in Africa.* Oxford: CABI publishers.

Snyman, S., Sumba, D., Vorhies, F., Gitari, E., Enders, C., Ahenkan, A., Pambo, A. F. K., & Bengone, N. (2021). *State of the wildlife economy in Africa.* Kigali, Rwanda: African Leadership University, School of Wildlife Conservation.

Spenceley, A. (2020). *Tourism and visitation in protected areas amid COVID-19: Guidance for protected area authorities and managers.* Brussels: Eurata Consortium.

Spenceley, A. (2021a). *COVID-19 and protected area tourism: A spotlight on impacts and options in Africa.* Brussels: Eurata Consortium.

Spenceley, A. (2021b). *The future of nature-based tourism: Impacts of COVID-19 and paths to sustainability.* Gland, Switzerland: Luc Hoffman Institute.

Spenceley, A., & Meyer, D. (Eds.) (2016). *Tourism and poverty reduction: Principles and impacts in developing countries.* London and New York: Routledge.

Spenceley, A., & Rylance, A. (2016). *The responsible tourist: How to find, book and get the most from your holiday.* Kindle e-book.

Spenceley, A., & Snyman, S. (2017). Can a wildlife tourism company influence conservation and the development of tourism in a specific destination? *Tourism and Hospitality Research,* 17 (1), 52–67. DOI: 10.1177/1467358416634158

Spenceley, A., et al. (2021). Tourism in protected and conserved areas amid the COVID-19 pandemic. *Parks,* 27, 103–118. (special issue). 10.2305/IUCN.CH.2021.PARKS-27-SIAS.en

Tabetando, R. (2020). Tourism and COVID-19 in Zambia. Retrieved from www. theigc.org/blog/tourism-and-covid-19-in-zambia/

United Nations Conference on Trade and Development (UNCTAD). (2020). COVID-19 and tourism: Assessing the economic consequences. Retrieved from https:// unctad.org/system/files/official-document/ditcinf2020d3_en.pdf

Vyawahare, M. (2020) As visitors vanish, Madagascar's protected areas suffer a 'devastating' blow. *Mongabay.* 5 May. Retrieved from https://news.mongabay.com/2020/ 05/as-visitors-vanish-madagascars-protected-areas-suffer-a-devastating-blow

Waithaka, J. (2020). The impact of COVID-19 pandemic on Africa's protected areas operations and programmes. Retrieved from www.iucn.org/sites/dev/files/content/documents/2020/report_on_the_impact_of_covid_19_doc_july_10.pdf

World Economic Forum. (2021). Global *risks report 2021,* 16th ed, World Economic Forum. Retrieved from www3.weforum.org/docs/WEF_The _Global_Risks_ Report_2021.pdf

World Tourism Organisation. (2020). Impact assessment of the COVID-19 outbreak on international tourism. Retrieved from www.unwto.org/impact-assessment-of-the-covid-19-outbreak-on-international-tourism

World Tourism Organisation. (2021). Tourism recovery tracker. Retrieved from www.unwto.org/unwto-tourism-recovery-tracker

WTTC (2020). Safe travels: Global protocols and stamp for the new normal. Retrieved from https://wttc.org/COVID-19/Safe-Travels-Global-Protocols-Stamp.

WWF-Namibia (2020). Mitigating the impacts of the COVID-19 virus to Namibia's communal conservancies. Unpublished report.

Part IV

Protected areas and tourism practices

Policy and practice

15 The adoption of community-based tourism in the proximity of protected areas

Implications for policy and practice

Oliver Mtapuri

Introduction

Tourism is vital for global economic growth. It generates income through the consumption of goods and services. It creates job opportunities, as well as opportunities to enhance infrastructure in host destinations, and enables cultural exchange. Tourism involves travelling for leisure or business. This creates a bond between citizens and tourists (United Nations Conference on Trade and Development, 2013). But these movements of people have the potential to strain the environment if not properly managed because humans, flora and fauna share the same ecosystem. In that ecosystem are living and non-living organisms which are interdependent. It is the interplay between these organisms that can ensure their sustainability or demise. In circumstances of mass tourism, tourism may cause deforestation that endangers animal, human and plant life.

Tourism relies on structures created by human beings such as roads, bridges and buildings. The problem is that, in the pursuit of money and survival, human beings have tended to over-harvest available resources, threatening the same flora and fauna that they depend on. On one hand, humans want to travel for leisure for which they pay money. On the other hand, the custodians of those resources need the money either for survival or to make profits and, at times spurred by greed, excessive profits regardless of the consequences. Over-harvesting of resources is detrimental to the overall ecosystem. With these conflicting interests, the immediate question is: what balance needs to be struck to ensure the sustainability of that ecosystem for the benefit of all species – living and non-living?

The world committed to the Sustainable Development Goals (SDGs) to reduce biodiversity loss and increase coverage of protected areas (in SDG 15) and to alleviate poverty (in SGD 1) by 2030. These goals are intertwined; hence achieving one goal impacts the other, while achieving them in isolation cannot yield the best results (Naidoo et al., 2019). Protected areas are poised to preserve wild species; and efforts are necessary to preserve and sustain the ecosystems within which the species live (Stolton et al., 2015). Protected areas

DOI: 10.4324/9781003193166-19

play an essential role in conserving ecosystems, natural habitats and biodiversity, besides playing an important role in tourism development.

Since tourism relies on nature, it is vital to conserve it. This chapter highlights the importance of protected areas (PAs) and argues that to ensure the accrual of benefits to local people, PAs need to be integrated with managing the surrounding landscapes and settings alongside local communities, with them, for them and, ideally, by them, through their assemblages such as community trusts. There are communities that live in or near PAs. PAs are sources of rivers, streams, and wildlife, and because of poverty in communities, some community members have continued to hunt and fish in PAs as their ancestors used to do. Under such circumstances, some challenges and opportunities come along with the creation of PAs. For example, the interests of communities may collide with the purposes of PAs when weighed against cultural values and traditional practices. For Joppa, Lourie, & Pimm (2008), PAs are the only defence mechanism against forest loss and species extinctions. For communities, PAs are a resource and asset for their utilisation and societal reproduction. Evidently, PAs are contested, but they play a big role in conserving nature and for their socio-economic impact on livelihoods for locals residing in their surroundings. On one hand, they may represent an admission that communities have failed to harvest their fauna and flora in a sustainable way as they over-hunt for survival as a means of last resort. There is also a school of thought that argues that the outcomes from PAs are unequally distributed (Brockington & Wilkie, 2015), resulting in uneven distribution of benefits (Oldekop et al., 2016). Braber, Evans, & Oldekop (2018) add that PAs can fuel poverty and inequalities as they were initially intended purely for nature and wildlife conservation. This chapter endeavours to answer the following questions: (1) How and what benefits can accrue to local communities from PAs and (2) what strategies can be employed to ensure the participation of communities in PAs? The chapter looks at experiences from selected Southern African countries, namely Botswana, South Africa and Zimbabwe, to address these questions.

Watson et al. (2014) argue that for PAs to fulfil their role effectively, there is a need for a new approach that ensures their proper recognition, funding, planning, and implementation. Oldekop et al. (2016) are of the view that PAs must adopt co-managing mechanisms and empower locals through participation, alleviation of poverty and reducing inequalities while maintaining local cultures and sustaining livelihoods. The value of PAs can transcend empowerment, poverty and inequality reduction to sustainability of livelihoods and the ecosystem itself if they are preserved and conserved. As such, PAs must provide the platform to empower communities, for conservation, continuous learning and education and tourism. Overall, recent experiences have shown that the effectiveness of PAs depends on the performance of management and how it works with communities (Watson et al., 2014).

Tourism is recognised for fostering economic diversification and as a vital driver for socio-economic progress; however, its growth is not synonymous with poverty and inequality reduction (Giampiccoli & Saayman, 2016).

Community-based tourism (CBT) is tourism that is owned and/or managed by communities to deliver wider community benefits (Zielinski et al., 2020). Geography, cultural heritage and customs are untapped resources that communities can use to create local livelihood opportunities through tourism (Nel, 2018). In short, the engagement of communities with CBT initiatives promotes the agency of communities and empowers community members (Satovuori, 2016). This chapter argues that CBT practices in and near PAs in Southern Africa can improve both nature and the well-being of citizens through the adoption of the finer qualities of CBT and PAs. This chapter is conceptual and relied entirely on secondary sources of data such as books, and journal articles for its compilation. The next section unpacks the nature of PAs.

Progressive realisation of PAs in Southern Africa

Countries in sub-Saharan Africa have adopted different practices to ensure the protection of the environment. The legal framework guiding wildlife in Southern Africa is built on Roman–Dutch Law with the legal status of res nullius, where wildlife belongs to the state (Chigonda, 2018). According to the IUCN (1980), protected areas are categorised in terms of their management objectives – for example, the Strict Nature Reserves are spaces for the protection of biodiversity and whose use is severely restricted (e.g. for scientific research). By legislation, South Africa permits different governance types of PAs to be practised, such that, besides the state land, the country allows private land to be used as PAs given the consent of the landowner (Nsukwini & Bob, 2019). As a result, PAs are categorised based on their ownership, namely, state-owned and privately owned PAs. According to De Vos et al. (2019), PAs have increased in number since their inception; by the year 2017, South Africa had 19 state-owned National Parks and more than 500 nature reserves. Chidakel et al. (2020) note that there are different levels of private reserves, with the lowest being individually owned parcels which also serve as tourist attractions. Beita and Andreu (2016) believe that PAs, regulation and local intervention can promote sustainability in the PA system with appropriate national policy.

The Global Environment Facility (GEF) funds developing countries as one of the main investors in the creation and effective management of PAs around the world (GEF, n.d.). Funding for conservation is necessary for PAs to be sustainably channelled towards the administration and management of facilities for the benefit of all. PAs are referred to as conservancies when they are collectively managed (Chidakel et al., 2020). Local people run conservancies for their benefit, the larger proportions of the returns on their investment should accrue to them. The estrangement and distancing of communities from their conservancies may result in communities taking negative actions such as over-grazing and hunting through desperation. This is in line with a finding by Mogomotsi et al. (2020) who observed that respondents in their study believed that governments prioritise the protection of wildlife over community livelihoods and as such some community members admitted to killing

208 *Oliver Mtapuri*

wildlife as an entitlement emanating from their customs, norms and beliefs. For example, local communities had sites they believed to host spiritual forces and people were prohibited to visit those sites. Traditional communities in pre-colonial Zimbabwe also assigned totems to groups of people to avoid wanton killing of birds and animals in which those who are recognised with, for example, the Eland or Buffalo are not allowed to harm or kill it. This resulted in peace and harmony between people and nature through balanced health between communities and the natural environment and these practices were used to instil fear while controlling natural resources and avoiding the overexploitation of certain preferred species (Chigonda, 2018).

Botswana is endowed with abundant wildlife resources and boasts one of Africa's largest herd of elephants. About 17% of its land is considered PAs, comprising the Kalahari Desert, Okavango Delta, the Makgadikgadi pans and the Chobe river. It is estimated that tourism employs about 92,300 people in Botswana, representing 10.9% of total employment of the country, and contributes 10.3% to the country's GDP (WTTC, 2020). In 1993, Botswana initiated its first Community-Based Natural Resources Management (CBNRM) projects to involve local communities in tourism and to raise consciousness regarding nature conservation while reducing human–wildlife conflicts (Mbaiwa, 2015). The first CBNRM project is the Chobe Enclave Conservation Trust, while the second CBNRM project is the Sankuyo Tshwaragana Management Trust (Mbaiwa, 2015). South Africa and Botswana formed the Kgalagadi Transfrontier Park in 1999 which is Africa's first post-colonial Transfrontier Conservation Area (TFCA) (Moswete & Thapa, 2018). It is made up of Kalahari Gemsbok National Park (South Africa) and Gemsbok National Park (Botswana). Such parks were created to conserve and manage natural resources through cross-border tourism. A TFCA is described as 'a large ecological area that traverses the borders of two or more countries, involving one or more protected lands as well as multiple resource use areas' (SADC, 1999: 10). CBNRM initiatives in Botswana facilitate community-based tourism (CBT) by combining natural resource protection with rural development and addressing human–wildlife conflict (Thakadu, 2005). CBT offers opportunities to boost local economies by creating jobs. Hence, for Mbaiwa et al. (2011), CBT development has vast economic advantages for communities.

Thapa et al. (2018) posit that soil and land degradation have occurred in Southern Africa, particularly in Zimbabwe, due to subsistence activities that rely solely on forest and rangeland ecosystems leading to searches for alternative livelihoods. To that end, the government of Botswana encourages the formation of wildlife-based trusts/CBOs to minimise stakeholder rivalry for resources. Local inhabitants in the Okavango Delta settlements of Khwai, Sankuyo and Mababe, and the southern Kalahari area, for example, have profited from ecotourism operations linked to wildlife through their CBOs/ trusts. The Kgalagadi Transfrontier Park is maintained as one biological region, despite the fact that it is regulated by two sets of rules and procedures (Lekgau

& Tichaawa, 2019). The Mier and the San population groups were given 25,000 hectares of land within the park on the South African side, and the management of different reserves as a unit is common in South Africa (Chidakel et al., 2020). For example, the Greater Kruger National Park (GKNP) is an integrated system of reserves that lies in the eastern region of South Africa, with the Kruger National Park as the anchor national park (Chidakel et al., 2020). The GKNP shares its borders with Mozambique and Zimbabwe and is part of a larger system of PAs known as Greater Limpopo Transfrontier Conservation Area. The free migration of animals permits the expansion of the wildlife's territory essential for forage and reproduction. The collaborative PA governance promotes partnership between the local communities, the private sector, government and NGOs, which yields more biodiversity and socio-economic benefits and allows for consensus-building and efficient use of resources (De Koning et al., 2017). Saarinen et al. (2019) observe that the Kgalagadi Transfrontier Park was established for conservation and to work with local people and cultures to build a responsible tourist industry. Mbaiwa (2015) notes that community trusts face the challenge of identifying their effectiveness on a practical level in improving livelihoods. What is important is to promote the wellness of human beings through shared benefits emanating from conservation and protection programmes.

Zimbabwe has the following: a large elephant population with Hwange National Park (HNP) holding twice its ecological carrying capacity at 45,000; a large black rhino population; and the highest concentration of the black eagle per unit area globally (Chibememe et al., 2014). Zimbabwe was the first African country to develop an alternative approach to managing natural resources outside PAs through the Community Areas Management Programme for indigenous Resources (CAMPFIRE) in the 1980s and CAMPFIRE enabled local communities to benefit from wildlife hunting revenue streams in their areas, including the rehabilitation of schools, clinics and sinking of boreholes and provision of bursaries to learners (Campfire, n.d.). Since the pre-colonial era, indigenous people of Zimbabwe have conserved natural resources through the use of traditional beliefs, taboos and customs (Chigonda, 2018).

In South Africa, some PAs have resulted in the gradual loss of traditional bodies of knowledge, practices and people have become homeless (IWPA, 2008). In Zimbabwe, the birth of colonialism marked a shift towards racially based control over natural resources. Fabricius (2004) claims that black people, caught in poverty, did not have political voice to air their concerns and so conservation became a tool of alienation. The colonial period introduced laws to exert control over natural resources and influenced the racially unequal distribution of land in Zimbabwe (Chigonda, 2018). This created further alienation of the people from their heritage. This exclusionary approach to conservation was an unfair system as it evacuated and denied people access to resources upon which they relied (Lele et al., 2010). As a result, conservation and PAs were seen as elitist.

Benefits of Transfrontier Conservation Areas (TFCA)

Transfrontier Conservation Areas (TFCAs) emerged as an alternative method to conservation (Sinthumule, 2016). TFCA are useful for biodiversity conservation, economic development, collaborations between nations and the free movement of animals. For Groom et al. (2006) biodiversity conservation is good for human survival. PAs are important for the survival of animal species and the conservation of the natural ecosystems. The TFCAs initiative calls for removing political boundaries amongst countries to permit integration of PAs and natural systems between two or more PAs (Sinthumule, 2016). Borders were removed between South Africa and Mozambique, making it possible for wildlife to roam from one country to another. Transboundary conservation provides large spaces for the conservation of the environment and the animals, and spaces for adaptation to climate change (Chassot, 2011). It is important for communities to be involved in all conservation efforts to ensure the sustainability of habitats, the environment, fauna and flora and their own survival. This opens up possibilities to start community-based tourism ventures in the precincts of TFCA so that the benefits accrue to communities from their own ventures as well as proceeds from the TFCAs. For Sandwith et al. (2001), this is another way of uniting communities split by colonial borders and supporting local traditions of being, cultures and indigenous institutions. The establishment of borders is political and not ecological, and therefore, the removal of borders provides a vehicle through which ecological integrity can be promoted (Sinthumule, 2016).

Botswana, South Africa and Zimbabwe have an opportunity to share experiences and lessons learned in the implementation of nature conservation policies and practices for the benefit of all countries and to bring social cohesion between communities who live adjacent to TFCAs on both sides of the borders. The migration of animals is important for their own survival as they search for conditions conducive for their survival, for example, for forage and water. Cumming (2008) observes that, when they return, should they return, they do not travel in a known and familiar pattern. Given the sensitivity of the matter, as it straddles sovereignty, the Peace Parks Foundation (PPF) works with governments at all levels, traditional authorities, private firms and other relevant stakeholders to craft a common strategy to guide the TFCA and its management (RETOSA, 2012).

Peace parks in Southern Africa will only be successful in the long run if local people living inside or next to them benefit significantly. CBT makes it possible for such communities to reap these benefits. Natural variety in Southern Africa is a major tourist attraction. In TFCA, CBT ensures that communities have a lot of influence over the activities that take place in their area, and as result they get a large share of the benefits (Wood, 2002). These advantages are significant in Southern Africa, where populations near PAs face high poverty rates, illiteracy, unemployment and skewed resource use patterns. Andersson et al. (2013) note that CBT projects inside Transfrontier Parks provide a number of benefits, including the potential for local populations to gain employment and revenue,

Community-based tourism: implications 211

as well as foreign money for national governments, while preserving the natural resource base.

Transfrontier parks allow CBT and conservation to take place beyond national borders. Community-based tourism within the boundaries of transfrontier parks in Zimbabwe, South Africa and Botswana has the potential to produce long-term economic growth through tourism. TFCA's overarching goal is to alleviate poverty, either directly or indirectly. The economic potential of transfrontier parks rests in the fact that tourism allows people living in these regions to benefit from existing natural resources without diminishing them. Van Aarde & Jackson (2007) are of the view that the creation of conservation areas inside TFCAs might be a solution to the issues connected to the management of large populations of animals, such as elephants, in Southern Africa. The idea behind the creation of TFCAs is that tourism would offer a financially viable exist-ence for the people who live in and around these parks. Evidently, transfrontier parks assist in protecting biodiversity and alleviating poverty for the people living in or near the TFCAs (Quinn et al., 2012). The New Partnership for Africa's Development (NEPAD) embraces notions of poverty alleviation and local socio-economic development and TFCAs as global rather regional platforms to achieve those ambitions in the SADC (NEPAD, 2010). TFCAs reduce the vul-nerability of fragmented habitat spaces, connected to PAs and rural communities, but open possibilities for the practice of community-based tourism.

In Zimbabwe, economic and political difficulties have made it extremely dif-ficult to practise and implement environmental sustainability as people become desperate to survive in the midst of poverty (Mawere, 2013). The unequal distribution of resources amongst citizens is problematic as socio-economic challenges make it difficult for the conservation to occur in earnest. The Peace Parks Foundation has been behind the establishment of TFCAs in Southern Africa, it assisted with the establishment of Kavango-Zambezi (KAZA) TFCA, which integrates Angola, Botswana, Namibia, Zimbabwe and Zambia, and the Great Limpopo Transfrontier Park (GLTFP), which integrates Mozambique, South Africa and Zimbabwe (Sinthumule, 2016). The advantages of manage-ment as a unit include the uniformity in the implementation of policy and greater control and management of wildlife and its movement. Therefore, PA governance means running the PA, conservation, protection of animals and being accountable to communities. However, some flaws have been acknowledged, such as the lack of coordination, outdated regulatory approaches, inadequate planning; insufficient resource allocation; and a failure to link conservation imperatives with the needs of local inhabitants (Rashid et al., 2017). These weaknesses hinder PAs from operating efficiently and effectively.

Community-based tourism (CBT) and protected areas: a coalescence

Chidakel et al. (2020) believe that tourism in PAs plays a vital role in the growth of local and regional economies. Tourism is vital for society to gain economic, environmental and social benefits; PAs contribute to revenue-sharing with adjacent communities including community empowerment through capacity building (Snyman & Bricker, 2019). Members of the community get jobs, which leads to poverty reduction, as a trade-off to hunting. For income generation, people from communities are encouraged to sell their craftwork to tourists and start their own accommodation businesses and enterprises (canoes and kayaks), work as guides and cooks. This is a dominant trend in Southern Africa countries, including South Africa and Zimbabwe, and engages other tourism-based activities (Shar et al., 2019). Snyman et al. (2019) opine that benefit-sharing in PA tourism requires good governance, a thorough understanding of community politics, hierarchies and how power is shared to develop a mechanism flexible for the empowerment of the marginalised and impoverished. To that end, it is also important to understand community practices, values, norms and traditions as well aspirations.

An integrated system also presents an economic advantage, given that all these reserves can be managed or governed together as a unit (Chidakel et al., 2020). Snyman et al., (2019) argue that central to benefit-sharing in PA tourism is equity, a vital component that ensures fairness and justice through recognition, procedure and distribution. The benefits acquired by communities also include intangible benefits, such as raising awareness among communities regarding conservation, enhanced decision-making skills and increased awareness regarding PAs. De Koning et al. (2017) call for collaborative environmental management as the major move towards effective benefit-sharing, as it opens opportunities for collaborative governance, for community engagement and trust-building mechanisms. Trust is needed between stakeholders and is a necessary condition for transparent, inclusive and participatory engagements. Snyman et al. (2019) maintain that, for many years, financial benefits from conservation fees have been the primary component of benefit-sharing in PA tourism directed to the community.

Collaborative governance of PAs presents a decentralised and democratic PA governance system that is built on customary rights (De Koning et al., 2017). Benefits should cascade to community members through their democratic assemblages and platforms. Other benefits related to PA tourism that accrue to communities include constructing health centres and schools (Snyman et al., 2019). As such, benefits acquired from PA tourism can be directed to develop initiatives within the community. Local communities in KwaZulu-Natal's National Park in South Africa collect levies from visitors for community development (Shar et al., 2019). Community trusts in Botswana collect revenue by selling wildlife quotas to safari companies, encouraging cultural tourism and increased benefit-sharing; PAs thus have positive impacts on biodiversity conservation and protection as the community feels the need to take part (Shar et al., 2019).

Discussion

According to Zielinski et al. (2020), CBT initiatives differ based on the level of community participation, ranging from the employment of community members in a business between a community member or family, and an outside business partner, to full control of the tourism operation. It is evident that the impacts of CBT permeate a larger part of a community and beyond. In the same way, the benefits of tourism can transcend the sector as money earned in tourism can be invested in the education and health of community members and beyond. As such, it means empowerment, self-reliance and self-determination also traverse it. The main idea behind CBT initiatives is that activities or initiatives must be community-based (Satovuori, 2016). CBT must thus be responsive to the social ills experienced in these often 'uneconomic' communities (Strydom, Mangope & Henama, 2018). Communities must take part in matters, processes and systems that affect them. It is imperative to understand the power dynamics in communities because they are heterogeneous and, therefore, context-specific, and any solutions must heed the same.

When people see the benefits and gains from tourism, they will guard and protect the asset. The training of community members must be sustained concerning their responsibilities as responsible citizens. Similarly, the cascading of indigenous knowledge regarding fauna and flora can be done in the context of CBT. Local myths, mores, values, cultures, habits and traditions are shared within the community and with tourists guaranteeing their longevity. Community member-to-member referrals, called peer-to-peer referrals, should be the order of the day for various services such as food, handicrafts and accommodation, so that money circulates within the community context of CBT. This will also enhance community cohesion. The introduction of CBT does not mean that it will resolve conflicts and tensions within communities. It provides a platform to work in harmony for the betterment of all using local resources.

This chapter argues that, when communities do not see the benefits accruing from community-based tourism initiatives, this may lead to their alienation and the adoption of reckless attitudes towards their natural resources, especially in communal resources in which they have a stake as a collective. In other words, they will be tempted to shift to a survival mode of taking care of themselves first at all costs, irrespective of community concerns, particularly in a context of poverty and inequality.

Seek & Sellier (2019, p. 57) indicate that PAs 'bring jobs, income, and know-how directly to residents in remote areas. They also bring new products into the tourism economy while establishing a shared responsibility for managing and protecting key assets – such as land, cultural heritage, and wildlife – to the local people and the private sector players.' However, when they do not deliver on these promises, it leads to frustration and a feeling of abandonment.

CBT ventures, including micro and small enterprises that operate under a common organisational umbrella and independent family-owned rural businesses under a community organisation, are categorised as CBT initiatives (Zielinski et al., 2020). When essential resources and assets are not available to communities through PAs, the survival of these small enterprises is threatened, and social cohesion may go into disarray, as everyone will work for their own survival and that of their business.

214   *Oliver Mtapuri*

Evidently, PAs have disrupted indigenous ways of living in circumstances in which hunting is now termed poaching and harvesting plants for medicinal remedies is criminalised under the banner of deforestation. It is upon the animals and trees that livelihoods depended. Without these, livelihoods are threatened, vulnerable and equally endangered. Additionally, when people see the benefits and gains, they will guard and protect the asset. The chapter theorises that people depend on their natural and physical resources and are likely to conserve and preserve them when they have enough to satisfy their basic and immediate needs. Conversely, people are likely to disobey traditions, mores and habits in using their natural and physical resources when their livelihoods and survival are threatened. Africans are stereotypically considered poachers when they harvest what their ancestors used to harvest in their normal course of life. Rich people enjoy exclusive and an unfair advantage because of their resources as they can hunt down animals as they wish because of their money. This hunting privilege is sometimes reinforced by law/legislation by national governments also to earn money from hunting fees charged against elitists. The experiences of these three countries have shown that: a) Communities can stay in PAs based on the SA experience as was done with the Mier and San groups. b) Decentralisation through trusts empowers communities as a strategy that was done in Botswana. c) Transfrontier parks permit the cross-border movement of both humans and animals and therefore promote cross-border tourism and this in turn permits collaborative governance in which different reserves are managed as a single unit, for example, the Greater Kruger National Park, as part of the Greater Limpopo Transfrontier Conservation Area. d) Collaborative governance nurtures consensus building and cohesion between countries by uniting people separated by political borders. e) The experiences from CAMPFIRE in Zimbabwe, as in the other countries, have shown that the benefits to communities are multiple, from income to rehabilitation of social infrastructure and the provision of bursaries to learners. f) It is through a combination of policy, regulation and community participation that these dividends from PAs and CBT initiatives can be realised.

Conclusion

Protected areas in Southern Africa play a role in improving the livelihoods of those living in communities adjacent to PAs. However, this chapter has demonstrated that, though there are advantages of living close to PAs, there are also disadvantages. The common disadvantage of PAs in Southern Africa is the eviction of people from their communities and fauna and flora, leading to alienation. The exclusion makes it difficult for the local people to access their natural resources to sustain their livelihoods. The experiences of these Southern African countries have demonstrated the harmony that transfrontier parks bring between countries by allowing animals to transverse political boundaries and uniting communities separated by the same. The common goal of PAs is to sustainably preserve the environment while ensuring the sustenance of livelihoods. How successful this plays out in these countries is determined by context, namely, the socio-economic rules and regulations prevailing in these countries, and how these countries work together as a region to preserve their fauna and flora.

References

Andersson, J. A., de Garine-Wichatitsky, M., Cumming, D. H. M., Dzingirai, V., & Giller, K. E. (Eds.) (2013). *Transfrontier conservation areas: People living on the edge.* London: Earthscan.

Beita, C. M., & Andreu, M. N. (2016). Local level policies for tourism management in protected areas: Experiences from Costa Rica. In Mukul, S. A., Rashid, A. Z. M. M. (Eds.), *Protected areas: Policies, management and future directions.* New York: Nova Science Publishers, 32–57.

Braber, B. den, Evans, K. L., & Oldekop, J. A. (2018). Impact of protected areas on poverty, extreme poverty, and inequality in Nepal. *Conservation Letters*, 11 (6), 25–46.

Brockington, D., & Wilkie, D. (2015). Protected areas and poverty. *Philosophical Transactions of the Royal Society B: Biological Sciences*, 370 (1681), 201–234.

Campfire. (n.d.). Community benefits. Retrieved from https://campfirezimbabwe.org/article/community-benefits-summary

Chassot, O. (2011). Ecological issues – transboundary conservation. GTCN: IUCN. Retrieved from www.tbpa.net/page.php?ndx=46

Chibememe, G., Dhliwayo, M., Edson, G., Mtisi, S., Never, M., & Laiza, K. O. (2014). *Review of national laws and policies that support or undermine indigenous peoples and local communities.* Harare: Natural Justice and Ford Foundation.

Chidakel, A., Eb, C., & Child, B. (2020). The comparative financial and economic performance of Protected Areas in the Greater Kruger National Park, South Africa: Functional diversity and resilience in the socio-economics of a landscape-scale reserve network. *Journal of Sustainable Tourism*, 28 (8), 1100–1119.

Chigonda, T. (2018). More than just story telling: A review of biodiversity conservation and utilisation from precolonial to postcolonial Zimbabwe. *Scientifica*, 2018, 24–45.

De Koning, M., Nguyen, T., Lockwood, M., Sengchanthavong, S., & Phommasane, S. (2017). Collaborative governance of Protected Areas: Success factors and prospects for hin nam no national Protected Area, central Laos. *Conservation and Society*, 15 (1), 87–99.

De Vos, A., Clements, H. S., Biggs, D., & Cumming, G. S. (2019). The dynamics of proclaimed privately Protected Areas in South Africa over 83 years. *Conservation Letters*, 12 (6), e12644.

Fabricius, C. (2004). *Rights, resources and rural development: Community-based natural resource management in Southern Africa.* London: Earthscan.

Giampiccoli, A., & Saayman, M. (2016). Community-based tourism: From a local to a global push. *Acta Commercii,* 16 (1), a372. h p://dx.doi. org/10.4102/ac.v16i1.372.

Groom, M. J., Meffe, G. K., & Carroll, C. R. (2006). *Principles of conservation biology.* Sunderland: Sinauer.

IWPA (Isimangaliso Wetland Park Authority). (2008). *Integrated management plan.* The Dredger Harbour, St Lucia: IWPA.

Joppa, L., Loarie, S. R., & Pimm, S. L. (2008). On the protection of 'Protected Areas'. *Proceedings of the National Academy of Sciences*, 105 (18), 6673–6678.

216   *Oliver Mtapuri*

Lekgau, R. J., & Tichaawa, T. M. (2019). Effects of institutional arrangements and policies on community participation in wildlife tourism in Africa. *GeoJournal of Tourism and Geosites*, 27 (44), 1280–1295.

Lele, S., Wilshusen, P., Brockington, D., Seidler, R. & Bawa, K. (2010). Beyond exclusion: alternative approaches to biodiversity conservation in the developing tropics. *Current Opinion in Environmental Sustainability*, 2 (1–2), 94–100.

Mawere, M. (2013). A critical review of environmental conservation in Zimbabwe. *Africa Spectrum*, 48 (2), 85–97.

Mbaiwa, J. E. (2015). *Community-based natural resource management in Botswana. Institutional arrangements for conservation, development and tourism in Eastern and Southern Africa.* Dordrecht: Springer.

Mbaiwa, J. E., Stronza, A. L., & Kreuter, U. (2011). From collaboration to conservation: Insights from the Okavango Delta, Botswana. *Society and Natural Resources*, 24 (4), 400–411.

Mogomotsi, P. K., Mogomotsi, G. E. J., Dipogiso, K., Phonchi-Tshekiso, N. D., Stone, L. S., & Badimo, D. (2020). An analysis of communities' attitudes toward wildlife and implications for wildlife sustainability. *Tropical Conservation Science*, 13, 1–9.

Moswete, N., & Thapa, B. (2018). Local communities, CBOs/trusts, and people–park relationships: A case study of the Kgalagadi Transfrontier Park, Botswana. *George Wright Forum*, 35 (1), 96–108.

Naidoo, R., Gerkey, D., Hole, D., Pfaff, A., Ellis, A. M., Golden, C. D., & Fisher, B. (2019). Evaluating the impacts of protected areas on human well-being across the developing world. *Science Advances*, 5 (4), 1–15.

Nel, H. (2018). A comparison between the asset-oriented and needs-based community development approaches in terms of systems changes. *Practice*, 30 (1), 33–52. DOI: 10.1080/09503153.2017.1360474

NEPAD. (2010). The new partnership for Africa's development. Action plan for the environment initiative. Retrieved from www.nepad.org/climatechangeandsustainabledevelopment/knowledge/doc/1463/actionplan-environment-initiative

Nsukwini, S., & Bob, U. (2019). Protected Areas, community costs and benefits: A comparative study of selected conservation case studies from northern KwaZulu-Natal, South Africa. *GeoJournal of Tourism and Geosites,* 27 (4), 1377–1391.

Oldekop, J. A., Holmes, G., Harris, W. E., and Evans, K. L. (2016). A global assessment of the social and conservation outcomes of Protected Areas. *Conservation Biology*, 30 (1), 133–141.

Quinn, M. S., Broberg, L., & Freimund, W. (Eds.) (2012). *Parks, peace, and partnership: Global initiatives in transboundary conservation.* Calgary: University of Calgary Press.

Rashid, A. Z. M. M., Craig, D., & Mukul, S. A. (2017). Shifting paradigm of governance in the natural resources management of Bangladesh: A centralist to pluralistic approach in the forest protected areas management. In Mukul, S. A. & Rashid, A. Z. M. M. (Eds.), *Protected areas: Policies, management and future directions.* New York: Nova Science Publishers, 36–54.

RETOSA. (2012). Regional Tourism Organisation of Southern Africa. Regional Initiatives. Retrieved from www.retosa.co.za/regional-initiatives

Saarinen, J. (2019). Communities and sustainable tourism development: Community impacts and local benefit creation tourism. In McCool, S. F., & Bosak, K. (Eds.), *A research agenda for sustainable tourism.* Cheltenham: Elgar, 206–222.

SADC. (1999). SADC protocol on wildlife conservation and law enforcement. Retrieved from www.tbpa.net/docs/pdfs/SecMan/SecManSADCProtocol.pdf

Sandwith, T., Shine, C., Hamilton, L., & Sheppard, D. (2001). *Transboundary Protected Areas for peace and co-operation.* Best Practice Protected Area Guideline Series, 7. Gland: IUCN.

Satovuori, A. (2016). *Applying asset-based community development to community-based tourism: The case of Beni Na'im in Palestine Oppiaine.* MA thesis, University of Helsiniki. https://helda.helsinki.fi/bitstream/handle/10138/160822/anna_satovuori_thesis.pdf?sequence=3&isAllowed=y Accessed 14 August 2020.

Seek, C., & Sellier, N., 2019. *Stimulating sustainable development through tourism concessions: Case studies on how tourism can benefit the environment and communities living in and around Protected Areas.* No. 139922. Washington, DC: World Bank. http://documents1.worldbank.org/curated/en/643981564580916089/pdf/Stimulating-Sustainable-Development-Through-Tourism-Concessions-Case-Studies-on-How-Tourism-Can-Benefit-the-Environment-and-Communities-Living-in-and-Around-Protected-Areas.pdf

Shar, P., & Mukhovi, S. M. (2019). Benefits of Protected Areas to adjacent communities: The case of Maasai Mara National Reserve in Kenya. Retrieved from http://erepository.uonbi.ac.ke/handle/11295/107788

Sinthumule, N. I. (2016). Multiple-land use practices in transfrontier conservation areas: the case of Greater Mapungubwe straddling parts of Botswana, South Africa and Zimbabwe. *Bulletin of Geography. Socio-Economic Series*, 34 (34), 103–115.

Snyman, S., & Bricker, K. S. (2019). Living on the edge: Benefit-sharing from Protected Area tourism. *Journal of Sustainable Tourism*, 27 (6), 705–719.

Stolton, S., et al. (2015). Values and benefits of protected areas. In Worboys, G. L., Lockwood, M., Kothari, A., Feary, S., & Pulsford, I. (Eds.), *Protected area governance and management.* Canberra: The Australian National University, 145–168.

Strydom, A. J., Mangope, D., and Henama, U. S. (2018). Lessons learned from successful community-based tourism case studies from the Global South. *African Journal of Hospitality, Tourism and Leisure*, 7 (5). 66–82. www.ajhtl.com/uploads/7/1/6/3/7163688/article_18_vol_7_5__2018.pdf

Thakadu, O. T. (2005). Success factors in community based natural resources management in Northern Botswana: Lessons from practice. *Natural Resources Forum*, 29 (3), 199–212.

United Nations Conference on Trade and Development. (2013). Sustainable tourism: Contribution to economic growth and sustainable development. In *Issues note presented at the Expert Meeting on Tourism's Contribution to Sustainable Development.* New York: United Nations.

Van Aarde, R. J., & Jackson, T. P. (2007). Megaparks for metapopulations: Addressing the causes of locally high elephant numbers in southern Africa. *Biological Conservation*, 134, 289–297.

Watson, J. E. M., Dudley, N., Segan, D. B., & Hockings, M. (2014). The performance and potential of protected areas. *Insight Review*, 515, 67–72.

Wood, M. E. (2002). *Ecotourism: Principles, practices and policies for sustainability.* Retrieved from https://books.google.co.za/books/about/Ecotourism.html?id=TaAsAQAAMAAJ&redir_esc=y

World Travel and Tourism Council (WTTC). (2020). *World tourism report.* London: WTTC.

Zielinski, S., Jeong, Y., Kim, S.-I., & Milanés, C. (2020). Why community-based tourism and rural tourism in developing and developed nations are treated differently? A review. *Sustainability*, 12 (15), 38–59.

16 Militarisation of conservation and 'shoot to kill' policies

An analysis of the rights of African states to protect and conserve wildlife

Goemeone E. J. Mogomotsi and
Patricia Kefilwe Mogomotsi

Introduction

Protected and conserved areas are viewed as the cornerstones of biodiversity conservation in various parts of the world (Boucher, Spalding & Revenga, 2013). Various governments have established protected areas (PAs) as a policy response to mitigate the loss and cause of biodiversity (Barnes et al., 2016). Approximately 22.5 million km^2 (16.64%) of the land surface and 28.1 million km^2 (7.74%) of coastal waters and the ocean have been declared protected areas (United Nations Environment Programme, 2020). The latest surface area coverage for PAs is within the targets of the Convention on Biological Diversity whose aim was to increase the global land coverage of PAs to 17% by 2020 (Barnes et al., 2016).

PAs play different roles in the conservation of biodiversity, such as maintaining refuge and ensuring the fundamental ecological mechanisms of dispersal and gene exchange (Landridge, Sordello & Reyjol, 2020). Further, PAs protect ecosystems and their constituent species, protect ecosystem services, populations of threatened species, and in some instances to protect the ways of life of some communities. For PAs to succeed in goals of preventing the extinction of flora and fauna and retaining the most-intact ecosystems, they must work together with Indigenous Peoples, communities living adjacent to PAs and other non-governmental players with interest in the successful conservation of biodiversity (Maxwell et al., 2020). This is in recognition of the reality that increasing PA networks alone does not lead to conservation success.

Notwithstanding the growth of PAs in Africa, the continent is experiencing a decline in wildlife populations in most countries. The levels of poaching of some animals such as elephants and rhinos for their tusks or horns is increasing in PAs (Duffy, 2014). Although PAs generally reduce the rate of poaching and mortality of mammals, they do not eliminate poaching incidences on their own. This has prompted governments to devise effective and deterrent forms of conservation efforts, the most controversial being the use of military tactics or the militarisation of conservation. The increasing use of military tactics in

DOI: 10.4324/9781003193166-20

wildlife protection efforts around the world is largely reflective of the desperation by government to save species on the verge of extinction (Humphreys & Smith, 2011). The militarisation of anti-poaching is not new in Africa. It became a policy tool of choice in the 1970s and 1980s due to high incidences of poaching which pressurised some governments to devise radical responses to poaching incidents (Mogomotsi & Madigele, 2017). The use of military tactics to reduce poaching is traceable to the colonial era when PAs were first established in sub-Saharan Africa (Neumann, 1998). From that era to the post-colonial or modern times, conservation-induced violence has been legitimised and normalised by colonial troops, and through the imposition of states of emergency in African states (Marijnen, 2017). The apartheid South African government which promoted white values of patriotism, self-sacrifice and self-defence increasingly adopted militarised anti-poaching as a part of the wider national defence strategy, to combat rhino poaching (Annecke & Masubelele, 2016). Conservation of biodiversity is important not only for ecological reasons but also for socio-economic purposes. In that regard, there is a clear link between advocated nature conservation, restoration ecology and sustainable economic development. (Royuela et al., 2019). Conservation and the establishment of PAs are important for the preservation of wildlife and livelihoods of communities dependent on nature-based tourism.

Prior to delving into the substance of this chapter it is worth noting that the militarisation of conservation of opposed by some scholars. Those against 'green militarisation', as it is often called, argue that the militarisation of conservation in Africa highlights the competition between morality and human rights vis-à-vis the responsibility of humankind to protect wild animals, forcing policymakers to choose between two moral 'goods' (Neumann, 2007). The opponents of militisation of conservation further state that the terms 'poacher' and 'poaching', although largely intended to refer to commercial poaching activities targeting high-value biodiversity, are difficult to narrow down as a result of the hybridisation of subsistence and commercial poaching, also the complicity of local communities in commercial poaching (Mushonga and Matose, 2020). In short, they argue that the local communities who hunt for subsistence purposes end up being unintended subjects of the wrath of the state apparatus (Mushonga and Matose, 2020; Ramutsindela, 2016). It is imperative to note that this chapter does not discuss the opposing views in detail besides acknowledging their existence.

Targeted killing is often used for the physical elimination of enemy combatants during hostilities but also of suspected terrorists in peacetime (Bachmann, 2013). In appropriate circumstances, targeted killing or shoot to kill may be justifiable as a lawful and legitimate method of warfare. Conversely, targeted killing operations executed outside an armed conflict may qualify as acts of extrajudicial killing, murder or assassinations liable for prosecution under international and domestic law. Targeted killings are not a new practice – governments have long sought to prevail over their enemies by engaging in premeditated killings of individual suspects (Heyns & Knuckey, 2013). It has been in use since World

War II, and what has essentially changed recently is its rapid proliferation as a combat strategy in non-traditional military operations (Heyns & Knuckey, 2013). The rapid invocation of targeted killing as a policy instrument is often attributed to the state of Israel in its pursuit against alleged Palestinian terrorists (David, 2003). Between late 2000, when the al-Aqsa *intifada* began, and the end of 2005, the state of Israel had target-killed almost 300 suspected terrorists, a fact that attracted widespread international condemnation and fuelled scholarly debates (Eichensehr, 2007). Due to the frequency of targeted killings by the state of Israel, it is understandable why it is one of the few countries to have put in place formal operational guidelines for the permissibility of targeted killing and have those guidelines confirmed or legitimised by the judiciary (Falk & Hefetz, 2019). This policy entails the use of the military to assassinate those people who are deemed to plan, launch or commit terrorist attacks in Israel and in the [occupied territories] against both civilians and soldiers. Similarly, the United States of America has over the years reserved the right to kill, and has indeed killed, those it believes to be terrorists (Foreman, 2013).

Further, the US Coast Guards, which is a branch of the US Armed Forces, is involved in the militarised combating of illegal, unreported and unregulated fishing, which at times involves the shooting and killing of illegal fishermen (Telesetsky, 2018). The use of force in wildlife protection presents a unique strategic challenge in that one side of the conflict is defenceless against its human opponent yet must rely on the altruism of other humans for its protection (Humphreys & Smith, 2011). It is clear that there exists a link between issues relating to sovereignty, statehood and combating wildlife crime. This relationship between sovereignty and the responsibility to protect natural resources with specific reference to wildlife is often linked to the United Nations-endorsed Responsibility to Protect agenda and the principle of just cause in war parlance (Bellamy, 2008). It is argued that the concept of Responsibility to Protect is equally applicable in instances of combating the degradation of the environment that is the basis of the livelihood of a defined group of people (Kleine, 2015).

The use of military tactics, weaponry and even personnel to patrol protected areas (PAs) against incursion by those wishing to extract wildlife and other resources, a dynamic termed 'green militarisation', has occupied a growing place in academic literature (Duffy, 2019). However, there is a dearth of legal scholarship in this contentious yet growing practice in wildlife conservation.

Permanent sovereignty over natural resources and its relationship to wildlife conservation

The sovereign rights of nation-states over natural resources within their territories were recognised over 50 years ago under the auspices of the United Nations through the adoption of General Assembly Resolution 1803 on the Permanent Sovereignty over Natural Resources (Ng'ambi, 2015). The right of permanent sovereignty over natural resources entails the abstraction rights

Militarisation of conservation   221

by states to attain economic development and the need to assert themselves on issues such as the control of their natural resources (Ng'ambi, 2015). Every nation–state has an absolute right to own and develop natural resources within its territory into equitable gains for the national polity or specific communities in a specific country (Mirandi, 2012).

The doctrine of permanent sovereignty over natural resources has attained the status of international law and has gained international recognition as a vehicle for developing countries to utilise and manage domestic natural resources (Chekera & Nmehielle, 2013). This is consistent with the conceptualisation of the doctrine of sovereignty at public international law which generally refers to the supremacy that the government of any state has over the people, resources and all other authorities within the territory it controls (Mogomotsi et al., 2020). In the context of this chapter, the meaning of 'sovereignty' in relation to the principle of permanent sovereignty over natural resources can be easily understood to mean the 'legal, governmental control and management authority over natural resources' (Schafer & Bell, 2002). Some of the sub-rights of states that devolve or flow from the overarching right of permanent sovereignty over natural resources are the rights of states to determine and control use conservation and management of natural resources (Enyew, 2017).

The right of permanent sovereignty over natural resources became mapped onto territorially circumscribed domestic legal orders. Each state retains internal jurisdiction over conflicts between governments and their people(s) about the exploitation and distribution of resource wealth. The argument of this chapter is that the permanent sovereignty as envisaged by the United Nations is applicable to the rights of states to protect the natural resources within their territories. This stems from the duty of a state at international law to be accountable to its citizenry and to the society of states for the protection of its population (Glanville, 2011). The permanent sovereignty over natural resources, among other duties, imposes the duty to use resources sustainably (Armstrong, 2015). Therefore, there is no doubt that the duty to ensure sustainable use of natural resources entails combating poaching of wildlife and the overharvesting of veldt products. The conservation territoriality is premised on the protected area model where authorities use practices of mapping, demarcating, legislating and the use of force and violence to produce the desired results for the conservation of wild flora and fauna (Massé, 2020).

Every state has a right to protect the integrity of its sovereignty and international borders (MacFarlane & Sabadze, 2013). In the context of the United Nations Charter, the concept of territorial integrity is twofold. First, it is aimed at the maintenance and protection of existing boundaries, with a view of preventing nation-states from promoting secessionism or border changes in other countries (Elden, 2005). Secondly, it provides for the respect of equal sovereignty by proscribing against interference in internal affairs of states and the preservation of domestic sovereignty. In recognition of the territorial integrity of states and the sacrosanctity of sovereignty, most written constitutions contain explicit clauses making direct reference to the sovereignty of national territory (Doyle, 2018).

Wildlife crime, specifically poaching, is a real and serious threat to the sovereignty of some nation-states (Kideghesho, 2016). It has been argued that the tendency to conceptualise the conservation of biodiversity without any reference to states is not realistic and is unsatisfactory (Okasnen & Vuorisalo, 2019). This is because states are self-determining actors and the principal possessors of biological resources in their territories. The fundamental idea is that each country, as a sovereign actor, oversees the biodiversity within its territory. It is herein argued that international humanitarian law or the law of armed conflict is equally applicable in armed anti-poaching law enforcement efforts.

International humanitarian law regulates the conduct of states during armed conflict. This field of international law is reflective of an inherent compromise between humanitarianism and military necessity. Even though it does not impose rights and obligations in the interests of the state parties, it exists to protect persons (Hill-Cawthorne, 2017). However, modern conflicts are drastically different from those envisioned when this law first evolved. As a result, the law of armed conflict, the *jus in bello*, applies from the moment a state of armed conflict does exist, be it as an international conflict between states or a non-international armed conflict between a state and non-state armed groups. The distinction between international and non-international armed conflicts is a much more historical fact not based on military necessity or humanitarian considerations (Watkin, 2004).

Over the centuries, some states have regulated both peace and wartime relations amongst themselves, while they have long been reluctant to subject their efforts to maintain law, order and public security within their territorial borders to the purview of international law (Watkin, 2004). In terms of Common Article 3 of the Geneva Conventions, non-international conflicts have been made the subject of international humanitarian law (International Committee of the Red Cross, 1949). The law of armed conflict is equally applicable in instances of conflict situations where the overall legality of the use of interstate force, the *jus ad bellum*, is questionable. Traditionally, international humanitarian law was aimed at governing state actions during war against other states. However, the dictates of modern society have transformed the conception of war, which was understood to be state versus state, to include state versus non-state conflicts. Modern conflicts between the states and non-state groups, such as the 'War on Terror' or the 'War on Poaching' between states and non-state actors, have resulted in new military tactics involving targeted killing (MacDonald, 2011).

Unlike the 'war on drugs' which is more figurative and often non-violent, it is possible to wage war on poaching since the armed perpetrator, being the poacher, is known and mostly in possession of arms of war (Gustafson et al., 2018). In the context of non-international hostilities, states may only resort to the use of force where there is concrete evidence that organised armed violence or crime exist (Kretzmer, Ben-Yehuda & Furth, 2014). There is no justification for not employing the rules relating to the conduct of hostilities merely on the strength of the argument that an armed conflict is taking place in the state's territory (Kretzmer, Ben-Yehuda & Furth, 2014). International humanitarian law provides that, when the use of force is resorted to, states must abide by three main principles which will limit their invocation of military action. These principles are applicable whether use of force for self-defence or on another basis. For military action to be lawful, it should be designed only to cause harm which is proportionate to the military objective and is not unnecessarily cruel or inhumane and which always distinguishes between civilians and combatants. These principles, which require states to ensure that their military responses must be necessary, proportionate and immediate, are known as the *Caroline* formula, named after a ship that was attacked and downed in the United States of America in 1837 (Wood, 2018).

The International Court of Justice confirmed that the *Caroline* formula is part of international law in the case of *Nicaragua v United States* (hereinafter 'the *Nicaragua* case': International Court of Justice, 1986). There is consensus that the *Nicaragua* case confirms that it is a requirement of customary international law that action taken as self-defence by states should satisfy the requirements of necessity and proportionality.

The law of targeted killings at international law and the conservation of African wildlife

International legal principles governing targeted killing

It is important to note that although the sources of international law are broad, it is apparent that in their development, it was not envisaged that a dimension of armed conflict would be the militarisation of anti-poaching efforts. Laws on conservation create and uphold specific territories in part by creating criminals, or '*homo penalis*, the man who can be legally punished' (Foucault, 2008). In the context of conservation, this entails the criminalisation of activities deemed inconsistent with the objectives of the preservation of wild flora and fauna (Massé, 2020). The creation of *homo penalis* established an institutional framework aimed at arresting and punishing individuals who break conservation laws, and punishment falls within the Foucauldian notions of sovereign power (Massé, 2020).

The use of military tactics in combating poaching seems to be a novel issue previously not envisaged by international lawyers and military strategies. At international law, under the law of armed conflict, states are obliged to take precautions and ensure that their use of force satisfies the three essential elements as set out in the *Caroline* incident and the *Nicaragua* case. State parties are under a duty to ensure that their military actions comply with the principles of distinction, least suffering and proportionally. States are entitled to invoke the right of self-defence if threatened with armed attack which presents a 'necessity of self-defence, instant, overwhelming, leaving no choice of means and no moment of deliberation' (Webster, 1841). These principles, therefore, are equally applicable in the use of force in defending the territorial integrity of states in the domestic context, including in anti-poaching operations. States are obliged to ensure that civilians are protected against such use. In instances where states have resorted to the militarisation of anti-poaching, they are under a duty to ensure that civilians are protected.

Despite the existence of criticisms from some quarters, targeted killing is an acceptable and legitimate part of warfare tactics under international law governing warfare (Duffy, 2016). The concept of targeted killings is often referred to as 'assassination' or 'extrajudicial execution' (Fisher, 2007). This is not advisable, as they are value-laden terms connoting immorality and illegality, and may prejudge any debate (David, 2003). It is worth noting that this chapter does not engage in the discussions about the morality or ethics of targeted killings, which are more appropriate in international human rights law focused writings. Targeted killing is controversial in international law, with its opponents arguing that it contravenes Article 6(1) of the International Covenant on Civil and Political Rights, and therefore contravenes international human rights law (Fisher, 2007). On the other hand, the proponents of targeted killing argue that the legal regime applicable should not be international human rights law, but rather international humanitarian law.

The argument in the preceding paragraph is anchored on the jurisprudence of the International Court of Justice, which stated that law applicable to armed conflict, as the *lex specialis* for the conduct of hostilities, determines the test of what is the arbitrary deprivation of life (Fisher, 2007). The basic argument adopted in this chapter is that, in terms of international humanitarian law, civilians lose their protected status and may be targeted under the law of belligerent occupation, applicable to international and non-international armed conflict, if they take part in hostilities (Hailbronner, 2016). The opposing attitudes taken towards 'targeted killings' are reflective of the fundamental disagreement not only regarding their morality or legality, but also on the issue of the legal regime by which that legality should be judged (Kretzmer, 2005).

The main limitation or the consideration for states' conduct during armed hostilities when devising their military tactics is the concept of proportionality (Hailbronner, 2016). This principle of customary international law was codified as part of international humanitarian law through the First Additional Protocol to the Geneva Conventions of 1949 (International Committee of the Red Cross, 1978). In the context of international humanitarian law, proportionality refers to the goods to be weighed, that is, the military advantage against the possible collateral damage to civilians (International Committee of the Red Cross, 1978) Proportionality in international human rights law and international humanitarian law are significantly different (International Committee of the Red Cross, 1978). At international humanitarian law, combatants are legitimate targets in armed conflict, whereas civilians are not (International Committee of the Red Cross, 1978). Under the law of armed combat, the level of combatant casualties is never an issue (Newton & May, 2014). The loss of lives of soldiers in *jus in bello* is not counted in proportionality calculations. Instead, *jus in bello* proportionality only concerns whether the soldiers are treated cruelly, in the sense that they experience unnecessary or superfluous suffering.

International human rights law starts from a very different assumption, namely that all people have the right to life. Therefore, international human rights law requires states only to take such measures as are proportionate to the pursuance of legitimate aims to ensure continuous and effective protection of human rights (Mandani, 2010). However, international human rights law and humanitarian law are mutually complementary and their use for ascertaining each other's content and scope is at times inevitable (Orakhelashvili, 2008). For the purposes of this chapter, international human rights law perspectives on the subject are not considered. In the law of armed combat, the principle of proportionality is aimed at protecting civilians and civilian objects against expected incidental harm from an attack that is excessive to the military advantage anticipated during armed hostiles.

The concept of proportionality is a critical component of the law on the use of force and the law of armed conflict – the *jus ad bellum* and the *jus in bello*. In the former, it entails the belligerent's response to a grievance (Gardam, 1993). In the latter, it refers to the balance to be struck between the achievement of a military goal and the cost in terms of life (Gardam, 1993). In invoking military action, agents of the states are required that, when targeting an individual with lethal force, they should ensure that the force will mitigate or eliminate the threat posed and is proportional to the threat and the need to deter it (Gustafson, Sandstorm & Townsend, 2018). It is an international law requirement that the military advantage to be obtained by an envisaged operation should outweigh the possibility of harm to civilians or damage to civilian objects due to the resultant military action (Bartels, 2013). Article 51(5) (b) of Protocol I of the Geneva Conventions further provides that a military action is to be considered disproportionate if

> [it is] – expected to cause incidental loss of civilian life, injury to civilians, damage to civilian objects or a combination thereof, which would be excessive in relation to the concrete and direct military advantage anticipated.

Essentially, military commanders are under a legal obligation to ensure that any possible civilian loss is not disproportionate to the expected military benefit. Any disproportionate loss to civilian life and assets that was foreseeable is in breach of an international law obligation.

National parks and other protected areas as the battlegrounds

The war on poaching has been presented by conservationists as a just war and a serious threat to peace and security in terms of Chapter VII of the United Nations Charter (Humpreys & Smith, 2011). The narratives and discourse of wildlife crime have become increasingly belligerent on the international policy stage. The war model has commonly been adopted because of the security implications posed by poaching and trafficking, which are comparable to the threat of terrorism (White, 2014). This increasing tendency to discursively frame poaching via reference to terrorism resonates with wider conceptual approaches to environmental security (Duffy, 2016).

Wildlife poaching has recently caught the attention of the United Nations Security Council or the Security Council which accepted that poaching is a threat to international peace and security. As a result, the Security Council passed two United Nations Security Council Resolutions (UNSCRs) 2134 and 2136 which authorised the implementation of targeted sanctions against poachers, wildlife product traffickers and against persons and entities pulling the strings (United Nations, 2016). These UNSCRs were primarily designed to target several armed rebel groups operating in the eastern region of the Democratic Republic of the Congo and the Central African Republic (Cogan, 2015). This approach of the Security Council may be deemed to remove any doubt that might have existed that poaching is the intrusion of territorial integrity with potential to weaken the states' sovereignty in a manner not any different from armed combat by state actors and terrorist groups.

It is herein submitted that the Security Council has legitimised the classification of wildlife poaching at the same level with international terrorism, thus requiring states to combat it in equal measures deserving to be implemented against terrorists. This is notable since the Security Council has, for the period following the terrorist attacks on the Twin Towers in the United States of America, occupied a crucial institutional position in the international combating of terrorist financing regimes. The Security Council decisions relating to the fight against terrorism are viewed by some as the manifestations of its newfound authority to pass binding legislative enactments or pronouncements (Whittle, 2015). Acting in terms of Chapter VII of the United Nations Charter, the Security Council has sweeping powers to pass binding decisions for the maintenance of international peace and security. Therefore, it can safely be argued that the world's legislative organ has recognised the devastating possible effects of wildlife poaching, and it is within the remit of states in the exercise of their sovereign powers to give effect to such recognition.

Based on the proposition that anti-poaching is a war *sui generis*, states are justified in using extraordinary approaches in protecting their resources, including wildlife. In war, the main obligation of the government to its citizens is to safeguard the states' territorial integrity (MacFarlane & Sabanadze, 2013). Laws of armed combat apply equally to citizens and foreigners. Therefore, states acting on verified intelligence should be able to kill their targets. Although some level of deterrence of terrorism is achievable, dissuading potential terrorists is not easy when they are eager to die for their cause (Mogomotsi & Madigele, 2017). In such situations, the best response to terrorism is to eliminate the threat before it can be launched. Although controversial, the fact remains that one of the most successful means of eliminating terrorists before they can strike is

Militarisation of conservation 227

targeted killing (David, 2003). The findings on the use of targeted killings in Afghanistan have shown that they resulted in diminishing the Taliban's success rates and weakened their morale (Wilner, 2010). It is becoming increasingly difficult to dispute that such research findings reflect the efficacy of targeted killings in counterterrorism and counterinsurgency (Wilner, 2010). Targeted killings of armed poachers has great potential to convince poachers to change behaviour or refrain from entering protected areas with the intention to shoot and kill endangered wildlife species (Kirchofer, 2016).

In the context of militarised anti-poaching operations, the principle of proportionality will require armed anti-poaching units to carry out intelligence-led operations to ensure the precision of their targets, so as to exclude the possibility of shooting at innocent civilians, especially members of local communities. To effectively enforce the law against armed poaching bandits operating in African protected areas, it is essential to have intelligence to allow military commanders to plan in respect of both pre-emptive and preventative target killings (Falk, 2014). It has been observed that the most effective intelligence gathering operations are those that have established and maintained local information networks in the communities and surrounding areas. It is important to highlight that, where operationally possible without risking the lives of law enforcement agents, arresting the perpetrators as opposed to killing them should be given priority (Falk, 2014).

Conclusion

This chapter has argued in support of the invocation of law of armed combat in non-international hostilities. It has characterised the operation by armed poachers in PAs as an act of hostility and infringement of sovereignty. Further, this chapter has adopted a position that excludes international human rights law as the default legal system applicable during wartime.

African states are entitled to declare growing levels of poaching within their territories to be akin to war. In the absence of international tribunal judicial decisions, the persuasive jurisprudence of the Israeli courts has been discussed and endorsed as useful in the formation of state practice in the use of targeted killings in non-international hostilities. It is further argued herein that the states practice of Israel, United States of America and the jurisprudence of the Israeli courts are crucial in shaping the direction of customary international law principles governing targeted killings in non-international disputes. It is the position of this chapter that terrorists are not any different from poachers: they threaten peace and violate the sovereignty of states in a similar manner. However, this is not to suggest that military commanders are to engage in indiscriminate killings. The conduct of military officers and other armed law enforcement officers executing anti-poaching operation in African PAs must be consistent with the limits set out in international law.

This chapter views militarised anti-poaching through the lenses of international law, especially international humanitarian law, which is rarely done.

The available and growing literature on green militarisation is largely from the perspective of international relations and political sciences with little legal reasoning made. It is essential for the development of international wildlife and conservation law to engage in further research on militarised conservation from a purely legal perspective. This topic raises serious questions of law which should be discussed in view of both international humanitarian law and international human rights law to contribute to international law-making. Although eminent legal scholars have built impressive scholarship on targeted killings, especially from the American and Israeli perspective, African legal scholars have not drawn lessons from such scholarship in the context of the burning issue of militarised conservation. This is particularly important as most of the poaching takes place in African soils.

References

Annecke, W., & Masubelele, M. (2016). A review of the impact of militarisation: The case of rhino poaching in Kruger National Park, South Africa. *Conservation & Society,* 14 (3), 195–204.

Armstrong, C. (2015). Against 'permanent sovereignty' over natural resources. *Politics, Philosophy & Economics,* 14 (2), 129–151.

Bachmann, S. (2013). Targeted killings: Contemporary challenges, risks and opportunities. *Journal of Conflict and Security Law,* 18 (2), 259–288.

Barnes, M. D., Craigie, I. D., Harrison, L. B., Geldmann, J., & Collen, B. (2016). Wildlife population trends in protected areas predicted by national socio-economic metrics and body size. *Nature Communications,* 7. doi:10.1038/ncomms12747

Bartels, R. (2013). Dealing with the principle of proportionality in armed conflict in retrospect: The application of the principle in international criminal trials. *Israel Law Review,* 46 (2), 271–315.

Bellamy, A. J. (2008). The responsibility to protect and the problem of military intervention. *International Affairs,* 84 (4), 615–639.

Boucher, T. B., Spalding, M. D., & Ravenga, C. (2013). Role and trends of protected areas in conservation. In Levin, S. (Ed.), *Encyclopedia of Biodiversity* (Vol. 6). Waltham, MA: Elsevier, 485–503. doi:10.1016/B978-0-12-384719-5.00348-8

Chekera, Y. T., & Nmehielle, V. O. (2013). The international law principle of permanent sovereignty over natural resources as an instrument for development: The case of Zimbabwean diamonds. *African Journal of Legal Studies,* 6, 69–101.

Cogan, J. K. (2015). Stabilization and the expanding scope of the Security Council's work. *American Journal of International Law,* 109 (2), 324–339.

David, S. R. (2003). Israel's policy on targeted killings. *Ethics & International Affairs,* 17 (1), 111–126.

Doyle, O. (2018). The silent constitution of territory. *International Journal of Constitutional Law,* 16 (3), 887–903.

Duffy, R. (2014). Waging a war to save biodiversity: The rise of militarized conservation. *International Affairs,* 90 (4), 819–834.

Duffy, R. (2016). War, by conservation. *Geoforum,* 69, 238–248.

Eichensehr, K. E. (2007). On target? The Israeli Supreme Court and the expansion of targeted killings. *Yale Law Journal,* 116 (8), 1873–1881.

Elden, S. (2005). Territorial integrity and the War on Terror. *Environment and Planning A: Economy and Space*, 37 (2), 2083–2104.

Enyew, E. L. (2017). Application of the right to permanent sovereignty over natural resources to Indigenous Peoples: Assessment of current legal developments. *Arctic Review on Law and Politics*, 8, 222–245.

Falk, O. (2014). Permissibility of targeted killings. *Studies in Conflict & Terrorism*, 37 (4), 295–321.

Falk, O., & Hefetz, A. (2019). Minimizing unintended deaths enhanced the effectiveness of targeted killing in the Israeli–Palestinian Conflict. *Studies in Conflict & Terrorism*, 42 (6), 600–616.

Foucault, M. (2008). *The birth of biopolitics: Lectures at the College de France, 1978–1979*. New York: Picador.

Fisher, W. J. (2007). Targeted killings, norms and international law. *Colombia Journal of Transnational Law*, 45 (3), 711–758.

Foreman, M. J. (2013). When targeted killing is not permissible: An evaluation of targeted killing under the law of war and morality. *Journal of Constitutional Law*, 15 (3), 921–960.

Gardam, J. G. (1993). Proportionality and force in international law. *American Journal of International Law*, 87 (3), 391–413.

Glanville, L. (2011). The antecedents of 'sovereignty as responsibility'. *European Journal of International Relations*, 17 (2), 233–255.

Gustafson, K., Sandstorm, T., & Townsend, L. (2018). The bush war to save the rhino: Improving counter-poaching through intelligence. *Small Wars & Insurgencies*, 29 (2), 269–290.

Hailbronner, M. (2016). Laws in conflict: The relationship between human rights and international humanitarian law under the African Charter on Human and Peoples' Rights. *African Human Rights Law Journal*, 16 (2), 339–364.

Heyns, C., & Knuckey, S. (2013). The long-term international law implications of targeted killing practices. *Harvard International Law Journal Online*, 104–114.

Hill-Cawthorne, L. (2017). Rights under international humanitarian law. *European Journal of International Law*, 28 (4), 1187–1215.

Humphreys, J., & Smith, M. L. (2011). War and wildlife: The Clausewitz connection. *International Affairs*, 87 (1), 121–142.

International Committee of the Red Cross. (1949). *Geneva Conventions of 12 August 1949*. Geneva: International Committee of the Red Cross.

International Committee of the Red Cross. (1978). *Protocol Additional to the Geneva Conventions of 12 August 1949 and relating to the protection of victims of international armed conflicts*. Geneva: International Committee of the Red Cross.

International Court of Justice. (1986). *Military and paramilitary activities in and against Nicaragua (Nicaragua v United States of America)*. The Hague: International Court of Justice.

Kideghesho, J. R. (2016) The elephant poaching crisis in Tanzania: A need to reverse the trend and the way forward. *Tropical Conservation Science*, 9 (1), 369–388.

Kirchofer, C. (2016). Targeted killings and compellence: Lessons from the campaign against Hamas in the second intifada. *Perspectives on Terrorism*, 10 (3), 16–25.

Kleine, K. (2015). Will R2P be ready when disaster strikes? The rationale of the Responsibility to Protect in an environmental context. *International Journal of Human Rights*, 19 (8), 1176–1189.

Kretzmer, D. (2005). Targeted killing of suspected terrorists: Extra-judicial executions or legitimate means of defence? *European Journal of International Law,* 16 (2), 171–212.

Kretzmer, D., Ben-Yehuda, A., & Furth, M. (2014). 'Thou shall not kill': The use of lethal force in non-international armed conflicts. *Israel Law Review,* 47 (2), 191–224.

Langridge, J., Sordello, R., & Reyjol, Y. (2020). Outcomes of wildlife translocations in Protected Areas: What is the type and extent of existing evidence? A Systematic Map Protocol. *Environmental Evidence,* 9 (16). doi:10.1186/s13750-020-00199-4

MacDonald, S. D. (2011). The lawful use of targeted killing in contemporary international humanitarian law. *Journal of Terrorism Research,* 2 (3), 126–144.

MacFarlane, N., & Sabanadze, N. (2013). Sovereignty and self-determination: Where are we? *International Journal,* 68 (4), 609–627.

Mamdani, M. (2010). Responsibility to protect or right to punish? *Journal of Intervention and Statebuilding,* 4 (1), 53–67.

Marijnen, E. (2017). The 'green militarisation' of development aid: The European Commission and the Virunga National Park, DR Congo. *Third World Quarterly,* 38 (7), 1566–1582.

Massé, F. (2020). Conservation law enforcement: Policing Protected Areas. *Annals of the American Association of Geographers,* 110 (3), 758–773.

Maxwell, S. L., Cazalis, V., Dudley, N., & Hoffman, M. (2020). Area-based conservation in the twenty-first century. *Nature,* 586, 217–227.

Mirandi, L. A. (2012). The role of international law in intrastate natural resource allocation. *Proceedings of the Annual Meeting,* 106, 75–78.

Mogomotsi, G. E. J., & Madigele, P. K. (2017). Live by the gun, die by the gun: Botswana's 'shoot-to-kill' policy as an anti-poaching strategy. *South African Crime Quarterly,* 60, 51–59.

Mogomotsi, G. E. J., Mogomotsi, P. K., & Mosepele, K. (2020). Legal aspects of transboundary water management: An analysis of the intergovernmental institutional arrangements in the Okavango River Basin. *Leiden Journal of International Law,* 3 (2), 391–408.

Mushonga, T., & Matose, F. (2020). *Geoforum,* 117, 216–224.

Neumann, R. P. (1998). *Imposing wilderness. Struggles over livelihood and nature preservation in Africa.* Berkeley, CA: University of California Press.

Neumann, R. P. (2007). Moral and discursive geographies in the biodiversity wars in Africa. *Political Geography,* 23 (7), 813–837.

Newton, M., & May, L. (2014). *Proportionality in international law.* Oxford: Oxford University Press.

Ng'ambi, S. P. (2015). Permanent sovereignty over natural resources and the sanctity of contracts, from the angle of *Lucrum Cessans. Loyola University Chicago International Law Review,* 12 (3), 153–172.

Oksanen, M., & Vuorisalo, T. (2019). Conservation sovereignty and biodiversity. In Casetta, E., da Silva, J. M., & Vecchi, D. (Eds.), *From assessing to conserving biodiversity, history, philosophy and theory of the life sciences.* Cham: Springer International Publishing, 435–445.

Orakhelashvili, A. (2008). The interaction between human rights and humanitarian law: Fragmentation, conflict, parallelism, or convergence? *European Journal of International Law,* 19 (1), 161–182.

Ramutsindela, M. (2016). Wildlife crime and state security in South(ern) Africa: An overview of developments. *Politikon,* 43 (2), 159–171.

Rovuela, J. B., Hervías-Parejo, S., de la Cruz, A., Geraldes, P., Costa, L. T., & Gil, A. (2019). The socio-economic impact of conservation: The Safe Islands for Seabirds LIFE project. *Oryx, 53* (1), 109–116.

Schafer, J., & Bell, R. (2002). The state and community-based natural resource management: The case of the Moribane Forest Reserve, Mozambique. *Journal of Southern African Studies*, 28 (2), 401–420.

Telesetsky, A. (2018). U.S. state practice: Taking a necessary long-arm approach to maritime enforcement. *Korean Journal of International and Comparative Law*, 6, 199–218.

United Nations Environment Programme, World Conservation Monitoring Centre, & International Union for Conservation of Nature. (2020). *Protected Planet Report 2020*. Cambridge: Protected Planet Report.

Watkin, K. (2004). Controlling the use of force: A role for human rights norms in contemporary armed conflict. *American Journal of International Law*, 98 (1), 1–34.

Webster, D. (1841). British–American diplomacy. Caroline Case, 29 British and Foreign State Papers (24 April 1841) 1137–1138. Washington, DC. Retrieved 5 July 2021, from https://avalon.law.yale.edu/19th_century/br-1842d.asp

White, N. (2014). The 'white gold of jihad': Violence, legitimisation and contestation in anti-poaching strategies. *Journal of Political Economy*, 21 (1), 452–474.

Whittle, D. (2015). The limits of legality and the United Nations Security Council: Applying the extra-legal measures model to Chapter VII action. *European Journal of International Law*, 26 (3), 671–698.

Wilner, A. S. (2010). Targeted killings in Afghanistan: Measuring coercion and deterrence in counterterrorism and counterinsurgency. *Studies in Conflict & Terrorism*, 33 (4), 307–329.

Wood, M. (2018). The Caroline incident – 1837. In Ruys, T., Corten, O., & Hofer, A. (Eds.), *The use of force in international law: A case-based approach*. Oxford: Oxford University Press, 5–14.

17 Implications of the 'high-value, low-volume' approach in conservation and tourism resources management

Lesego Senyana Stone and Moren Tibabo Stone

Introduction

Travel and tourism has become an important sector globally. Contributing 10.3% to the global Gross Domestic Product (GDP), 330 million jobs and growing by more than 3.5% in 2019, the travel and tourism sector is more significant for over 90 countries where the sector contributes more than 10% of GDP and a substantial share of employment (World Travel and Tourism Council (WTTC), 2016, 2020). Consequently, tourism is significant to economies of both developed and developing countries (Eshliki & Kaboudi, 2012). For many countries, especially in the developing world, tourism is promoted to contribute to poverty alleviation (Scheyvens & Russell, 2012; Pratt, Suntikul & Dorji, 2018). Due to the estimated growth in international tourist arrivals for many emerging economies, international development organisations like the WTTC and the United Nations World Tourism Organisation (UNWTO) acknowledge the importance of tourism to the attainment of the Sustainable Development Goals (SDGs) (Scott, Hall & Gössling, 2019).

The tourism sector has enjoyed steady growth over the years. This growth can be attributed to improvements in travel and communication systems, changes in economic and social statuses of people in the industrialised world which have enabled many people to take part in overseas travel and the introduction of different tourism products to cater to different niche markets (Mbaiwa, 2017). Such niche markets include safari and wildlife and wilderness tourism, which are popular in many countries in East and Southern Africa (Mbaiwa, 2017) and are characterised by visits to 'pristine areas' (Higham, Kearsley & Kliskey, 2001). While for many countries, especially those in the Global South, these are promoted for economic reasons, for those in the Global North, engaging in these niche activities may be for conservation purposes and to escape from city life (Stone & Nyaupane, 2016a). As a result, many developing countries have chosen tourism as a development strategy. For many, it is a source of foreign exchange earnings, infrastructure development, economic development and employment (DeLacy, 2009; Khan & Rasheed, 2016).

DOI: 10.4324/9781003193166-21

Implications of HVLV approach 233

Just like other countries in the Global South, Botswana has adopted tourism as an economic development strategy and to diversify the economy. Consequently, travel and tourism has become an important sector in the country, contributing 9.6% to the GDP and 8.4% to total employment in 2019; the sector is the second largest economic sector after diamond mining (Mathambo, 2014; WTTC, 2021). Even during the era of COVID-19, tourism remains an important economic sector for the country despite declines of 48.6% in its contribution to GDP, 76.8% in international tourist spending and 33.6% in domestic tourists' spending (WTTC, 2021). Despite these declines, Botswana is a major tourist destination for international tourists predominantly from North America and Europe. In 2019, international tourist spending contributed 9.2% to the country's total exports (WTTC, 2021).

Tourism development in Botswana mainly takes place in the northern part, known for its wildlife and wilderness. Due to the tourism product promoted by the country, sustainable tourism development is an important aspect of the travel and tourism sector in Botswana. To that end, the country has adopted a high-value low-volume tourism policy (HVLV) aimed at promoting sustainable tourism and consequently conserving the natural resources the sector depends on (Government of Botswana, 1990). The policy advances a HVLV strategy to restrict deleterious environmental and social impacts on pristine and relatively undisturbed wildlife and wilderness areas, while promoting socio-economic benefits for rural communities (Stone et al., 2021). The high prices (fees) are expected to lead to low demand for tourists, thereby reducing environmental degradation. This strategy is enshrined in the principles of conservation and sustainable tourism development. However, it has yielded unintended consequences and stifled and limited the domestic market to visit Botswana's most sought-after destinations. The value over volume is a strategy sought to attract tourists with an average daily expenditure greater than that of an average visitor's total holiday expenditure, the intention being to maximise benefits while at the same time conserving the environment (Government of Botswana, 1990). Although the country has recently released a revised tourism policy which calls for the promotion of domestic tourism, increased participation of citizens in the tourism sector and the diversification of tourism products, until all these are achieved the HVLV strategy remains (Government of Botswana, 2021). In fact, the creation of Ngamiland district as a tourism economic zone may continue to entrench the strategy (Government of Botswana, 2021).

High-value, low-volume (HVLV) policy strategy and sustainable tourism development

Since the 1980s, sustainable development has become a popular development option, and tourism research has also been part of this movement (Liu, 2003). Tourism is considered sustainable if it:

234   *Lesego Senyana Stone and Moren Tibabo Stone*

1   Optimally uses resources from the environment which are natural and that establish a vital part in the advancement and growth of tourism while conserving important environmental processes and aiding culture.

2   Makes certain achievable, economic operations in the long-term, makes available socio-economic remunerations to stakeholders and are evenly spread, includes stable employment and job opportunities and social services to host communities, and supports poverty alleviation.

3   Respects the social and cultural sincerity of the people, protects their environment, their living and traditional heritage and values and enhances either inter-cultural knowledge and acceptance (WTO, 2014; Okonkwo & Odey, 2018, p. 94).

The sustainable tourism movement is characterised by the notion that, if conservation projects can bring benefits to local people and assist in the alleviation of poverty, locals will appreciate and value the conservation of natural resources (Brandon & Wells, 1992). To achieve this, several conservation and development integrated strategies such as Community-Based Natural Resource Management (CBNRM) adopted by many nature-based tourism-dependent countries, have been put in place to ensure biodiversity conservation benefits communities and provides them with new income streams for conservation management (Hutton & Leader-Williams, 2003; Naidoo & Adamowicz, 2005; Walpole & Thouless, 2005). An HVLV tourism model is preferred by many conservation planners due to perceived economic returns for conservation and a reduction in … through reductions in visitor numbers reducing negative environmental impacts by reducing visitor numbers (Sandbrook, 2009). The HVLV tourism strategy aims to promote sustainability by limiting the number of tourists (i.e. low volume) and charging high prices (i.e. high value), thereby making tourism areas exclusive reserves for elites who can afford the high prices charged.

Countries such as Bhutan and Botswana have adopted the HVLV strategy for the same reasons advanced by conservation planners. In Botswana, sustainable tourism is promoted and supported by institutional frameworks that advance sustainable development through tourism. These include the CBNRM policy, Botswana Tourism Master Plan of 2000, the Ecotourism Strategy of 2002, and the Tourism Policy of 1990 (Government of Botswana, 1990, 2000). Such frameworks have been adopted in Botswana to promote the conservation of natural resources and to promote the livelihood of communities, especially those living adjacent to wildlife and wilderness areas (Government of Botswana, 1990, 2007). This is because 'sustainability in ecological and economic terms … is necessary in Botswana's tourism … because tourism tends to destroy or at least endanger its own assets, the protection and conservation of its own natural environment is imperative' (Government of Botswana, 2000, p. 9). Through the CBNRM policy, sustainable tourism development is promoted 'to improve community livelihoods through sustainable management and utilisation of natural resources in their environs' and ensuring that benefits from the natural resources far exceed the costs of living with those resources (Government of

Botswana, 2007, p. 1). Sustainable tourism encompasses measures and management practices relevant to all types of tourism and should not be misconstrued as one type of tourism (Weaver, 2006).

Likewise, Bhutan follows an HVLV tourism model grounded on the belief that 'uncontrolled tourism will overburden Bhutan's limited facilities and threaten the traditional culture, values and the environment' (Khamrang, 2013, p. 7). The use of the HVLV policy by the country is intended to protect the country's natural environment and curb the progression of acculturation (Khamrang, 2013). The number of tourists to Bhutan is controlled through a daily set minimum tariff of US$200, mandatory guided tours, specific established spatial restrictions, the difficulties related to the visa application process and the packaging of prepaid tours paid through official agents in Bhutan (Nyaupane & Timothy, 2010). The high costs and other mandatory requirements bar low-spending tourists from extending their visits to the country and disturbing the environment and local culture (Nyaupane & Timothy, 2010; Suntikul & Dorji, 2016).

The HVLV tourism strategy has contributed to community development and has drawn attention to Botswana in the global arena as a haven for wildlife and conservation (Mogomotsi et al., 2020). However, despite its intended goals, the HVLV tourism strategy tends to create exclusions that have led to tourism spaces frequented by older, educated and wealthy tourists who are willing to spend more money for unique tourism experiences (Gurung & Seeland, 2008). Using the concept of sustainable tourism, this article aims to analyse the HVLV tourism development strategy as advanced by Botswana to determine its contribution to the country's tourism sector. Using data from studies carried out by the authors and secondary sources, the study adopts a qualitative approach to determine (a) the implications of following the HVLV strategy on tourism development in Botswana and (b) the effectiveness of the strategy in promoting the conservation of natural resources and improving community livelihoods.

Community development, livelihoods improvement and conservation

The HVLV has facilitated opportunities that enhance the livelihoods of community members. These include employment opportunities, creating opportunities for community development. For instance, the Chobe Enclave Community Trust (CECT) communities have formed handicraft groups that sell souvenirs a traditional dancing troupe that performs for tourists (Elijah, 2014; Stone & Nyaupane, 2016b). However, although the HVLV strategy adopted by the country has led to employment opportunities for local communities, they occupy low-paying jobs which do not require any advanced skills; high-paying jobs with good benefits are occupied by expatriate employees (Mbaiwa, 2005; Stone & Stone, 2011).

In the Okavango Delta, the HVLV has led to the establishment of Santawani Lodge, Shandrika cultural tourism village and Kazikini campsite by the Sankoyo community. This has diversified the communities' income streams

(Mbaiwa, 2004). Furthermore, it has facilitated the communities' acquisition of modern facilities such as modern housing and televisions (Mbaiwa, 2015; Stone & Nyaupane, 2016b). The HVLV strategy, through the promotion of CBNRM, has enabled poverty alleviation projects which have been possible through revenue generated from land rentals from partnerships with private enterprises and wildlife hunting quotas. With the revenue, communities have been able to provide social services such as housing for the elderly, the destitute and orphans, water supply, annual household dividends, scholarships, funeral assistance and game meat (Mbaiwa, 2015; Mbaiwa & Stronza, 2010; Sebele, 2010).

Another positive to come out of the HVLV strategy is the contribution to the conservation of natural resources in the country. For instance, in the CECT area, poaching incidents are low in areas where there are tourism activities compared to areas where there are none (Stone & Nyaupane, 2016b). Mbaiwa (2015) reports reduced illegal hunting incidents related to people's changing that attitudes towards wildlife resources. This has developed due to benefits people have derived from the sector, leading them to develop positive attitudes towards wildlife conservation and tourism. The use of community escort guides has also led to communities observing regulations that promote environmental management (Schuster, 2007).

Contribution to the emergence of enclave tourism development

Contrary to its positive contribution, results indicate that the HVLV strategy promotes the development of enclave tourism. Enclave tourism refers to 'tourism that is concentrated in remote areas, and its all-inclusive nature means that the facilities, services, and physical location fail to take into account the needs of the local communities' (Nunkoo & Ramkissoon, 2016, pp. 557–558). Enclave tourism reinforces dependency and is ingrained in the tenets of colonialism where 'pleasure peripheries' located in the economic and political periphery of the global economic system have developed as leisure spaces for tourists primarily from the Global North; the spaces are separated from the surrounding area (Judd, 1999; McFarlane-Morris, 2021; Weaver, 2006). Researchers acknowledge that enclave tourism developed following a move from agriculture as the main economic activity to tourism characterised by 'all-inclusive packages', minor forward and backward economic linkages with the local economy and benefits from tourism mostly found within the limits of the enclaves (Britton, 1982; Brohman, 1996; Mbaiwa, 2005; Shaw & Williams, 2002). Furthermore, enclaves are often externally controlled ' by global capital and transnational organisations through a series of spatial networks, which unless they are strongly regulated by the local state, allow only limited economic benefits to accrue to the host communities' (Shaw & Shaw, 1999, 68).

In Botswana, the development of enclave tourism has led to a tourism sector that is largely driven by the international market. The country's tourism industry is one driven by dependency dynamics where there is a large dependence on international tourists and internationally owned facilities to drive the tourism sector (Stone et al., 2017). This is especially true in the Okavango Delta region where there is little to no interaction between host communities and the tourism sector, resulting in poor forward and backward economic linkages between the sector and the local economy, high revenue leakages, low domestic tourism rates and low local participation in tourism (Mbaiwa, 2005; Mbaiwa, 2011, Stone, 2014). Baatweng (2014) attributes the high revenue leakages to the handling of most of the country's international tourists' bookings in South Africa. This phenomenon has led to economic leakages estimated to be approximately 70 to 90% of business transactions (Baatweng, 2014). Furthermore, foreign companies and investors have ownership and control of approximately 82% of accommodation facilities in the Okavango Delta, thereby contributing to the repatriation of profits to their countries of origin and evading tax in Botswana (Mbaiwa, 2017).

Britton (1982) indicates that the promotion of tour packages offered by foreign-owned hotels and airlines leads to a loss of income, with only 22–25% of the revenue received from the tour package reaching the destination. The reliance on international tourists perpetuates enclave tourism by facilitating the revenue leakages since international tourists spend less money in the country. On the other hand, a stronger domestic market can boost visitor spending within the domestic economy and can assist in countering the effects of the revenue leakages (Stone et al., 2017).

Stifling and limiting effects on the domestic market

Indications are that the HVLV tourism strategy adopted by the country has led to the under-valuing of domestic tourism and more significance being assigned to international, high-spending tourists (Stone & Nyaupane, 2020). The preference for international tourism over domestic tourism has led to exclusions of locals as tourists and tourism entrepreneurs from the tourism sector of Botswana. In studies by Stone & Nyaupane (2016a, 2020), such exclusions are said to be perpetuated by undeveloped infrastructure that requires a four-wheel drive vehicle to navigate, the foreign ownership of tourism enterprises, the charging of exorbitant prices (in US dollars) for tourism products and services, clearly denying access to locals and sidelining them at the expense of the international market. Such practices promote the needs of international tourists and disenfranchise locals. The exclusionary nature of the HVLV tourism strategy is associated with colonial governments that set up protected areas as recreational spaces for Whites. These ideals have been adopted by independent African states, thereby maintaining the narrative that such spaces are a prerogative for White-upper-middle class and not for locals who are excluded from such spaces. In

238   *Lesego Senyana Stone and Moren Tibabo Stone*

most African states, national parks were set up for the White-upper-middle class; the same continues in Botswana, indicating the continued marginalisation of other groups (Byrne & Wolch; 2009; Fletcher, 2014; Roberts, 2009).

The reliance on the international market has proven to be unsustainable especially during the COVID-19 pandemic and its associated movement restrictions. With such measures in place, the tourism sector was put in disarray since international tourism came to a halt and the sector experienced booking cancellations and requests for refunds (Hambira et al., forthcoming). The curtailing of tourism due to COVID-19 affected community livelihoods since communities could not sell their wildlife hunting quotas to professional hunters and consequently, business and jobs were lost (Stone et al., 2021). As a result, the country has started to promote strategies aimed at increasing domestic tourism, including promoting a 'Rediscover Botswana' initiative aimed at sparking local travel, developing urban sites with tourism potential, promoting nature-based tourism sites to citizens and residents at discounted prices and facilitating agri-tourism (Ker & Downey, 2020; Ministry of Finance & Economic Development, 2020; Presidential COVID-19 Task Force Bulletin, 2020). However, it has not been determined yet how effective these strategies are, partly because some are still in the process of being developed and because research/studies have not been carried out yet to determine their effectiveness.

Minimal local participation and decision-making powers

Due to the HVLV strategy promoted, the sector requires skills that locals do not have, to cater to the needs of the high-end market. Participation by locals is often through CBNRM. However, due to a lack of business skills and capacity, communities' participation is often limited to communities selling their hunting quotas and receiving land rentals for the concession areas they lease out to private entities (Stone & Nyaupane, 2018). Furthermore, partnerships which were created to bridge the knowledge gap between local communities and private entities are not empowering and have not equipped communities to fully participate in the sector as was envisioned at the inception of CBNRM (Rozemeijer, 2009). The tourism policy calls for improvements in the management and ownership of tourism enterprises (Government of Botswana, 1990), however, this has not been achieved yet.

Moreover, despite the government's assertion that CBNRM devolves decision-making powers regarding natural resources to communities, this has not occurred as powers are still with government agencies and community-based organisations must abide by what the government decides. Although CBNRM is touted as a bottom-up approach, the situation on the ground indicates it is still a top-down approach. For instance, the Department of Wildlife and National Parks (DWNP) still has decision-making powers on regulating and allocating wildlife hunting quotas, despite the community living with the wildlife and probably knowing more about what is on the ground (Mogomotsi et al., 2020: Stone, 2015). The government of Botswana remains the custodian of natural resources found in the country, hence they make decisions even where powers are said to have been devolved to local communities (Government of Botswana, 2007; Lenao, 2017). Furthermore, the promotion of Technical Advisory Committees [TAC], made up of civil servants, to advise local communities engaged in tourism business, also limits decision-making capacities by community-based organisations. The TAC is responsible for making decisions on CBNRM matters affecting community-based organisations, including tendering processes and awarding tenders; this makes communities powerless as decisions are made for them. The devolution of power is therefore an illusion (Lenao, 2017).

Discussions

Based on results from this chapter, the HVLV strategy has brought mixed results for the tourism sector in Botswana. Institutional frameworks adopted in the country promote sustainable development through tourism. This has proven, to a certain extent, to be an effective strategy in Botswana since it has led to improvements in community livelihoods. It has contributed to the alleviation of poverty in rural communities and has led to changes in community attitudes towards wildlife conservation. Scheyvens and Hughes (2019) allude to the important role that tourism plays in poverty alleviation and assisting in the attainment of the sustainable development goals (SDGs). Although the wages from tourism may be low and employment opportunities for locals are mainly those requiring low skills, the benefits derived from such wages are widely spread and are used to buy food, clothes, construct houses, support families and pay school fees and members and parents (Mbaiwa & Stronza, 2010; Sebele, 2010).

On the other hand, the HVLV strategy has led to the exclusion of locals from participating in tourism and owning tourism facilities. Since the sector caters to high-end tourists, high level skills are needed to service the market. As a result, the sector is dominated by foreign owners and management (Mbaiwa, 2005). Similar results where the sector is dominated by westerners and power lies with outsiders have been observed in Bhutan where a similar strategy is followed (Nyaupane & Timothy, 2010). As a result of this, the sector has poor forward and backward economic linkages with the local economy, leading to high revenue leakages due to evasion of tax, foreign-based bookings, and the foreign ownership of facilities. Britton (1982) and Weaver (2006) attribute this enclave development to colonialism and the development of associated global economic systems that are divisive and are symbolised by exclusions.

Related to this is the relegation of locals to landlords who lease out their wildlife concession areas to foreign-owned tourism entrepreneurs. This has come about due to partnerships that do not empower locals, as was initially intended. At inception of the CBNRM programme, partnerships with private entities were envisaged to impart tourism knowledge and skills to locals so that they might ultimately take over the sector when contracts end (Rozemeijer, 2009). This has not worked out as communities still lack skills, and the sector continues to be foreign dominated. Consequently, while the call for 'low-volume'

240 *Lesego Senyana Stone and Moren Tibabo Stone*

takes care of resources' conservation, the 'high-value' part has led to exclusions of locals from visiting places of interest (Nyaupane & Stone, 2016a), compromising yet another principle of sustainability, social equity and justice. The HVLV strategy is a 'double-edged sword' as it has shown how unsustainable it is, especially during the era of COVID-19. It also continues to reinforce exclusions of the local market in tourism activities (Stone & Nyaupane, 2019). While the HVLV tourism strategy is envisioned as best practice, it has unintended repercussions on tourism performance, conservation and tourism resources management. Despite the introduction of the revised Tourism Policy in April 2021, it is still too early to determine whether the situation will change. However, what the new policy calls for has long been suggested by other institutional frameworks, such as the Tourism Masterplan Plan and the Ecotourism Strategy. Commitment must be shown by policymakers for these instruments to work and for change to occur in the tourism landscape.

Conclusion and way forward

This chapter analysed the implications of the HVLV strategy on conservation and tourism resources management. The results indicate that the strategy has mixed results. Although the HVLV strategy has contributed to the conservation of natural resources and poverty alleviation, it has also brought about unintended consequences. These include contributions to the development of enclave tourism in the country. This is exacerbated by the promotion of high-end tourism which calls for skills that locals do not have. Furthermore, this has contributed to the foreign control and ownership of facilities and poor forward and backward economic linkages to the external sourcing of goods and services to cater for the high-end market. Foreign ownership has also contributed to external bookings and tax evasion. Essentially the country is losing a lot of money; revenue leakages remain high.

Any hopes of changing the tourism landscape of Botswana for the better rest with the current revised tourism policy that calls for the promotion of domestic tourism, more local involvement, diversification of tourism products, equitable distribution of tourism benefits, sustainable use of tourism resources, etc. Hence, in line with the revised tourism policy, concerted efforts need to be put in place to address current problems. These include but are not limited to the following. (1) Promoting domestic tourism to nature-based tourism sites within acceptable limits during the low season to cater for seasonal variations created by international tourism. This will cater for low and middle-income local tourists. (2) Providing incentives such as reduced hotel rates, organised group tours, to promote domestic tourism (3) Although revenue maximisation should not come before social equity and access to national parks resources, it should also be noted that international tourists are the main source of revenue for national parks. Revenue from high-income visitors should ensure high-quality tourism products are maintained to meet visitor expectations and satisfaction. (4) Promoting tourism to in popular areas to spread the benefits of tourism to

Implications of HVLV approach   241

other parts of the country, for example, develop dry area tourism in the Kalahari Desert and give locals opportunities to operate small-scale establishments.

Government policy currently allows only locals to own small-scale establishments such as bed and breakfasts and guest houses. However, monitoring and enforcement must take place to ensure that the standards set by Botswana Tourism Organisation are abided by. Furthermore, to promote conservation, all facilities should be graded and eco-certified.

References

Baatweng, V. (2014). Botswana loses up to 90% of tourism revenue. *Botswana Sunday Standard*, 10 July. www.sundaystandard.info/article.php/ email.php?NewsID= 20498

Brandon, K., & Wells M. (1992) Planning for people and parks: Design dilemmas. *World Development,* 20, 557–570.

Britton, S. (1982). The political economy of tourism in the third world. *Annals of Tourism Research*, 9 (3), 331–358.

Brohman, J. (1996). New directions in tourism for third world development. *Annals of Tourism Research*, 23 (1), 48–70.

Byrne, J., & Wolch, J. (2009). Nature, race, and parks: Past research and future directions for geographic research, *Progress in Human Geography*, 33 (6), 743–765.

DeLacy, T. (2009). Pacific tourism adaptation to climate change risks. Presentation to UNDP conference on climate change in the Pacific: Impacts on local communities, Apia, 1 August.

Elijah, B. (2014). Assessment of benefits and challenges of community-based tourism: A case study of the Moremi-Mannonnye Conservation Trust. Undergraduate thesis, University of Botswana, Gaborone.

Eshliki, S. A., & Kaboudi, M. (2012). Community perception of tourism impacts and their participation in tourism planning: A case study of Ramsar, Iran. *Procedia-Social and Behavioral Sciences*, 36, 333–341.

Fletcher, R. (2014). *Romancing the wild: Cultural dimensions of ecotourism.* Durham, NC: Duke University Press.

Government of Botswana. (1990). *Tourism policy: Government paper no. 2 of 1990.* Gaborone: Government Printer.

Government of Botswana, (2000). *Botswana tourism master plan: Final report.* Gaborone: Consulting.

Government of Botswana, (2007). *Community-based natural resource management policy.* Gaborone: Government Printers.

Government of Botswana. (2021). *Tourism policy.* Gaborone: Government Printer.

Gurung, D. B., & Seeland, K. (2008). Ecotourism in Bhutan extending its benefits to rural communities. *Annals of Tourism Research*, 35 (2), 489–508.

Hambira, W. L., Stone, L. S., & Pagiwa, V. (forthcoming). Botswana nature-based tourism and COVID-19: Transformational implications for the future. *Development Southern Africa*, 1–17. DOI: 10.1080/0376835X.2021.1955661

Higham, J., Kearsley, G., and Kliskey, A. (2001). Multiple wilderness recreation management: Sustaining wilderness values – maximizing wilderness experiences. In Cessford, G. (Ed.), *The state of wilderness in New Zealand*, 81–93, Wellington: Department of Conservation.

242 *Lesego Senyana Stone and Moren Tibabo Stone*

Hutton, J., & Leader-Williams N. (2003) Sustainable use and incentive-driven conservation: Realigning human and conservation interests. *Oryx,* 37, 215–226.

Judd, D. (1999). Constructing the tourist bubble. In Judd D. & Fainstein, S. (Eds.), *The tourist city.* New Haven, CT: Yale University Press, 35–53.

Ker & Downey. (2020). Explore the wildlife rich Okavango Delta and Moremi Game Reserve. Gaborone: Ker & Downey.

Khamrang, L. (2013). Modernisation, globalisation and development in Bhutan: Tourism as a catalyst. *Journal of Management & Public Policy,* 5 (1), 5–11.

Khan, R. E. A., & Rasheed, M. K. (2016). Political economy of tourism in Pakistan: The role of terrorism and infrastructure development. *Asian Development Policy Review,* 4 (2), 42–50.

Lenao, M. (2017). Community, state and power-relations in community-based tourism on Lekhubu Island, Botswana. *Tourism Geographies,* 19 (3), 483–501.

Liu, Z. (2003). Sustainable tourism development: A critique. *Journal of Sustainable Tourism,* 11 (6), 459–475.

Mathambo, K. (2014). *Botswana budget speech of 2014/15 financial year.* Gaborone: Botswana Parliament, Government Printer.

Mbaiwa, J. E., 2004. The success and sustainability of community-based natural resource management in the Okavango Delta, Botswana. *South African Geographical Journal,* 86 (1), 44–53.

Mbaiwa, J. E. (2005). Enclave tourism and its socio-economic impacts in the Okavango Delta, Botswana. *Tourism Management,* 26 (2), 157–172.

Mbaiwa, J. E. (2011). Cultural commodifcation and tourism: The Goo-Moremi community, Central Botswana. *Tijdschrift voor Economische en Sociale Geografe,* 2 (3), 290–301.

Mbaiwa, J. E. (2015). Ecotourism in Botswana: 25 years later, *Journal of Ecotourism,* 14 (2/3), 204–222.

Mbaiwa, J. E. (2017). Poverty or riches: Who benefits from the booming tourism industry in Botswana? *Journal of Contemporary African Studies,* 35 (1), 93–112.

Mbaiwa, J. E., & Stronza, A. L. (2010). The effects of tourism development on rural livelihoods in the Okavango Delta, Botswana. *Journal of Sustainable Tourism,* 18 (5), 635–656.

McFarlane-Morris, S. (2021). 'Come this close, but no closer!' Enclave tourism development and social change in Falmouth, Jamaica. *Journal of Tourism and Cultural Change,* 19 (1), 132–146.

Ministry of Finance and Economic Development. (2020). *2020/21–2022–2023 Economic recovery and transformation plan.* Gaborone: MFRD.

Mogomotsi, P. K., Stone, L. S., Mogomotsi, G. E. J., & Dube, N. (2020a). Factors influencing community participation in wildlife conservation. *Human Dimensions of Wildlife,* 25 (4), 1–15.

Naidoo, R., & Adamowicz W. (2005) Economic benefits of biodiversity exceed costs of conservation at an African rainforest reserve. *Proceedings of National Academy of Sciences USA,* 102, 16712–16716.

Nunkoo, R., & Ramkissoon, H. (2016). Stakeholders' views of enclave tourism: A grounded theory approach. *Journal of Hospitality & Tourism Research,* 40 (5), 557–558.

Nyaupane, G. P., & Timothy, D. J. (2010). Power, regionalism and tourism policy in Bhutan. *Annals of Tourism Research,* 37 (4), 969–988.

Okonkwo, E. E., & Odey, A. O. (2018). Impact of sustainability on tourism development in Nigeria: A case study of cross river state, Nigeria. *International Journal of Tourism Sciences,* 18 (2), 89–109.

Implications of HVLV approach   243

Pratt, S., Suntikul, W., & Dorji, U. (2018). Economic sustainability? Examining the linkages and leakages between agriculture and hotels in Bhutan. *International Journal of Tourism Research*, 20 (5), 626–636.

Presidential COVID-19 Task Bulletin. (2020). Tourism sector threatened by COVID-19. Issue 111, 3 September.

Roberts, N. S. (2009). Crossing the color line with a different perspective on whiteness and (anti) racism: A response to Mary McDonald. *Journal of Leisure Research*, 41 (4), 495.

Rozemeijer, N. (2009). CBNRM in Botswana. In Suich, H., Child, B., and Spenceley, A. (Eds.), *Evolution and innovation in wildlife conservation: Parks and game ranches to transfrontier conservation areas.* London: Earthscan, 243–256.

Sandbrook, C. G. (2009). Local economic impact of different forms of nature-based tourism, *Conservation Letters*, 3, 21–28.

Scheyvens, R., & Hughes, E. (2019). Can tourism help to 'end poverty in all its forms everywhere'? The challenge of tourism addressing SDG1. *Journal of Sustainable Tourism*, 27 (7), 1061–1079.

Scheyvens, R., & Russell, M. (2012). Tourism and poverty alleviation in Fiji: Comparing the impacts of small- and large-scale tourism enterprises. *Journal of Sustainable Tourism*, 20 (3), 417–436.

Schuster, B (2007). Proceedings of the 4th national CBNRM conference in Botswana and the CBNRM status report, IUCN Botswana, Gaborone, 20–23 November.

Scott, D., Hall, C. M., & Gössling, S. (2019). Global tourism vulnerability to climate change. *Annals of Tourism Research*, 77, 49–61.

Sebele, L.S (2010). Community-based tourism ventures, benefits and challenges: Khama rhino sanctuary trust, central district, Botswana, *Tourism Management*, 31 (1), 136–146.

Shaw, B. J., & Shaw, G. (1999). 'Sun, sand and sales': Enclave tourism and local entrepreneurship in Indonesia. *Current Issues in Tourism*, 2 (1), 68–81.

Shaw, G., & Williams, A. (2002). *Critical issues in tourism: Geographic perspectives.* London: Blackwell.

Stone, L. S. (2014). *Perceptions of nature-based tourism, travel preferences, promotions and disparity between domestic and international tourists: The case of Botswana.* PhD thesis, School of Community Resources and Development, Arizona State University.

Stone, M. (2015). Community-based ecotourism: A collaborative partnerships perspective. *Journal of Ecotourism*, 14 (2–3), 166–184.

Stone, L. S., & Nyaupane, G. P. (2019). The tourist gaze: Domestic versus international tourists. *Journal of Travel Research*, 58 (5), 877–891.

Stone, L. S., & Nyaupane, G. P. (2020). Local residents' pride, tourists' playground: The misrepresentation and exclusion of local residents in tourism. *Current Issues in Tourism*, 23 (11), 1426–1442.

Stone, M. T., & Nyaupane, G. P. (2018). Protected areas, wildlife-based community tourism and community livelihoods dynamics: Spiraling up and down of community capitals. *Journal of Sustainable Tourism*, 26 (2), 307–324.

Stone, L. S., & Nyaupane, G. (2016a). Africans and protected areas: North-South perspectives. *Annals of Tourism Research*, 58, 140–155.

Stone, M. T., and Nyaupane, G. P. (2016b). Protected areas, tourism and community livelihoods linkages: A comprehensive analysis approach. *Journal of Sustainable Tourism*, 24 (5), 673–693.

Stone, L. S., & Stone, T. M. (2011). Community-based tourism enterprises: Challenges and prospects for community participation; Khama Rhino Sanctuary Trust, Botswana. *Journal of Sustainable Tourism*, 19 (1), 97–114.

Stone, L. S., Stone, M. T., Mogomotsi, P. K., & Mogomotsi, G. E. J. (2021). The impacts of COVID-19 on nature-based tourism in Botswana: Implications for community development. *Tourism Review International*, 25, 263–278.

Stone, T. M., Mbaiwa, J. E., & Stone, L. S. (2017). Tourism in Botswana in the last 50 years: A review. *Botswana Notes and Records*, 49, 57–72.

Suntikul, W. & Dorji, U. (2016). Tourism development: The challenges of achieving sustainable livelihoods in Bhutan's remote reaches. *International Journal of Tourism Research*, 18, 447–457.

Walpole, M. J., & Thouless, C. R. (2005) Increasing the value of wildlife through non-consumptive use? Deconstructing the myths of ecotourism and community-based tourism in the tropics. In Woodroffe, R., Thirgood, R., & Rabinowitz, A. (Eds.), *People and wildlife: Conflict or coexistence?* Cambridge: Cambridge University Press, 122–139.

Weaver, D. (2006). *Sustainable tourism: Theory and practice.* Oxford: Butterworth Heinemann.

World Tourism Organization. (2014). *Tourism highlights.* Madrid: UNWTO.

World Travel and Tourism Council. (2016). Global tourism data gateway. Retrieved from www.wttc.org/datagateway

World Travel and Tourism Council. (2020). Botswana: 2020 annual research: Key highlights. Retrieved from https://wttc.org/Research/Economic-Impact

WTTC. (2021). Botswana, (2021). *Annual research: Key highlights.* London: WTTC.

18 Promotion of pro-poor tourism in Southern Africa

Conservation and development critical issues

Owen Gohori, Peet van der Merwe, and Andrea Saayman

Introduction

In the Southern Africa region, 88 million people (45% of the population) are estimated to live in extreme poverty (Porter, 2017). This is despite abundant natural resources in the region. Sachs and Warner (2001) argue that countries with natural resource wealth tend to have a higher proportion of poor people; this is called the natural resource curse. Likewise, the African Development Bank (2016) observed that, in the past 15 years, resource-poor countries in Africa outperformed their resource-rich counterparts in reducing poverty. The United Nations (UN) Sustainable Development Goals (SDGs) have no poverty as the first goal, and they regard tourism as one sector that has the potential to alleviate poverty through job creation and empowerment of vulnerable groups such as the youth and women (United Nations World Tourism Organisation (UNWTO), 2018).

The new millennium saw the popularity of the pro-poor tourism (PPT) approach, which 'aims to increase net benefits for the poor from tourism and ensures that tourism growth contributes to poverty reduction' (Ashley, Roe & Goodwin, 2001, p. viii). PPT has poverty as its key focus, and any tourism product or attraction can meet PPT objectives (Ashley et al., 2001). This has prompted governments from developing countries to use tourism as a tool for poverty alleviation in economically marginalised communities.

The abundant natural resources in Southern Africa resulted in the formulation of a strategy to use these resources in addressing poverty whilst conserving them at the same time. However, conservation planning often employed 'top-down' and centrally planned approaches that excluded local communities (UN, 2009). These 'command-and-control' strategies tended to perpetuate poverty, inequality and power structures that hindered the realisation of biodiversity conservation and sustainable well-being goals (UN, 2009).

It has now been recognised that it is neither politically feasible nor ethically justifiable to deny local communities the use of natural resources without providing them with alternative means of livelihood, or to manage protected

DOI: 10.4324/9781003193166-22

areas without their empowerment and support (Kothari et al., 2015). According to the authors, the growth of common property scholarships since the late 1980s has shown the ability of local people to manage natural resources and ecosystems sustainably and effectively. Community participation has therefore been identified as fundamental to the attainment of economic, political, social and environmental objectives that underpin conservation, whereas excluding local communities is considered detrimental to the sustainability of natural resources (Saberwal, Rangarajan & Kothari, 2001).

Although some scholars (e.g. Galvin and Haller, 2008) argue that community participation does not always translate into economic benefits for local people, participation is still regarded as one of the essential factors for conserving natural resources while providing economic benefits to local people (Kothari et al., 2015). This led to the emergence of the community-based natural resource management (CBNRM) paradigm, which represents a shift from centralised to more devolved approaches. It denotes a wide range of practices whereby local collective institutions or groups of people, organised formally or informally, manage and utilise their lands, resources and common property, which may or may not involve a protected area (Kothari et al., 2015).

Poverty is mainly a rural phenomenon and rural people depend on natural resources for survival (International Fund for Agricultural Development, 2010). This has prompted the assumption that conserving natural resources can help in addressing poverty (Davies et al., 2014). Adams et al. (2004) argue that there is a need to address the dual goals of biodiversity conservation and poverty reduction in these rural areas. They recommend an approach known as pro-poor conservation (PPC). It is defined as 'harnessing conservation to deliver on poverty reduction and social justice objectives' (Roe & Elliot, 2006, p. 58). PPC is a people-centred approach that has poverty reduction and livelihood security as core objectives, while involving different stakeholders and empowering vulnerable groups with assets, rights and entitlements they need to improve their lives through sound environmental management (Adams et al., 2004). It takes different forms and encompasses various approaches such as community-based conservation, integrated conservation and development projects (ICDP), direct payments (REDD+) and protected areas (PAs) (Roe & Elliot, 2006; Davies et al., 2014).

Africa has the largest proportion of land allocated for PAs in the world (Popova, 2014). A protected area is 'a clearly defined geographical space, recognised, dedicated and managed, through legal or other effective means, to achieve the long-term conservation of nature with associated ecosystem services and cultural values' (International Union for Conservation of Nature (IUCN), 2008). PAs vary in size, location, management approaches and objectives. Some examples include national parks, nature reserves, private game reserves, game farms, wilderness areas, wildlife management areas, protected landscape areas (Scherl et al., 2004) and transfrontier conservation areas (TFCAs). The Southern African Development Community (SADC) Programme for TFCA emphasises the importance of community participation in the development of tourism and its benefits, as it is deemed an opportunity to enhance livelihoods and thus contribute to poverty reduction (SADC Secretariat, 2013).

As other interventions were initiated to address the goals of conservation and development simultaneously, communities outside protected areas began to establish community-based tourism (CBT) projects and joint ventures with private operators to generate revenues as incentives for conservation (Scherl et al., 2004). These have proliferated in Southern Africa and are called by different names in different countries.

This chapter provides a link between tourism development, poverty alleviation, conservation, and development through an overview of various PPT and PPC initiatives from Southern Africa. As per the Vth IUCN World Parks Congress recommendations, the chapter contributes towards the argument that protected areas and subsequent tourism development should contribute to poverty reduction at the local level. The chapter does not offer new empirical data but discusses and critically evaluates existing literature. The chapter also highlights the challenges faced by Southern African countries in their endeavour to use tourism as a tool for poverty alleviation, conservation and development. Despite focusing on the Southern African region, this chapter may offer some learning points to other developing countries globally that might want to use tourism as a tool for poverty alleviation, conservation and development.

Pro-poor tourism, conservation and development in Southern Africa

The relationship between tourism, poverty alleviation and community development is complex. At times, it appears positive but at other times negative. Stone and Nyaupane (2016) argue that PA tourism facilitates linkages between biodiversity conservation and community livelihood, thus achieving conservation and development simultaneously. Likewise, Gohori and Van der Merwe (2020, 2021) posit that tourism can bring about community development and empowerment in rural areas. Since most PAs are in remote and rural areas, tourist expenditures may provide an alternative income for local communities (Souza et al., 2019). Nevertheless, tourism can only be sustainable around protected areas if it can improve the livelihood of local communities (Stone & Nyaupane, 2016).

The concepts of development and poverty are multi-dimensional. Poverty entails the lack of both income and non-income aspects, such as having no voice or recognition for participating in community issues and being vulnerable socially, economically and politically (Chambers, 1995). According to Carr (2008), community participation and empowerment are therefore critical to poverty alleviation. Similarly, community development entails empowerment, participation, partnership, community capacity and community change (Telfer, 2003). For tourism development to alleviate poverty, it should promote community participation, community empowerment and the use of indigenous

248　*Owen Gohori et al.*

knowledge and culture (Gohori & Van der Merwe, 2020). A developed community is therefore both improved and empowered (Gohori & Van der Merwe, 2020). Consequently, for any CBNRM initiative to alleviate poverty, conserve natural resources and bring about community development, communities should be empowered, participate in tourism and have their indigenous knowledge systems (IKS) incorporated in tourism development. Attention is subsequently given to initiatives in Southern Africa that promote community participation, empowerment and the use of IKS.

Indigenous knowledge systems

In Africa, culture is intricately bound with the use, management and conservation of natural resources, as traditional knowledge plays a crucial role in using and managing these natural resources. For many generations, traditional institutions have created rules to control the use of natural resources and develop sanctions that restrain and govern their consumption (Fabricius, 2004). The Communal Areas Management Programme for Indigenous Resources (CAMPFIRE) programme in Zimbabwe, which is considered the pioneer of the CBNRM initiatives in Southern Africa (Child, 2003), regards IKS to be of paramount importance to natural resource management (Zimbabwe Trust, 1990). The Nyaminyami CAMPFIRE project incorporates the Tonga values, IKS and practices, as hunting of female animals is prohibited and the Tonga hunting seasons are recognised (Sibanda, 2004).

Other examples of the incorporation of IKS can also be found in Southern Africa. For example, a lodge in the Mozambican side of the Chimanimani TFCA was named Ndzou (which means elephant in the local Ndau language) at the request of local people who wanted to show their cultural ties with elephants (Dondeyne, Kaarhus & Allison, 2012). In Namibia, traditional rules control the harvesting of palm leaves in the conservancies in the absence of conservancy-level natural resource management plans (Jones & Mosimane, 2000). The Basarwa in Botswana's Okavango Delta know how to use fire to attract wildlife and maintain the ecosystem in a constant state of renewal. They also believe that hunting is essential to keep the animal population manageable and healthy (Fabricius, 2004). Kothari et al. (2015) opined that information from traditional science or knowledge systems and cultural practices could be effective in resource management if combined with Western scientific methods.

Community participation

In terms of community participation, authority over wildlife and tourism have been devolved to lower levels of government (e.g. Zimbabwe) and even directly to local communities (e.g. Botswana and Namibia) (Jones & Mosimane, 2000). According to Campbell and Shackleton (2001), the best examples of community participation in the region are found in Botswana (trusts), Namibia (conservancies) and Makuleke in South Africa (communal property associations) as local residents have received proprietary rights over natural resources and have authority to make rules, approve developments, enter into partnerships with the private sector, receive revenues and distribute benefits. In Eswatini, the Mhlumeni community involved with the Lubombo Conservancy-Goba (LCG) TFCA formed the Mhlumeni Trust to ensure that the community participates in tourism (Üllenberg et al., 2015). Most of the benefits in these examples are returned to the communities. In the Caprivi (Namibia), safari operators deal directly with conservancy management committees of a particular conservancy. For example, in the Salambala Conservancy, the management committee consulted the community and the traditional structures before giving a final decision to the safari operator (Jones & Mosimane, 2000).

As earning an income is one of the ways to alleviate poverty, most CBT projects in Southern Africa have generated income for the participating communities. In South Africa, the Rocktail Bay Lodge in Kwa-Zulu Natal, which falls under the Mqobela community, receives lease payment from Wilderness Safaris (Dodds, Ali & Galaski, 2018). The Mahenye/Chilo Gorge Safari Lodge in Manicaland Province, Zimbabwe, has a similar arrangement with their private partner (Gohori & Van der Merwe, 2020). In Namibia, the Khoadi Hoas Conservancy distributes revenue from the Grootberg Lodge to the community (Asheeke & Katjiuingua, 2007). The CAMPFIRE programme in Zimbabwe receives 92% of its revenue from trophy hunting (Booth, 2016). The Sankuyo community trust from the Okavango Delta earned US$220,000 in two years from trophy hunting and part of this was distributed to the households involved in the project (Boggs, 2004). Besides receiving income, living conditions of local people have also been improved by tourism development. In the Western Cape, South Africa, 250 houses were built for local people in the small coastal town of Still Bay, while there was also improvement in the educational facilities (Binns & Nel, 2002). Similarly, the CAMPFIRE in Zimbabwe constructed clinics and drilled boreholes in participating communities (Tchakatumba et al., 2019).

Trophy hunting has been known to be resilient to external shocks, as it is not affected by political instability the way mass tourism is (Loveridge, Reynolds & Milner-Gulland, 2007). Although Zimbabwe has been experiencing political instability and harsh economic conditions for the past two decades, trophy hunting remained the major source of income for the CAMPFIRE programme (Booth, 2016), even though most other ecotourism projects were closed. Mbaiwa and Tshamekang (2012) found that most people (about 122) from the Chobe Enclave Villages were employed by four CBT projects in the Chobe Enclave in Botswana. The Songimvelo-Malolotja (SM) TFCA, which integrates the Songimvelo Nature Reserve in South Africa and Malolotja Nature Reserve in Eswatini, also employs 60 people, the majority being from the surrounding villages (Üllenberg et al., 2015).

Tourism development around PAs has been key in conserving flora and fauna. All consumptive tourism CBT projects adhere to quota setting to promote the sustainable killing of animals. Besides the quota setting, the anti-poaching units formed in each CBT project and the natural resource monitors

250 *Owen Gohori et al.*

play a crucial role to ensure the conservation of natural resources (Campbell & Shackleton, 2001). Previous research done in Mahenye, Zimbabwe, indicate that the establishment of the CBT project in 1982 reduced poaching cases, prompting the government to increase the hunting quota for elephants in 1986 (Murhree, 2000). In Namibia's Kunene Region, the community ended up being allowed to hunt surplus game (Jones & Mosimane, 2000). There has also been greater conservation awareness for the participating communities in Mozambique and Eswatini's LCG TFCA (Üllenberg et al., 2015). Dondeyne et al. (2012) observed that, since the establishment of the Chimanimani TFCA, wildlife populations on the Mozambican side have been stable, as the locals came to realise that they can receive economic benefits from conserving wildlife. The revenue from sport hunting in the Lupande Game Management Area in Zambia has also raised awareness of wildlife conservation (Kapungwe, 2000). Loveridge et al. (2007) argue that consumptive tourism in Africa has increased the habitat available for wild species, as the land was converted from cattle ranching to extensive game ranching, largely for trophy hunting.

Community empowerment

The final aspect that symbolises both poverty alleviation and community development is empowerment, as discussed. Empowerment in tourism comprises four dimensions, which include economic, psychological, social and political empowerment (Scheyvens, 1999). Examples of employment opportunities and revenue generated from trophy hunting are evidence of economic empowerment. Consumptive tourism also brings about community development by providing meat to local communities, thus ensuring food security; in this way, local people are economically empowered (Gohori & Van der Merwe, 2021). The Mahenye community always get meat when an elephant is killed by trophy hunters (Loveridge et al., 2007; Gohori & Van der Merwe, 2020). The recognition and incorporation of local people's IKS in tourism development are examples of psychological empowerment (Gohori & Van der Merwe, 2021), whereas the construction of social projects from tourism revenues is a sign of social empowerment. Revenues from tourism were used to construct houses for the elderly in the Chobe Enclave community-based tourism projects in Botswana (Mbaiwa & Tshamekang, 2012) and in Zimbabwe, schools, clinics and grinding mills were built from tourism revenues generated by the CAMPFIRE projects (Gohori & Van der Merwe, 2021).

Examples of political empowerment can be found in Namibia's conservancies, where women and youth were elected to serve on committees where they could make decisions concerning the use of wildlife. They were further empowered through training, for example, at the Grootberg Lodge in the Khoadi Hoas Conservancy (Jones & Mosimane, 2000; Asheeke & Katjiuingua, 2007). In Lesotho, women are also being elected to serve on committees of community-based projects, taking up positions as vice-chairpersons, secretaries and treasurers (Matela & Ntlale, 2000). Members of the Makuleke community

Promotion of pro-poor tourism 251

in South Africa benefited from training opportunities, which they later used to gain employment due to improved skills and knowledge (Dodds et al., 2018).

Challenges facing pro-poor tourism, pro-poor conservation and community development in Southern Africa

Despite efforts made and some noted successes, using tourism as a tool for poverty alleviation, conservation and community development is not without difficulties. The main obstacles that local communities face in securing development from tourism are due to conflict of interest, lack of skills, limited financial resources, access to information and human–wildlife conflict.

Conflict of interest

The heterogeneous nature of communities is a cause for concern. The different groups found within communities, such as the poor, the rich, women, men and the youth, have different competing interests, thereby prompting conflicts (Jones & Mosimane, 2000). Although CBNRM initiatives expect people to speak with one voice and have a single vision, this has proven difficult to achieve. Jones and Mosimane (2000) give the example of the Khomani San in the southern part of the Kalahari Desert, on the border of Botswana and Namibia, who fought for their land in solidarity, but once they received the land, they split into two groups due to different interests.

The policy framework used by most Southern African countries' governments, which does not empower local people, negatively affects PPT, PPC and community development. In Zimbabwe and Zambia, devolution of power and authority remains within government institutions and is not delegated to communities (rural district councils in the former and the district councils in the latter). In Namibia, Zambia and Zimbabwe, the quota for trophy hunting is determined by the governments without involving the communities (Campbell & Shackleton, 2001; Gohori & Van der Merwe, 2020). Therefore, communities are not empowered to make decisions.

In some instances, there are conflicts of interest between communities and other stakeholders. For example, in Namibia, a San community ended up throwing out two NGO staff members, accusing them of making decisions without consulting the community (Jones & Mosimane, 2000). The Lupande Game Management Area in Zambia ended up being perceived as belonging to NORAD by local people, as they were side-lined in the day-to-day running of the project (Kapungwe, 2000).

Skills

Local people also lack basic management skills, for example, marketing and product knowledge, to manage the projects successfully. Hence, in many instances, they cannot reach their target market. They also do not have skills and access to online booking systems such as Expedia or TripAdvisor because of low literacy levels and an absence of entrepreneurial skills (Asheeke & Katjiuingua, 2007; Dodds et al., 2018).

The Makulele community in South Africa has received training provided by non-governmental organisations (NGOs), which assisted the community in expanding their offering to tourists. However, they remain dependent on tour operators to transport tourists to the community, which influences their revenues negatively (Makandwa, 2021).

Finance

Due to the lack of financing, the CBT projects end up being funded by NGOs and they struggle or even go defunct when the funders withdraw (Dodds et al., 2018). Some Southern African governments (e.g. Namibia, Zambia and Zimbabwe) maintain ownership of communal lands, communities cannot borrow from financial institutions using land as collateral, thus they cannot be equal partners with private partners due to a lack of assets (Asheeke & Katjiuingua, 2007). In Lesotho, communities are required to pay a joining fee plus a yearly subscription to become a member of the Grazing Association (Campbell & Shackleton, 2001). Likewise, the Gairezi Ecotourism project in Zimbabwe requires a joining fee from local people for them to become members (Gohori & Van der Merwe, 2021). This entails that those who cannot afford the joining fee will not be eligible to receive benefits, thereby remaining economically disempowered.

Elite domination

The lack of financing often leads to elite domination, which comes in different forms. In some cases, men dominate women. For example, in the Fish River in the Eastern Cape, South Africa, women are not involved in decision-making, as they do not hold positions in the committees (Cocks, 2000). Similarly, Kapungwe (2000) noted the low participation of women in the ADMADE programme in Zambia, whereas in Botswana, the boards of trustees in some communities form close alliances with safari operators, thus neglecting the wishes of their constituencies (Campbell & Shackleton, 2001). Mbaiwa (2004) also found that the Okavango Community Trust board members and a few elites from the village technical committees receive high sitting allowances, while the rest of the board members receive nothing. On the Mozambican side of the Chimanimani TFCA, the community of Tse Tserra is dominated by wealthy people (Tornimbeni, 2008).

Access to information

In some CBNRM initiatives, information about the projects is not readily available to local people. At the Khama Rhino Sanctuary Trust (KRST), Botswana,

Stone and Stone (2011) observed that management did not give information about the project to the community members, and this hampered their participation. In Namibia's conservancies, poor information flow between committee members and the community members was noted, which compromised their participation in decision-making (Jones & Mosimane, 2000; Campbell & Shackleton, 2001). The Richtersveld Community from the South African side of the Ais-Richtersveld Transfrontier Park (ARTP), which straddles the border between Namibia and South Africa, criticised their community representatives for not disseminating information regarding park management (Üllenberg et al., 2015).

Human wildlife-conflict (HWC)

The rampant HWC in the region is also a challenge to the success of the CBT initiatives in alleviating poverty, conserving natural resources and bringing about community development. HWC is socially disempowering, as it results in food shortages (Stone, 2015). Tchakatumba et al. (2019) found that all forms of HWC (carnivores killing livestock, wildlife killing or injuring humans and wildlife raiding crops) worsened in the Chiredzi district, Zimbabwe, during the post-donor era. The widespread HWC instigates communities to advocate that more animals should be sold for trophy hunting (Jones & Mosimane, 2000) and this might affect the PPC objective of CBNRM negatively. This antagonism has been exacerbated by the lack of proactive processes to deal with HWC (Gohori & Van der Merwe, 2021), as well as the absence of ways to compensate affected communities. Trophy hunting, which is supposed to eliminate problem animals, usually takes place in the dry season, whereas most crop raids take place in the wet season (Loveridge et al., 2007). The chances of eliminating the problem animals are thus slim. In Savuti, Botswana, trophy hunting had a negative effect on conservation, as male lions became rare because they were allocated for trophy hunting. This exposed female lion groups to kleptoparasitism by spotted hyenas (Loveridge et al., 2007).

These challenges that bedevil CBNRM initiatives have led some scholars (e.g. Hulme & Murphree, 1999) to conclude that success in formal CBNRM is elusive and that its long-term success cannot be guaranteed. They further argue that CBNRM is not a panacea to development and conservation and suggest that it is time to look for other development pathways and conservation strategies. On the other hand, Fabricius (2004, p. 23) postulates that there will always be a mix of losses and gains when dealing with CBNRM, and that 'all-out success or failure seldom occurs when dealing with people-natural resource relationships'.

The way forward

This chapter has provided an overview of PPT initiatives in Southern Africa in relation to PPC and development. Following one of the Vth IUCN World

Parks Congress recommendations, which advocates poverty alleviation through protected area establishment, the chapter has given examples from across the region in which this goal has been achieved. The chapter has argued that poverty is multi-dimensional and has pointed out that community participation and empowerment are key in poverty reduction. Furthermore, these two aspects and the use of and recognition of IKS and culture have been cited as symbolising development. Impediments to the achievement of PPT, PPC and development have been identified as the main obstacles to poverty alleviation. This section subsequently presents recommendations based on the successes and identified challenges.

In order to avert the lack of skills, NGOs, private partners and governments should offer training programmes to communities. However, from previous research (see Gohori & Van der Merwe, 2021), it has been found that the training programmes given to communities have been top-down and didactic. Incorporating local people's IKS in the programmes may address this problem and promote skills and knowledge that are relevant and home grown.

There is also a need to craft and implement policies that promote community empowerment regarding the use and management of natural resources, especially land tenure rights and the devolution of power and authority to grassroots levels. This will assist in addressing the lack of finances, as communities will be able to borrow from financial institutions and to make decisions. This, however, should be done in consultation with community members to avoid a 'one-size-fits-all' approach (Gohori & Van der Merwe, 2021), which is one of the contributors to the current challenges.

Most CBNRM initiatives have been focusing on accommodation. Although this is critical, as tourists need a place to stay, there is a need to diversify and even cater for day-trippers, which requires identifying tours/activities that can be done in a day. However, this calls for partnerships with the private sector (mostly tour operators and accommodation establishments) that will expose the projects to the market (Dodds et al., 2018).

Since one of the key attractions in rural communities is culture, communities should ensure that they pass on their culture to the next generation so that tourists continue to visit their projects. An example can be found in the Okavango Delta, Botswana, where the Basarwa promote the inter-generational transfer of knowledge, as young men work alongside old men and female children accompany their mothers to gather wild fruits, cut grass or collect reeds (Madzwamuse & Fabricius, 2004). Makandwa (2021) states that the Sengwe community in Zimbabwe and the Makulele community in South Africa pass on the skills of making handicrafts to new generations and most households from the communities have been involved in these handicrafts for generations.

The discussed challenges and the given recommendations offer a useful starting point for policymakers and practitioners involved with CBT development to engage in discussion that can lead to policies and strategies that are pro-poor and promote PPC and community development. This chapter adds

Promotion of pro-poor tourism 255

to the growing academic literature on PPT by highlighting not only successes, but also challenges faced in using tourism as a tool for poverty alleviation and community development.

References

Adams, W. M., Aveling, R., Brockington, D., Dickson, B., Elliott, J., Hutton, J., Roe, D., Vira, B., & Wolmer, W. (2004). Biodiversity conservation and the eradication of poverty. *Science,* 306 (5699), 1146–1149.

African Development Bank. (2016). *African development report 2015: Growth, poverty and inequality nexus: Overcoming barriers to sustainable development.* Abidjan, Ivory Coast: AfDB.

Asheeke, J. W., & Katjiuingua, O. (2007). *A sustainable tourism country report: Namibia.* Windhoek, Namibia: Federation of Namibian Tourism Associations.

Ashley, C., Roe, D., & Goodwin, H. (2001). *Pro-poor tourism strategies: Making tourism work for the poor: A review of experience.* Nottingham: IIED.

Binns, T., & Nel, E. (2002). Tourism as a local development strategy in South Africa. *The Geographical Journal,* 168 (3), 389–408.

Boggs, L. (2004). Community-based natural resource management in the Okavango Delta. In Fabricius, C., Koch, E., Magome, H., & Turner, S. (Eds.), *Rights, resources and rural development: Community-based natural resource management in Southern Africa.* London: Earthscan, 147–159.

Booth, V. (2016). The role of trophy hunting of elephant in support of the Zimbabwe CAMPFIRE Programme. 28 June. Retrieved from www.campfirezimbabwe.org/content/role-trophy-hunting-elephant-support-zimbabwe-campfire-programme

Campbell, B., & Shackleton, S. (2001). The organizational structures for community-based natural resource management in Southern Africa. *African Studies Quarterly,* 5 (3), 87–114.

Carr, E. R. (2008). Rethinking poverty alleviation: A 'poverties' approach. *Development in Practice,* 18 (6), 726–734. doi:10.1080/09614520802386363

Chambers, R. (1995). Poverty and livelihoods: Whose reality counts? *Environment and Urbanisation,* 7 (1), 173–204.

Child, B. (2003). Origins and efficacy of modern community based natural resources management (CBNRM) practices in the southern African region. 21 October. Retrieved from www.iucn.org/backup_iucn/cmsdata.iucn.org/downloads/cca_bchild.pdf

Cocks, M. (2000). Empowering communities to manage natural resources: Where does the new power lie? Fish River case study: Eastern Cape, South Africa. In Shackleton, S., & Campbell, B. (Eds.), *Empowering communities to manage natural resources: Case studies from Southern Africa.* Pretoria: CSIR, 111–125.

Davies, T. E., Fazey, I. R. A., Cresswell, W., & Pettorelli, N. (2014). Missing the trees for the wood: Why we are failing to see success in pro-poor conservation. *Animal Conservation,* 17, 303–312. doi:10.1111/acv.12094

Dodds, R., Ali, A., & Galaski, K. (2018). Mobilizing knowledge: Determining key elements for success and pitfalls in developing community-based tourism. *Current Issues in Tourism,* 21 (13), 1547–1568. doi:10.1080/13683500.2016.1150257

Dondeyne, S., Kaarhus, R., & Allison, G. (2012). Nature conservation, rural development and ecotourism in Central Mozambique: Which space do local communities get? In

256   *Owen Gohori et al.*

Convery, I., Corsane, G., & Davies, P. (Eds.), *Making sense of place: Multidisciplinary perspectives*. Woodbridge, England: Boydell Press, 291–301.

Fabricius, C. (2004). The fundamentals of community-based natural resource management: Historical background to community-based natural resource management. In Fabricius, C., Koch, E., Magome, H., & Turner, S. (Eds.), *Rights, resources and rural development: Community-based natural resource management in Southern Africa*. London: Earthscan, 3–43.

Galvin, M., & Haller, T. (2008) *People, Protected Areas and global change: Participatory conservation in Latin America, Africa, Asia and Europe*. Bern, Switzerland: University of Bern.

Gohori, O., & Van der Merwe, P. (2020). Towards a tourism and community-development framework: An African perspective. *Sustainability, 12* (5305), 1–34. doi:10.3390/su12135305

Gohori, O., & Van der Merwe, P. (2021). Tourism and community empowerment: The perspectives of local people in Manicaland Province, Zimbabwe. *Tourism Planning & Development*, 1–19. doi:10.1080/21568316.2021.1873838

Hulme, D., & Murphree, M. (1999). Communities, wildlife and the 'new conservation' in Africa. *Journal of International Development, 11*, 277–285.

International Fund for Agricultural Development. (2010). *Rural poverty report 2011*. Rome: International Fund for Agricultural Development.

International Union for Conservation of Nature. (2008). Protected areas. 25 March. Retrieved from www.iucn.org/theme/protected-areas/about

Jones, B. T. B., & Mosimane, A. W. (2000). Empowering communities to manage natural resources: Where does the new power lie? Case studies from Namibia. In Shackleton, S., & Campbell, B. (Eds.), *Empowering communities to manage natural resources: Case studies from Southern Africa*. Pretoria: CSIR, 80–110.

Kapungwe, E. M. (2000). Empowering communities to manage natural resources: Where does the new power lie? Case studies from Mumbwa Game Management Area and Lupande Game Management Area, Zambia. In Shackleton, S., & Campbell, B. (Eds.), *Empowering communities to manage natural resources: Case studies from Southern Africa*. Pretoria: CSIR, 169–189.

Kothari, A., et al. (2015). Managing resource use and development. In Worboys, G. L., Lockwood, M., Kothari, A., Feary, S., & Pulsford, I. (Eds.), *Protected Area governance and management*. Canberra: ANU Press, 789–822.

Loveridge, A. J., Reynolds, J. C., & Milner-Gulland, E. J. (2007). Does sport hunting benefit conservation? In MacDonald, D. W., & Service, K. (Eds.), *Key topics in conservation biology 1*. Oxford: Blackwell Publishing, 224.

Madzwamuse, M., & Fabricius, C. (2004). Local ecological knowledge and the Baraswa in the Okavango Delta: The case of Xaxaba, Ngamiland District. In Fabricius, C., Koch, E., Magome, H., & Turner, S. (Eds.), *Rights, resources and rural development: Community-based natural resource management in Southern Africa*. London: Earthscan, 160–173.

Makandwa, G. (2021). Sustainable community-based tourism: The entrepreneurial skills of the rural women in Southern Africa. Doctoral thesis, North-West University, Potchefstroom, SA.

Matela, S., & Ntlale, N. (2000). Empowering communities to manage natural resources: Where does the power lie? The case of Lesotho. In Shackleton, S., & Campbell, B. (Eds.), *Empowering communities to manage natural resources: Case studies from Southern Africa*. Pretoria: CSIR, 33–52.

Mbaiwa, J. E. (2004). The success and sustainability of community-based natural resource management on the Okavango Delta, Botswana. *South African Geographical Journal,* 86 (1), 44–53. doi:10.1080/03736245.2004.9713807

Mbaiwa, J. E., & Tshamekang, T. E. (2012). Developing a viable community-based tourism project in Botswana: The case of the Chobe Enclave Conservation Trust. In Ahmed, A. (Ed.), *2012 world sustainable development outlook: Innovate and lead for a siustainable future.* London: World Association for Sustainable Development, 519–536.

Murphree, M. W. (2000). The lesson from Mahenye. In Hutton, J., & Dickson, B. (Eds.), *Endangered species threatened convention: The past, and future of CITES, the Convention on International Trade in Endangered Species of Wild Fauna and Flora.* London: Earthscan, 181–196.

Popova, U. (2014). Conservation, traditional knowledge, and indigenous peoples. *American Behavioural Scientist,* 58 (1), 197–214. doi:10.1177/0002764213495043

Porter, A. (2017). Extreme poverty set to rise across Southern Africa. 23 March. Retrieved from https://issafrica.org/iss-today/extreme-poverty-set-to-rise-across-southern-africa

Roe, D., & Elliot, J. (2006). Pro-poor conservation: The elusive win–win for conservation and poverty reduction? *Policy Matters,* 14 (3), 53–63.

Saberwal, V., Rangarajan, M., & Kothari, A. (2001) *People, parks and wildlife: Tracts for the times.* New Delhi: Orient Longman.

Sachs, J. D., & Warner, A. M. (2001). Natural resources and economic development: The curse of natural resources. *European Economic Review,* 45, 827–838. doi:10.1016/S0014-2921(01)00125-8

SADC Secretariat. (2013). SADC programme for Transfrontier Conservation Areas. Gaborone, Botswana. 20 October. Retrieved from https://www.sadc.int/files/4614/2122/3338/SADC_TFCA_Programme_FINAL_doc_Oct_2013.pdf

Scherl, L. M., Wilson, A., Wild, R., Blockhus, J., Franks, P., McNeely, J. A., & McShane, T. O. (2004). *Can protected areas contribute to poverty reduction? Opportunities and limitations.* Gland, Switzerland: IUCN.

Scheyvens, R. (1999). Ecotourism and the empowerment of local communities. *Tourism Management,* 20 (2), 245–249. doi:10.1016/S0261-5177(98)00069-7

Sibanda, B. (2004). Community wildlife management in Zimbabwe: The case of CAMPFIRE in the Zambezi Valley. In Fabricius, C., Koch, E., Magome, H., & Turner, S. (Eds.), *Rights, resources and rural development: Community-based natural resource management in Southern Africa.* London: Earthscan, 248–258.

Souza, T. S. B., Thapa, B., Rodrigues, C. G. O., & Imori, D. (2019). Economic impacts of tourism in protected areas of Brazil. *Journal of Sustainable Tourism,* 27 (6), 735–749. doi:10.1080/09669582.2017.1408633

Stone, L. S., & Stone, M. T. (2011). Community-based enterprises: Challenges and prospects for community participation; Khama Rhino Sanctuary Trust, Botswana. *Journal of Sustainable Tourism,* 19 (1), 97–114. doi:10.1080/09669582.2010.508527

Stone, M. T. (2015). Community empowerment through community-based tourism: The case of Chobe Enclave Conservation Trust in Botswana. In Van der Dium, R., Lamers, M., & Van Wijk, J. (Eds.), *Institutional arrangements for conservation, development and tourism in Eastern and Southern Africa: A dynamic perspective.* London: Springer, 81–100.

Stone, M. T., & Nyaupane, G. P. (2016). Protected areas, tourism and community livelihoods linkages: A comprehensive analysis approach. *Journal of Sustainable Tourism,* 24 (5), 673–693. doi:10.1080/09669582.2015.1072207

258 *Owen Gohori et al.*

Tchakatumba, P. K., Gandiwa, E., Mwakiwa, E., Clegg, B., & Nyasha, S. (2019). Does the CAMPFIRE programme ensure economic benefits from wildlife to households in Zimbabwe? *Ecosystems and People,* 15 (1), 119–135. doi:10.1080/26395916.2019.1599070

Telfer, D. J. (2003). Development issues in destination communities. In Sign, S., Timothy, D. J., & Dowling, R. K. (Eds.), *Tourism in destination communities.* Oxford: CABI, 155–180.

Tornimbeni, C. (2008). Negotiating the state through inclusion in the community. Elite formation in decentralised resource management in Chimanimani, Mozambique. *Afriche e Orienti,* 2, 85–103.

Üllenberg, A., Buchberger, C., Meindl, K., Rupp, L., Springsguth, M., & Straube, B. (2015). *Evaluating cross-border natural resource management projects: Community-based tourism development and fire management in conservation areas of the SADC region.* Berlin: Deutsche Gesellschaft für Internationale Zusammenarbeit (GIZ) GmbH.

United Nations. (2009). *State of the world's Indigenous Peoples.* New York: UN.

United Nations World Tourism Organisation. (2018). *Tourism and the sustainable development goals: Good practices in the Americas.* Madrid: UNWTO and OAS.

Zimbabwe Trust. (1990). *The CAMPFIRE programme in Zimbabwe.* Harare: Zimbabwe Trust.

19 Contrasting safari and bushmeat hunting in Southern Africa

Conservation and development issues

Julia Laura van Velden

Introduction

The hunting of wild animals has been practised throughout humanity's history (Alves et al., 2018). Although the advent of industrialised agriculture has allowed many people to shift from this mode of survival towards relying on industrial livestock farming for protein needs, this is not the case everywhere (Alves et al., 2018). Hunting is still conducted in many regions of the world out of necessity to provide food and income, but also for recreation, and to satisfy cultural and social mores (Van Vliet et al., 2016). However, wildlife populations around the world are struggling to sustain current levels of extractive use (Ripple et al., 2019). Therefore, conservationists have attempted to manage hunting, whether conducted recreationally or for subsistence protein or income. Wildlife tourism has been a way of generating money for such conservation management, and extractive tourism such as safari hunting forms a part of this (Lindsey et al., 2006).

There is a relationship between the management of unsustainable, unregulated hunting and the practice of allowing wildlife hunting, if sold on a formal economic market via safari hunting. This juxtaposition between illegal hunting for human survival and legal hunting for recreation is interesting to explore both in terms of their impacts on wildlife conservation and in terms of impacts on people who live with such wildlife. This chapter explores the positive and negative ecological and social impacts of both safari hunting and bushmeat hunting, as well as the intersection of these activities. It will also discuss how the exclusion of local communities' rights and viewpoints from the wider conversation about these controversial issues may impact wildlife, communities and tourism. This review follows the targeted literature review approach, where current research and debates are presented and evaluated.

Safari hunting, also known as 'sport hunting' or 'trophy hunting', is hunting conducted by tourists for the purpose of recreation who pay premium prices for the opportunity to hunt individuals with exceptional physical attributes, such as large body size or tusks (Lindsey et al., 2007). This industry operates by selling hunts to clients, with wildlife sourced from game farms or wildlife conservation areas. The revenue is then split by the operator and the organisation selling the

DOI: 10.4324/9781003193166-23

licence to hunt the animal (Lindsey et al., 2007). Hunting can target common species such as impala; however, most revenue is generated from hunting charismatic species such as 'the big five' (lion, leopard, elephant, buffalo and the two rhinoceros species) (Di Minin et al., 2016). In contrast, the term 'bushmeat', also known as 'wild meat' or 'game meat' is defined as any non-domesticated terrestrial mammal, bird, reptile or amphibian which is harvested for the purpose of providing food for humans (Nasi et al., 2008). This term is inclusive of all the steps in the supply chain: acquisition (or hunting), trade, and consumption of meat (Nasi et al., 2008). Bushmeat hunting is distinct from recreational or safari hunting based on two (contested) criteria, namely the *main purpose* and *legality* of the activity.

First, safari hunting's primary purpose is for the hunter's pleasure, and can be a leisure or status activity (Leader-Williams, 2009). Safari hunting is therefore experiential, rather than conducted to meet existential needs such as protein or income. Secondly, safari hunting generally requires some form of permit or legal ownership of land or animals, and is conducted within the legal sphere, or is supposed to be (Lindsey et al., 2007). Conversely, bushmeat hunting is generally conducted for the specific purpose of generating meat for consumption and is mostly conducted outside of the legal sphere (Nasi et al., 2008). There are grey areas to this definition, as hunting may also fulfil multiple roles, including those of status and culture (Van Vliet & Nasi, 2008). It is important to recognise that the illegality of bushmeat hunting may stem more from the unjust systematic exclusion of local communities from ownership of wildlife resources than any real conservation concern (Duffy, 2010).

The costs and benefits of safari hunting

Safari hunting is a highly contested issue, with both positive and negative aspects. The proponents of safari hunting are often in favour of the activity due to its practical, large-scale potential to provide conservation benefits. Safari hunting can provide key funding for conservation activities in many countries, where state funding is insufficient and tourism makes up this shortfall (Lindsey et al., 2017; Lindsey et al., 2018). Because safari hunting commands higher pricing and attracts tourists to areas that may be unattractive to other non-consumptive tourists (e.g. photographic tourists), it may serve to address these shortfalls. Safari hunters may be willing to visit politically unstable countries (Lindsey et al., 2006), and land use which is viable for photographic tourism can comprise a relatively small proportion of the wildlife estate in Africa (Lindsey et al., 2016; Winterbach et al., 2015).

Safari hunting is meant to be a primary contributor to the operational costs of Community-Based Natural Resource Management (CBNRM), such that external support is no longer necessary (Jones & Weaver, 2009). A particular case for safari hunting as a conservation benefit is the use of private land to preserve natural habitat, which may otherwise be transformed for other uses. For example, in South Africa, where safari hunting is a key revenue generator

Contrasting safari and bushmeat hunting   261

(Parker et al., 2020), private land conservation covers double the land that state protected areas cover (Taylor et al., 2020). Local community ownership of wildlife and inclusion into wildlife markets has also been highlighted as a way to ensure appropriate benefits are received in exchange for the sometimes severe consequences of living with such wildlife (Leader-Williams & Hutton, 2005).

On the negative side, first, safari hunting can only achieve its conservation goals if it is ecologically sustainable and does not negatively impact animal population demographics. Excessive quotas for hunting male lions in Zimbabwe have, for example, impacted population densities and sex ratios (Davidson et al., 2011), although more sustainable management options are known to be possible (Lindsey et al., 2013a). Secondly, its ability to mitigate the effects of human wildlife conflict and generate benefits to communities living alongside wildlife are dependent on the level of benefits and their equitable distribution to those most affected. Drake et al. (2021) found that sustainable safari hunting only offsets approximately 30% of the economic cost of crop destruction by elephants. Thirdly, there are the moral and ethical dimensions of such a practice and their attendant public perception. Ethically, it has been argued that safari hunting is incongruous with conservation, as it is based on an extractive and objectifying relationship with animals, as well as being a Western imperialist practice (Batavia et al., 2019). This can cause reputational risks to tourism, where public outrage has led to calls by Western nations to ban safari hunting imports, as well as the practice altogether, and, therefore, effectively to eliminate the primary motivation of safari hunters to pay for such an activity (Di Minin et al., 2016).

Safari hunting in Namibia

Namibia's CBNRM programme provides an example of how safari hunting is used to achieve conservation and community goals. This programme is based on the concept of sustainable use of wildlife, using economic instrumentalism, rights devolution and collective proprietorship (Jones & Weaver, 2009). By devolving property rights to collective management by local communities, this approach gives legal empowerment to rural people, who would otherwise be unable to significantly benefit from wildlife. By strengthening incentives to conserve wildlife it also helps to develop local governance institutions (Boudreaux & Nelson, 2011). Beginning in the 1990s, this programme has since been widely recognised as contributing to the strong recovery of wildlife in Namibia (Naidoo et al., 2011).

Safari hunting plays a large role in this programme, by providing substantial contributions to the economic welfare of local communities. These contributions have been found to be of a different kind to those that can be provided by non-extractive tourism, where hunting provides for governance structures and management costs of conservancies, while photographic tourism provides for employment and wages (Naidoo et al., 2016). Additionally, hunting benefits are generated more quickly, within a few years of formation, as this activity is not as reliant on infrastructure in the same way photographic tourism is (Naidoo et al., 2016). A study has also found that communities receiving substantial benefits from hunting have a more favourable attitude towards wildlife than those living in similarly performing conservancies utilising photographic tourism (Störmer et al., 2019). This may be because meat from hunted animals provides a significant benefit to communities, which gives a clear and direct link between the action (conserving wildlife) and the benefit (meat), something which is often unclear in other schemes.

However, despite these benefits, other research has found that benefits are inconsistent and can be distributed unequally. Furthermore, dependence on safari hunting can increase the vulnerability of communities if there are market changes (e.g. via bans) (Thomsen et al., 2021). Continuing human–wildlife conflicts can also undermine successes, as can insecurities in long-term land tenure (Boudreaux & Nelson, 2011). Therefore, for safari hunting to provide a viable method of conserving wildlife and mitigating land transformation and illegal hunting, the costs of human–wildlife conflict need to be mitigated and rights need to be further devolved from government and NGOs to communities, with appropriate support for their aspirations to manage wildlife.

The costs and benefits of bushmeat hunting

Bushmeat can play multiple roles in local people's livelihoods (Van Vliet et al., 2016), including economic, nutritional, social and cultural roles. In economic terms, bushmeat is important to actors all along its supply chain, including hunters, transporters, wholesale/local traders and consumers (Cowlishaw et al., 2007). For hunters, the economic role bushmeat plays often blurs the line between subsistence and the commercial, as meat can both be sold for income and used at home for personal consumption (Knapp et al., 2017). Hunting may lift households out of poverty, with some studies suggesting that households do not hunt *because* they are wealthy, but rather *they are wealthier because they hunt* (Travers et al., 2019). The economic role that bushmeat plays for consumers varies depending on context, as wealthier households consume more bushmeat in urban areas, while the opposite holds true for rural areas (Brashares et al., 2011).

For rural consumers, the role of bushmeat can vary between a primary source of their protein requirements (Martin et al., 2012) and acting as a safety net in lean conditions (Brashares et al., 2004). Apart from economic and food security roles, bushmeat may simply be preferred in many societies because of its taste (Schenck et al., 2006). Hunting can also have a role in developing symbolic/social capital, as hunters may have high status in their community (Lindsey et al., 2013b) and many cultures use bushmeat for celebrations or ceremonies (Van Vliet & Nasi, 2008).

Despite these positive contributions to people's livelihoods, the hunting, trade and consumption of wild animals is one of the top threats facing wildlife around the world today. Harvesting for human consumption is the largest threat to 98% of threatened megafauna, (Ripple et al., 2019). Declines in abundances of both bird and mammals in hunted areas are stark, with an average of a 58% reduction in abundance in hunted areas relative to unhunted areas (Benítez-López et al., 2017). The term 'the Bushmeat Crisis' (Bowen-Jones et al., 2003) has been coined due to the scale and the intensity of hunting around the world, constituting a crisis for both conservation and human welfare.

First, in terms of conservation, the ecological impacts of bushmeat hunting are wide-ranging, including generalised wildlife population declines (Lindsey & Bento, 2012) and disproportionate impacts on specific species (Becker et al., 2013). Despite the benefits that bushmeat may provide to local communities in the short term in terms of income and protein, the loss of wildlife can have longer term effects. The supply of meat from African forests, for example, is expected to drop by 81% within the next 50 years (Fa et al., 2003). Given the unsustainable rate of hunting in many areas, this short-term gain may mean that no wildlife will be available in future, if wildlife is reduced to such low densities as to be reproductively unviable. Additionally, as discussed previously, safari hunting, game ranching and ecotourism are valuable and profitable enterprises (Taylor et al., 2016). However, formal wildlife-based land uses will not be able to succeed without medium densities of wildlife. An example of the economic ramifications of bushmeat hunting can be found in a Mozambiquan protected area, where historical and current illegal hunting leads to an estimated loss of US$1.62 million per year in revenue (Lindsey & Bento, 2012).

Finally, the risk of zoonotic disease transmission from the butchering and consumption of wild animals is a growing concern, and has been linked with a number of emerging human diseases (Karesh & Noble, 2009). These outbreaks demonstrate the large risks that bushmeat consumption poses to local communities and the world at large, and is especially pertinent due to the loss of tourism revenues from international travel restrictions, expected to severely impact conservation activities across Africa (Lindsey et al., 2020).

Bushmeat hunting in Malawi

The south-east African country of Malawi has diverse and important terrestrial and freshwater biodiversity (Government of Malawi, 2014), despite its small size. There are 99 protected areas in Malawi, approximately 16.8% of the land area (World Bank Group, 2018). Wildlife tourism does not, however, currently play a large role in Malawi's economy, due to poor infrastructure and low densities of wildlife. This is contrary to the situation in many East and Southern African countries, and the development of these protected areas into profitable enterprises is a top priority for the Malawian government.

The political and organisational context of protected areas in Malawi is evolving rapidly. The Department of National Parks and Wildlife (DNPW) suffers from acute financial shortages. In 2014, DNPW's budgetary ceiling was US$ 315,000, excluding salaries. In comparison the annual budget for the Kenya Wildlife Service is ~US$ 50 million (Waterland et al., 2015). The very minimum budget that DNPW requires to function at the most fundamental level is US$ 1,050,000 (Waterland et al., 2015). These financial shortages have large effects on the ability of protected areas to function, and to undertake community-based interventions to reduce bushmeat hunting.

Within the last five to ten years, however, large international conservation NGOs have become involved with many protected areas in Malawi. The NGO African Parks (AP) is responsible for the management of four protected areas in a delegated co-management arrangement with the Malawian government (African Parks, 2019). The aim of such partnerships is to inject funding and management capacity into protected areas operating in a semi-collapsed state with very low wildlife populations, due to a previous lack of enforcement. Tourism numbers have risen at all AP-managed protected areas since takeover. For example, Majete rose from virtually no tourists in 2003 to over 11,000 per year in 2019 (African Parks, 2019).

Currently, Malawi does not allow any safari or recreational hunting from its protected areas, apart from the occasional culling of 'problem animals' (Jere, 2017). The government also supplies a small number of licences to hunt wildlife outside protected areas (Jere, 2017). It is however likely that the amount of protein able to be supplied from these licences is relatively small. Malawi is somewhat limited in its options to provide sustainable and legal bushmeat outside protected areas, in the form of sustainable use areas such as those used in Zambia, Tanzania and Namibia, due to rapid land transformation to agricultural areas (van Velden et al., 2020a).

Recent research in Malawi has indicated the scale of bushmeat hunting and consumption. Van Velden et al. (2020a) found that up to 39% of the population living around protected areas may consume bushmeat and between 4 and 19% may hunt for bushmeat. Hunting and consumption exist at levels high enough for conservation concern, even in protected areas with substantial budgets for community-based livelihood projects (van Velden et al., 2020a). Increasing involvement in such projects did not reduce these activities in some instances. Importantly, it was found that consumption was more prevalent in poorer households, while hunting occurred more often in wealthier households.

These results indicate, first, that conservation projects may not be adequate in providing alternative proteins for poorer households, and that wealthier households are not incentivised to switch from hunting to another income-generating activity (van Velden et al., 2020a). Van Velden et al. (2020b) found that community-based projects that provide products in the short term (e.g. Non-timber Forest Product schemes or regulated hunting) were less preferred and have fewer positive impacts on causing switches to other forms of income activities than programmes which give the opportunity for long-term economic empowerment, such as business creation projects.

Malawian conservation (and attendant wildlife tourism) is currently at crossroads. Having seen significant wildlife recoveries in some parks due to stringent enforcement (African Parks, 2019), while others without those resources have struggled to maintain wildlife populations viable for tourism, there is some concern that conservation in Malawi may swing towards a more militant, enforcement-based conservation model (van Velden et al., 2020a). Growing human populations and a lack of employment opportunities in many areas are creating increasing pressure on all protected areas. Hunting in some legalised format, although not viable currently due to recovering wildlife populations, may become possible in the future and act as an important source of revenue to help to make up for the drastic shortfalls in conservation funding currently. Therefore, it is recommended that the Malawian conservation sector carefully evaluate this possibility, in terms of how to ensure economic and ecological sustainability and whether extractive use is an ethos that this sector is willing to adopt.

The intersection of bushmeat and safari hunting

Bushmeat hunting and safari hunting intersect in important ways. First, bushmeat hunting and safari hunting are connected because safari hunting enlarges the wildlife conservation estate, by providing an economic incentive to private individuals for this land use, or for governments to create large areas conserved as hunting blocks (Parker et al., 2020). However, economic losses from bushmeat hunting may push private actors from this system, causing this land to be converted to agriculture (Lindsey et al., 2013b). Secondly, tourism may be impacted by both safari and bushmeat hunting in different and connected ways, which then influences conservation funding and success. Bushmeat hunting, by creating so-called 'empty forests' or 'empty savannas' (Wilkie et al., 2011), limits tourism opportunities, because tourists will be unwilling to pay entry fees if there are low chances of seeing wildlife, especially charismatic species or megafauna. An example of this is the exceptionally low tourism numbers to certain Malawian protected areas in the past, primarily because wildlife was so depleted (African Parks, 2019).

In contrast, tourism may be affected by public perception of safari hunting, a so-called 'reputational risk' to countries which allow hunting. Kenya provides an example of a country that does not allow any safari hunting but also suffers from much illegal bushmeat hunting (Ottichilo et al., 2000), which has been argued to have been caused by limited opportunities for communities to legally benefit from wildlife (Lewis & Jackson, 2005). Finally, safari hunting is often allowed on the premise that the benefits it provides to local communities allow them to shift away from relying on bushmeat hunting or consumption, towards more formalised market-based interactions with protected areas (Naidoo et al., 2011). This mitigation is however extremely context-dependent, assuming that protein needs are met by using safari hunting meat for cheap sale to communities, that creation of jobs in the sector allows for past bushmeat hunters to shift professions and that other revenue streams such as photographic tourism are not endangered (Naidoo et al., 2011).

Local agency and ownership in the hunting debate

Safari hunting, and to a lesser extent bushmeat hunting, are part of a wide public debate on the acceptability of extractive human–wildlife relationships. Safari hunting is often attended by public outrage, driven by social media. Social movements, called 'cyberactivism', where participants are mobilised online to create petitions, share content and call for change, have been particularly influential in the safari hunting debate (Mkono, 2018). Perceptions on human–animal relationships have large attendant impacts on tourism, as the wider public increasingly views any violence towards animals with repugnance. Tourists may choose to not support countries where such practices take place and banning hunting imports to other countries will take away incentives for safari hunters to visit African countries (Dickman et al., 2019).

In terms of bushmeat hunting or hunting of high-value species such as rhinos, 'poachers' are often dehumanised and stigmatised in the public arena, and the use of extrajudicial lethal force is rising with the attendant militarisation of conservation, as part of a so-called 'war on poaching' (Duffy et al., 2019). However, the voices that are conspicuously missing from the mainstream debate are those of local African people, who live with wildlife. Such a failure to understand how local people view the trade-offs of hunting may ultimately negatively impact both conservation and tourism, if local people perceive that the benefits of living with wildlife are exceeded by the costs. For example, Angula et al. (2018) found that, in Namibia, 91% of community members at communal conservancies were not in favour of a safari hunting ban and only 11% would continue to support wildlife conservation if such a ban were put in place.

Enforcing Western views of wildlife management deprives local people of their agency and ultimate ownership of wildlife. Indeed, studies have found that, to many Africans, safari hunting is not viewed as objectionable because of any moral imperatives, but rather because it is seen to privilege Western elites in accessing wildlife resources (Mkono, 2019). Other studies have also found that some local people view bushmeat hunting and consumption as a right and that wildlife, despite being protected by the state on behalf of their country, is ultimately a common good of the people (van Velden et al., 2020a). Eating game meat is a fundamental part of many cultures, including those already marginalised (LaRocco, 2020), a factor that cannot be dismissed. However, recently there have been calls for a more inclusive debate, which actively recognises the right of African countries and people to make decisions over their wildlife (Cassidy & Salerno, 2020). Botswana, which lifted a five-year hunting moratorium in 2019, reinstating safari hunting, is an instance where the decision to manage wildlife in their own way was taken in the face of international backlash (LaRocco, 2020).

Conclusion

This chapter does not argue for safari hunting and bushmeat hunting to be accepted without debate, but rather argues that it is necessary to ensure that

Contrasting safari and bushmeat hunting 267

international (and often Western) views are not privileged over local people's perspectives. Increasing local agency and devolving rights to benefit from wildlife will ultimately improve conservation outcomes (Oldekop et al., 2016). Conserving African wildlife therefore requires a careful dance between use and protection and can only be achieved with the recognition of what local communities want and need, and acceptance of their rights to make decisions concerning the wildlife they live alongside. This includes recognising both the positive and negative impacts of safari and bushmeat hunting, as well as how they are interlinked.

References

African Parks. (2019). Annual report 2019. Retrieved from www.africanparks.org/sites/default/files/uploads/resources/2020-06/AFRICAN%20PARKS%20-%202019%20Annual%20Report%20-%20WEB%20READY%20v1%20-%20Low%20Res.pdf

Alves, R. R. N., Souto, W. M. S., Fernandes-Ferreira, H., Bezerra, D. M. M., Barboza, R. R. D., & Vieira, W. L. S. (2018). The importance of hunting in human societies. In *Ethnozoology*. New York: Academic Press, 95–118.

Angula, H. N., Stuart-Hill, G., Ward, D., Matongo, G., Diggle, R. W., & Naidoo, R. (2018). Local perceptions of trophy hunting on communal lands in Namibia. *Biological Conservation*, 218, 26–31.

Batavia, C., Nelson, M. P., Darimont, C. T., Paquet, P. C., Ripple, W. J., & Wallach, A. D. (2019). The elephant (head) in the room: A critical look at trophy hunting. *Conservation Letters*, 12 (1), e12565.

Becker, M., McRobb, R., Watson, F., Droge, E., Kanyembo, B., Murdoch, J., & Kakumbi, C. (2013). Evaluating wire-snare poaching trends and the impacts of by-catch on elephants and large carnivores. *Biological Conservation*, 158, 26–36.

Benítez-López, A., Alkemade, R., Schipper, A. M., Ingram, D. J., Verweij, P. A., Eikelboom, J. A. J., & Huijbregts, M. A. J. (2017). The impact of hunting on tropical mammal and bird populations. *Science*, 356 (6334), 180–183.

Boudreaux, K., & Nelson, F. (2011). Community conservation in Namibia: Empowering the poor with property rights. *Economic Affairs*, 31 (2), 17–24.

Bowen-Jones, E., Brown, D., & Robinson, E. (2003). Economic commodity or environmental crisis? An interdisciplinary approach to analysing the bushmeat trade in central and west Africa. *Area*, 35 (4), 390–402.

Brashares, J. S., Arcese, P., Sam, M. K., Coppolillo, P B., Sinclair, A. R. E., & Balmford, A. (2004). Bushmeat hunting, wildlife declines, and fish supply in west Africa. *Science*, 306, 1180–1183.

Brashares, J. S., Golden, C. D., Weinbaum, K. Z., Barrett, C. B., & Okello, G. V. (2011). Economic and geographic drivers of wildlife consumption in rural Africa. *Proceedings of the National Academy of Sciences of the United States of America*, 108, 13931–13936.

Cassidy, L., & Salerno, J. (2020). The need for a more inclusive science of elephant conservation. *Conservation Letters*, 13 (5), e12717.

Cowlishaw, G., Mendelson, S., & Rowcliffe, J. (2007). Livelihoods and sustainability in a bushmeat commodity chain in Ghana. In Davies, G., & Brown, D. (Eds.), *Bushmeat and livelihoods: Wildlife management and poverty reduction*. Oxford: Blackwell Publishing, 32–46.

268 *Julia Laura van Velden*

Davidson, Z., Valeix, M., Loveridge, A. J., Madzikanda, H., & Macdonald, D. W. (2011). Socio-spatial behaviour of an African lion population following perturbation by sport hunting. *Biological Conservation,* 144 (1), 114–121.

Di Minin, E., Leader-Williams, N., & Bradshaw, C. J. A. (2016). Banning trophy hunting will exacerbate biodiversity loss. *Trends in Ecology & Evolution,* 31 (2), 99–102.

Dickman, A., Cooney, R., Johnson, P. J., Louis, M. P., & Roe, D. (2019). Trophy hunting bans imperil biodiversity. *Science,* 365 (6456), 874.

Drake, M. D., Salerno, J., Langendorf, R. E., Cassidy, L., Gaughan, A. E., Stevens, F. R., … Hartter, J. (2021). Costs of elephant crop depredation exceed the benefits of trophy hunting in a community-based conservation area of Namibia. *Conservation Science and Practice,* 3 (1), e345.

Duffy, R. (2010). *Nature crime: How we're getting conservation wrong.* New Haven, CT: Yale University Press.

Duffy, R., Massé, F., Smidt, E., Marijnen, E., Büscher, B., Verweijen, J., … & Lunstrum, E. (2019). Why we must question the militarisation of conservation. *Biological Conservation,* 232, 66–73.

Fa, J. E., Currie, D., & Meeuwig, J. (2003). Bushmeat and food security in the Congo Basin: Linkages between wildlife and people's future. *Environmental Conservation,* 30 (1), 71–78.

Government of Malawi. (2014). Fifth national report to the convention on biological diversity. Lilongwe, Malawi. Retrieved from www.cbd.int/doc/world/mw/mw-nr-05-en.doc

Jere, R. (2017). National parks and wildlife (amendment) act. Lilongwe: Ministry of Justice Malawi. Retrieved from www.lilongwewildlife.org/wp-content/uploads/NATIONAL-PARKS-AND-WILDLIFE-AMENDMENT-BILL.pdf

Jones, B., & Weaver, C. (2009). CBNRM in Namibia: Growth, trends, lessons and constraints. In Suich, H. & Child, B. (Eds.), *Evolution and innovation in wildlife conservation: Parks and game ranches to transfrontier conservation areas.* London: Earthscan, 223–242.

Karesh, W. B., & Noble, E. (2009). The bushmeat trade: Increased opportunities for transmission of zoonotic disease. *Mount Sinai Journal of Medicine: A Journal of Translational and Personalized Medicine,* 76 (5), 429–434.

Knapp, E. J., Peace, N., & Bechtel, L. (2017). Poachers and poverty: Assessing objective and subjective measures of poverty among illegal hunters outside Ruaha national park, Tanzania. *Conservation and Society,* 15, 24–32.

LaRocco, A. A. (2020). Botswana's hunting ban and the transformation of game-meat cultures, economies and ecologies. *Journal of Southern African Studies,* 46 (4), 723–741.

Leader-Williams, N. (2009). Conservation and hunting: Friends or foes? In Dickson, B., Hutton, J., & Adams, W. A. (Eds.), *Recreational hunting, conservation and rural livelihoods: Science and practice.* Chichester: John Wiley & Sons.

Leader-Williams, N., & Hutton, J. M. (2005). Does extractive use provide opportunities to offset conflicts between people and wildlife? In Woodroffe, R., Thirgood, S., & Rabinowitz, A. (Eds.), *People and wildlife, conflict or co-existence?* (Vol. 9). Cambridge: Cambridge University Press, 140.

Lewis, D., & Jackson, J. (2005). Safari hunting and conservation on communal land in southern Africa. In Woodroffe, R., Thirgood, S., & Rabinowitz, A. (Eds.), *People and wildlife, conflict or co-existence?* (Vol. 9). Cambridge: Cambridge University Press, 239–251.

Lindsey, P. A., Alexander, R., Frank, L. G., Mathieson, A., & Romañach, S. S. (2006). Potential of trophy hunting to create incentives for wildlife conservation in Africa where alternative wildlife-based land uses may not be viable. *Animal Conservation,* 9 (3), 283–291.

Lindsey, P. A., Allan, J., Brehony, P., Dickman, A., Robson, A., Begg, C., ... & Tyrrell, P. (2020). Conserving Africa's wildlife and wildlands through the COVID-19 crisis and beyond. *Nature Ecology & Evolution,* 4 (10), 1300–1310.

Lindsey, P. A., Balme, G. A., Funston, P., Henschel, P., Hunter, L., Madzikanda, H., ... & Nyirenda, V. (2013a). The trophy hunting of African lions: Scale, current management practices and factors undermining sustainability. *PLoS One,* 8 (9), e73808.

Lindsey, P. A., Balme, G. A., Funston, P. J., Henschel, P. H., & Hunter, L. T. B. (2016). Life after Cecil: Channelling global outrage into funding for conservation in Africa. *Conservation Letters,* 9, 296–301.

Lindsey, P. A., Barnes, J., Nyirenda, V., Pumfrett, B., Tambling, C., Taylor, W., & t'Sas Rolfes, M. (2013b). The Zambian wildlife ranching industry: Scale, associated benefits, and limitations affecting its development. *PLoS One,* 8 (12), e8176.

Lindsey, P.A., & Bento, C. (2012). *Illegal hunting and the bushmeat trade in central Mozambique. A case-study from Coutada 9, Manica province.* Harare: TRAFFIC Eastern/Southern Africa.

Lindsey, P. A., Chapron, G., Petracca, L. S., Burnham, D., Hayward, M. W., Henschel, P., ... & Macdonald, E. A. (2017). Relative efforts of countries to conserve world's megafauna. *Global Ecology and Conservation,* 10, 243–252.

Lindsey, P.A., Miller, J. R., Petracca, L. S., Coad, L., Dickman, A. J., Fitzgerald, K. H., ... & Knights, K. (2018). More than $1 billion needed annually to secure Africa's protected areas with lions. *Proceedings of the National Academy of Sciences,* 115, E10788–E10796.

Lindsey, P. A., Roulet, P., & Romanach, S. (2007). Economic and conservation significance of the trophy hunting industry in sub-saharan Africa. *Biological Conservation,* 134 (4), 455–469.

Martin, A., Caro, T., & Mulder, M. B. (2012). Bushmeat consumption in western Tanzania: A comparative analysis from the same ecosystem. *Tropical Conservation Science,* 5 (3), 352–364.

Mkono, M. (2018). The age of digital activism in tourism: Evaluating the legacy and limitations of the Cecil anti-trophy hunting movement. *Journal of Sustainable Tourism,* 26 (9), 1608–1624.

Mkono, M. (2019). Neo-colonialism and greed: Africans' views on trophy hunting in social media. *Journal of Sustainable Tourism,* 27 (5), 689–704.

Naidoo, R., Weaver, L. C., De Longcamp, M., & Du Plessis, P. (2011). Namibia's community-based natural resource management programme: An unrecognized payments for ecosystem services scheme. *Environmental Conservation,* 38 (4), 445–453.

Naidoo, R., Weaver, L. C., Diggle, R. W., Matongo, G., Stuart-Hill, G., & Thouless, C. (2016). Complementary benefits of tourism and hunting to communal conservancies in Namibia. *Conservation Biology,* 30 (3), 628–638.

Nasi, R., Brown, D., Wilkie, D., Bennett, E., Tutin, C., van Tol, G., & Christophersen, T. (2008). *Conservation and use of wildlife-based resources: The bushmeat crisis.* Montreal: Secretariat of the Convention on Biological Diversity; Center for International Forestry Research (CIFOR)

Oldekop, J. A., Holmes, G., Harris, W. E., & Evans, K. L. (2016). A global assessment of the social and conservation outcomes of protected areas. *Conservation Biology,* 30, 133–141.

270 *Julia Laura van Velden*

Ottichilo, W. K., Grunblatt, J., Said, M. Y., & Wargute, P. W. (2000). Wildlife and livestock population trends in the Kenya rangeland. In Prins, H. H. T., Grootenhuis, J. G., & Dolan, T. T. (Eds.), *Wildlife conservation by sustainable use*. Dordrecht: Springer, 203–218.

Parker, K., De Vos, A., Clements, H. S., Biggs, D., & Biggs, R. (2020). Impacts of a trophy hunting ban on private land conservation in South African biodiversity hotspots. *Conservation Science and Practice*, 2 (7), e214.

Ripple, W. J., Wolf, C., Newsome, T. M., Betts, M. G., Ceballos, G., Courchamp, F., … & Worm, B. (2019). Are we eating the world's megafauna to extinction? *Conservation Letters*, e12627.

Schenck, M., Effa, E., Starkey, M., Wilkie, D., Abernethy, K., Telfer, T., … & Treves, A. (2006). Why people eat bushmeat: Results from two-choice, taste tests in Gabon, Central Africa. *Human Ecology*, 34, 433–445.

Störmer, N., Weaver, L. C., Stuart-Hill, G., Diggle, R. W., & Naidoo, R. (2019). Investigating the effects of community-based conservation on attitudes towards wildlife in Namibia. *Biological Conservation*, 233, 193–200.

Taylor, A., Lindsey, P., & Davies-Mostert, H. (2016). *An assessment of the economic social and conservation value of the wildlife ranching industry and its potential to support the green economy*. Johannesburg: Endangered Wildlife Trust.

Taylor, W. A., Lindsey, P. A., Nicholson, S. K., Relton, C., & Davies-Mostert, H. T. (2020). Jobs, game meat and profits: The benefits of wildlife ranching on marginal lands in South Africa. *Biological Conservation*, 245, 108561.

Thomsen, J. M., Lendelvo, S., Coe, K., & Rispel, M. (2021). Community perspectives of empowerment from trophy hunting tourism in Namibia's Bwabwata national park. *Journal of Sustainable Tourism*, 1–18. DOI: 10.1080/09669582.2021.1874394

Travers, H., Archer, L. J., Mwedde, G., Roe, D., Baker, J., Plumptre, A., … & Milner-Gulland, E. J. (2019). Understanding complex drivers of wildlife crime to design effective conservation interventions. *Conservation Biology*, 33, 1296–1306.

van Velden, J., Wilson, K., Lindsey, P., McCallum, H., Moyo, B. H. Z., & Biggs, D. (2020a). Bushmeat hunting and consumption is a pervasive issue in African savannahs: Insights from four protected areas in Malawi. *Biodiversity and Conservation*, 29, 1443–1464.

van Velden, J. L., Travers, H., Moyo, B. H. Z., & Biggs, D. (2020b). Using scenarios to understand community-based interventions for bushmeat hunting and consumption in African savannas. *Biological Conservation*, 248, 108676.

Van Vliet, N., Cornelis, D., Beck, H., Lindsey, P., Nasi, R., LeBel, S., … Jori, F. (2016). Meat from the wild: Extractive uses of wildlife and alternatives for sustainability. In *Current trends in wildlife research*. Dordrecht: Springer, 225–265.

Van Vliet, N., & Nasi, R. (2008). Hunting for livelihood in northeast Gabon: Patterns, evolution, and sustainability. *Ecology and Society*, 13 (2), 1–33.

Waterland, S., Vaughan, J., Lyman, E., & Jurisic, I. (2015). *Illegal wildlife trade review*. Lilongwe, Malawi: Department of National Parks and Wildlife of Malawi.

Wilkie, D. S., Bennett, E. L., Peres, C. A., & Cunningham, A. A. (2011). The Empty Forest revisited. *Annals of the New York Academy of Sciences*, 1223, 120–128.

Winterbach, C. W., Whitesell, C., & Somers, M. J. (2015). Wildlife abundance and diversity as indicators of tourism potential in northern Botswana. *PLoS One*, 10 (8), e0135595.

World Bank Group. (2018). Terrestrial protected areas. Retrieved from https://data.worldbank.org/indicator/ER.LND.PTLD.ZS

Part V

Conclusion

20 A synthesis of protected areas and tourism contributions to conservation and community livelihoods goals in Southern Africa

A conclusion

Moren Tibabo Stone, Lesego Senyana Stone, Patricia Kefilwe Mogomotsi and Goemeone E. J. Mogomotsi

Introduction

In this concluding chapter, we synthesise debates on the conservation and development centred on protected areas (PAs) and tourism. This debate is informed by the useful insights generated by contributing chapters to this volume. Information derived from the chapters focuses on issues dealing with theory and practice, policy, institutions and diverse stakeholders. It is therefore evident that to understand the relationship between PAs and tourism development, it is important to understand their dynamic interconnections. There is no debate as to whether PAs provide attractions that serve the tourism sector and that in turn tourism development serves communities living within and around PAs by providing them with alternative livelihood options. The debate is on how best PAs and tourism can serve both conservation and development objectives sustainably without yielding detrimental outcomes that undermine the same efforts. This volume indicates that the understanding of the relationship between PAs, tourism and livelihoods is not conclusive and is still up for further debate. To end this debate, we first must find robust theory(ies) or conceptual framework(s) that can articulate the social–ecological relationship that exists between PAs, tourism and community livelihoods to inform the practical execution of conservation/development projects.

Success in conservation depends on whether PAs are effectively managed and can mitigate threats to fulfil their multiple roles of enhancing biodiversity conservation and promoting community development (Bhammar et al., 2021). This is fundamental in the face of growing pressure on PAs, especially from anthropogenic undertakings aimed to improve livelihoods (Geldmann et al., 2019). Well-managed PAs are a critical component of any biodiversity conservation strategy (Cazalis et al., 2020). However, well managed PAs were easy to recognise during times when their roles were solely based on conservation, without the added role of community development through tourism, hence

DOI: 10.4324/9781003193166-25

274 Moren Tibabo Stone et al.

only conservation indicators were used to measure their performance. Bringing in tourism was one way to finance PAs based on a win–win management fashion (Spenceley et al., 2017). This win–win strategy must be successful for sustainability to occur, as losing income generation opportunities from tourism can reduce funds for PA management and community benefit, and as a result, increase conservation threats (Lindsey, 2020). This edition has highlighted some emerging issues which are discussed in the next section.

Protected areas, tourism and livelihoods: emerging issues

Nearly all PAs in Africa are inadequately funded. Snyman (2012) argues that a deficit of US$ 1 billion annually must be addressed to save iconic species and landscapes. The World Travel and Tourism Council (WTTC, 2019) indicates that wildlife tourism hosted by PAs directly contributed US$ 120.1 billion in GDP to the global economy and sustained 21.8 million jobs in 2018, demonstrating its market viability. Given competing demands over limited public financial resources, governments often do not prioritise investments in PAs, including tourism, in part because although these investments generate conservation benefits, they do not further development goals (Bhammar et al., 2021). There is an overall gap in estimating the contribution and impacts of PAs. Such gaps include direct, indirect and induced revenues to local and national economies through tourism. This data gap makes it difficult to establish a return on public investments in PA management, reinforcing governments' perception that PAs are 'financial sinks' or that they only generate conservation benefits, and have limited economic and development outcomes (Bhammar et al., 2021).

Based on theories and conceptual frameworks used by different chapter contributors to this volume, there is a shortage of comprehensive or robust underpinnings that can help to illuminate the understanding of the complex relationship between conservation, tourism and livelihoods, without yielding unintended consequences. This volume identifies theory and practice, policy instruments, institutional landscapes and diverse stakeholders as key proponents that influence PAs and tourism to achieve success and/or fail to meet conservation and development objectives. The four components are discussed below.

Theory and practice

Moving from theory to practice is never an easy task. Hall (1996) argues that collaborative partnership methodologies in tourism planning have the potential to take in a wide range of stakeholders, escalate political participation and social equality, and contribute to more sustainable forms of tourism. Hall (1996) also cautions that theoretically informed collaborative arrangements may not be adequately inclusive in nature. Extant literature has proposed different theoretical frameworks to analyse residents' perceptions, attitudes, behaviour and participation in relation to PAs and tourism initiatives (see Ntuli & Muchapondwa in this volume; Ntuli et al., 2019; Snyman, 2014). The frameworks allow researchers

Conclusion   275

to identify and analyse variables that affect this relationship. Bragagnolo et al. (2016) observed a relatively high degree of concordance between studies with certain variables showing strong associations with attitudes. The authors recommend a more rigorous model-building approach based on a clear conceptual framework drawing from extensive empirical data on conservation and development.

Green initiatives are needed to promote sustainable and continue the support of biodiversity conservation and socio-economic development. More empirical research is also needed to navigate, direct and yield science-informed materials that inform both theory/conceptual underpinnings and sustainable practice. An adaptive management approach would add flexibility and accommodate inconsistences that currently prevail. Thus far, an inclusive approach to PA management remains a key focus that still faces many challenges.

Policy instruments

As is evident from some of the contributions in this volume, in response to perceived shortcomings of the dominant PAs approach in Southern Africa, the 1980s and 1990s witnessed an upsurge in people-centred conservation approaches to bridge the conservation–development gap (van der Duim & Pellis in this volume). Such policy instruments yielded integrated conservation development programmes (ICDP) such as CBNRM, CAMPFIRE and conservancies in Southern Africa. For instance, in Botswana, the CBNRM Policy of 2007 was developed to guide the newly people-centred conservation and development approach. Despite this growing tendency toward integrated approaches at the landscape level, inherent complexities of landscapes will always present persistent and significant challenges, such as balancing multiple objectives, equitable inclusion of all relevant stakeholders, dealing with power and gender asymmetries, and moving beyond existing administrative, jurisdictional and sectorial silos (Ros-Tonen et al., 2018). Moreover, in governance and partnership literature, power has often been neglected as a useful concept in analysing and understanding evolving conservation and development governance processes. In fact, governance and partnerships tend to be presented as depoliticised and consensual policymaking by independent actors in seemingly power-free processes (Kuindersma et al., 2012).

Though policy instruments have spelt out how to transit from exclusive to inclusive conservation and development approaches, doing this remains unclear given the lack of common systemic practices and understanding of these approaches (Reed et al., 2015). Pellis et al. (2018) argue that in conservation and development implementation projects, what is considered as 'solved' in one location and moment in time may form the stage for yet another problem if we move out from one landscape to another. Hence, policy instruments in the conservation and development agenda need to be informed by in situ rather than ex situ contextual settings, as each landscape is different from another.

276 *Moren Tibabo Stone et al.*

Besides, inclusive policies and programmes are criticised elsewhere as promoting elitism (Dubbink, 2013), being exclusionary and favouring the interests of specific partners (Rhodes, 1997). This leads to power imbalances (Visseren-Hamakers, 2009) and the favouring of 'capable' partners while others in governance processes become excluded (Bitzer & Glasbergen, 2015).

Stone and Stone (in this volume) discuss the high-value, low-volume (HVLV) strategy adopted by Botswana to guide her conservation and tourism development agenda. They highlight that the HVLV tourism strategy adopted by the country has led to the undervaluing of domestic tourism and more significance being assigned to international high-spending tourists. The strategy's preference for international tourism over domestic tourism has led to the exclusion of locals as tourists and tourism entrepreneurs. While the HVLV tourism strategy is envisioned as best practice, it has yielded unintended repercussions on tourism performance, conservation and resources management. To appreciate the magnitude of problems engulfing PAs, KC (2021) reports that there are currently many PAs that operate without management plans. The development of relevant policies and regulations to foster sustainability is necessary to guide PAs and help them nurture their many functions and roles.

Institutions

One of the vital subjects in the debate on sustainable development addresses the question of what institutional arrangements are the most promising in advancing the process of progressive transformation (Glasbergen, 2007). Organisational scholars have hyped collaborative partnerships of institutions as a useful and necessary instrument for problem-solving within a problem realm (Selin & Beason, 1991). Institutions are considered important and effective when people realise their benefits, when they are ready to listen to, discuss and make decisions in consultation with people and when they can provide the right solutions to their problems (Shoo & Songorwa, 2013).

Collaboration describes interactions between institutions based on at least some agreed rules or norms, intended to address a common issue (Bramwell & Lane, 2000). The domination of and over-reliance on certain individual institutions in most cases affects the degree of participation of all institutions. For instance, donors and NGOs who sometimes sponsor conservation and development projects dominate collaborative partnership arrangements (Stone, 2015). Although various authors have examined the effectiveness of institutional partnerships, especially at the global level (Visseren-Hamakers, 2013), there is limited understanding of how partnerships contribute to governing integrated landscapes across sub-Saharan Africa (van der Duim & Pellis in this volume). It is not clear what institutions can do to discharge their functions to help PAs achieve their many functions and roles. An array of recommendations exists on institutions' involvement in guiding PAs. For instance, Badola (2018) posits that weak institutions and governance systems may lead to mass tourism development in PAs controlled by powerful stakeholders. The authors also argue

Conclusion 277

that local institutions with strong intrinsic spatial linkages are most adaptive to challenges of PAs, and that traditional local institutions, assisted by governments and NGOs, are best suited to achieve PAs' mandate. Like Badola (2018), some chapters in this volume illustrate that it is important to appreciate the importance of involving all relevant institutions, but also underline how difficult it is to manage power relations that emerge due to the involvement of many institutions (see Mogomotsi and Mogomotsi, Mtapuri, Mutanga, Mwakiwa, Stone and Stone, etc.).

Diverse stakeholders

In a diversified community setting, each stakeholder controls resources such as knowledge, expertise and capital, but on their own is unlikely to possess all the resources necessary to achieve its objectives and to plan effectively for its future in relation to a significant development project (Jamal & Stronza, 2009). The interdependence of stakeholders means that there are potentially mutual or collective benefits from stakeholders collaborating with each other (Selin & Beason, 1991). Stakeholders may work together if they consider that the probability of realising their goals and creating new opportunities in a problem domain are greater by performing jointly rather than acting alone (Czernek, 2013). A variety of terms are used to describe different collaborative and partnership arrangements in the tourism development literature. These include coalitions, forums, alliances, task forces, community–private partnerships, community–private agreements, joint venture partnerships and public–private partnerships (Bramwell & Lane, 2000; Jamal & Stronza, 2009; Jones, 2002; Rozemeijer, 2001).

As demonstrated by contributions to this volume and extant literature, all these arrangements have been adopted and put to the test, but the outcomes have been mixed. Bramwell and Lane (2000) caution that the definition of collaborative partnerships makes no assumptions about which stakeholders will participate, how much power they may have, how representative they may be or about the total number of stakeholders involved. Furthermore, Stone and Stone (this volume) posit that the issue of power relations in projects usually comes up, as some stakeholders by virtue of their existence possess more power than others, hence they always influence conservation and tourism stakeholders' collaborative partnership projects. Bramwell and Lane (2000) argue that the complexity of engaging diverse stakeholders in collaborative partnerships makes it difficult to involve them all equally, hence some partners' power may be too great, leading to the creation of cartels.

It is important to note the role power plays in collaborative efforts. Gerschick, Israel and Checkoway (1990) challenge the assumption that power is a zero-sum commodity. Increasing the power of one community or individual or partner implies decreasing the power of another (Bartunek & Keys, 1982). Due to the involvement of diverse stakeholders in PAs and tourism development projects and what is to be developed and conserved, the inclusiveness of

278 *Moren Tibabo Stone et al.*

stakeholders' opinions and the array of goals become very wide-ranging and difficult to accomplish equitably. Contingent on this volume's outcomes, we can fairly remark that the structural design of PAs and tourism development may not in itself guarantee the achievement of environmental conservation and development.

Is the future gloomy?

It is paramount to appreciate the role played by PAs in the conservation and development nexus. It is anticipated that the current biodiversity crisis would be much more severe had the establishment of PAs not taken place in the last century. Conversely, it would have been worse had PAs not provided alternative forms of livelihood to many communities that are today dependent on them (PAs) for various means of support. Hence, backing the global protected area estate is instantly and constantly needed if it is to fully deliver its promises and potential. In practice, it seems PAs can make much wider ecological, social and economic contributions to human society. However, it is not yet clear what the general impacts of these increasing demands on PAs will be, or whether additional demands will arise in the future and add on to already existing complications and pressures PAs are already subjected to. Despite the effect of unanticipated outbreaks like the COVID-19 pandemic, PA tourism is anticipated to grow. If not informed by sustainable tourism development principles, PA tourism can easily become one of the human-led threats to the existence of PAs. Efforts are needed to promote a reconciliation in the multiple roles played by PAs in their quest to deliver conservation and development intents.

In view of these discussions, theoretically, PAs accepting tourism as another land use they host sounds like a noble idea. However, others view it as an example of a community development 'imposter' driven by economic imperatives and a neoliberal agenda purported to further exploit local communities (Blackstock, 2005). All the same, the loss of biodiversity resources hosted by PAs will equally lead to the loss of revenue from tourism, adversely affecting communities who live around PAs. Many such communities are already living in extreme poverty, are dependent on tourism benefits and face added challenges of food security, human welfare and human–wildlife conflicts. Efforts to assist in the promotion of PAs as contributors to conservation and tourism development and to reconcile resultant unintended outcomes are a necessity. Otherwise the contribution of PAs to regional conservation and development will remain a controversial issue.

Lastly, the issue of pandemic outbreaks has brought another dimension of risks. Taking a leaf from COVID-19, it has taught us much about PAs and tourism interdependence. For example, KC (2021), highlights that there are serious risks associated with (i) an overdependence on tourism, particularly for destinations that rely on mass tourism, (ii) PA destinations that depend on small-scale tourism to support rural livelihoods due to their vulnerability and (iii) PA destinations that are still struggling to enter the tourism market because they will face additional obstacles in accessing the interrupted tourism industry.

To this end, we do not have any doubts that the overall findings of the chapters in this volume have implications for PAs managers, policy architects, tourism and community planners whose goal is to design programmes or projects that aim to assist protected areas sustain their conservation and community development goals. The volume is also relevant to academics, professors and students alike, especially graduate students who are interested in conservation, tourism and community livelihood dynamics.

References

Badola, R., Hussain, S. A., Dobriyal, P., Manral, U., Barthwal, S., Rastogi, A., & Gill, A. K. (2018). Institutional arrangements for managing tourism in the Indian Himalayan protected areas. *Tourism Management*, 66, 1–12.

Bartunek, J., & Keys, C. (1982). *Power equalization in schools through organizational development*. London: Sage.

Bhammar, H., Li, W., Molina, C. M. M., Hickey, V., Pendry, J., & Narain, U. (2021). Framework for sustainable recovery of tourism in Protected Areas. *Sustainability*, 13 (5), 2798.

Bitzer, V., & Glasbergen, P. (2015). Business–NGO partnerships in global value chains: Part of the solution or part of the problem of sustainable change? *Current Opinion in Environmental Sustainability*, 12, 35–40.

Blackstock, K. (2005). A critical look at community-based tourism. *Community Development Journal*, 40, 39–49.

Bragagnolo, C., A., Malhado, C. M., Jepson, P. & Ladle, R. J. (2016). Modelling local attitudes to Protected Areas in developing countries author(s). *Conservation & Society*, 14 (3), 163–182.

Bramwell, B., & Lane, B. (2000). Collaboration and partnerships in tourism planning. In Bramwell, B., & Lane, B. (Eds.), *Tourism collaboration and partnerships: Politics, practice and sustainability*. Clevedon: Channel View, 1–19.

Cazalis, V., Princé, K., Mihoub, J.-B., Kelly, J., Butchart, S. H. M., & Rodrigues, A. S. L. (2020). Effectiveness of protected areas in conserving tropical forest birds. *Nature Communications*, 11, 1–8.

Czernek, K. (2013). Determinants of cooperation in a tourist region. *Annals of Tourism Research*, 40, 83–104.

Dubbink, W. (2013). *Assisting the invisible hand: Contested relations between market, state and civil society*. Dordrecht: Springer Science & Business Media.

Geldmann, J., Manica, A., Burgess, N. D., Coad, L., & Balmford, A. (2019). A global-level assessment of the effectiveness of protected areas at resisting anthropogenic pressures. *Proceedings of National Academy of Sciences USA*, 116, 23209–23215.

Gerschick, T., Israel, B., & Checkoway, B. (1990). *Means of empowerment in individuals, organizations, and communities*. Ann Arbor, MI: Program on Conflict Management Alternatives, University of Michigan.

Glasbergen, P. (2007). Setting the scene: The partnership paradigm in the making. In Glasbergen, P., Biermann, F., & Mol, P. J. (Eds.), *Partnerships, governance and sustainable development*. Northampton, MA: Edward Elgar, 29–48.

Hall, C. M. (1996). *Introduction to tourism in Australia: Impacts, planning and development.* Melbourne: Addison, Wesley & Longman.

Jamal, T., & Stronza, A. (2009). Collaboration theory and tourism practice in protected areas: Stakeholders, structuring and sustainability. *Journal of Sustainable Tourism*, 17 (2), 169–189.

Jones, B. (2002). *Chobe Enclave, Botswana: Lessons learnt from a CBNRM project 1993–2002.* Gaborone: IUCN/SNV CBNRM Support Programme.

KC, B. (2021). Complexity in balancing conservation and tourism in protected areas: Contemporary issues and beyond. *Tourism and Hospitality Research*, 146735 84211015807.

Kuindersma, W., Arts, B., & van der Zouwen, M. (2012). Power faces in regional governance. *Journal of Political Power*, 5 (3), 411–429.

Lindsey, P., et al. (2020). Conserving Africa's wildlife and wildlands through the COVID-19 crisis and beyond. *Nature Ecology and Evolution,* 4, 1300–1310.

Ntuli, H., Jagers, S. C., Linell, A. Sjöstedt, M., & Muchapondwa, E. (2019). Factors influencing local communities' perceptions towards conservation of transboundary wildlife resources: The case of the Great Limpopo Transfrontier Conservation Area. *Biodiversity Conservation*, 28, 2977–3003.

Pellis, A., Pas, A., & Duineveld, M. (2018). The persistence of tightly coupled conflicts. The case of Loisaba, Kenya. *Conservation & Society*, 16 (4), 387–396.

Reed, J., Deakin, L., & Sunderland, T. (2015). What are 'integrated landscape approaches' and how effectively have they been implemented in the tropics: A systematic map protocol. *Official Journal of Collaborative Environmental Evidence.* Retrieved from: https://link.springer.com/article/10.1186/2047-2382-4-2

Rhodes, R. A. (1997). *Understanding governance: Policy networks, governance, reflexivity and accountability.* London: Open University Press.

Ros-Tonen, M. A., Reed, J., & Sunderland, T. (2018). From synergy to complexity: The trend toward integrated value chain and landscape governance. *Environmental Management*, 62 (1), 1–14.

Rozemeijer, N. (2001). *Community-based tourism in Botswana: The SNV experience in three community-tourism projects.* Botswana: SNV/IUCN CBNRM Support Programme.

Selin, S., & Beason, K. (1991). Inter-organizational relations in tourism. *Annals of Tourism Research*, 18 (4), 639–652.

Shoo, R., & Songorwa, A. (2013). Contribution of ecotourism to nature conservation and improvement of livelihoods around Amani nature reserve, Tanzania. *Journal of Ecotourism*, 12 (2), 75–89.

Snyman, S. (2014). Assessment of the main factors impacting community members' attitudes towards tourism and protected areas in six southern African countries. *Koedoe*, 56 (2), 1–12.

Snyman, S. L. (2012). The role of tourism employment in poverty reduction and community perceptions of conservation and tourism in southern Africa. *Journal of Sustainable Tourism*, 20, 395–416.

Spenceley, A., Snyman, S., & Eagles, P. (2017). *Guidelines for tourism partnerships and concessions for protected areas: Generating sustainable revenues for conservation and development. In Report to the Secretariat of the Convention on Biological Diversity and IUCN.* Gland, Switzerland: IUCN.

Stone, M. T. (2015). Community-based ecotourism: A collaborative partnerships perspective. *Journal of Ecotourism*, 14 (2–3), 166–184.

Visseren-Hamakers, I. J. (2009). Partnerships in biodiversity governance: An assessment of their contributions to halting biodiversity loss. *Nederlandse Geografische Studies*, 1–177.

Visseren-Hamakers, I. J. (2013). Partnerships and sustainable development: The lessons learned from international biodiversity governance. *Environmental Policy and Governance*, 23 (3), 145–160.

WTTC. (2019). The *economic impact of global wildlife tourism*. Accessed 12 July 2020 at https://travesiasdigital.com/wp-content/ uploads/2019/08/The-Economic-Impact-of-Global-Wildlife-Tourism-Final-19.pdf

Index

abbreviations xvi–xviii
accommodation businesses 212
Addo Elephant National Park 107
African Charter on Human and Peoples
  Rights 91
African Development Bank 245
African Elephant Coalition 178, 179
African painted dogs 108
African Parks (AP) 264
African voice 152
Afrikaners 17
aggressive animals, removing 35, 117
agricultural communities and wildlife
  conflicts 105
agricultural water demand 169
airlines banning trophies 155
Ais-Richtersveld Transfrontier Park 253
Amboseli 81, 83
Amboseli Ecosystem Management Plan
  (AEMP) 76, 80, 83
Amboseli Ecosystem Trust (AET) 73, 75–6,
  79, 80, 81
Amboseli national park 79
ancestral land 88, 89, 90, 97; rights to 92
animal rights groups 118, 131, 134, 136,
  135, 137
Animal Trophies Act 157
Annan, Koffi 150, 154
anti-hunting groups 132
anti-poaching 222, 225–6, 226, 266
anti-poaching militarisation 219
anti-poaching patrols 77; armed 227
apartheid 18
aquatic life, threats to 169
arid and semi-arid regions 106, 109, 110
armed conflict, international and
  non-international 222
attitude formation 29
attitudes 33–4

attitudes, positive and negative, of host
  communities 57, 115
attitudes towards protected areas 28, 29, 30,
  115
attitudes, perceptions and behaviour links
  29, 30
attitudes to conservation, positive 47

Balete tribe 89
barriers against wildlife 102
Basarwa people 135, 137, 248, 254
Bechuanaland Protectorate (Botswana)
  15–16, 20
behaviour 28, 29–30; retaliatory 35;
  variables affecting 31–3, 34
behaviour, perceptions and attitudes links
  29, 30
benefit sharing 35, 57, 198, 212
benefits, indirect 34
benefits, intangible 212
benefits, non-economic 35
Bhutan tourism 234, 235, 239
Big Five 108, 260
big game hunters 133
Big Life Foundation (BLF) 76, 79, 80, 81, 83
biodiversity 133, 263; crisis 278
black eagles 209
Black Rhinoceros Guardianship Program
  176
black South Africans 18
'Blood law' 137
borders, removed 210
boreholes 249
Bornfree 137
Botswana, best in conservation 131, 136, 235
Botswana, Chinese in 154
Botswana, community trusts 58
Botswana economy 131
Botswana, elephant debate 6

Index 283

Botswana elephant population 131, 132, 139, 181
Botswana GDP 23, 134, 208, 233
Botswana government 22; decision making 238–9
Botswana hunting ban 132, 134–7; loss of revenue 136–7; lifting 133, 137
Botswana, land as protected areas 131, 208
Botswana, land disputes 89
Botswana, luxury ecotourism 136, 208
Botswana, poverty alleviation projects, Botswana 236
Botswana tourism 8, 23, 131; *see also* Chobe National Park
Botswana, wildlife management areas (WMAs) 131
Botswana relocation policies 90
Botswana San people 6, 89, 90, 95, 97, 209, 251; legal challenge re land 90–1
Botswana, trophy hunting 131
Botswana wildlife conservation 131
'bottom-up' approach 36, 58, 62
Buffalo, protected 208
bush encroachment 165–6, 170
bush meat hunting 9, 137
bushmeat 260; consumption 264, 266
'Bushmeat Crisis' 263
bushmeat hunting 260, 266
bushmeat hunting in Malawi 263–5
bushmeat hunting, costs and benefits 262–3
Bushmen 90–1; *see also* San people of Botswana
business opportunities 46

Cape Town 162
Caprivi 62, 249
Caroline formula 223
carrying capacity 22, 209
cattle grazing 81
cattle industry expansion 140
Cecil the lion: as a focusing event 150, 151, 157; killing of 133, 147, 148; legislation after 151, 157; media coverage of 147; reaction in southern Africa 147, 152, 153
Central Kalahari Game Reserve (CKGR) 90, 139
challenges of tourism 45
chemical methods of killing 117, 118, 122; dangers of 118
chilli trees to deter crop raiding 121
China importing trophies 153, 154
Chobe Enclave community-based tourism projects 250

Chobe Enclave Conservation Trust 22, 208, 235, 236
Chobe Enclave Villages 249
Chobe National Park 19–21, 23, 179
Chobe river 208
Chomsky, Noam 150, 153
civilians as legitimate targets 224
civilians, harm to 225
climate change 7; and tourism 162, 164–9
climatic patterns (2010-2021) 163
clinic construction 249
collaborative governance 212
collaborative nature reserves 108
collaborative partnerships 277
colonial period, hunting in 15
colonial settlers 87
combat strategy in non-military operations 220
common pool dilemmas 57
common pool resources (CPR) 57
common property 104
Communal Areas Management Programme for Indigenous Resources (CAMPFIRE) 22, 56–7; challenges 170–1; human-wildlife conflicts 122; hunting rights 118; and indigenous knowledge 248; infrastructure facilities 105; programmes 105–6
communal conservancies, Namibia 106
communal conservation programmes, requisite factors 105
Communal Property Association (CPA) 107
communities made powerless 239
communities, discontented, undermining conservation 18
communities, displacement and exclusion of 58
Community Based Natural Resource Management (CBNRM) 6, 8, 22, 44, 56–7, 58–9; challenges 66, 253; criticism of 105; consumptive tourism 122; hunting rights 135; paradigm 246; programmes 62–3, 104; in Namibia 77, 82, 106; rights to benefits from natural resources 119
community conservation 82
community empowerment 250–1
community participation 246, 248–50
community tolerance to wildlife, opportunities for enhancing 60–4
community-based organisations (CBOs) 119, 136, 209

284 Index

community-based projects 264
community-based tourism (CBT) 43–4, 56, 59, 207; and protected areas 211–12; ventures 213
compensation for land forcibly taken 19, 104
compensation for wildlife damage 22, 102, 123; challenges from 102–3
concept of proportionality 224, 225
Conference of the Parties (CoP18) Meeting 179
conservancies 207; benefits of 110–11
conservancies in Kenya 76–7
conservancy approach, criticism of 110
conservancy beneficiaries 78
conservation and agricultural land conflicts 100–1
conservation and development debate 1
conservation costs 3
conservation funds diverted to health 189
Conservation International 136, 138
conservation interventions 101–4
conservation laws 223
conservation objectives, local communities resisting 133
conservation projects 176
conservation, indigenous methods of 15, 16
conservation, militarisation of 8
conservation-induced violence 219
consultation, lack of 36
'contractual parks' 104, 106, 107–8
Convention on Biological Diversity (CBI) 4
Convention on International Trade in Endangered Species (CITES) 21, 138, 147, 154, 176; agreement to 'one-time' export of stockpiled ivory 177–8
CITES records on trophy imports 153
CITES, no to selling stockpiled ivory 182
CITES, poaching and elephant surveys 178–9
"conservation, fortress" 17, 56
CoP18 181
corruption 50
cost-benefit analysis (CBA) framework 31, 33
costs and benefits 30, 34
costs and benefits of sustainable tourism 234
COVID-19 pandemic 7#, 23#, 38, 168#, 188–94; impacts on the environment 191; impacts on tourism 189–94; financial losses 190, 191; report 195

craftwork 212
criminalisation 223
crop damage, compensation for 140
crop destruction 115, 261
crop loss 101
crop raiding 102, 105, 121, 122
cultural tourism 46
culture 248, 254
Community Wildlife-Based Tourism (CWBT) 56, 57, 62, 63; challenges faced 63–4; role 60–1; successes and failures 59; stakeholders in 62–3
cyberactivism 266
cyclones 163, 168

damming effects 169
dancing troupe 235
Day Zero 162, 168
deforestation 49, 205
Democratic Republic of the Congo 226
Department of National Park and Wildlife (DNPW), Malawi 263–4
Department of Nature Conservation 109
Department of Wildlife and National Parks (DWNP), Botswana 22, 238
desertification 169
diamond mining, Botswana 20, 23
disease transmission 122; prevention 102, 110; zoonotic 263
donor withdrawal 105, 106
Douglas-Hamilton, Dr Iain 177
drought 84, 161–2, 163, 165, 166#, 168; extended 170; leading to poaching 169; prolonged 169; recurring 169

ecological capacity 169
ecological carrying capacity 22, 209
ecological factors 36
ecologically sound tourism 43
economic conservation interventions 102–3
economic globalization 88
economic recovery 197–8
ecosystems, wildlife 132–3
ecotourism 5, 42–3; benefits and costs 182; challenges to 47–51; employment from 46; failure of 48–9; opportunities 45–7; project 252; and traditional culture 51; unintended consequences 51
ecotourism and private enterprise 49
ecotourism, socio-cultural impact of 48
education 120; effect of 34, 35; low levels of 48, 51
El Niño events 163, 164

Eland, protected 208
elephant death 175
elephant deterrence 121
elephant hunting ban 181
elephant hunting debate 131
elephant poaching 49, 178
elephant population: decline in 177; depletion 15; increase 138, 139, 180; land capacity for 180
elephant sanctuaries 166
elephant slaughter 15
Elephant Trade Information System (ETIS) 179
Elephant Without Borders (EWB) 135
Elephant-Human Relations Aid 181
elephants killing people 182
elephants, appetite 182
elephants, cost of living with 132
elephants, desert 180–1
elephants, destruction by 139
elephants, export of baby to China 147
elephants, hunting and culling 24
elephants, killing 177
elephants, mysterious deaths 147
elephants, threats to 166
elephants, proportion of illegally killed (PIKE) 179
elitism 209, 214, 252
employment 212
employment loss owing to COVID 191, 192
employment opportunities 50, 109, 110, 114
'empty forests and savannah' 265
enclave tourism 23–4, 239, 236–7
enclosures 101
endangered species 102, 176; trade prohibition 176–7
Endangered Species Act 148
enforcement conservation interventions 103
enterprises, small 212, 213, 241
environmental crime 190
environmental degradation 161; reducing 233
environmental recovery 198
equations, perceptions, attitudes and behaviour 30, 33perceptions
erosion 169
Eswatini, community participation 249
export of stockpiled ivory 177–8
extinction, species facing 36, 117, 219
extreme weather events 168

fairness 34
farming, unsustainable 109
fences 89, 101, 102; biological 102; electric 110; elephant damage to 121
finance, borrowing 254
'financial sinks', protected areas as 274
financing, lack of 252
fire frequency 163, 165
fire impact 165–6
firearms, weapons and traps in game reserves 21
Fish River 252
fishermen, killing illegal 220
fishing 21
flooding 162, 163, 168
focusing events 150–1, 153, 157
foreign exchange earnings 191, 232
foreign ownership 239
forest reserves 22
"fortress conservation" 17, 56
funds, trickle down to households 105
future 278–9

Gairezi Ecotourism project 252
game guards 77
Garden Route National Park 164
gene pools 170
Geneva Conventions 222, 225
Global Environment Facility (GEF) 207
Global North-South dynamics 138, 141
global warming 163
globalization, economic 88
Google Scholar 44, 116, 162
governance by landowners 75
governance issues 36
governance mechanisms 49–50
governance model 35–6; top-down 36, 37; bottom-up 36; inclusive 37
government support 82
government supremacy over people and resources 221
grazing 169
Grazing Association 252
grazing pressure 170
Great Limpopo Transfrontier Conservation Area (GLTFTA) 34
Great Limpopo Transfrontier Park (GLTFP) 211
Greater Kruger National Park (GKNP) 209
Greater Limpopo Transfrontier Park and Conservation Area 168, 209
greed, human 176
'green militarisation' 219, 220, 228

286 *Index*

Griquas 15
Gross Domestic Product (GDP) 189–90;
   Botswana 23, 134, 208, 233; global 232,
   274; loss owing to COVID 191; tourism
   contributions 44
guard dogs 121

habitat manipulation 101, 102
handicrafts 235, 254
Healthy Parks Healthy People Initiative
   195, 198
heatwaves 163
herbivores 169
high-quality, low-impact tourism 109
High-Value, Low-Volume (HVLV) tourism
   8, 233, 234–6, 237, 238, 239–40; lack of
   skills for 238, 239, 240
honeybees 102
hostilities, conduct of 223
hostilities, non-international 222
human encroachment 49
human fatalities by elephants 139
human population, increasing 63, 180, 265
Humane Society International 177, 178
Humane Society of the US 137
human-elephant conflict 138, 140, 180,
   181, 182
human-wildlife conflict 17, 19, 22, 49, 115,
   253
human-wildlife conflict, mitigating 115,
   116, 117; lethal approaches 116–20;
   non-lethal approaches 120–2
hunted to local extinction 109
hunter-gatherer lifestyle 90
hunting and fishing as traditional practices
   206
hunting ban, Botswana 132, 134–7; loss of
   revenue 136–7; reversal 133, 137
hunting in the colonial period 15
hunting debate 6, 266
hunting, employment 134
hunting lobby 132
hunting for pleasure 259, 260
hunting from necessity 259
hunting quotas 22, 119, 238, 250
hunting restrictions 120
hunting rights, selling 119
hunting, regulated and unregulated 117,
   118
hunting, reinstating 137 international
   outrage
hunting, sustainable 249
hunting, unpredicted consequences 122

hunting, unsustainable 263
Hwange National Park 59, 148, 166, 209

illegal resource harvesting 58
illegal wildlife trafficking 31
implications for sustainability 64–5
inbreeding 170
incentives 57, 105
incentives to behave sustainably 31
incentivising conservation 38
indigeneity 92, 93
indigenous knowledge 62, 63–4, 97
indigenous knowledge systems (IKS) 248,
   250; incorporation into programmes 254
indigenous people losing land 6
Indigenous Peoples and the State 6, 87–8,
   93, 94, 95
Indigenous Peoples: as conservationists
   95; dispossession of 87, 88, 93;
   marginalisation of 87, 88; participation
   in international affairs 93, 94; resisting
   eviction 90; rights 6, 93; right to self-
   determination 94–5, 96; threats to culture
   and land 87–8; transgressions against 95;
   understanding sustainability 89
inequality 19, 31
information, access to 252–3
informed consent 96
infrastructure, poor 46–7, 50, 237
injustice to marginalised communities 93
injustices, redressing 94
institutional partnerships 276
institutions 276–7
integrated conservation and development
   projects (ICDPs) 56, 58, 246
international community 149–50, 151,
   153–5; role of 146–7
International Ecotourism Society (TIES)
   42
international funding cuts 79
international human rights law 94, 224,
   225, 228
international humanitarian law 222, 223,
   224–5, 226, 228
international law 88, 93, 221, 228
international trade agreement 176
International Union for Conservation of
   Nature (IUCN) 4, 138, 139, 141, 176,
   207; African Elephant Status Report 179;
   World Parks Congress 247, 253–4
interstate force 222, 225
Israel, targeted killing 220, 227
ivory, demand for 178

ivory exports 177–8
ivory markets 178, 179; closing 179
ivory money for conservation 180
ivory sales ban 176, 180
ivory sales debate 182
ivory stockpiles 7, 177–8; efforts to sell 181, 182; inability to sell 179–80, 182; sale of 147
ivory trade 176, 177, 178, 179; banning 177; application to lift ban 181; illegal 179
ivory-carving incident 178

jobs, high- and low-paying 235
joint venture partnerships (JVPs) 119
jus ad bellum 222, 225
jus in bello 222, 223, 224–5, 226, 228

Kariba, Lake 162
Kasane Forest Reserve 22
Kavango Zambesi Transfrontier Conservation Area (KAZATFCA) 165, 211
Kenya, Chinese in 154
Kenya, Conservation and Wildlife Management Act 75
Kenya, elephant deterrence 121
Kenya, land disputes 89, 90
Kenya, landscape approaches 75
Kenya 2010 Constitution 75, 90
Kenya, no safari hunting, but illegal bushmeat hunting 265
Kenya, partnerships in 73–7, 79–80
Kenya Wildlife Conservancies Association (KWCA) 75, 76–7, 80, 83
Kenya Wildlife Services (KWS) 75, 80; budget 263
Kenyan conservancies 79
Kenyan government, role of 83
Kenya relocation policies 90
Kenyan Wildlife Act 80
Kgalagadi Transfrontier National Park 165, 208–9
Khama, Lieutenant General Ian 131, 135, 136, 181
Khama Rhino Sanctuary Trust (KRST) 236, 252–3
Khoadi Hoas Conservancy 249
Khomani San people 251
Kilimanjaro, rural 47
killing elephants 179
killing of non-target species 117; terrorist killings 220

killing wildlife: as entitlement 207–8; customs/traditions 207–8; indiscriminate 122; outcry against 122
kraals 121
Kruger National Park (KNP) 17–19, 107, 175; and climate change 161–2; communities adjacent to 18, 120; and drought 164; damage by floods 168; poaching in 17, 18
Kunene, Namibia 77, 81, 83
Kwa-Zulu Natal 249; National Park 212

La Niña 166
lack of support for conservation 22
Laikipia 80, 81
Laikipia Wildlife Forum (LWF) 73, 77, 80
land claim backs in South Africa 107
land communal ownership 91
land conflicts 19
land converted to agriculture 265
land degradation 208
land disputes 87
land expropriation 35
land favouring wildlife over crops 106
land grievances 89–90
land issues 17, 18
land litigation 89, 90
land management, stakeholder classes 100
land restitution programme 19
land rights 18
land taken by force 88, 106
land transformation 49, 264
land use change 47, 103, 107, 108, 109
land use options, economically viable 104–5
land, agricultural to ecotourism 47
land, denial of access 92
land, non-monetary value 88
landscape 'trespass' 81
landscape governance 73–5; partners 79; roles 74
landscape partnerships 74–7
landscape, definition 74
law of armed combat 222, 223, 224–5, 226, 228
legal challenges re land 90–2
legislation after Cecil's death 151
leopard populations 134
leopard study 123
Lesotho 250, 252
lethal control methods, unacceptability 123
lethal force, use of 225
Lewa Wildlife Conservancy (LWC) 76
lion populations 134

288 *Index*

lion trophy imports 148, 153; bans 148
lions, killing 117, 253
literacy levels, low 252
literacy problems 51
livelihood and conservation trade-offs 94
livelihood vs conservation 89–90
livestock depredation by carnivores 100, 101
livestock diseases from wildlife 115
livestock farms, former 108–9
livestock guarding dogs 121
livestock loss 101
local communities: exclusion of 8, 16; inclusion of 36–7; made criminals 21; withholding support for conservation 16
loss of human life 115
loss of livestock 115
loss of livestock and crops from wildlife 49
low humidity 166
low income households 34
Lubombo Conservancy-Goba (LCG) TFCA 249
Lupande Game Management Area 250, 251

Maasai 20
Maasailand Preservation Trust (MPT) 76, 81
Madagascar 193
Mahenye community 62, 250
Makgadikgadi pans 208
Makulele community 107, 250–1, 252
Malawi 264
marginalisation of Indigenous Peoples 87, 88
Masisi, President Mokgweetsi 131, 137, 138–9, 181
mass tourism 205
Mau Forest, Kenya 90, 91, 92
Maun 139
Mbirikani Group Ranch 76, 83
meat from hunted animals 110, 262
media, African 147, 149, 152
media coverage of Cecil the lion 147
media, definition 147–8
media, influence of 149; coverage of environmental issues 149
media power 157
media, putting pressure on authorities 152
media, role of 146–7, 148, 151, 156–7
media setting agenda 151–2
media, Western 149
Mhlumeni community 249
micro credits 51–2
Mier population 209

migrant communities 81
migration corridors 170
migration of animals 209, 210
migration patterns, disturbance to 165, 168
migratory patterns, changes in 168
militant enforcement-based conservation 265
militarisation of conservation 218–19; opponents of 219
military action, proportionate 223
military tactics in wildlife protection 218–19, 223
minimal interference with constant monitoring 109
Mnangagwa, President Emmerson 177
mobile pastoralists 81
Monitoring the Illegal Killing of Elephants (MIKE) 178, 179
Mozambique: elephant deterrence 121; hunting in protected areas 263; residents in protected areas 104

Namibia 77–8; and CBNRM 106; challenges 83–4; Chinese in 154; communities 81–2; conservancies 77, 80, 253; increase in wildlife populations 134; partnerships in 73–4; poaching in 79; safari hunting in 261–2
Namibian Association of CBNRM (NACSO) 77–8, 79, 80, 82
Namibian Conservation model 106
Namib-Nauklft National Park 109
NamibRand Nature Reserve 108, 109–10
national parks and game reserves, introduction of 15, 16, 20
Natron, Lake 50
natural resource curse 245
natural resource wealth 245
natural resources 161; traditional control of 248
needs of local communities, failure to consider 16
needs theory 30, 33
nepotism 18
New Partnership for Africa's Development (NEPAD 211
Ngamiland district 233
Ngorongoro Crater 20
niche markets 232
non-governmental organisations (NGOs) 59, 75, 79, 83, 138, 252, 264; financing CBT projects 252
NORAD 251

Northern Rangelands Trust (NRT) 73, 76–7, 80, 83

Ogiek people 6, 89, 90, 95, 97; and Kenya Government 91–2
Okavango Community Trust 252
Okavango Delta: bush meat hunting 137; climate change 161–2; development 235; earnings from trophy hunting 249; ecotourism in 46; elephant deterrence 121; foreign control 237; poaching 120
Ol Donyo Wuas Trust 76
'one-time' export of stockpiled ivory 177–8
opportunities from tourism 45
Ostrom, Elinor 31, 32, 33, 36, 132
over-grazing 207
over-harvesting 103, 205
over-hunting for survival 206
over-tourism 4, 190, 192, 194
ownership, sense of 37

Palmer, Walter 148
park regulations, contravention of 18, 19
partnerships 73–4, 78, 79, 80; dominant partners 80, 82; with government 79
Peace Parks Foundation (PPF) 210, 211
perceptions 28, 29, 30, 36; attitudes and behaviour links 29, 30; forming 31, 32, 33, 34; and economic benefits 34–5; negative 31, 34, 36, 38; in Zimbabwe 37
Permanent Sovereignty over Natural Resources 220
pesticides 117
plants harvested for medicine criminalised 214
'pleasure peripheries' 236
poacher turned ranger 176
poachers 8, 226, 266
poaching 30, 49, 120, 133; decrease in 59, 65; of elephants 49, 178; in Kruger National Park 17; in Namibia 79; networks 21; for subsistence 21, 31, 120; war on 222, 225–6, 226, 266
poisoning 117, 137, 139
policy change window 150, 151, 157
policy instruments guidance 275
policy options 37–8
political boundaries, removal 210
post-COVID-19 strategy 195
poverty 37, 42; alleviation 8, 236, 245; extreme 245
poverty status 30
power dynamics 95, 96

power imbalances 75, 155, 276, 277
power relations 73–4, 80–2, 93
power sharing, asymmetric 49
power, devolution of 239
Predator Compensation Fund (PCF) 76
predators and crop-raiders 6
predators killing livestock 49
private enterprise and ecotourism 49
private land conservation 261
private land used as protected areas 207
private nature reserves 108–10
'problem animals' 264
propaganda techniques 137–8
property rights, violation of 92
pro-poor conservation (PPC) 246; challenges facing 251–3
pro-poor tourism (PPT) 245; challenges facing 251–3
proportion of illegally killed elephants (PIKE) 179
Protected Area Approach (PAA) 73
protected areas 2, 3–4, 16; attitudes towards 33; as battlegrounds 225–7; definition 246; as 'financial sinks' 274; inadequate funding of 274; and local conflicts 19–20, 21; loss to poor people living adjacent to 114–15; conflicting demands on 49; percentage of land and water area 114, 218; ; perceived value of 31; populations near 210; as recreational spaces for Whites 237; as resources and assets 206; restricted access to 35; shortcomings of 73; in Tanzania 42; threats to sustainability 56; variety 246
protectionists 118

quotas for hunting 103, 104, 135, 249, 251

radio 149
rainfall, extreme 162, 167–8
rainfall patterns, shift in 165
rational choice theory 31
recommendations 45, 51–2, 111, 124, 240
regulations, use of strict 36
relocation of traditional communities 48, 90
replacement animals after killing 117
resentment 35
resource use, illegal 103
resource-poor and resource-rich countries 245
resources, demands for 88
responsibility to protect 220

290 Index

retaliation hunting and poaching 63, 106, 119–20, 123#
revenue leakages 237, 239
revenue sharing 22
rhino horn, trade in 154
rhino hunting 154, 266
rhino poaching 18, 39; combating 219; Kruger National Park 24
rhinos 108, 209, 236
Richtersveld Community 253
right to own and develop natural resources 221
rights to make decisions about wildlife 267
royal game 134

safari hunting 9, 259; ban 266; calls to ban imports 261; costs and benefits 118, 260–1; meat from 265; in Namibia 261–2; and public outrage 261, 266; public perception of 265; revenue from 119, 135; *see also* trophy hunting
San people of Botswana 6, 89, 90, 95, 97, 209, 251; legal challenge re land 90–1
Sankoyo community 235
Sankuyo community trust 249
Sankuyo Tshwaragana Management Trust 208
Savannah Vulture Project 176
Save the Rhino Trust (SRT) 81
Save Valley Conservancy 108–9, 110
Security Council 226
self-defence by states 223–4
self-determination, Indigenous People's right to 94–5, 96
self-sustaining reserves 109
Serengeti National Park 20, 168
Sesana case 90
settlement, unplanned 109
settler colonialism 87
severe weather events 163
shared ownership of wildlife resources 24
"shoot to kill" policies 8, 219–20, 223–5, 226–7
skills, lack of 238, 239, 240, 251–2
skills, passing on 254
snares 117
social ecological systems (SESs) 31, 132–3; variables 31–3, 34
social exchange theory (SET) 30, 33, 57, 64, 65
social inequalities 19

social media 149, 266; giving Africans a voice 152–3; about Cecil the lion; 148, 149; about hunting 131, 132, 137, 138
social movements 266
social recovery 198–9
social services 236
socio-cultural impact of ecotourism 48
soil degradation 208
Songimvelo-Malolotja (SM) TFCA 249
South Africa National Parks (SANParks) 107
South Africa National Parks and nature reserves 164, 165, 168, 207; *see also* Kruger National Park, Table Mountain National Park
South Africa, contractual parks in 106–8
South Africans, black 18; white 17
Southern Africa Development Community (SADC) 43, 44, 211
sovereignty 94, 221–2, 226; over natural resources 220, 221; threat to 222
Special Game Licences (SGL) 91, 134–5
species abundance 36
species die-offs 164
species reintroduction 109
species, overabundant, harvest of 110
species, rare and exotic, desire to own 176
stakeholder-based wildlife interventions 103–4
stakeholders, diverse 277–8
State use of force 222, 223, 224
State, "unfair actions" by 18
State's right to protect its sovereignty and borders 221
ivory stockpiles 7, 177–8; efforts to sell 181, 182; inability to sell 179–80, 182; sale of 147
Strict Nature Reserves 207
study themes 45
subsistence and commercial poaching hybrid 219
subsistence hunting 192, 219; criminalised 214
subsistence poaching 21, 31, 120
sustainability implications 60–1
sustainable tourism 114, 119, 233–5

Table Mountain National Park 162, 164, 166, 167
Tanzania: government power 49; protected areas 42
targeted killing 8, 219–20, 223–5, 226–7

Index 291

tax evasion 237, 239
tax incentives 197
Technical Advisory Committees (TAC) 239
temperature extremes 166, 168
temperature increase 164
temperatures at Cape Point 167
territorial integrity 221, 224, 226
terrorism, response to 226
terrorist killings 220
threatened megafauna 262–3
Tonga hunting 248
'top-down' approach 36, 37, 58, 63, 133, 245, 254
tourism add-ons 190, 197
tourism, alternatives to 197
tourism, beginnings 15
tourism, decline in 168, 169, 189, 191
tourism demands 50
tourism development goals 23
tourism, domestic 197, 237, 238
tourism, ecologically sound 43
tourism, empowerment in 250–1
tourism, ethical 135
tourism global jobs 232
tourism growth 278
tourism, halt to 188–94
tourism industry: alternatives to 194; problems 23; resilience 194
tourism infrastructure 50
tourism interdependence 278
tourism jobs 189
tourism linked to other economic sectors 50
tourism, low numbers 265
tourism management 4
tourism opportunities 45, 190
tourism overdependence on 278
tourism, photographic 119, 135
tourism, positive and negative consequences of 114
tourism pre-COVID 189–90
tourism, pro-poor (PPT) 245; challenges facing 251–3
tourism recovery strategy 194, 195
tourism resorts, water-based 161–2
tourism sector, sustainable recovery 196–8
tourism for socio-economic progress 206
tourism spin-offs 213
Tourism Supporting Conservation (TOSCO) 77
tourism, sustainable 114, 119, 233–5
tourism, use of revenue 46
tourism, virtual 198–9
tourism, way forward 195–6

tourist accommodation 254
traditional control of natural resources 248
traditional economic activities 48 foregoing
traditional food, change from 48
traditional hunting 120; termed poaching 214
traditional knowledge, loss of 209
traditional livelihood, loss of 87
traditional practices 206
transboundary conservation 210#
Transfrontier Conservation Areas 208, 248, 249, 250, 253; benefits of 210–11; goals of 211; flaws of 211
transnational organisations, control by 236
traps 117
travel restrictions 189
trophy bans by airlines 155
trophy hunting 6, 122, 148; critics of 140; debates 131, 133–4; earnings from 249; in marginal areas 141; moratorium 131; in Namibia 80; opponents of 134; views 132; see also safari hunting
trophy imports 153, 157; proposed ban on 151–2, 155
trust building 104

unfairness 35, 36
unintended consequences 8, 51, 233, 239
United Nations Conference on Environment and Development 149
United Nations Declaration on the Rights of Indigenous Peoples 92, 93, 94, 97; Articles 32, 94, 96
United Nations Environment Programme (UNEP) 114, 218
United Nations Security Council 226; Resolutions (UNSCRs) 226
United Nations World Tourism Organisation (UNWTO) 56, 232, 245
United Nations-endorsed Responsibility to Protect 220

value over volume strategy 8, 233, 234–6, 237, 238, 239–40
vegetation destruction 169
vegetation, global impact on 161
Victoria Falls and climate change 162
violence towards animals 266
virtual tourism 198–9
vultures 117

walking safaris 110
war, conception of 222
war on poaching 222, 225–6, 226, 266

292 *Index*

water demand, human 169
water shortages 169
water stress 166
water, downstream ecology 169
Western lifestyle adopted by youths 51
'white cowboys' 80
white South Africans 17
White upper-middle classes 237–8
wildebeest die-offs 140
wildfires 163–4, 166
wildlife as belongs to the State 207
wildlife bio-physical characteristics 106
wildlife control, lethal and non-lethal
    means 101–2
wildlife crime 222, 226
wildlife decline 133, 135, 218, 263
wildlife ecosystems 132–3
wildlife grey and black markets 152
wildlife, injured 122
wildlife, loss of 263
wildlife killing: indiscriminate 122; outcry
    against 122
wildlife management, Western views 266
wildlife migratory routes 140

wildlife poaching 226
wildlife quotas 212
wildlife trade, illegal 153–4; market for 154
wildlife trafficking 154, 226
wildlife translocation 121–2
wildlife trophy imports 153
wildlife, *res nullius* status 207
'woke' corporates 155
women, sidelined 252
World Conference on Human Rights 93
World Tourism Organisation (WTO) 114,
    189
World Travel and Tourism Council
    (WTTC) 232, 274
World Wide Fund for Nature (WWF) 138,
    154
World Wildlife Fund 77

Zambia 59, 193, 251
Zanzibar 50
Zimbabwe: elephant population 209;
    government control 251; human survival
    211; income from trophy hunting 249;
    national parks 168; people of 209

Printed in the United States
by Baker & Taylor Publisher Services